STUDIES IN ROMAN PRIVATE LAW

STUDIES IN ROMAN PRIVATE LAW

ALAN WATSON

THE HAMBLEDON PRESS
LONDON AND RIO GRANDE

Published by The Hambledon Press, 1991
102 Gloucester Avenue, London NW1 8HX (U.K.)
P.O. Box 162, Rio Grande, Ohio 45672 (U.S.A.)

ISBN 1 85285 047 7

British Library Cataloguing in Publication Data

Watson, Alan *1933-*
Studies in Roman Private law.
1. Roman Empire. Private law.
I. Title
343.70602632

Library of Congress Cataloging-in-Publication Data

Watson, Alan
Studies in Roman private law/Alan Watson.
Includes bibliographical references and index.
1. Roman law. I Title.
KJA2190.W39 1991
340.5″4 – dc20 91-16529 CIP

Printed on acid-free paper and bound in Great
Britain by Bookcraft Ltd., Midsomer Norton, Somerset

Contents

Acknowledgements

The essays reprinted here first appeared in the following places and are reprinted by kind permission of the original publishers.

1. *Daube Noster*, edited by Alan Watson (Scottish Academic Press, Edinburgh and London, 1974), pp. 331-341.
2. *Maior Viginti Quinque Annis, Essays in Commemoration of the Sixth Lustrum of the Institute for Legal History of the University of Utrecht*, edited by J.E. Spruit (Van Gorcum, Assen, 1979), pp. 195-201.
3. *Tijdschrift voor Rechtsgeschiedenis* (1965), pp. 38-50.
4. *Tijdschrift voor Rechtsgeschiedenis* (1961), pp. 243-258.
5. *The Irish Jurist* (1966), pp. 313-315.
6. *The Classical Review* (1973), pp. 127-128.
7. *Tijdschrift voor Rechtsgeschiedenis* (1961), pp. 1-21.
8. *Law Quarterly Review* (1962), pp. 205-227.
9. *Studia et Documenta Historiae et Iuris* (1967), pp. 189-209.
10. *IURA* (1961), pp. 210-221.
11. *Festschrift Klaffenbach, Klio* (1970), pp. 473-475.
12. *Revue Internationale des Droits de l'Antiquité* (1967), pp. 455-465.
13. *The Irish Jurist* (1969), pp. 378-391.
14. *Revue Internationale des Droits de l'Antiquité* (1963), pp. 69-91.
15. *Revue Internationale des Droits de l'Antiquité* (1961), pp. 391-416.
16. *Studia et Documenta Historiae et Iuris* (1963), pp. 285-287.
17. *Tijdschrift voor Rechtsgeschiedenis*(1966), pp. 175-193.
18. *Sein und Werden im Recht, Festgabe Ulrich von Lübtow* edited by W.G. Becker & L.S. von Carolsfeld (Duncker & Humblot, Berlin, 1970), pp. 381-387.

19. *Tijdschrift voor Rechtsgeschiedenis* (1975), pp. 211-220.

20. *IURA* (1966), pp. 174-178.

21. *Tijdschrift voor Rechtsgeschiedenis* (1960), pp. 197-210.

22. *Law Quarterly Review* (1961), pp. 526-532.

23. *Studia et Documenta Historiae et Iuris* (1962), pp. 331-341.

24. *Studi in Onore di Edoardo Volterra*, ii, (Giuffrè, Milan, 1969), pp. 445-449.

25. *Labeo* (1975), pp. 193-196.

26. *Zeitschrift der Savigny-Stiftung (romanistische Abteilung)* (1961), pp. 392-402.

27. *Mélanges Philippe Meylan*, i, (Imprimerie Centrale de Lausanne, Lausanne, 1963), pp. 66-69.

28. *Tijdschrift voor Rechtsgeschiedenis* (1971), pp. 73-83.

29. *Tijdschrift voor Rechtsgeschiedenis* (1962), pp. 209-242.

30. *Synteleia Arangio-Ruiz* (Jovene, Naples, 1965), pp. 290-292.

Preface

The articles in this volume all concern issues in understanding Roman private law. They include my earliest piece on Roman law, '*Arra* in the Law of Justinian', which was published in 1959, and which had its roots in a paper written for the class of Professor J.A.C. Thomas at the University of Glasgow.

Over the years the study of Roman law has given me enormous pleasure, and this seems an appropriate place to thank my teachers for all their encouragement and help: Sir John Spencer Muirhead, who first introduced me to the subject; Professor J.A.C. Thomas, under whom I took an advanced course on the Roman law of sale; David Daube, who supervised my D. Phil. thesis. I also want to express my gratitude to my friends and colleagues of many lands for the stimulation of their writings and conversation.

Alan Watson

For David and Caroline

I

Persons

1

Enuptio gentis

WHILE she was still a slave Hispala Faecenia plied the prostitute's trade and continued to support herself so even after she had been manumitted.[1] When her patron died and she was under no one's tutelage she sought from the tribune of the plebs and the praetor, and was granted, a *tutor dativus*.[2] She made a will instituting as sole heir her lover, Publius Aebutius,[3] who was the son of a deceased *eques equo publico*.[4] Aebutius was already supported by her since he was not well provided for by his relatives.[5]

Aebutius's *tutores* had died and he had come under the tutelage of his step-father,[6] who so maladministered the estate that he could not render an accounting. Livy also says Aebutius was under the *tutela* of his mother but this cannot be technically accurate since women could not be *tutores*. Probably Livy should be taken to mean that he was brought up by her (and her husband). Step-father and mother therefore decided to corrupt Aebutius by means of the Bacchanalia.[7] Hispala Faecenia warned Aebutius of the dangers, he refused to be initiated into the Bacchic rites, and was driven from home. The next day he reported the matter to Spurius Postumius, one of the consuls of that year, 186 B.C., who eventually dragged the story of the Bacchanalian orgies from the very reluctant Hispala Faecenia.[8] The cult and its adherents were investigated and put down with great severity,[9] and Publius Aebutius and Hispala Faecenia rewarded.

Livy, 39.19.3. Sp. Postumius aliquanto post Romam venit: eo referente de P. Aebutii et Hispalae Faeceniae praemio, quod eorum opera indicata Bacchanalia essent, senatus consultum factum est, (4) uti singulis his centena milia

1. Livy, 39.9.5.
2. Livy, 39.9.7. This kind of *tutor* was instituted by the *lex Atilia*, probably in 210 B.C.: cf. Rotondi, *Leges publicae populi romani* (reprinted Hildesheim, 1966), pp. 275f; Kaser, *Das römische Privatrecht*, i, 2nd edit. (Munich, 1972), p. 357 and n. 42.
3. Livy, 39.9.7.
4. Livy, 39.9.2.
5. Livy, 39.9.6.
6. Livy, 39.9.2.
7. Livy, 39.9.3,4.
8. Livy, 39.10.1–39.14.3.
9. Livy, 39.14.4–39.18.9.

aeris quaestores urbani ex aerario darent; utique consul cum tribunis plebis ageret, ut ad plebem primo quoque tempore ferrent, ut P. Aebutio emerita stipendia essent, ne invitus militaret neve censor ei invito equum publicum assignaret; (5) utique Faeceniae Hispalae datio, deminutio, gentis enuptio, tutoris optio item esset, quasi ei vir testamento dedisset; utique ei ingenuo nubere liceret, neu quid ei qui eam duxisset ob id fraudi ignominiaeve esset; (6) utique consules praetoresque, qui nunc essent quive postea futuri essent, curarent ne quid ei mulieri iniuriae fieret, utique tuto esset. Id senatum velle et aequum censere, ut ita fieret. (7) Ea omnia lata ad plebem factaque sunt ex senatus consulto; de ceterorum indicum impunitate praemiisque consulibus permissum est.

This text of Livy, and this text alone, mentions *gentis enuptio*, which seems to be, apparently, the right to marry outside the *gens*. The grant, of course, implies that without it Hispala Faecenia could only have married a member of her own *gens*. But we have no other evidence for any such restriction on freedom of marriage.

The purpose of the present article is to try to clarify the nature of both the special grant and the ordinary restriction. It should be emphasised that, given the sparseness of our information, no certainty should be expected. But any conjecture to be plausible must have at least three major qualities. First it must be able to explain the total lack of information for the years prior to 186 B.C. We should be looking perhaps for a rule of law which had little fundamental significance or which was of relatively recent introduction in 186, or was indeed both uncommon and new. Secondly, the conjecture must be able to explain the complete absence of sources for the period after 186. Unimportance of the rule would not be a wholly satisfactory explanation since from the second century B.C. on, legal rules become better and better documented. Hence the rule in question should have been abandoned, and shortly after 186 B.C. at that. The nearer the date of disappearance can be placed to 186 the better, both because the longer the rule survived the more likely it was to be mentioned a second time, and because our sources improve for the late second and the first centuries B.C., and for the Empire. Further, it would be preferable if the rule's disappearance was not due to an express provision of statute or edict – likely to be recorded! – but was the indirect result of some such provision, or of simple desuetude. Thirdly, the conjecture must be in complete harmony with the wording given by Livy for the *senatus consultum*. Livy's knowledge and understanding of law are very faulty and in this story itself there are at least two major howlers: he appears to think that a woman could be a *tutor* (39.9.2); and that *manus* was a power which could be exercised over an unmarried woman by her *patronus* or *tutor* (39.9.7). Hence the obvious technical precision of the wording given for the *senatus consultum* is even more striking and can leave little doubt that Livy is doing nothing more than put into indirect speech the direct wording of the decree.

Mommsen first deduced from the passage that a widow could be given by her husband the right of freely alienating her property and of marrying outside the *gens*, as well as the right of freely choosing her tutor. Hence he observed that a woman did not have the unfettered right of marrying a person who did not belong to her *gens*. He also thought the obstacle could not be removed at the simple wish of the father or *tutores* since otherwise there would have been no greater difficulty in marrying outside than inside the *gens*. Rather he suggested that the consent of the *gentiles* was necessary for marriage outside of the *gens*.[10] Later he modified his opinion and thought that legally a statute was necessary for *gentis enuptio*: support for this he found in the allusion to the *testamentum* which was originally a comitial act and which was regarded as such.[11]

But neither of Mommsen's theories will really do. To begin with, no attempt is made to explain the absence of sources before 186, yet presumably the rule on either theory was then very important. Indeed the second theory presupposes the antiquity of the rule since it was only in early times that the main form of will was a comitial act. This revised theory can also be discounted since it is likely that the *testamentum calatis comitiis* was already obsolete in 186,[12] yet that form of will was the only one which could be regarded as legislation. Secondly, neither theory can account for the absence of references after 186. It should be remembered that the succession rights of the *gentiles* were still very important at least as late as the first quarter of the first century B.C.[13] Thirdly, neither theory is really in harmony with Livy's Latin. The *item* in *tutoris optio item esset* separates that privilege from the foregoing, the *datio*, *deminutio*, *gentis enuptio*, and ties it alone to the *quasi ei vir testamento dedisset*. Thus, the Latin would not support the view that *gentis enuptio* was a right which was given to a widow by a husband's will. In favour of this proposition moreover, it should be noticed that *datio*, *deminutio* and *gentis enuptio* all go together, that if *quasi ei vir testamento dedisset* applied to one it would apply to all, and that nowhere is there any sign that a husband by will ever gave his widow the right of giving or diminishing her property. On the other hand, and significantly, we know it was well established that a husband by will could leave to his widow who had been in his *manus* the right of choosing her own tutor, the *optio tutoris*.[14] Once it is recognised that in Livy's text *enuptio gentis* has no connection with a *testamentum* then any

10. 'Die römischen Eigennamen der republikanischen und augusteischen Zeit' now in *Römische Forschungen* i (Berlin, 1864), pp. 1ff at p. 9 n. 5.
11. *Römisches Staatsrecht* iii (Leipzig, 1887), p. 21 n. 1; followed by Marquardt, *Das Privatleben der Römer* i (Leipzig, 1886), p. 30 n. 3.
12. Cf. Watson, *Roman Private Law around 200 BC* (Edinburgh, 1971), p. 100 n. 1.
13. Cicero, *de orat.* 1.39.176; *in Verrem II*, 1.45.115; *pro Flacco*, 34.84; Suetonius, *Divus Iulius*, 1.2; Catullus, 68.119ff; *Laudatio Turiae*, i. 13-26. Cf. Watson, *The Law of Succession in the Later Roman Republic* (Oxford, 1971), pp. 180f.
14. G.1.151ff.

remaining support for the idea that a comitial act was relevant for *enuptio gentis* also disappears.

Mommsen, however, was able to dispose of the idea that the restriction on marriage outside of the *gens* applied only to freedwomen. As he observes, we would have expected the position in early times to be the reverse, namely that women who were not members of the *gens* by birth – that is freedwomen and women married *cum manu* – could marry out of the *gens* more easily than those who were born into it.[15]

Kübler, who relies heavily on Mommsen, thought a decree of the *curiae* or of the senate was needed for marriage outside her *gens* by a woman who was *sui iuris*.[16] He further observed that in the earliest period the resolution of the *curiae* could occur through the *testamentum*, and considered this was the usual method. The idea that the restriction applied only to women *sui iuris* is, of course, not in conflict with the passage of Livy, and may be a valuable insight. But there is to this view, too, the wellnigh insuperable obstacle that the rule is evidenced neither before, nor after, 186. The difficulty is especially great, of course, because of the formalities and publicities of the procedures said to be involved. It is very hard to believe that if a woman *sui iuris* could marry outside her *gens* only by a decree of the *curiae* or the senate, this rule could exist, presumably for a long time, and then disappear some time after 186 B.C., without any clear trace. And as already argued, the text of Livy shows no connection between *gentis enuptio* and a *testamentum*, hence there is no link between the *curiae* and *gentis enuptio*. It should also be observed that the grant of *gentis enuptio* was not made to Hispala Faecenia by a decree of the senate. Rather the decree of the senate was to the effect that the consul should take up with the tribunes of the plebs the putting forward of these proposals to the people. That is, the grant of *datio*, *deminutio*, *gentis enuptio*, etc. was in fact made by a *plebiscitum*.[17]

Kaser thinks that very important reasons weighed against a woman *sui iuris* coming into the *manus* of her husband and that where the woman was *sui iuris* such marriages would be uncommon and only rare exceptional cases. He suggests that possibly Mommsen's conjecture that *gentis enuptio* required a comitial act should be linked with this proposition where a daughter had become the sole heir.[18] This opinion, which restricts the need for *gentis enuptio* to the sup-

15. 'Eigennamen', p. 9 n. 5. The further objection of Weissenborn and Müller [*Titi Livi ab urbe condita* ix (Berlin, 1962), p. 4] that there is no other example or proof that the marriage restriction applied only to freedwomen, has no force since we have no other evidence at all either for the restriction or the right of *gentis enuptio*.
16. *RE* 7, s.v. *gens* at 1186.
17. Why the procedure to be adopted was a *plebiscitum* and not a resolution of the *comitia centuriata* is discussed in Watson, *Law Making in the Later Roman Republic* (Oxford, 1974), pp. 6ff.
18. 'Ehe und *conventio in manum*', *IURA* i (1950), pp. 64ff at p. 101.

posedly rare case of marriage *cum manu* by a woman *sui iuris*[19] who was also an heiress, might explain why we have so little information on the subject, but leaves untouched the very considerable problem of how the legal rules involved disappeared without trace. And again nothing links *gentis enuptio* with a comitial act.

But a further fundamental objection can be levelled at all the foregoing views, especially that of Mommsen. A Roman *gens* was basically either patrician or plebeian,[20] yet intermarriage between patricians and plebeians was always permitted except between the years 450[21] and 445 B.C.[22] The plebs' insistence on the restoration of the right of intermarriage is not understandable if one could still not marry outside one's *gens* without approval whether of the *gentiles*, the senate or the *curiae*. The right of intermarriage between plebs and patricians is meaningless if there was not also, generally at least, the free right of marrying outside one's *gens*. Again, from a very early date long before 186 B.C., the right of intermarriage existed between Romans and the citizens of certain Latin communities at least.[23] But the Romans would be members of a *gens*, and the Latins would not be members of the same *gens*. This also is hard to reconcile with a general rule against marriage outside one's *gens*.

The preceding paragraph gives us a fourth quality to look for in the rule restricting the freedom of marriage with a member of another *gens*. Either it concerned only a small group of people and was not of general application, or it was not an absolute rule which could be set aside only by a decree of the senate, by the consent of the *gentiles* or by something like a legislative act. Or it was a rule which at one and the same time was easily waived and affected only a small group of people.

The text of Livy itself can afford much information about *gentis enuptio*. The grant included the right of *datio* and *deminutio*. The former is best taken as

19. It is not necessary or appropriate here to discuss the main propositions put forward by Kaser in his article but, in general, I do not find them convincing. Nor is it entirely plausible that marriage *cum manu* of a woman was a rare exception: for instance, the grant of *tutoris optio* to Hispala Faecenia clearly envisages that she, who is *sui iuris*, might enter a husband's *manus*.
20. Cf. e.g. Kübler, *RE* 7, s.v. *gens* at 1180ff; Scullard, *A History of the Roman World, 753–146 BC*, 3rd ed. (reprinted London, 1969), p. 41.
21. That the limitation was due to an innovation of the tyrannous second set of *decemviri* appears from all the surviving texts: Cicero, *de re pub.* 2.37.63; Livy, 4.4.5,9,10; 4.5.5; 4.6.2; Dionysius of Halicarnassus, 10.10.5; cf. above all, Last, 'The Servian Reforms', *JRS* xxxv (1945), pp. 30ff at pp. 31f; and also, e.g., Palmer, *The Archaic Community of the Romans* (Cambridge, 1970), p. 290. The argument that the provision was an innovation holds, whether or not one thinks that the formal distinction between patrician and plebeian was also of recent date.
22. By the *lex Canuleia*: Cicero, *de re pub.* 2.37.63; Livy 4.1-6.
23. See the instances cited by Mommsen, *Römisches Staatsrecht*, iii (Leipzig, 1887), p. 633 n. 1. The traditions inherent in the stories are significant even if the instances are not historical. We need not be precise about which communities had *conubium*.

meaning the right of transferring ownership;[24] the latter the right of contracting and alienating property (including money) even when this results or may result in a loss. Now there was no absolute prohibition on a woman *sui iuris* – as Hispala Faecenia was – transferring ownership or entering contracts which might result in loss. Rather, a woman *sui iuris* required the consent of her *tutor* to manumit a slave,[25] promise anything by stipulation[26] or indeed enter into any contract, or transfer anything by *mancipatio*.[27, 28] And, needless to say, *tutoris optio* also concerned tutelage, and had the purpose of making it simpler for the woman to obtain her *tutor*'s consent when this was necessary. Now in the reward to Hispala Faecenia the grant of *gentis enuptio* occurs in the midst of these three: after *datio* and *deminutio*, before *tutoris optio*. It therefore is plausible to assert that *gentis enuptio*, too, has some connection with tutelage, and this can only be in relation to the *tutor*'s consent. Just as the grants of *datio* and *deminutio* do not allow Hispala Faecenia to do something which otherwise was absolutely forbidden, but only to transfer ownership or diminish her substance without the authority of her *tutor*, so *gentis enuptio* does not permit something otherwise impossible but simply allows Hispala Faecenia to marry outside her *gens* without obtaining her *tutor*'s consent.

But for what in relation to marriage was the consent of the *tutor* normally required? It would seem it was not needed for marriage *sine manu*,[29] but was for marriage *cum manu* formed by *confarreatio* or by *coemptio*.[30] However, even when the marriage was to be *sine manu* the approval of the woman's *tutor* and her relatives would be sought and their strong disapproval, or disagreement among themselves, was perhaps not without legal importance. This is suggested for much later by a rescript of the Emperors Severus and Antoninus in the year A.D. 199.

> C.5.4.1. Cum de nuptiis puellae quaeritur nec inter tutorem et matrem et propinquos de eligendo futuro marito convenit, arbitrium praesidis provinciae necessarium est.

24. Or, of making a conveyance. Many texts show *datio* with the meaning of 'transference of ownership', 'conveyance': e.g. D.12.1.2.2; 46.3.68; 29.2.74.1; 15.1.47.6; 36.1.2. A similar sense for the verb, *dare*, is outstandingly clear in G.4.4.
25. Cicero, *pro Caelio*, 29.68.
26. Cicero, *pro Caecina*, 25.72.
27. Cicero, *pro Flacco*, 34.84; *ad Att.* 1.5.6 (cf. Watson, *The Law of Persons in the Later Roman Republic* (Oxford, 1967), pp. 137f); *Vat. Fr.* 1 (cf. Hausmaninger, *Die Bona Fides des Ersitzungsbesitzers im klassischen römischen Recht* (Vienna, Munich, 1964), pp. 13ff).
28. Since the text of Livy appears, to me, to make sense I would reject the far-reaching emendation and interpretation of Voigt, 'Zu Livius xxxix, 19, 5', *Rheinisches Museum für Philologie*, xxxiii (1878), pp. 483ff.
29. But it was for the constitution of a dowry (Cicero, *pro Caecina*, 25.73) except for a *dotis datio* which contained no *res mancipi*.
30. Cf. Watson, *Persons*, pp. 46f.

Thus we are told that when a girl's *tutor* and her mother and relatives cannot agree on the choice of a husband for her the decision is needed of the governor of the province. This would imply that relatives and *tutores*, for sufficient reason, could stop a marriage taking place.[31] Very possibly for a much earlier period we can call in aid the incident in Ardea in 443 B.C. when according to Livy a plebeian girl was courted by a patrician who won the mother's support, and by a plebeian who had the approval of her *tutores*. The resulting quarrel could not be settled privately and the matter was taken to court.[32] The report is only relevant for us, of course, if either the law of this Latin town was the same as that of Rome on this point, or if Livy has assimilated the law of Rome to that of Ardea.[33]

The important question for us, though, is where, in all this, does the consent of the *tutor* to *gentis enuptio* fit? I should like to produce a hypothesis and then examine, so far as necessary, the details.

I suggest that when a woman *sui iuris* was to be married *cum manu* the consent of her *tutor* was needed but it could not be unreasonably withheld. When the woman in question was in the first class of citizens because of her wealth she was expected to marry inside the *gens* and so keep her fortune within the family group. If she wished to marry *cum manu* outside the *gens* then not only could the *tutor* withhold his consent but it was considered perfectly reasonable and proper for him to do so, he could not be compelled to give his consent and the marriage would not be valid without it. The grant by the *senatus consultum* of one hundred thousand *asses* to Hispala Faecenia[34] put her in the first class of citizens and the further award of *gentis enuptio* freed her from the necessity of having her *tutor*'s consent to marriage outside her *gens*.

The legal rules contained in this hypothesis have the four general qualities which earlier I maintained were necessary for any satisfactory explanation of the problem. First, we can see why there is no information on the subject before 186 B.C. The requirement of the *tutor*'s consent to *gentis enuptio* is only an extension of the requirement of his consent to marriage *cum manu* and differs only in that it is regarded as self-evidently reasonable for him to withhold it. Thus it would not be specially prominent. The requirement of his consent to *gentis enuptio* would not be the result of express legislation but develop gradually in practice – hence no evidence for its introduction – and it would apply only to a tiny fraction of the population.[35] Moreover, social conditioning was presumably

31. Cf. e.g. Corbett, *The Roman Law of Marriage* (Oxford, 1930), pp. 61f. Volterra is inclined to take the decision in C.5.4.1. as applicable to a rule of local, and not Roman, law; 'Sul diritto familiare di Ardea nel V secolo A.C.', *Studi in onore di Antonio Segni* (Milan, 1966), pp. 3ff at pp. 20f.
32. Livy 4.9.4–6.
33. Cf. now on the whole story, Daube, *Roman Law, Linguistic, Social and Philosophical Aspects* (Edinburgh, 1969), pp. 113ff, and the authorities he cites.
34. Livy, 39.19.4.
35. Though socially and politically this was the most important fraction.

such that only very rarely would an extremely wealthy woman *sui iuris* consider marrying out of the *gens*. Such social conditioning would be far less strong in the case of a freedwoman like Hispala Faecenia who had no ties of blood, history or sentiment with the *gens* to which she was attached. Secondly, we can explain the total absence of sources after 186 B.C. The anti-feminist *lex Voconia* of 169 B.C.[36] forbade persons who were assessed in the census as having more than one hundred thousand *asses* from instituting a woman as heir.[37] This rule applied even where the testator's sole child was a daughter.[38] After the *lex Voconia*, then, the class of women who owned more than one hundred thousand *asses* would be virtually extinct.[39] Thus, after 169 there would scarcely be a woman who needed her *tutor*'s consent to marriage outside her *gens*, in so far as this requirement was above the normal requirement of the *tutor*'s consent to her marriage. And, since this was the indirect result of legislation which aimed at something else, there would naturally be no trace of an express provision abolishing the requirement. Thirdly, the rules are in harmony with the wording of the *senatus consultum* as reported by Livy. Fourthly, they constitute neither an absolute bar to marriage outside the *gens* (which could be set aside only by a resolution of the senate, the *curiae* or of the *gentiles*) nor were they of general application.[40]

Something more must be said about some of the details of the hypothesis. The proposition that the *tutor*'s consent for *gentis enuptio* was needed only for very rich women *sui iuris*, in particular those with a fortune of at least one hundred thousand *asses*, is easily explained. The purpose of the rule is, of course, the preservation of the fortune for the benefit of the *gens* or at least for particular members of it, and hence the rule is appropriate only where the woman is wealthy. It should again be stressed that for at least another century the succession rights of the *gens* remained very important.[41] Here we might appropriately compare this rule with the Attic law of marriage of an ἐπίκληρος or 'heiress': when a citizen died leaving no issue but a daughter (or daughters) and he had not taken the step of adopting a son and marrying him to the daughter, then the right to marry her went to the nearest male relative, in a fixed order of precedence. If the ἐπίκληρος was already married her male relative could still claim her as his bride and force the dissolution of her existing marriage, and according

36. Cf. Watson, *Succession*, pp. 29ff.
37. G.2.274. Though Dio Cassius, 56.10, speaks of 25,000 *drachmae* which would be one hundred thousand sesterces of Roman money.
38. Cicero, *de fin*. 2.17.55; Augustine, *de civ. Dei*, 3.21.
39. Until legal force was given to *fideicommissa* (cf. G.2.274) in the reign of Augustus, by which time marriage *cum manu* itself had almost entirely disappeared.
40. Even if one thinks a large proportion of patrician girls *sui iuris* would have fortunes of more than one hundred thousand *asses* and would require the *tutor*'s consent for *gentis enuptio*, the presumably larger number of patrician males who had so much money would be able to marry less wealthy plebeian girls who needed no such consent.
41. See supra, p. 5 n. 13.

to Isaeus this was of frequent occurrence.[42] In this case, too, the special restriction on the woman's choice in marriage applied only to those with money and had the purpose of keeping her wealth within the family circle.[43, 44] The proposition that the Roman restriction applied only to women with a fortune of at least one hundred thousand *asses* is more conjectural, and indeed need not be rigidly insisted upon. But it is suggested by two facts. First, that is the sum of money decreed to Hispala Faecenia by the senate and the grant of *gentis enuptio* may be dictated in part by the desire to free her from the restriction imposed upon her by the very generosity of the senate itself. Secondly, as a result of the *lex Voconia* of 169 B.C., the disappearance of the rule without trace becomes somewhat easier to explain if the restriction applied only to women of that degree of wealth.

The hypothesis also postulated that in the usual case the consent of the *tutor* to marriage by *conferreatio* or *coemptio* could not be unreasonably withheld. There is no textual evidence for this, but that should not distress us unduly since there is, in fact, scarcely any textual evidence that the *tutor*'s consent to such a marriage was needed at all. The earliest evidence for consent is in Cicero, *pro Flacco*, 34.84, by which time *manus* itself had become uncommon.[45] The very strong *a priori* probability is that the *tutor* could not act in a wholly arbitrary fashion, and for his own personal gain withhold his consent from any marriage to be contracted *cum manu*, no matter how reasonable it might be. Such a situation would have been intolerable.

Finally on the details of the hypothesis, it was also postulated that the *tutor*'s consent to *gentis enuptio* was needed only when the marriage from the outset was to be *cum manu*. One reason for this is that the words *gentis enuptio* imply that the woman is actually moving out of her *gens* which would not be the case where she was married *sine manu*. Again, so long as a marriage was *sine manu*, the rights of the *gens* to succeed to her property would not technically be affected.[46] Further, the *tutor*'s consent was needed for a marriage which was constituted *cum manu* but not for one formed *sine manu*. Nonetheless, it should be said that there is a possibility that the *tutor*'s consent to *gentis enuptio* by a wealthy woman was needed even when the marriage at the outset was *sine manu*. The requirement of this consent may have developed because it might happen that the woman would eventually have come under her husband's

42. *Pyrrhus*, 63ff.
43. For all this see Harrison, *The Law of Athens*, *i*, *The Family and Property* (Oxford, 1968), pp. 9ff, 132ff.
44. Cf. for Jewish law, Numbers 36, especially verse 8: 'And every daughter that possesseth an inheritance in any tribe of the children of Israel, shall be wife unto one of the family of the tribe of her father, that the children of Israel may enjoy every man the inheritance of his fathers.'
45. For this see Watson, *Persons*, pp. 21ff, 46f.
46. This is so for 186 B.C. but not, of course, for the late first century B.C. when intestate succession was fundamentally altered by edicts: cf. Watson, *Succession*, pp. 181ff.

manus by *usus*.[47] Livy 4.9.4-6 and C.5.4.1[48] might be an indication that in some circumstances a *tutor* could block the woman's marriage even when this was without *manus*. This possibility does not affect the main structure of the hypothesis.

To return for a moment to the situation of 186 B.C. Hispala Faecenia was a freedwoman whose *patronus* had died and to whom a *tutor dativus* had been appointed. This means that the patron had left no son (not even one under puberty) who could succeed to the tutelage of Hispala Faecenia.[49] Hence, if the *patronus* had no other direct descendants[50] Hispala Faecenia's inheritance would go on her death intestate[51] to the *gens* of which she was in some sense a member. This appears clearly from Cicero, *de orat.* 1.39.176 which concerns the *hereditas* of a freedman's son.[52] All this despite the fact that she herself would not be regarded as a *gentilis*, within the terms of the definition given by Cicero, *top.* 6.29.[53]

If the above explanation of *gentis enuptio* is correct then it seems we may have been attributing too much power to the *gens* and making marriage within the *gens* more significant than it really was.[54] Rather, what we have is another rule which shows the importance of the rights of succession of the *gens*.

No paper dedicated to my master David Daube would be appropriate without at least a passing reference to wider matters. The grant to Hispala Faecenia of *datio*, *deminutio*, *gentis enuptio* and *tutoris optio* has the aim of making her more independent of her *tutor*'s control. Nothing would better show the hollowness of any claim that at that time *tutela mulierum* existed to protect a woman from her own weakness.[55] Again, the seriousness with which the Roman authorities regarded the Bacchanalian orgies is well displayed. Only that explains the very generous grant of money and other privileges made to a prostitute who revealed what she knew unwillingly and only under severe threats,[56] and to a young man who, not to put too fine a point on it, was living off her immoral earnings and had made his complaint to the consul out of self-interest.[57]

47. For the argument that it was only around the beginning of the first century B.C. that *auctoritas tutoris* was needed if the woman was to come under the husband's *manus* by *usus* see Watson, *Persons*, pp. 21ff; idem, *Legal Origins and Legal Change*, chapter 3, pp. 11ff.
48. Cf. supra.
49. Cf. G.1.177ff.
50. For the rules of the XII Tables which were then still in force see G.3.45f; cf. Watson, *Succession*, pp. 185f.
51. Since she was a woman she could have no *suus heres*. And a woman could never make a will without the consent of her *tutor* (and even then only when she had undergone *capitis deminutio*); cf. Watson, *Succession*, pp. 23f.
52. The obscurities in that situation do not affect us but see Watson, *Succession*, p. 182.
53. Cf. e.g. Treggiari, *Roman Freedmen during the Late Republic* (Oxford, 1969), pp. 81f and 82 n. 1.
54. Cf. e.g. Watson, *Roman Private Law*, pp. 19f.
55. See for a later period G.1.190.
56. Livy, 39.12-13.
57. Livy, 39.11.3-7.

Finally, if we could believe Livy's whole account we would learn something more about Roman law and Roman sexual morality. It should be observed that Aebutius's step-father *quia tutelam ita gesserat ut rationem reddere non posset, aut tolli pupillum aut obnoxiam sibi vinculo aliquo fieri cupiebat.*[58] What one might suspect from the first clause quoted is confirmed by the word *pupillus*. This forward young man, Aebutius, was still under tutelage! The text of Livy, indeed, might be adduced as evidence that the view – later held by the Proculians[59] – was already widespread that tutelage of boys came to an end at fourteen, not when they reached physical maturity.[60] Only with difficulty could it be maintained that Aebutius had not reached puberty! Unfortunately I doubt whether Livy's dignified narrative, so sympathetic to Publius Aebutius and Hispala Faecenia, can be regarded as trustworthy. Despite the impression deliberately created by Livy, these two were, as we have noticed, very shady characters. It seems to me highly likely that Hispala's master had freed her because as a *libertina* she could attract better-paying customers, and that after the manumission he continued to run her as a whore. I suspect that on his death Aebutius became Hispala's pimp as well as her lover – a traditional arrangement – and that he was neither so young nor inexperienced in the ways of the world as Livy suggests.

It is sometimes suggested, on the sole authority of Livy, 39.19.4, that despite the financial compensation provided by the state, exemption from the *equus publicus* was regarded as a privilege.[61] But if the view of Publius Aebutius expressed here is correct, then we should not conclude too hastily that the exemption conferred on him after he became wealthy by the grant from the *aerarium* was a benefit which would be eagerly desired by young *equites*.

58. Livy, 39.9.3.
59. G.1.196.
60. This is denied for marriage by boys by Watson, *Roman Private Law*, p. 20.
61. Cf. Gelzer, *The Roman Nobility*, translated by Seager (Oxford, 1969), p. 5.

2

Two Notes on Manus

1. Usus, trinoctio abesse and the Lemuria

The most important text for *usus* is G. 1.111.

> Usu in manum conueniebat quae anno continuo nupta perseuerab*at*; *quia* enim veluti annua possessione usucapiebatur, in familiam viri trans*i*bat filiaque locum optinebat. itaque lege duodeci*m* tabularum cautu*m* est ut, si qua nollet eo modo in manu*m* mariti convenire, ea quotannis trinoctio abesset atque eo modo <*usum*> cuiusque anni interrumperet. sed hoc totum ius partim legibus sublatum est, partim ipsa desuetudine oblitteratum est.

Thus, according to Gaius *manus* was acquired by *usus* if a woman remained married (*nupta*) for a year unless she stayed away from her husband for three nights. J. G. A. Wilms[1] advanced the view that the nights in question were not any three nights, but the three nights of the *Lemuria*, 9-10, 11-12 and 13-14 May, when it was believed that the ghosts of ancestors came to homes and had to be warded off by the head of the family. This opinion can, I submit, be confidently rejected. To begin with there is nothing in the texts on the *Lemuria* which indicates or implies in any way that absence on these nights would prevent the acquisition of *manus*.

> Ovod, *Fasti*, 5.429. nox uni iam media est somnoque silentia praebet,
> et canis et variae conticuistis aves,
> ille memor veteris ritus timidusque deorum
> surgit – habent gemini vincula nulla pedes –
> signaque dat digitis medio cum pollice iunctis,

1. *De vrouw sui iuris, Cicero, pro Flacco 34, 84 en de manusvestiging door usu,* Gent, 1938, pp. 28ff: aproved as a probability by P. Koschaker, ZSS 63 (1943, p. 477; and by Th. Mayer-Maly, '*Studien zur Frühgeschichte der Usucapio* II', ZSS (1961), pp. 221ff at p. 260. The question is left open by Kaser, *Das römische Privatrecht* I, 1955, p. 69 n. 9; A. Watson, *The Law of Persons in the Later Roman Republic* Oxford, 1967, p. 20 n. 1.; D. Daube, *Dividing a Child in Antiquity,* California Law Review 54 (1966), pp. 1630 ff at p. 1634.

occurrat tacito ne levis umbra sibi,
cumque manus puras fontana perluit unda,
vertitur et nigras accipit ante fabas
aversusque iacit, sed dum iacit, 'haec ego mitto,
his' inquit 'redimo meque meosque fabis.'
hoc novies dicit nec respicit; umbra putatur
colligere et nullo terga vidente sequi.
rursus aquam tangit Temesaeaque concrepat aera
et rogat, ut tectis exeat umbra suis.
cum dixit novies 'manes exite paterni!'
respicit et pure sacra peracta putat. –

Festus, *Fabam* nec tangere, nec nominare Diali flamini licet, quod ea putatur ad mortuos pertinere. Nam et Lemuralibus iacitur larvis, et Parentalibus adhibetur sacrificiis, et in flore eius luctus litterae apparere videntur.

Nonius 135, *Lemures*, larvae nocturnae et terrificationes imaginum et bestiarum. Varro de Vita Populi Romani lib. 1: 'quibus temporibus in sacris fabam iactant noctu ac dicunt se Lemurios domo extra ianuam eicere'.

Secondly, nothing in these texts suggests that the *Lemuria* were significant in any way for the power of a Roman *paterfamilias* over his dependants, for instance, for loss of *patria potestas* if a *filiusfamilias* was absent. The whole ritual is directed towards preventing the ghosts acquiring any sort of sway over the members of the family; not to giving power over individuals to the *pater*. Thirdly, there is no indication and no reason to think that whatever effect the ritual might have had for a dependant in a family was produced only if the dependant was actually present, at the ceremony or in the house. The words of Ovid, in fact, suggest that the head of the household alone arose from his bed and performed the ritual. Fourthly, if the *Lemuria* had been significant for *manus* we would have expected the point to be different. The wife's presence in the matrimonial home on these nights would have brought her within her husband's *manus*, and the passage of a whole year would have been irrelevant. Fifthly, a text of Aulus Gellius shows that for Quintus Mucius, in the late 2nd century B.C. absence for any three nights sufficed to break the *usus*.

N.A. 3.2.12. <Q.> quoque Mucium iureconsultum dicere solitum legi non esse usurpatam mulierem, quae, cum Kalendis Ianuariis apud virum matrimonii causa esse coepisset, ante diem IV Kalendas Ianuarias sequentes usurpatum isset: 13. non enim posse impleri trinoctium, quod abesse a viro usurpandi causa ex duodecim tabulis deberet, quoniam tertiae noctis posterioris sex horae alterius anni essent, qui inciperet ex Kalendis.

It is not satisfactory simply to suggest that this was the result of a change due to juristic interpretation. G.1.111 implies that the *trinoctio abesse* rule was an innovation of the XII Tables,[2] and we can at least accept from what he says that the codification contained an express provision on the subject. But the wording (modernised) of the XII Tables was still very well known in Quintus Mucius' time – slightly later Cicero mentions that in his childhood the codification was learnt by heart at school.[3] In the circumstances evidence for a change in interpretation would have to be produced. And there seems to be no such evidence.[4] A similar argument from Aulus Gellius, *N.A.* 3.2.13 lies against any view that the XII Tables contained no provision on *usurpatio*.

Thus, the wife's absence from the matrimonial home for any three nights would prevent the acquisition of *manus*.[5] The point is of considerable importance, and so is the existence of a specific provision on *usurpatio* in the XII Tables, because the emphasis is then on the avoidance of *manus*, not, as might seem to be inherent in Wilm's theory, on the acquisition of *manus*. In other words, there was already a desire in some cases on the part of the woman or her *paterfamilias* to avoid *manus* and this desire was given legal recognition.

This last conclusion then involves us in a further point, namely that before the introduction of *usurpatio* the standard marriage was one where the husband had *manus* over the wife. *Usus* was not a device invented to turn a permanent or semi-permanent marriage where there was no *manus* into a marriage where there was *manus*, but from the start was intended for marriages which were to be *cum manu*.[6]

The XII Tables provision also means, of course, that it was possible to have a permanent marital union in which the woman did not ever come under the *manus* of the man. Since positive steps had to be taken to avoid *manus* occurring, and since even as late as the beginning of the 2nd century B.C. marriage with *manus* was probably more common than marriage *sine manu*,[7] we can be confident that at the time of the XII Tables most marital unions involved the woman's being in manus.[8] But

2. Tomulescu arbitrarily suggests that Gaius was mistaken and the *trinoctio abesse* rule was much later: *Gaius 1.111 und die Ehe usu*, Sein und Werden im Recht, Festgabe von Lübtow, Berlin, 1970, pp. 401ff at pp. 504ff.
3. *de leg.* 2.4.9.
4. For this and other serious arguments against Wilms see already R. Yaron, *De usurpationibus*, Studi Grosso II, Turin, 1968, pp. 553 ff, at pp. 554f.
5. Filhol fails to establish any connection between this *trinoctium* and the rule of sacral law (cf. Aulus Gellius, *N.A.* 10.15.14) that the flamen Dialis should not sleep away from his bed for a *trinoctium continuum*: *Usurpatio Trinoctii (Aulu-Gelle, Nuits Attiques, X.15)*, Hommages à L. Herrmann, Brussels, 1960, pp. 359ff.
6. Cf. Kaser, *AI*, p. 319.
7. Cf. A. Watson, *Roman Private Law around 200 B.C.*, Edinburgh, 1971, p. 17 and n.6.
8. Cf. e.g. Kaser, *loc. cit.*; R. Yaron, *Minutiae on Roman Dicorce*, *TR* 28 (1960), pp. 1ff at p. 5.

there is no reason to doubt that such unions where there was no *manus* were nonetheless regarded as true and proper marriages. This is the clear implication of G.1.111[9] and there is no evidence to the contrary.[10]

2. *In manu filii*

When a wife was *in manu* and the husband was a *filiusfamilias,* was she in the *manus* of her husband or of his *paterfamilias*? For early law we have no direct information, but we have six texts from the Empire.

> G.2.159. Idem iuris est et <*in*> uxoris persona quae in manu est, quia filiae loco est, et in nuru quae in manu filii est, quia neptis loco est.

> G.3.41. Qua de causa postea praetoris edicto haec iur*is* iniquitas em*e*ndata est. sive enim faciat testamentum libertus, iubetur ita testari ut patrono suo partem dimidiam bonorum suorum relinqua*t*, et si aut nihil aut minus quam partem dimidiam reliquerit, datur patrono contra tabulas testamenti partis dimidiae bonorum possessio; si vero intestatus moriatur suo herede relicto adoptivo filio, <vel> uxore quae in manu ipsius esset, vel nur*u* quae in manu filii eius fuerit, dat*ur* aeque patrono adversus hos suos heredes partis dimidiae bonorum possessio. prosunt autem liberto ad excludendum patronum naturales liberi, non solum quos in potestate mortis tempore habet, sed etiam emancipati et in adoptionem dati, si modo aliqua ex parte heredes scripti *sint, aut praeteriti con*tra tabulas testamenti bonorum possessionem ex edicto petierint; nam exheredat*i* nullo modo repellunt patronum.
>
> *Coll.* 16.2.3 (Gaius *institutionum libro* III) Uxor quoque, quae in manu est, *ei cuius in manu est* sua heres est, quia filiae loco est: item nurus quae in filii manu est, nam et haec neptis loco est. Sed ita demum erit sua heres, *si* filius, cuius in manu sit cum pater moritur, in potestate eius non sit. Idemque dicimus et de ea, quae *in* nepotis manu matrimonii causa sit, quia proneptis loco est.[11].

> *Epit. Ulp.* 22.14. Sui heredes instituendi sunt vel exheredandi. Sui autem heredes sunt liberi, quos in potestate habemus, tam naturales quam adoptivi; item uxor, quae in manu est, et nurus, quae in manu est filii, quem in potestate habemus.

> Aulus Gellius, *N.A. 18.6.9.* Matrem autem familias appellatam esse eam solam, quae in mariti manu mancipioque aut in eius, in cuius maritus, manu mancipioque

9. Even though it can be asserted that words and phrases like *nupta perseverabat* and *maritus* need not be used by Gaius inevitably of valid marriages, the natural understanding is that they are so used, unless there are counter-indications.
10. Cf. e.g. P. E. Corbett, *The Roman Law of Marriage,* Oxford, 1930, pp. 86ff. Tomulescu, however, argues from Aulus Gellius *N.A.* 3.2.12, that such relationships in the 5th century B.C. were not marriage and that the woman was, for the time being, a sort of concubine: *Gaius, 1.111*, pp. 401ff. In that text he takes *matrimonii causa* as 'with the intention of a future marriage' ('zwecks späterer Ehe'). But just as easily the phrase can mean 'on account of marriage': cf. e.g. Varro, *de ling. lat.* 5.175; G.1.115b; 2.63; *Coll.* 16.2.3. So the text is not positively for him.

esset, quoniam non in matrimonium tantum, sed in familiam quoque mariti et in sui heredis locum venisset.

Servius *in Verg. Aen.* 11.476 . . . *Matrem vero familias eam esse, quae in mariti manu mancipioque, aut in cuius maritus manu mancipioque esset, quoniam in familiam quoque mariti et sui heredis locum venisset.*

The first four texts unequivocally say that the wife is *in manu filii,* the last two that she is *in manu mancipioque* of his *pater.* The first four are from legal works, the remaining two from non-legal writers. But of this first four three originate in the Institutes of Gaius, and the *Epitome Ulpiani* from which the fourth comes is very dependent upon Gaius. So it might be felt that the view expressed is very much that of one jurist, though in an elementary work like the Institutes one could expect simple unqualified statements to give the general opinion.[12] On the other hand, of the two non-legal texts, that of Servius comes directly or indirectly from that of Aulus Gellius as the wording shows. And both, with their *manu mancipioque,* are very untechnical. Therefore, any conflict for classical law has to be resolved in favour of the view in the first four texts.

But, then, what is the significance of the four texts? First of all, pace Bonfante[13] it is not that Gaius and Ulpian are talking of succession when the *paterfamilias* is dead and the *filiusfamilias* – become in turn *paterfamilias* – has been invested with *manus* over his wife, and that clarity demands such a way of speaking to avoid confusion with the relationship of the wife to the dead *paterfamilias.* Such a view is just contrary to the tenor of the texts.[14] Moreover, we must not forget that in every legal text where *manus* is spoken of when the husband is a *filiusfamilias,* the wife, we are told, is in the *manus* of the husband. It would be an amazing coincidence if this did not really represent what was felt to be the case but was due to such particular facts as Bonfante suggests. Secondly, these legal texts should not be taken as indicating a factual, but not a legal, situation: that is, that although the *paterfamilias* alone has legal power over the menbers of the family he in practice allows a married *filius* a greater or less amount of the de facto control over his wife in *manu.*[15] Legal texts should be primarily concerned with

11. This text is used to reconstruct what is now G. 3.3. in the editions of Gaius' *Institutes.*
12. Against Solazzi's suggestion of interpolations, *Glosse a Gaio,* Studi Riccobono, Palermo, 1936, pp. 71ff at pp. 172ff, see Volterra, *'Nuove ricerche sulla conventio in manum',* Atti della Accademia Nazionale dei Lincei (*Classe di Scienze morali, storiche e filologiche* 12, Rome, 1966, pp. 251ff. at p. 257 n. 17.
13. *Corso di diritto romano, i, Diritto di famiglia,* reprinted Milan, 1963, pp. 67f.
14. Volterra thinks Bonfante's view rather forced: *Nuove ricerche,* p. 256 n. 13 (at. p. 257).
15. This seems to be the suggestion of Kaser, *RPR* I, p. 55 and n.17.

the law, not the social situation. And again it is important to stress that it is not some but all of the legal texts which talk of the wife's being *in manu filii.* Moreover, a view such as that which is here being opposed would also involve holding that the two non-legal texts give the legal, not the factual, situation.

We must accept, I think, that in classical law a wife married *cum manu* to a *filiusfamilias* was regarded juristically as being in the *manus* of the *filius.*[16] But, as G.2.159 and *Coll.* 16.2.3 tell us, she was in the position of a granddaughter, *neptis loco,* to her husband's *paterfamilias*; and if the husband should leave the *patria potestas* of his father, then his wife, as all four texts make plain, would be a *sua heres* of the *pater.* Obviously then, the wife was very much within the family of the *paterfimilias,* though no text actually calls his relationship to her *patria potestas.* Just as the four legal texts which we have looked at give us the legal position so the two non-legal texts which talk of the woman's being *in manu mancipioque* of the husband's *pater* tell us something of practical importance. The woman was in practice much subject to him.

One further explanation of the legal texts which should be rejected is that the wife was *in manu* of her husband in the sense that, like a daughter to him, she would not become independent on the death of the hisband's *pater* but would then be within his power. Support for such a view might be found in the statement that she was *neptis loco* to her husband's *paterfamilias* and *filiae loco* to her husband. But the fundamental weakness of any such hypothesis lies in the different use of language in respect of *patria potestas;* a granddaughter (or grandson) is never said to be *in potestate* of her father, but always *in potestate* of the grandfather.[17] Again, two other and famous texts, G.2.157 and D.28.2.11 (Paul *2 ad Sab.*), are a flimsy basis for any view that in contemporary legal theory – as distinct from a vague, floating idea – *sui heredes* were regarded as in some sense already owners or quasi-owners of the property of the *pater*; and these two texts cannot be used to support the view that the *filius* has a (similar) sort of passive or silent power over his wife *in manu.*[18]

If, as has been argued, it was a juristic concept in the time of Gaius

16. Cf. above all, Volterra, *Nuove ricerche.*
17. *Cf. e.g. G. 2.156; Coll.* 3.2.2; D.1.6.4 (Ulpian *1 inst.*).
18. Pace Kaser [*Ruhende und verdrängende Hausgewalt im älteren römischen Recht*], ZSS 59 (1939), pp. 31ff at p. 31, the texts do not 'berichten, daß in alter Zeit die Hauskinder schon zu Lebzeiten des paterfamilias 'gewissermaßen' Eigentümer des Vermögens waren'. Nothing is said in the texts about earlier times, and there is no particular reason to hold that they are giving a theory which was held in early law.

that a wife was *in manu* of her *filius* husband this must have had consequences, benefiting the husband.[19] It is hard to find these in private law. They do not exist in respect of property, which all belongs to the *pater*. Again so far as the husband is concerned, Augustus' *lex Iulia de adulteriis coercendis,* probably of 18 B.C., seems to have drawn no distinction between a marriage where there was *manus* and one where there was not. Likewise there is no reason to think that in the Empire a *filius* husband could divorce his wife more easily if he were married *cum manu* than if he were married *sine manu*. It is clear that he could divorce his wife without his father's consent if he was married *sine manu*. Though there is no evidence the same was probably true where he was married *cum manu*. The father's right to dissolve a son's marriage – if the right still existed[20] – was apparently independent of whether there was *manus* or not.

The explanation lies elesewhere. Gaius tells us that *usus* no longer existed.[21] Tacitus[22] says that the habit of marrying by *confarreatio* had been dropped or was confined to a few families, and so there was no longer enough candidates for certain priesthoods. Hence a *senatusconsultum* was issued that by *confarreatio* a wife passed into her husband's *manus* only for sacred purposes but in other respects remained free of *mnaus.*[23] Gaius speaks of *coemptio* as still creative of *manus,*[24] but it must have become rare.[25] Hence, it can be said that *manus* was rather unimportant in private law in the time of Gaius. What was important and obvious were the sacred law consequences of *confarreatio* and these benefited the husband, not his father if he had one. Thus, it is very reasonable to think that it is on this account – unimportance of *manus* in private law, significance of *manus* in sacred law – that our four legal texts say that a wife is *in manu* of a husband who is a filiusfamilias.

To turn now to early times. Then, no doubt, the sacred consequences of *confarreatio* would be at least as significant as they were in the time of

19. I.e. while he was still a *filius*.
20. The right disappeared as a result of legislation under the Antonines. The Emperor responsible is a matter for doubt, but the problem does not directly concern us: P.S. 5.6.15; D. 24.1.32.19 (Ulpian *33 ad Sab.*); cf. Corbett, *Marriage* pp. 239ff.
21. G. 1.111.
22. *Ann.* 4.16.
23. G. 1.136.
24. G. 1.136.
25. Cf. e.g. De Zulueta, *The Institutes of Gaius* II, Oxford, 1953, p. 36. The *senatusconsultum* on *confarreatio* shows that it was not the actual ceremony nor its sacred law consequences which caused its unpopularity, but its effects on the private law rights of the wife. These were the same for *coemptio* as for *confarreatio,* and must also have resulted in the virtual disappearance of *coemptio*.

Gaius, and they would be for the benefit of the husband even when he was a *filius.* But the private law consequences would be enormously important since *manus* was the rule, not the exception, and the advantages here would accrue to the husband's *paterfamilias.* The private law results of *manus* would be much more important than those of sacred law and hence we can confidently assert that at the time of the XII Tables and throughout most of the Republic a wife would be regarded as *in manu* of the *paterfamilias* of her husband's family.

3

The Divorce of Carvilius Ruga

I.

An attempt to trace the main outline of the history of divorce in Rome in the very early period is largely an attempt to explain two conflicts or, at least, two apparent conflicts in the texts, both of which are connected with the divorce of Carvilius Ruga.

II.

First. On the one hand it would appear and is generally accepted [1]) that the XII Tables contained a provision about divorce. The main text adduced for this view is Cicero *Phil.* 2.28.69:

> . . . illam suam suas res sibi habere iussit ex duodecim tabulis, clavis ademit, exegit [2]).

The other text cited in this connexion, D. 48.5.44, from Gaius' third book on the XII Tables, with its *si ex lege repudium missum non sit* confirms the existence in the XII Tables of some provision on the subject of divorce [3]). On the other hand, there is the very strong Roman tradition that the first divorce was that of Spurius Carvilius Ruga. It is so described by Dionysius of Halicarnassus, Plutarch, Valerius Maximus and Aulus Gellius [4]).

---

1) Cf most recently, Yaron *Minutiae on Roman Divorce*, Tijd. 28 (1960) p. 1ff; C. Herrmann *Le rôle judiciaire et politique des femmes sous la république romaine* (Bruxelles-Berchem, 1964) p. 30f. Nothing significantly new on early law is to be found in Meira *A Legislação romana do divórcio* Romanitas 3—4 (1961) p. 199ff. To these is to be added Yaron *De divortio varia, 3. Iterum D. 48.5.44*, Tijd. 32 (1964) 554 ff.; I am very grateful to Professor Yaron for allowing me to read in typescript this part of his article.

2) This is the punctuation adopted by most modern jurists: but see *infra p.* [5].

3) Cf Yaron Tijd. 28 *cit.* p. 1. Volterra in *Intorno a D. 48.5.44(43)* to appear in Studi in onore di Biondo Biondi holds that *ex lege* here does not refer to the XII Tables; but see the criticisms of Yaron in Tijd. 32 *cit.*

4) Cf Tertullian *Apol.* 6; *De monog.* 9.

Dionysius *Antiq.* 2.25.7:

Καὶ μέχρι πολλοῦ διέμεινε χρόνου ταῦτ' ἀμφότερα παρὰ Ῥωμαίοις ἀπαραιτήτου τυγχάνοντα ὀργῆς. μάρτυς δὲ τοῦ καλῶς ἔχειν τὸν περὶ τῶν γυναικῶν νόμον ὁ πολὺς χρόνος. ὁμολογεῖται γὰρ ἐντός ἐτῶν εἴκοσι καὶ πεντακοσίων μηδεὶς ἐν Ῥώμῃ λυθῆναι γάμος. κατὰ δὲ τὴν ἑβδόμην ἐπὶ ταῖς τριάκοντα καὶ ἑκατὸν ὀλυμπιάσιν ὑπατευόντων Μάρκου Πομπωνίου καὶ Γαΐου Παπιρίου πρῶτος ἀπολῦσαι λέγεται τὴν ἑαυτοῦ γυναῖκα Σπόριος Καρουΐλιος ἀνὴρ οὐκ ἀφανής, ἀναγκαζόμενος ὑπὸ τῶν τιμητῶν ὀμόσαι τέκνων ἕνεκα γυναικὶ συνοικεῖν (ἦν δ'αὐτῷ στεῖρα ἡ γυνή), ὅς ἐπὶ τῷ ἔργῳ τούτῳ καίτοι δι' ἀνάγκην γενομένῳ μισούμενος ὑπὸ τοῦ δήμου διετέλεσεν.

Plutarch *Quaest. Rom.* 14 [5]):

.... ἱστορεῖται γοῦν ὅτι πρῶτος μὲν ἐξέβαλε γυναῖκα Σπόριος Καρβίλιος ἐπ' ἀτεκνίᾳ, ...

Theseus-Romulus. 35. [6]. 3,4:

Οὕτω συνέμειξεν ἀλλήλοις καὶ συνέπηξε τὰ γένη, καὶ παρέσχε πηγὴν τῆς εἰς αὖθις εὐνοίας καὶ δυνάμεως τοῖς πράγμασιν. αἰδοῦς δὲ καὶ φιλίας καί βεβαιότητος, ἣν εἰργάσατο περὶ τοὺς γάμους, ὁ χρόνος ἐστὶ μάρτυς. 4. ἐν γὰρ ἔτεσι τριάκοντα καὶ διακοσίοις οὔτε ἀνὴρ ἐτόλμησε γυναικὸς οὔτε γυνὴ κοινωνίαν ἀνδρὸς ἐγκαταλιπεῖν, ἀλλ' ὥσπερ ἐν Ἕλλησιν οἱ σφόδρα περιττοὶ τὸν πρῶτον ἔχουσιν εἰπεῖν πατροκτόνον ἢ μητροφόνον οὕτω Ῥωμαῖοι πάντες ἴσασιν, ὅτι Καρβίλιος Σπόριος ἀπεπέμψατο γυναῖκα πρῶτος, ἀπαιδίαν αἰτιάσμενος.

Lycurgus-Numa 25. [3]. 12, 13:

ὡς γὰρ παρ' ἡμῖν οἱ ἱστορικοὶ γράφουσι τοὺς πρώτους ἢ φόνον ἐμφύλιον ἐργασαμένους ἢ πολεμήσαντας ἀδελφοῖς ἢ πατρὸς αὐτόχειρας ἢ μητρὸς γενομένους, 13 οὕτω Ῥωμαῖοι μνημονεύουσιν ὅτι πρῶτος μὲν ἀπεπέμψατο γυναῖκα Σπόριος Καρβίλιος, μετὰ τὴν Ῥώμης κτίσιν ἔτεσι τριάκοντα καὶ διακοσίοις οὐδενὸς τοιούτου γεγονότος, πρώτη δὲ γυνὴ Πιναρίου Θαλαία τοὔνομα διηνέχθη πρὸς ἑκυρὰν αὐτῆς Γετανίαν Ταρκυνίου Σουπέρβου βασιλεύοντος. οὕτω καλῶς καὶ κοσμίως τεταγμένα τὰ τῶν γάμων ἦν ὑπὸ τοῦ νομοθέτου.

Valerius Maximus *Mem.* 2.1.4:

Repudium inter uxorem et virum a condita urbe usque ad centesimum et quinquagesimum annum nullum intercessit. Primus autem Sp. Carvilius uxorem sterilitatis causa dimisit. Qui, quamquam tolerabili ratione motus videbatur, reprehensione tamen non caruit, quia ne cupiditatem quidem liberorum coniugali fidei praeponi debuisse arbitrabantur.

---

[5]) Cf *Quaest. Rom.* 59.

Aulus Gellius *N.A.* 4.3.1:

> Memoriae traditum est quingentis fere annis post Romam conditam nullas rei uxoriae neque actiones neque cautiones in urbe Roma aut in Latio fuisse, quoniam profecto nihil desiderabatur, nullis etiamtunc matrimoniis divertentibus. 2. Servius quoque Sulpicius in libro, quem composuit de dotibus, tum primum cautiones rei uxoriae necessarias esse visas scripsit, cum Spurius Carvilius, cui Ruga cognomentum fuit, vir nobilis, divortium cum uxore fecit, quia liberi ex ea corporis vitio non gignerentur, anno urbis conditae quingentesimo vicesimo tertio M. Atilio P. Valerio consulibus. Atque is Carvilius traditur uxorem, quam dimisit, egregie dilexisse carissimamque morum eius gratia habuisse, set iurisiurandi religionem animo atque amori praevertisse quod iurare a censoribus coactus erat uxorem se liberum quaerundum gratia habiturum.

N.A. 17.21.44:

> Anno deinde post Romam conditam quingentesimo undevicesimo Sp. Carvilius Ruga primus Romae de amicorum sententia divortium cum uxore fecit, quod sterila esset iurassetque apud censores uxorem se liberum quaerundorum causa habere, . . .

In the first text of Aulus Gellius it is not expressly said that the divorce of Carvilius was the first in Rome but that is the clear implication of what is said in §§ 1 and 2. The date of the first Roman divorce is estimated differently in the texts [6]) but a Spurius Carvilius Ruga was consul in 234 B.C. and again in 228 [7, 8]) and both Aulus Gellius and Dionysius place the divorce in question around 230 B.C. This date is generally accepted as correct [9]). How are we to reconcile the evidence that the XII Tables contained a provision about divorce with the tradition that the first Roman divorce took place over 200 years after the XII Tables?

---

6) As early as 604 B.C. according to Valerius Maximus: cf Corbett, *The Roman Law of Marriage* (Oxford, 1930) p. 227.

7) Cf Münzer *R.E.* III 1630.

8) Valerius Maximus 2.9.2 tells us that L. Annius repudiated his wife. With the help of Livy 9.43.25 this can be dated to 307—306 B.C.: cf Corbett *op. cit.* p. 218.

9) *E.g.* Kaser, *Das römische Privatrecht* I (Munich, 1955) p. 279: but see Corbett *op. cit.* p. 227. The early dating of Plutarch and Valerius Maximus might be a rationalisation, *i.e.*, it was realised that the first divorce could not be around 230 B.C., so Carvilius' divorce was made to take place much earlier.

III.

The second conflict or apparent conflict involves no fresh texts. It is widely accepted that the XII Tables contained a provision on divorce which used a form of words like *res suas sibi habeto* or *res tuas tibi habeto* [10]). This provision is, I think, generally taken as relating in some way, at least, to the separation of the wife's property from her husband's [11]). How is this to be squared with Gellius' statement in *N.A.* 4.3.1 that for almost five centuries from the founding of Rome there were no *cautiones rei uxoriae* and no *actiones rei uxoriae* and with his report in 4.3.2 that according to Servius *cautiones rei uxoriae* first became necessary with the divorce of Carvilius?

IV.

Before a solution is proposed, a little more must be said about the conflicts.

In the case of the first conflict, it is most likely that the XII Tables did contain a provision about divorce and that divorce was permitted at that time. One would expect Cicero and Gaius to have considerable knowledge of the provisions of the XII Tables even if at times they misunderstood them. Again, there is some evidence that divorce was allowed in Rome even before the XII Tables [12]). The Roman tradition that the divorce of Carvilius was the first must therefore be inaccurate and this, indeed, is generally accepted [13]). There is, in fact, considerable evidence of a divorce in Rome in 307—306 B.C. [14]). But if the tradition is wrong, Carvilius' divorce must nonetheless have had great significance and it must have been important enough to

---

10) Cf the authors cited in note 1 and the references they give. This phrase was certainly very common from at least the time of Plautus: Plautus *Am.* 928; *Tri* 266; Martial 10.41.2; Quintilian *Decl.* 262; Apuleius *Met.* 5.26; Seneca *Suas.* 1.6; D. 24.2.2.1 (Gaius *11 ad ed. prov.*).

11) Cf *infra* p. 28f.

12) Cf *infra* p. 30f.

13) *E.g.* Kaser *loc. cit.*

14) Cf *supra* p. 25 n. 8.

give rise to the tradition. Kaser says that, of course, the case of Carvilius was not the first case of divorce but was the first without fault of the wife, the divorce being for childlessness [15]). This, I suggest, is not wholly convincing. It is hard to believe that whereas some wives had, between the XII Tables and about 230 B.C., been divorced for some matrimonial offence, no husband had, during that long period, divorced his wife where she had not misbehaved and where the husband himself was behaving badly. Even if there were extremely severe penalties for unjustified divorce, one would expect it to occur: the prospect of a very large dowry — or even love of another woman — could prove irresistible. And a husband might well hope to escape the penalties of wrongfully divorcing his wife by falsely alleging that she was guilty of an offence and the truth might emerge later.

As for the second conflict, very considerable doubt must be expressed as to whether a clause like *res suas sibi habeto* was in the XII Tables at all. The sole text which on any interpretation supports the proposition that some such words were in the XII Tables is Cicero *Phil.* 2.28.69 and the interpretation of that depends very much on the punctuation adopted [16]). If we insert a comma after *tabulis* and not after *iussit*, then some such clause was in the XII Tables. If we insert a comma after *iussit* and not after *tabulis*, the text is no evidence that a clause like *suas res sibi habeto* was in the XII Tables. The provision of the XII Tables would then be concerned with the taking away of the keys from the wife. The latter punctuation in fact is the one generally preferred by modern editors of Cicero [17]). Indeed, it has in its favour the rhetoric of the situation for then the acts would be given in order of importance — Antony uttered the traditional formula of divorce, took away the keys as laid down by the XII Tables, drove her out. If *ex duodecim tabulis* is attached to *suas res sibi*

---

15) Cf Herrmann *op. cit.* p. 50f.

16) Cf Corbett *op. cit.* p. 218f.

17) Cf Mueller, *M. Tulli Ciceronis scripta quae manserunt omnia* II. 3 (Leipzig, 1893) p. 398; Clark, *M. Tulli Ciceronis Orationes* II (Oxford, 2nd edit. reprinted 1946) *ad h.l.*; Boulanger & Wuilleumier, *Cicéron, Discours* XIX (Paris, 1959) p. 126 (these last have, in fact, a semi-colon after *iussit*).

habere iussit, the act which comes in the middle, *clavis ademit*, looks very unimportant [18]. If the clause were not in the XII Tables it might be relatively late — it is not otherwise evidenced as existing before the time of Plautus — and if such were the case there would be no second conflict. Nonetheless, we cannot exclude the possibility that the XII Tables did contain such a clause and we must act, contrary to our interest, as if they did. Yaron [19] has shown the implausibility of the view that the XII Tables' clause, *res suas sibi habeto*, if it existed, related to marriages *sine manu*. He himself sees it not as being concerned with the form of the divorce but as „regulating the property relationship of the couple about to separate" [20] in marriages *cum manu*. I would agree with him that there is no real difficulty for his view in the fact that logically a wife in marriage *cum manu* owns no property [21] but nonetheless I am unconvinced by his thesis. Above all, it is most unlikely that a clause intended to regulate the property relationship between spouses who are about to part would take the form of a command by the husband to the wife to take away her property [22]. She might easily take too much! The husband will naturally be very interested in the property arrangements. Moreover, the property relationship between the spouses might be very complex and not at all suitable for a peremptory command. Again, one would just not expect, I think, that a phrase of this kind would be seriously

---

18) Mr Robert Ogilvie of Balliol College, Oxford, who kindly read this note would be much more definite in placing the comma after *iussit*. He tells me that in three-verb sentences in Cicero in which a prepositional phrase appears between the first and second verbs, the phrase, so far as he can discover, is always attached to the second verb. Moreover, he says, the construction of the balanced clauses of *suam . . . iussit* (11 syllables), *ex . . . ademit* (12 syllables), followed by a shorter phrase is regular in Cicero.

19) Tijd. 28 *cit.*

20) *Op. cit.* p. 3. He goes on, "it is only reasonable that divorce should be accompanied by the reversal, as far as possible and practicable, of the relationship created by marriage."

21) *Op. cit.* p. 5f.

22) The texts cited by Yaron from other Mediterranean sources do not show a command to the wife to remove her property.

considered as a basis of property rights and construed as a conveyance. Secondly, Yaron's interpretation emphasises the conflict with Aulus Gellius 4.3.2 [23]). If this provision of the XII Tables (if it did exist there) was concerned with the regulation of property between the spouses, why does Servius say that *cautiones rei uxoriae* were not needed before the divorce of Carvilius? And if the XII Tables had laid down detailed rules for the regulation of property, what was there in the case of Carvilius which meant that thereafter *cautiones* had to be taken? Similar objections may be raised to the view of Herrmann who does not distinguish between marriages *cum manu* and marriages *sine manu* and who sees the clause as allowing the wife to take back her *res nec mancipi* whether she was at fault or not [24]).

V.

A solution to the difficulties may be found, I think, if we can attach some weight to Plutarch *Romulus* 22. 3:

> Ἔθηκε δὲ καὶ νόμους τινάς, ὧν σφοδρὸς μέν ἐστιν ὁ γυναικὶ μὴ διδοὺς ἀπολείπειν ἄνδρα, γυναῖκα δὲ διδοὺς ἐκβάλλειν ἐπὶ φαρμακείᾳ (και) τέκνων ἢ κλειδῶν ὑποβολῇ καὶ μοιχευθεῖσαν· εἰ δ' ἄλλως τις ἀποπέμψαιτο, τῆς οὐσίας αὐτοῦ τὸ μὲν τῆς γυναικὸς εἶναι, τὸ δὲ τῆς Δήμητρος ἱερὸν κελεύων· τὸν δ' ἀποδόμενον γυναῖκα θύεσθαι χθονίοις θεοῖς.

According to this text, Romulus enacted a rigorous law whereby a wife could not divorce her husband, but a husband could divorce his wife for poisoning a child, for substitution of keys or for adultery. If a husband turned out his wife for any other

---

23) Which Yaron does not bring into his discussion.

24) *Op. cit.* p. 30. "Il s'agit ici de la description de la répudiation. Nous y voyons deux choses: la première est que la femme a le droit — et sans doute quelle que soit sa faute —, de reprendre ses effets. Il s'agit là, bien entendu, des *res nec mancipii*, de ses vêtements, de ses bijoux. Dès cette époque, il faut noter (comme déjà dans les lois royales) le souci d'éviter la fraude du mari qui consisterait à répudier sa femme pour s'enrichir à ses dépens. Selon les lois royales, le mari en cas de répudiation illégitime, devait donner à la femme la moitié de ses biens, mais les droits de la femme n'étaient pas précisés dans le cas où la répudiation était légitime. A présent la femme semble avoir le droit de reprendre ses effets en cas de répudiation légitime."

reason, he was compelled to give one half of his property to his wife and the other half to Ceres. The word ἐκβάλλειν is ambiguous, but points to repudiation rather than to *de facto* expulsion [25]). Which is the correct translation does not really affect us. The passage certainly cannot be taken at its face value and it is doubtful how much weight should be given to it [26]). But it would be sufficient for our purpose if it can be taken as showing that before or even at the time of the XII Tables a husband was allowed to divorce his wife with impunity on account of certain specified offences and that where he repudiated her (or, alternatively, expelled her *de facto*) for any reason other than one of those specified he had to give her a fixed proportion of his fortune. So long as this continued to be the position there would be no need and no scope for agreements between the parties to regulate property if there was a divorce. If a wife were divorced for one of the reasons specified in the statute, she would, I think we can assume [27]), forfeit her dowry. If she were divorced or, it might be, turned out when she was not guilty of one of the offences specified she was entitled to a fixed proportion of her husband's property. The regulating of property where a marriage broke down was not in the hands of the parties but was controlled by the state. The crisis came when Carvilius wished to divorce his wife. She had not committed a matrimonial offence but was divorced because she could not have any children. This is expressly stated by all the writers on the subject — Dionysius, Plutarch, Valerius Maximus and Aulus Gellius. Consequently, Carvilius ought to have had to pay a fixed proportion of his

---

25) Cf Corbett *op. cit.* p. 219. It may well be a rendering of *i foras* or *baete foras*

26) Cf *infra* p. 32f.

27) Cf Kaser *op. cit.* pp. 71 and 287. But there is no direct evidence. Yaron kindly writes to me: "I should hesitate to hold categorically . . . that the wife divorced for good reason necessarily loses her dowry. The very odium of having been divorced is no mean punishment in an early society, and it seems to me quite possible that she would have retained what was hers to begin with." But I suggest it would be too sophisticated for an early society to see any punishment in the odium of having been divorced. Dionysius *Antiq.* 2.25.1 expressly tells us that Romulus made no provision for the returning or recovery of the dowry.

property to his wife [28]) but he also was not behaving improperly. Far from it! The divorce was wanted by Carvilius because he had had to give an oath to the censors that he would have a wife in order to produce children [29]). Carvilius' concept of piety was so strict that he regarded it as wrong to remain married to a woman who could not have children. The legal problem then was, was a husband who divorced his wife who had not committed any of the specified matrimonial offences liable to lose part of his property to her when the cause of the divorce was the oath which the husband was compelled to give by the censors, the guardians of Roman morality? The answer would seem to be that he was not so liable. This decision would raise a second question, namely, what means were at the disposal of the divorced wife or her father for the recovery of the dowry? So far as we can tell, the answer to this question would be: „None". A new and unforeseen situation had developed.

The divorce would have created a sensation. There is the romantic element. A man of noble birth divorces his innocent wife whom he loves — *egregie dilexisse carissimamque morum eius gratia habuisse* [30]) — because of an oath compelled by the censors. And Dionysius says that although his action was based on necessity he was ever afterwards hated by the people. There is its legal significance. Henceforward, in certain cases at least, an innocent wife might be divorced by her husband who would not be compelled to pay to her the proportion of his property demanded under the old law and there would be no action available for the reclaiming of the dowry. This would cause general doubt as to the comprehensiveness of the existing law and in future parties to a marriage will want to make their own provisions for the distribution of property in the event of divorce, at least for

---

28) And, if we attach full weight to Plutarch, the rest of his fortune was to go to Ceres: but see Mommsen, *Römisches Strafrecht* (Leipzig, 1899) p. 689 n. 4, Kaser, ZSS 58 (1938) p. 71 f and the references he gives, p. 71 n. 5.

29) Not, of course, that the censors would have compelled the divorce: cf Savigny, *Ueber die erste Ehescheidung in Rom* in Vermischte Schriften I (Berlin, 1850) p. 81ff.

30) Aulus Gellius *N.A.* 4.3.2.

cases which might not be adequately covered by the old law [31]). *Cautiones rei uxoriae* will thus come into existence. Also, an action independent of agreements, will have to be invented to cover those cases where the husband should not forfeit his property nor the wife her dowry and where the parties have not made special arrangements. This will become the *actio rei uxoriae*. Carvilius' case and the development of *cautiones* and *actio* might also lead to doubt as to whether the old law was even satisfactory for the situations which it covered. If a husband divorcing his wife for some reason other than one of the faults specified in the old legislation might not have to forfeit a proportion of his property to her, was it necessarily always fair that a wife guilty of one of these faults should lose all of her dowry? A trend towards less stringent penalties could have been started.

Such a case as Carvilius' might well become rooted in tradition. Admittedly, we would have to say that in transmission the tradition has been corrupted. But there is no great difficulty here especially since, whatever view is taken of the divorce of Carvilius, the tradition cannot possibly be correct. Indeed, on the view here suggested, it may be possible to trace some of the steps in the corruption of the tradition. In 4.3.2, Aulus Gellius quotes Servius, and none of our other sources for the tradition clearly goes back so far. Servius here says nothing of this being the first divorce, but only that *cautiones rei uxoriae* were not needed before the divorce of Carvilius. Original statements of this kind might have been interpreted by later writers as meaning that the divorce of Carvilius was the earliest. Again, the form of the text of Valerius Maximus may be significant. The form is not "There were no divorces in Rome for 150 years until Carvilius first divorced his wife on the ground of sterility." But it has "150 years passed from the foundation of Rome without a single divorce. Sp. Carvilius first repudiated his wife for sterility." This could derive from an original source which contained only the second sentence —

31) The legal significance of the case is discussed in general terms *infra* p. [13]. It is not necessary to discuss here the difficult question of the original nature of the *actio rei uxoriae*. See for all, Esmein *La nature originelle de l'action rei uxoriae*, N.R.H. 17 (1893) p. 145ff.

Primus [*autem*] *Sp. Carvilius uxorem sterilitatis causa dimisit* — and the original author might have meant not that this was the first divorce ever, but only that it was the first divorce on the ground of sterility. Such a statement again could have been misinterpreted and could have played its part in the formation of the tradition. Moreover, on this view, the tradition, as one might expect, has exaggerated the significance of Carvilius' divorce.

To turn to the second conflict. On the view here proposed, the statement in Aulus Gellius 4.3.1,2 that there were no *cautiones rei uxoriae* and no *actiones rei uxoriae* before the divorce of Carvilius is accurate. So a new interpretation is needed of *res tuas tibi habeto* if some such clause were in the XII Tables. This cannot refer to the regulating of property. It simply means "Take your things!", *i.e.* your clothing and personal objects. It is a particularly curt way of telling the wife to get out [32]). The imperative directed to the wife is completely appropriate — which it is not if it refers to the regulating of property. Even in a marriage *cum manu* where everything legally belongs to the husband it would be natural to regard the wife's clothing and small personal items as her own. If the clause were in the XII Tables it merely illustrated the wording for divorce but it was not a compulsory form. Against this interpretation of the clause it might be objected that as early as Plautus, in *Amphitruo* 928, it is the woman, Alcumena, who says *Valeas, tibi habeas res tuas, reddas meas*. But this is not a serious objection. For the clause, once established, would tend more and more to be used primarily to show that a divorce was intended. The original precise meaning would tend to be obscured and the clause would be used even where it was not really appropriate. Secondly, with the development of marriage *sine manu* and the divorce of Carvilius there would be a natural tendency to interpret the clause as relating

---

32) Exactly the same flavour seems to be found in Juvenal 6.146: '*collige sarcinulas*' *dicet libertus* '*et exi*'. One might also compare the curt way in which nowadays a labourer will be dismissed from a building site. He will merely be ordered "Collect your cards!" (*i.e.*, national insurance card etc.).

to a division of the property of the spouses though the command would not be taken literally and would not be understood as forming the basis of the spouses' property rights.

VI.

There is an obstacle to the view, however, in Dionysius 2.25.1,2:

1. ὁ δὲ Ῥωμύλος οὔτε ἀνδρί κατὰ γυναικὸς ἐγκλήματα δοὺς φθαρείσης ἢ τὸν οἶκον ἀδίκως ἀπολιπούσης οὔτε γαμετῇ κατ' ἀνδρὸς αἰτιωμένῃ κάκωσιν ἢ ἄδικον ἀπόλειψιν οὔτε περὶ προικὸς ἀποδόσεως ἢ κομιδῆς νόμους θεὶς οὔτε ἄλλο τῶν παραπλησίων τούτοις διορίσας οὐδ' ὁτιοῦν, ἕνα δὲ νόμον ὑπὲρ ἁπάντων εὖ ἔχοντα ὡς αὐτὰ τὰ ἔργα ἐδήλωσε, καταστησάμενος εἰς σωφροσύνην καὶ πολλὴν εὐκοσμίαν ἤγαγε τὰς γυναῖκας. 2. ἦν δὲ τοιόσδε ὁ νόμος· γυναῖκα γαμετὴν τὴν κατὰ γάμους ἱεροὺς συνελθοῦσαν ἀνδρὶ κοινωνὸν ἅπαντων εἶναι χρημάτων τε καὶ ἱερῶν. ἐκάλουν δὲ τοὺς ἱεροὺς καὶ νομίμους οἱ παλαιοὶ γάμους Ῥωμαϊκῇ προσηγορίᾳ περιλαμβάνοντες φαρραχείους ἐπὶ τῆς κοινωνίας τοῦ φαρρός ὃ καλοῦμεν ἡμεῖς ζέαν. αὕτη γὰρ ἦν ἀρχαία καὶ μέχρι πολλοῦ συνήθης ἅπασιν αὐτοῖς ἡ τροφή. φέρει δὲ πολλὴν καὶ καλὴν ἡ Ῥωμαίων γῆ (τὴν ζέαν). καὶ ὥσπερ (ἡμεῖς οἱ) Ἕλληνες τὸν κρίθινον καρπὸν ἀρχαιότατον ὑπολαμβάνοντες ἐπὶ τῶν θυσιῶν κριθαῖς καταρχόμεθα οὐλὰς αὐτὰς καλοῦντες, οὕτω Ῥωμαῖοι τιμιώτατόν τε καρπὸν καὶ ἀρχαιότατον εἶναι νομίζοντες τὰς ζέας διὰ τούτων ἁπάσης ἐμπύρου θυσίας κατάρχονται. μένει γὰρ ἔτι καὶ οὐ μεταπέπτωκεν εἰς πολυτελεστέρας ἀπαρχὰς τὸ ἔθος.

§ 1 expressly states that Romulus did not permit divorce. § 2 talks of marriage by *confarreatio* but the tenor of § 1 strongly suggests that Dionysius thinks of the prohibition of divorce as applying to all marriages. There would thus appear to be a certain conflict on the point between Plutarch and Dionysius [33]). It is not, I think, possible to disentangle the degree of accuracy of each writer and so I do not intend to go into the matter further. As was said before, it is enough for the purpose of this article if it can be held that at the time of the XII Tables or before a husband was allowed to divorce his wife (or *de facto* send her away) with impunity for certain faults but otherwise had to pay her a fixed proportion of his property, and the passage of Dionysius is not directly against that. The best argument for holding

---

33) For proposed solutions, cf, for instance, Corbett *op. cit.* p. 219ff.

that this was the position and that some weight, if not very much, should be given to Plutarch's account is that it enables sense to be made of the evidence on divorce from the XII Tables to the time of Carvilius.

VII.

In conclusion, something might be said — without going into detail — about the wider significance of the divorce of Carvilius. It was a big step in the direction of free marriage. Previously, a wife who was divorced for one of certain specified faults lost all of her dowry. Where the wife was divorced and had not committed any of these specified faults — or, it may have been, was merely sent away, divorce of a wife innocent of these misdemeanours being impossible — the husband had to pay her a fixed proportion of his property. The decision in Carvilius' case breached this. In later law, there were no fixed grounds for divorce and the financial penalties for divorce were far less stringent. The exact steps of this development probably cannot be traced, but it recalls the disappearance of the actionability of *sponsalia* during the Republic and the increasing rarity of marriages *cum manu* [34]).

---

34) I am indebted to a number of friends, especially Professor Reuven Yaron and Mr J. K. B. M. Nicholas, who kindly read this note and gave me their criticisms.

4

Captivitas and Matrimonium

Despite Corbett's dissenting voice [1]), modern jurists are agreed that generally *captivitas* ended a Roman marriage and that *postliminium* did not apply [2]).

> D. 24.2.1 (Paul 35 *ad ed.*): Dirimitur matrimonium divortio morte captivitate vel alia contingente servitute utrius eorum [3]).

> D. 49.15.12.4 (Tryphoninus 4 *disp.*): Sed captivi uxor tametsi maxime velit et in domo eius sit, non tamen in matrimonio est [4]).

This second text is especially significant since it comes from the middle of Tryphoninus' discussion of *postliminium* and there is no sign of the doctrine of *pendens*. Moreover, it is unlikely that any account of such has been cut out since Justinian favoured the survival of the marriage.

> D. 49.15.14.1. (Pomponius 3 *ad Sab.*): Non ut pater filium, ita uxorem maritus iure postliminii recipit: sed consensu redintegratur matrimonium.

This text is usually rightly taken as showing that *postliminium* does not apply, but that the former husband and wife, if they so desire, begin a new union. Corbett dissents from this view and says that the text means 'that the effective operation of *postli-*

---

1) *The Roman Law of Marriage*, Oxford 1930, pp. 212—215. *Cf* Rasi, *Consensus facit Nuptias*, Milan 1946, pp. 115—118.

2) *E.g.* Buckland, *The Roman Law of Slavery*, Cambridge 1908, p. 296; Bonfante, *Corso di diritto romano*, 1: *Diritto di Famiglia*, Rome 1925, pp. 240—242; Imbert, *Postliminium*, Paris 1945, pp. 99—106; Solazzi, *Scritti Ferrini*, 2, pp. 349—355; Di Marzo, *Studi Solazzi*, pp. 1—5; Amirante, *Captivitas e Postliminium*, Naples 1950, pp. 149—152.

3) *Vel — servitute* is generally held interpolated: *Cf* Amirante, *op. cit.*, p. 149. n. 3: but see *infrà*, p. 42, n. 20.

4) Whether, as is generally agreed (Amirante, *loc. cit.* and n. 4) *tametsi maxime velit* is an interpolation need not concern us.

minium was subject to the condition of the other consort's consent' [5]). But if *postliminium* had applied even conditionally one would have expected the position to have been significantly different. The marriage would have been regarded as retroactively valid for the period of captivity unless the other spouse dissented.

> D. 49.15.8 (Paul 3 *ad legem Iuliam et Papiam*): Non ut a patre filius, ita uxor a marito iure postliminii recuperari potest, sed tunc, cum et voluerit mulier et adhuc alii post constitutum tempus nupta non est: quod si noluerit nulla causa probabili interveniente, poenis discidii tenebitur.

There can be little doubt that the text is interpolated from *sed tunc* to the end and originally was a plain statement that there was no *postliminium* [6]). Otherwise it would conflict with the other text of Paul, D. 24. 2. 1. It cannot possibly have been Paul's opinion that captivity *ipso facto* ended the marriage, but that if on the prisoner's return his wife wished the marriage to continue it was retroactively validated. This would be unbelievable confusion and is all the more unlikely since, if the jurists had felt it appropriate, they could have called the doctrine of *pendens* into action. Corbett agrees that the text has been tampered with but says 'We need not therefore agree that Paul denied *postliminium*.' This might be so if D. 49. 15. 8. were our only text, but taken in conjunction with D. 24. 2. 1. and the text of Tryphonimus, D. 49. 15. 12. 4, (neither of which texts Corbett cites in this connection) the conclusion that he did, is inescapable [7]).

From these four texts it can be established that the general rule in classical law was that marriage was ended by *captivitas* and *postliminium* did not apply.

We have, however, two exceptional cases.

> C. 8.50.(51).1 (*Impp. Severus et Antoninus AA. Ovinio*): Ex duobus captivis Sarmatia nata patris originem ita secuta videtur, si ambo parentes in civitatem nostram redissent. quamquam enim iure proprio postliminium

---

5) *Op. cit.*, p. 213.

6) *Cf Index Itp.*

7) *Cf* also D. 24.3.56; *infra*, pp. 254, 255.

habere non possit quae capta non est, tamen parentum restitutio reddet patri filiam. 1. Qui cum ab hostibus interemptus sit, matris dumtaxat condicionem, quae secum filiam duxit, videtur necessario secuta. nam fictio legis Corneliae, quae legitimos apud hostes defuncto constituit heredes, ad eam quae illic suscepta est non pertinet, cum eo tempore quo captus est diem suum pater obisse existimetur. *PP. sine die et consule.*

As Amirante points out [8]), there are three texts in the Digest deriving from this passage [9]).

D. 38.17.1.3 (Ulpian 12 *ad Sab.*) . . . Sed et si apud hostes conceptus a captiva procreatus cum ea rediit, secundum rescriptum imperatoris nostri et divi patris eius ad Ovinium Tertullum poterit ex hoc senatus consulto admitti quasi vulgo quaesitus.

D. 49.15.9 (Ulpian 4 *ad leg. Iul. et Pap.*) Apud hostes susceptus filius si postliminio redierit, filii iura habet: habere enim eum postliminium nulla dubitatio est post rescriptum imperatoris Antonini et divi patris eius ad Orvinium Tertullum praesidem provinciae Mysiae inferioris.

D. 49.15.25 (Marcian 14 *Instit.*) Divi Severus et Antonius rescripserunt, si uxor cum marito ab hostibus capta fuerit et ibidem ex marito enixa sit: si reversi fuerint, iustos esse et parentes et liberos et filium in potestate patris, quemadmodum iure postliminii reversus sit: quod si cum matre sola revertatur, quasi sine marito natus, spurius habebitur.

Although Amirante quotes these texts in his chapter on '*Matrimonium*' he does not comment on them as being exceptions to the general rule, although various theories have been put forward. It is clear, to begin with, that the parents were married before capture. The older explanation of the general rule and of the present texts is as follows. Roman marriage demanded for its formation and continuance the possibility of physical cohabitation. This is impossible during the captivity of one of the spouses; hence the general rule. But cohabitation is possible where both husband and wife are taken prisoner; hence the exception in our present texts. There the marriage is retroactively validated by *postliminium* [10]).

---

8) *Op. cit.*, p. 152.

9) *Cf* also D. 4.6.15.1; 28.3.6.

10) *E.g.* Imbert *op. cit.*, p. 103; *Cf* Buckland, *Slavery*, *cit.*, p. 296.

Orestano, on the other hand, has shown convincingly that Roman marriage was not merely a matter of fact and could continue and even begin (provided there was *deductio in domum*) where the parties were physically separated [11]. His explanation of the general rule is that the *voluntas* of the parties is necessary for the continuance of the marriage and since a *captivus* is a slave he can have no *voluntas* [12]. And the present texts, especially the fundamental one, C. 8. 50. (51). 1, he rightly claims are concerned not with the parents' marriage but with the *postliminium* of the child [13]. The problem envisaged is that the child was born in captivity and is therefore not entitled to *postliminium* and so, strictly, should not become a Roman citizen whether she returns with both her parents or with her mother only. He quotes with reserved approval Perozzi's view [14] that the text does not say that the marriage continued during captivity if the spouses lived together nor that the marriage continued if they returned together; the text presupposes that the parties continued to live together after their return and so the marriage was restored to its former condition. Orestano's final conclusions are that in the first place, throughout the classical period marriage was ended by the captivity of both parties. And in the second place, even if one had to admit in this case —which to him does not appear certain—reintegration of the marriage *iure postliminii*, this would not be the result of a general principle, but of an innovation, exceptional in character, which has all the marks of a true *ius singulare*. But, *pace* Perozzi, there is nothing in the text to warrant saying that there is a presupposition that the spouses will continue to live together. Such a presupposition, moreover, cannot account for the decision. If such were the *ratio decidendi* there would be no ground for the case being decided differently, in respect of *postliminium*, from the

---

11) *La Struttura giuridica del Matrimonio romano*, 47 *B.I.D.R.* (1940), pp. 154 *et seq.* reprinted as part of a book of the same name, Milan 1951, pp. 85 *et seq.*; future references will be to the latter.

12) *Op. cit.*, pp. 115—149. Solazzi says, reasonably, that although Orestano could be right, the texts do not prove his case. *op. cit.*, p. 350.

13) *Op. cit.*, pp. 120—131.

14) *Istituzioni di diritto romano*, 2nd ed., Rome 1928, 1. p. 361. n. 2.

general rule. And, contrary to Orestano's view, the text does show that the marriage was retroactively validated by *postliminium* if both parties returned. If the Emperors, without considering other matters merely gave the child the *ius postliminii*, this would not explain why they decided she was legitinate. This demands a recognition of the validity of the marriage even if only retroactively. And it would not help to say that the parents on their return married again but there was no resurgence of the former marriage, since at that time there was no legitimation *per subsequens matrimonum* [15]).

That neither of the above explanations is satisfactory is confirmed by the text, D. 23. 2. 45. 6 (Ulpian 3 *ad leg. Iul. et. Pap.*), which deals with the other exception and which is not fully treated in either of the two recent monographs on *postliminium* [16]).

> Si ab hostibus patronus captus esse proponatur, vereor ne possit ista conubium habere nubendo, quemadmodum haberet, si mortuus esset. et [sed: Mommsen] qui Iuliani sententiam probant, dicerent non habituram conubium: putat enim Iulianus durare eius libertae matrimonium etiam in civitate propter patroni reverentiam. certe si in aliam servitutem patronus sit deductus, procul dubio dissolutum esset matrimonium.

The text seems to show a dispute between Ulpian and Julian. The former seems to hold that *captivitas* ends a marriage between a patron and his *liberta*, the latter that such a marriage continues. But Julian's view, with which we are primarily concerned, is usually held interpolated [17]). Bonfante excises *durare — esset matrimonium* on the ground that in classical law the marriage did not endure but did in Justinian's law [18]). But if by this is meant that he did not think *postliminium* applied in this special case in classical law, that is what we are investigating, and he has produced

---

15) *Cf* Buckland, *A Textbook of Roman Law*, 2nd ed., Cambridge 1932, p. 129.

16) Mentioned en passant by Imbert, *op. cit.*, p. 104 and n. 2; Amirante, *op. cit.*, p. 191; he gives a valuable bibliography, n. 38.

17) *Cf Index Itp.*, and the authors cited in nn. 18—20: *Cf* also Volterra, *Sul divorzio della Liberta*, Studi Riccobono 3, p. 201 *et seq.* at p. 217.

18) *Corso*, 1, *cit.*, p. 242 and n. 3.

no evidence. If his objection is to *durare* which should, strictly, mean in the context 'to continue during the captivity' it is also not serious. Ulpian may be using convenient, if not strictly accurate, language for Julian's position that the marriage is in suspense and therefore nothing contrary to it must be done. Solazzi also holds the text interpolated as to substance [19]. He exercises *certe — esset matrimonium* because of the change of construction and because the distinction between *captivitas* and *servitus* is not classical. As to the second objection, the text makes no distinction between *captivitas* and *servitus*. It is merely contrasting captivity by the enemy with other forms of slavery. The former is still slavery. And that there was a difference in certain circumstances is shown in the fact which is relevant to us, namely that in the former in some circumstances *postliminium* applied, which it certainly did not in the latter [20]. As to the first point there is no harsh change of style. *Certe etc.* plus the subjunctive may be a continuation of Julian's opinion in indirect speech, or it may be Ulpian expressing his opinion or the joint opinion of himself and Julian, in either of which latter cases the subjunctives would be explained by being still dependent on *proponatur*. But whether it is genuine or a gloss or a Justinianic interpolation need not concern us here too much, since its substance is in accordance with the law from at least the classical period onwards. Solazzi further attacks *propter patroni reverentiam* which he says, rightly, cannot be the reason for the decision attributed to Julian. It must be a later addition. Solazzi also says he cannot see any reason for the decision in the case of the capture of a patron married to his own *liberta* being different from the general rule, and of course he believes the substance has been altered. Beseler

---

19) *Studi sul Divorzio*, 34 *B.I.D.R.* (1926), pp. 295 *et seq.* at pp. 300, 301, p. 300. n. He does not seem to deal with the text in his later study on the same subject, *La legge augustea sul divorzio della liberta*, 51—52 *B.I.D.R.* (1948), p. 327 *et seq.*

20) The fact that *postliminium* operated in many fields, though not in all, to restore a Roman who had been a prisoner of the enemy to his former position, but did not where he had been reckoned a slave for some other reason may well account for *vel alia contingente servitute* in D. 24.2.1, which, therefore, may not be interpolated.

holds the whole text interpolated from *esse proponatur*, and says that *putat Iulianus durat matrimonium* derives from a false interpretation of the first sentence of D. 24. 2. 6. (Iulianus 62 *dig.*) [21].

But in substance the view attributed to Julian must be genuine [22]. It is impossible to understand why if, as is alleged, it were introduced by the compilers because they had changed the law and this was their opinion, it is put in second place quite clearly as the unsuccessful view while the main statement of the law is given in the contrary decision of Ulpian. And secondly, if it were not the opinion of the compilers and was not in the text, why should they invent it? [23].

Before we attempt to fit this exception of Julian into the general theory of *postliminium*, we must first understand the reason for the conflict between Julian and Ulpian. The solution is found in D. 24. 2. 11 pr. (Ulpian *3 ad leg Iul. et. Pap.*):

> Quod ait lex: 'divortii faciendi potestas libertae, quae nupta est patrono, ne esto', non infectum videtur effecisse divortium, quod iure civili dissolvere solet matrimonium. quare constare matrimonium dicere non possumus cum sit separatum. denique scribit Iulianus de dote hanc actionem non habere. merito igitur, quamdiu patronus eius eam uxorem suam esse vult, cum nullo alio conubium ei est. nam quia intellexit legis lator facto libertae quasi diremptum matrimonium, detraxit ei cum alio conubium. quare cuicumque nupserit, pro non nupta habebitur. Iulianus quidem amplius putat nec in concubinatu eam alterius patroni esse posse.

This text is considered heavily interpolated and probably no attempt at reconstruction could ever be fully accepted [24].

---

21) 45 ZSS (1925), pp. 198—199.

22) *Cf* Wolff, 17 Tijd. (1941), p. 174. n. 1.

23) On this understanding, *propter patroni reverentiam* must be a gloss, not a Justinianic interpolation. This objection also applies to the view of Levy, 'Verschollenheit und Ehe in antike Rechten' *Gedächtnisschrift für Emil Seckel* Berlin 1927, pp. 144 *et seq.* at pp. 149—50. Although he does not say that the view attributed to Julian is interpolated, such must be his opinion since he maintains that Julian's view was that the marriage was ended but the *liberta* had no *conubium* for a second marriage, and this is not what is stated in the text.

24) See Solazzi, 51—52 *B.I.D.R.* (1948), pp. 329—331; Volterra, *op. cit.*, pp. 205—210 and the works he cites nn. 4—25. Because of the wealth of literature on

Mostly, however, the inelegancies in the text are that sentences do not follow on the ones which precede and this is perhaps best explained as the result of excision rather than of additions. It seems reasonable to draw the following conclusions from the texts. Firstly, there is a dispute between Ulpian and Julian as to the effect of the *lex Julia et Papia*. This is shown by the words *Julianus quidem amplius putat*. The emphatic use of both *amplius* and *quidem* can only mean that the view put forward is one which Ulpian does not share and that it refers back to another point where the two jurists disagreed. There seems no reason for inserting *quam* after *amplius*[25]) or for suppressing the *quidem* and adding*<si liberta duobus communis sit>. Denique scribit Iulianus de dote hanc actionem non habere* is no obstacle to the idea that there was a conflict of opinion. *Denique* probably relates back to a sentence in which Julian's basic opinion was expressed, and which has been cut out. *De dote* should, of course, be *rei uxoriae*. Apart from this routine alteration, Julian's opinion cannot be interpolated, again because it would be pointless to invent an unsuccessful view and ascribe it to a jurist. If Julian refused the *liberta* the *actrio rei uxoriae* the reason must be that he regarded the marriage as still subsisting [26]). Hence his further opinion that she could not even be the concubine of another patron. A woman cannot be at the same time a wife to one person and concubine to another [27]). Ulpian's view seems no less clear. On the face of the text his position seems to be that he considers the marriage to

---

the subject it would be tedious and probably pointless to refer continually to the opinions of other writers.

[25]) *Cf* Volterra, *op. cit.*, pp. 209—210. nn. 23, 24.

[26]) Modestinus thought likewise, D. 24.2.10 (*l. reg.*): *Patrono invito liberta, quam in matrimonio habuit, ab eo discedere non potest, nisi ex causa fidei commissa manumissa sit: tunc enim potest, licet eius fit liberta.*

[27]) This is never stated directly in the texts, but it would be unreasonable to hold any other opinion in view of the rule that a man could not have a wife and a concubine at the same time. *Cf* Buckland, *Textbook, cit.*, p. 128; the contrary view put forward by Schulz is the result of a failure to distinguish between mere illegitimate intercourse and *concubinatus*. He does not refer to the main text, P.S. 2.20.1, *Classical Roman Law*, Oxford 1951, p. 138.

be dissolved but the *liberta* without consent cannot remarry. That is, despite the seemingly clear wording of the *lex*, he feels that the civil law rule that marriage is ended when one of the parties wishes it to, prevails. Despite the muddled state of the text this must also in substance have been Ulpian's view. First, because it is impossible to understand why Justinian who was hostile to divorce should have introduced it in a case where it was not permitted in classical law. And secondly, because otherwise there would not be, as there must be, a disagreement with Julian. The reason for his decision Ulpian tells us in *merito igitur, quamdiu patronus eius eam uxorem suam esse vult, cum nullo alio conubium ei est. nam quia intellexit legis lator facto libertae quasi diremptum matrimonium, detraxit ei cum alio conubium.* In other words, if the marriage were not dissolved at the wish of the *liberta* it would be pointless for the *lex* to say that so long as the patron wished her to be his wife she could not without his consent marry another. The two interpretations of this part of the *lex* are probably explicable on the supposition that the *lex Julia de maritandis ordinibus* said that the *liberta* could not marry another so long as her patron wished her as his wife, and the *lex Papia Poppaea nuptialis* (which is the later) declared that the *liberta* could not divorce her patron. Confusion arose when the two *leges* were fused and commented on as one piece of legislation [28]). The contrary view of Levy demands special treatment since his arguments are on a different level from those of the other advocates. He maintains [29]) that no clause such as *ne invito patrono alii nubere potestas esto* could have existed in the *lex Julia de maritandis ordinibus* since if the prohibition on divorce were perfect a second marriage would have been void and so the statute could not discuss a second

---

28) As I have said, the text seems to have been shortened and I consider the original plan of it to have been as follows: 1. The phrase of the statute which is to be commented on. 2. Ulpian's opinion that the *lex* does not alter the civil law of divorce. 3. Julian's contrary opinion and the main consequences which he draws from it. 4. Ulpian's refutation of Julian with arguments based on the wording of the *lex*. 5. Julian's other deduction that the *liberta* cannot even be the *concubina* of another patron, which also may have been explicitly denied by Ulpian.

29) *Der Hergang der römischen Ehescheidung*, Weimar 1925, p. 137 *et seq.*

marriage, and if the prohibition on divorce were imperfect it would be intended to prevent a second marriage so again there would be no reason to lay down the invalidity of such a marriage. The textual support for such a clause, he says, is very weak. The words at the beginning of D. 23. 2. 45. which contain the wording are, in his opinion, without doubt of unclassical origin but the only evidence he produces is that most of the clauses introduced by *in* = "with regard to" [30]) serve to link up the ends of a break in the discussion. He would reconstruct the wording of the *lex* like this: *divortii faciendi potestas libertae, quae nupta est patrono, invito eo ne esto quamdiu patronus eam uxorem esse volet*. But a number of points can be brought against Levy's case. First, his argument that both clauses could not exist is only valid if there were only one statute, not if there were two. Secondly, the fact that *in* = 'with regard to' is suspect and does show a shortening of the discussion is no indication that after *quod dicit* we are not given the actual words of the statute. The phrase *invito patrono* with the words presumably in that order does certainly occur in a statute relating to the ending of the marriage of a *liberta* with her patron [31]). Levy, at the very least has to transpose these words to suit his case. Thirdly, on Levy's reconstruction *invito eo* must occur in the statute between *patrono* and *ne esto*. For this reconstruction to be correct, we must assume that important as these words were they were omitted by Ulpian when he was giving the wording of the clause in D. 24. 2. 11. pr. [32])

Returning now to *postliminium*, we can understand the nature of the conflict between Ulpian and Julian in D. 23. 2. 45. 6, and we can explain why in this case Julian made an exception to the general rule of the effect of *captivitas* on *matrimonium*. We can also see the reason for the general rule and exceptions.

First, it must be said that the fact that Julian insists that the marriage of a *liberta* to her patron is not, *ipso facto*, dissolved

---

30) In German, 'bei', 'in bezug auf'.

31) D. 23.2.45.5.

32) And, of course, his explanation of the view ascribed to Julian in D. 23.2.45.6. is unacceptable: *cf supra* n. 23.

by the patron's capture disproves both theories advanced as to the reason for the general rule. It cannot be that marriage requires cohabitation for its continuance, nor that *voluntas* is necessary and inevitably fails when one of the parties is a prisoner. The real reason is the nature of *postliminium* itself. *Postliminium* is the automatic retention or recovery of the rights or duties of the captive. If the rights or duties are dependent on the unfettered wish of any other person there can be no question of automatic retention. Hence, marriage in general is ended by capture and is not revived by *postliminium* because usually the continuance of marriage is at all times dependent on the wishes of both parties, and since the one who is not a captive may decide that he or she does not wish to be considered the spouse of the other there can be no question of automatic retention or recovery. But of course, the parties are free to remarry. And thus where husband and wife are captured and return together, the marriage subsists by *ius postliminii*. It is wrong to say that marriage continues by *consensus*. There seems to be no text which says so, but if there is it would merely show a convenient way of speaking. It would be absurd if a wife charged with adultery could deny it on the score that before the act she ceased to have *affectio maritalis*. Rather, marriage continues until there is an expression of *dissensus*. And so where husband and wife are captured together and return together their marriage is retroactively regarded as having subsisted during the captivity because, since they were captives and therefore not Roman citizens, neither had the capacity to express *dissensus*. The continuance of the marriage in such circumstances is so much taken for granted that it is not discussed in the rescript in C. 8. 50. (51). 1, which concentrates on the innovation in giving the *ius postliminii* to the child born in captivity. In the same way, Julian holds that the marriage of the *liberta* is not ended by the capture of her *patronus* husband. She has no power of terminating the marriage and during his captivity he has no capacity to, hence it must be retroactively preserved by *postliminium*. But for Ulpian, the *liberta* can always divorce her husband, and since she has this power one cannot say that the marriage must automatically revive on the husband's return. Therefore, for him, *postliminium* does not apply and capture ends the marriage without qualification.

Justinian's Law.

Modern opinion is generally agreed that as in classical law so in Justinian's law captivity ended the marriage [33]). This is shown above all in the classical texts already cited which appear in the Corpus Iuris, and especially D. 24. 2. 1 which, as Kreller points out [34]), is placed by Justinian at the head of the Title '*de divortiis et repudiis*' But other texts tell the same story.

> D. 24.3.56 (Paul 6 *ad Plautium*): Si quis sic stipuletur a marito: 'si quo casu Titia tibi nupta esse desierit, dotem dabis?' hac generali commemoratione et ab hostibus capta ea committetur stipulatio vel etiam si deportata fuerit vel ancilla effecta: hac enim conceptione omnes hi casus continentur. plane quantum veniat in stipulatione, utrum quasi mortua sit an quasi divortium fecerit? humanius quis id competere dixerit, quod propter mortem convenit.

Heavily interpolated as this text undoubtedly is [35]), the basic fact for us is that captivity is clearly regarded as ending the marriage completely both in classical and Justinianic law.

But some texts do show Byzantine innovations.

D. 49. 15. 8 which is quoted above [36]), is interpolated from *sed tunc* to the end. This tells us that the marriage is not automatically renewed by the husband's return but only if the wife wishes it to and has not remarried *post constitutum tempus* [37]); but if she does not want it to without good reason, she will be liable to the

---

[33]) Solazzi, *op. cit.*, pp. 354—355; Kreller, *Die Ehe des römischen Kriegsgefangenen*, Juristische Blätter, (12) 1948, pp. 284 *et seq.* (not seen — cited by Amirante, *op. cit.*, p. 189. n. 31.); Amirante, *op. cit.*, pp. 189—201, and the authorities he cites.

[34]) *Op. cit.*, p. 284.

[35]) *Cf Index Itp.*

[36]) p. 244.

[37]) The reference to *post constitutum tempus* is perhaps odd since it only applied in cases where it was not certain whether the husband were a captive or dead: *cf* D. 24.2.6.

penalties for divorce. It is doubtful whether one can speak of *postliminium* here: *sed tunc* may refer back to the phrase *recuperari potest* and not necessarily to *iure postliminii recuperari potest.* More important, there is no sign of retroactiveness. Futher, the reference to *poenae discidii* must not be taken to imply that the marriage was in existence. It is simply a sanction to force the wife to return to the marriage and really means that she has to pay her husband the sum she would have had to if she had divorced him without good reason.

> D. 24.2.6 (Iulianus 62 *dig.*) Uxores eorum, qui in hostium potestate pervenerunt, possunt videri nuptarum locum retinere eo solo, quod alii temere nubere non possunt. et generaliter definiendum est, donec certum est maritum vivere in captivitate constitutum, nullam habere licentiam uxores eorum migrare ad alium matrimonium, nisi mallent ipsae mulieres causam repudii praestare. sin autem in incerto est, an vivus apud hostes teneatur vel morte praeventus, tunc, si quinquennium a tempore captivitatis excesserit, licentiam habet mulier ad alias migrare nuptias, ita tamen, ut bona gratia dissolutum videatur pristinum matrimonium et unusquisque suum ius habeat imminutum: eodem iure et in marito in civiatate degente et uxore captiva observando.

This text, too, is heavily interpolated[38]). Kreller's conservative restoration of the text[39]) is impossible. Julian cannot have written: *Uxores eorum, qui in hostium potestate <m> pervenerunt, possunt videri nuptarum locum retinere eo solo, quod alii* [*temere*] *<sine poena edicti> nubere non possunt.* Even if the Edict did establish a penalty for divorce without good cause, and even if Julian could write in such a way of a marriage which at the most is in suspense, the greater difficulty remains that even in another way the text could not correctly state the classical law. If the marriage were considered as still subsisting or in suspense and remarriage was punishable as a result, it would be both illogical and unfair not to attribute to the spouse who remained in Roman territory the benefits of a married woman. And of course, since Augustus,

---

38) *Cf Index Itp.*; Amirante, *op. cit.*, pp. 191—193, and the works he cites nn. 43—45.

39) *Op. cit.*, p. 285. Quoted in Amirante, p. 192. n. 43.

a married man or woman was in a better position as regards succession than a single person. Hence, in Julian's time a woman could also be seen to be married (if she were) by her greater power to accept inheritances and legacies. I submit that Julian originally wrote something like *Uxores eorum, qui in hostium potestate <m>pervenerunt, <non> possunt* [] *nuptarum locum retinere.* But we are mainly concerned with Justinian's law. And the text does show innovations. A wife whose husband is a prisoner cannot remarry without herself giving rise to a *causa repudii.* This in view of the texts cited above, cannot mean that Justinian considers the marriage continued during captivity, and need not, even when taken with the first sentence, indicate that there was *postliminium.* It may simply be a penalty imposed for remarriage contrary to law calculated as being financially the same as the penalty for conduct giving rise to a suit for divorce. Justinian goes on to say that when it is doubtful whether a spouse is a prisoner or dead, the other can remarry freely after five years.

> D. 48.5.14.7 (Ulpian 2 *de adulteriis*): Si quis plane uxorem suam, cum apud hostes esset, adulterium commisisse arguat, benignius dicetur posse eum accusare iuri viri: sed ita demum adulterium maritus vindicabit, si vim hostium passa non est: ceterum quae vim patitur, non est in ea causa, ut adulterii vel stupri damnetur.

The substance of this text is undoubtedly Justinianic and contrary to the classical law[40]). At first sight it might be thought that it is complete proof of the continuance or retroactive validation of the marriage since otherwise the husband should have no right to bring an action against his wife for adultery just as he would not if the marriage had been ended in any other way. But here again another explanation is plausible. If the conduct of the wife (and likewise of the husband) had been blameless during the captivity, the husband (or wife) could not on her return object to the recommencement of the marriage without incurring the penalties of a causeless divorce. Hence, in this case, in order *inter alia* to free the innocent husband from these penalties; he is allo-

40) *Cf Index Itp*; especially Volterra, Studi Bonfante 2, pp. 122—126.

wed to sue his wife for adultery and it is reasonable by Justinian's standards, if he could punish a spouse who without good reason refused to begin the marriage again, also to punish a spouse who gave the other reasonable cause not te begin again. Moreover, if *postliminium* had applied, the wife would on principle have been liable for her adultery and there would have been no reason to introduce the decision by *benignius* which suggests an exception to the rule.

The texts quoted in this section do not in fact provide proof that Justinian had by this time introduced *postliminium* in the case of a captive 's marriage or made it valid retroactively. Rather he only punished a spouse who refused to let the marriage begin again or gave just grounds for the other's refusal. Any other interpretation fails to take into account the texts in the first part of this article.

A change, however, does appear with Nov. 22 c. 7 of 536 A.D.:

Ἀλλὰ καὶ τῆς αἰχμαλωσίας τοιοῦτόν ἐστιν ὁποῖον bona gratia *διαλύειν τὸν γάμον εἴτε γὰρ ἀνδρὶ συμβαίη τοιοῦτον ἀγύχημα, τῆς γυναικὸς ἐν τῇ πολιτείᾳ μενούσης, εἴτε αὖθις γυνὴ μὲν εἰς αἰχμαλωσίαν ἀπίοι, μένοι δὲ ὁ ἀνὴρ ἐν πολιτείᾳ, ὁ μὲν ἀκριβής τε καὶ λεπτὸς λόγος διαλύει τὸν γάμον δουλείας γὰρ ἅπαξ ἐπιγενομένης θατέρῳ ἡ τῆς τύχης ἀνισότης τήν ἐκ τῶν γάμων ἰσότητα μένειν οὐ συγχωρεῖ πλὴν ἀλλὰ φιλανθρωπότερον τὰ τοιαῦτα θεωροῦντες, ἕως μέν ἐστι φανερὸν περιεῖναι ἢ τὸν ἄνδρα ἢ τὴν γαμετήν, μένειν ἄλυτα τὰ συνοικέσια συγχωροῦμεν, καὶ οὐκ ἐλεύσονται πρὸς δευτέρους γάμους οὔτε γυναῖκες οὔτε ἄνδρες, εἰ μὴ βούλοιντο δοκεῖν κατά προπέτειαν τοῦτο πρᾶξαι καὶ ὑποπεσεῖν ταῖς ποιναῖς, ὁ μὲν τῇ τῆς πρὸ γάμου δωρεᾶς φαμὲν ἐκτίσει, ἡ δὲ τῆς προικός. Εἰ δὲ ἄδηλον καθεστήκοι, πότερον περίεστιν ἢ μὴ τό εἰς πολεμίους ἀφικόμενον πρόσωπον, τηνικαῦτα πενταετίαν μενετέον εἴτε τῷ ἀνδρὶ εἴτε τῇ γυναικί, μεθ' ἥν, εἴτε σαφῆ γένοιτο τὰ τῆς τελευτῆς εἴτε ἄδηλα μένοι, γαμεῖν ἔξεστιν ἀκινδύνως. Καὶ τοῦτο γὰρ δὴ ταῖς καλουμέναις* bona gratia *διαλύσεσι παρὰ τῶν πρὸ ἡμῶν συνηρίθμηται, καί ἡμεῖς δὲ εἰς τοῦτο σύμφαμεν ὥςτε ἐνταῦθα οὐδὲ διαίσιῳ γίνεται καιρὸς οὕτω τῶν προσώπων διεστώτων ἀλλήλων, καὶ οὐδεὶς ἐντεῦθεν κερδανεῖ, οὔτε ὁ ἀνὴρ τὴν προῖκα οὔτε ἡ γυνὴ τὴν προγαμιαίαν δωρεάν, ἀλλ' ἕκαστος ἐπὶ τῶν οἰκείων μενεῖ.*

Sed etiam captivitatis casus talis est, quale est bona gratia distrahere matrimonium. Sive enim contingat tale infortunium viro, muliere in republica manente, sive rursus mulier quidem in captivitatem ducatur, maneat autem vir in republica, scrupulosa quidem et subtilis ratio transigit nuptias: servitute namque semel superveniente alteri personae fortunae inaequalitas

> aequalitatem ex nuptiis manere non sinit. Attamen humanius talia contemplantes, donec quidem est manifestum superesse aut virum aut uxorem, manere insoluta matrimonia sinimus, et non venient ad secundas nuptias neque mulieres neque viri, nisi volunt videri ausu temerario hoc egisse et poenis succumbere, ille quidem ante nuptias donationis dicimus exactioni, illa vero dotis. Si vero incertum sit, utrum superest an non quae ad hostes persona devenit, tunc quinquennium expectandum est sive a viro sive a muliere, post quod, sive manifestum fiat de morte sive incertum maneat, nubere licebit sine periculo. Et hoc enim nuncupatis bona gratia transactionibus a praecentibus connumeratum est, nos quoque in hoc consentimus, ut hic neque repudio fiat opus, ita personis distantibus ab alterutris, et nullus ex hoc lucrabitur, neque vir dotum neque mulier antenuptialem donationem, sed unusquisque in suis manebit.

Despite Di Marzo [41]), the text does tell us that the marriage continues during the captivity. The argument is: captivity is the sort of thing which ends marriage; and when this misfortune happens, precise and subtle reasoning puts an end to the marriage; nevertheless, taking a more humane view, so long as it is clear that the husband or wife is still alive, we permit the marriage to remain in existence. It is noteworthy that Justinian does not say that captivity ends marriage but 'is the sort of thing which does'. And the emphasis on 'the subtle and precise reasoning' weakens the case for the dissolution of the marriage. Di Marzo would be on much stronger ground if the text has simply said *ratio transigit nuptias*. Nor does the reference back to our text in Nov. 22. c. 10. really help Di Marzo since it is concerned only with the first general statement. Thus Justinian takes the step which was required of him after his introduction of penalties for failure to recommence the marriage. But it is striking that did not bring in *postliminium*, probably because the spouse who remained free still had unrestricted power to end the marriage at will [42]).

---

41) *Dirimitur Matrimonium captivitate*, Studi Solazzi, p. 1 *et seq*. See also the references given by him and add Amirante *op. cit*., p. 201.

42) The texts on *dos* and *donatio inter virum et uxorem* do not affect the arguments brought forward in this article: D. 24.3.56 (see supra, pp. 48 sq.); D. 24.3. 10.pr. (Amirante, *op. cit*., p. 155, is wrong when he says that even if the *filia* had not died the *pater* could always recover *dos profecticia* from the husband. The death

of the *filia* is a necessary element of the case, since during her lifetime the *pater* could only sue for recovery of *dos profecticia* with her consent: *cf* Solazzi, *Sul Consenso della filia familias all'actio rei uxoriae exercitata del padre*, 70 *Rendic. real. ist lombardo* (1937), pp. 261 *et seq.*) C. 5.18.5 (*cf* Amirante, *op. cit.*, p. 156); D. 24.1.32.14 (*cf* Solazzi, Scritti Ferrini *cit.*, pp. 352—353.

5

The Identity of Sarapio, Socrates, Longus and Nilus in the Will of C. Longinus Castor

The will of the Roman veteran, C. Longinus Castor of the village of Caranis, was sealed on the 17th November, 189 A.D. We do not possess the will itself, but we have the translation into Greek made for the official record at Arsinoe on 21st February, 194. The translation begins:

> [1]['Ερμηνί]α διαθ(ήκης). [2][Γάιος Λογγῖνος Κάστωρ οὐε]τρανὸς ἐντίμως ἀπολυθε[ὶ]ς [3][ἐκ κλάσσης πραιτωρί]ας Μισηνῶν [δια]θήκην ἐποί[ησ]εν. [4][ἐλευθέρας εἶναι κελεύω] Μαρκέλλαν·δού[λη]ν μ[ο]υ μίζονα ἐ[τ]ῶν [5][τριάκοντα καὶ Κλεοπάτραν] δούλην μου μ[ίζονα] ἐτῶν τριάκ[οντ]α [6][καὶ ἑκάστη ἔστω κληρο]νόμος ἐξ ἴσου μ[έρους] ἐμοῦ. {κληρον[ομ.].}. [7][οἱ δὲ λοιποὶ πά]ν[τε]ς ἀποκληρόνομοί [μου] ἔστωσαν. προσε[ρ]χέσ-[8][θωσάν τε τῇ κληρονομίᾳ] μου ἑκάστη ὑπὲρ τοῦ ἰδίου μέρους ὁπότ[α]ν [9][φαίνηται ἑκάστη μα]ρ[τύ]ρασθαι ἑαυτὴν ἐμοῦ κλ[η]ρονόμον εἶναι, μὴ ἐξῖ-[10][ναι δὲ] π[ι]π[ρά]σκειν μηδὲ ὑποτίθεσθαι. ἀλλ' εἴ τι ἐὰν ἀν[θ]ρώπιν[ο]ν πά-[11]θῃ Μαρκέλλ[α] ἡ προγεγραμμένη, τότε τὸ μέρος τῆς κληρονομίας ἑαυτῆς [12][πρ]ὸς Σαραπίωνα καὶ Σωκράτην καὶ Λόγγον καταντῆσαι θέλω. ὁμοίως [13][Κλε]οπάτραν τὸ μέρος αὐτῆς πρὸς Νεῖλον καταντῆσαι θέλω.

Thus, Longinus orders his two slave-women, Marcella and Cleopatra, to be free and, to show that he is acting in accordance with the *lex Aelia Sentia* (*1*), he declares that they are both over the age of thirty. These two women are instituted his heirs in equal shares and everyone else is disinherited. Further down, the testator declares that if Marcella should die her share of the inheritance is to go to Sarapio, Socrates and Longus, and likewise if Cleopatra should die her share is to go to Nilus. These four gentlemen are not further described, they are not referred to later in the will, and they are not left legacies. The clauses which concern them have given rise to some difficulty. The general view is that the clauses are nothing other than *substitutiones vulgares* (2). The imperative words of the Roman rules,

(*1*) G.1.17.
(2) See now the references given by Arangio-Ruiz, *FIRA* III, p. 148 n. 3; and most recently, Taubenschlag, *The Law of Greco-Roman Egypt in the Light of the Papyri*, 2nd ed. (Warsaw), 1955), p. 195.

it is said (3) have been departed from and we have a faithful imitation of the Hellenistic forms. A minority view is that a *fideicommissum* is imposed on the two heirs to restore the whole inheritance when they die to the four men (4). We are not concerned with the correctness of these views but with a point made by Arangio-Ruiz who supports the minority view. He says (5) that we cannot guess who these four men are—their names alone are given—and therefore he suspects that this part of the official translation has been shortened.

But is it in fact impossible to guess who these four men are? The real question, of course, should be rather different, namely, is there sufficient evidence in the document for it to have been unambiguously apparent at the time who these four men were? I submit that even at this distance of time it is not difficult to make a plausible suggestion as to the identity of these men and that, therefore, there is no need to postulate that the translation of the will is abbreviated.

The translation contains one very important clue to their identity, namely that Sarapio, Socrates and Longus are to succeed to Marcella, while Nilus alone is to succeed to Cleopatra. This is not consistent with a simple hypothesis that Longinus wished Nilus to have a share three times as large as that of Sarapio, Socrates or Longus. If this had been his intention, one would not have expected the gifts to the men to be related to the deaths of the two women in the way that they are. One might have expected rather that in the event of the death of either woman, or of both of them, Nilus was to succeed to one-half share, the other three each to one-sixth. Moreover, on that hypothesis, if the provisions are in fact *substitutiones vulgares,* the testator's intentions are likely to be upset if one, but only one, of the women were to die before the will took effect. And, likewise on that hypothesis, if the provisions are really *fideicommissa,* the danger ought to have been foreseen that one of the women might prove to be improvident. The dependence of the bequests to Sarapio, Socrates and Longus on the one hand and to Nilus on the other on the deaths of Marcella and Cleopatra respectively is explicable only on the hypothesis that there was a particular connexion between the three first named men and Marcella, and between Nilus and Cleopatra. The best clue to the nature of this connexion is that the four men are apparently free—at least there is no sign that they were slaves either of Longinus (6) or of another. Since three men are to succeed to Marcella one can exclude the possibility that the men were free men who were allowed to associate with the slave-women in a manner akin to marriage. Again if one suggests that

(3) Taubenschlag, loc. cit.
(4) Cf. Arangio-Ruiz, loc. cit.
(5) Loc. cit.: "Ceterum qui sint viri, quorum nomina summatim enunciantur, divinari non potest: quocirca suspicamur hanc interpretationis partem in breve coactam esse."
(6) If they were slaves of Longinus the provisions, which contain no gift of liberty, are absurd.

the men are the brothers or cousins of the women it is very difficult to understand why the former should be free and the latter slaves. How would such a factual situation come about? But one form of blood relationship would explain the situation, namely that Sarapio, Socrates and Longus are the sons of Marcella, and Nilus is the son of Cleopatra; and that *Longinus* is the natural father of all four males and hence has manumitted them. That a manumittens was the natural father was treated as a *iusta causa* under the *lex Aelia Sentia* for allowing a slave freed under the age of thirty to be a Roman citizen (7). This suggestion would also explain why Longinus freed Marcella and Cleopatra and made them his heirs—they were or had been his mistresses.

This solution meets no obstacle in the fact that there is only a general clause of *exheredatio*. Natural sons who were not in their father's *potestas* did not have to be disinherited *nominatim* (8). Nor is it really an obstacle that the will in a later provision shows that Cleopatra had a daughter, Sarapias, who had not been previously manumitted but is to be freed by a *fideicommissum* under the will and given property. She may not have been the child of Longinus and even if she were (9) he may not have felt the same desire to manumit her. A more serious objection might be that Longinus could have been expected to state that Sarapio, Socrates, Longus and Nilus were his sons whom he had manumitted. But one can appreciate that a man might not wish to declare expressly in his will that four of the beneficiaries are his illegitimate children by his slave-girls and that the two principal beneficiaries are not only his slaves but his mistresses. This attitude is understandable even though Longinus would have had to declare at the time of the manumissions that the slaves were his natural children. On this hypothesis it would have been tasteless for Longinus to describe the four males simply as the manumitted sons of Marcella and Cleopatra.

If this suggestion is correct then it will be seen that there was really no need—for the sake of identification—to describe Sarapio, Socrates, Longus and Nilus more closely in the will; on the contrary, an argument can be found to explain why they were *not* more fully described.

(7) G.1.19.
(8) For the rules see Buckland, *A Textbook of Roman Law*, 3rd ed. by Stein (Cambridge, 1963), pp. 321ff.
(9) Cf. e.g., Arangio-Ruiz, *La successione testamentaria secondo i papiri greco-egizii* (Naples, 1906) p. 227 and n. 2.

6

Vespasian: Adsertor Libertatis Publicae

In A.D. 71 Vespasian issued at Rome[1] a *sestertius* inscribed on the reverse SPQR ADSERTORI LIBERTATIS PUBLICAE[2] in four lines within an oak-wreath, the *corona civica*. The purpose of this note is to clarify the exact claim being made by Vespasian. M. Grant has already called attention to a possible relationship with the inscription on a tetradrachm issued at Ephesus by Augustus in 28 B.C.: IMP CAESAR DIVI F COS VI LIBERTATIS P(opuli) R(omani) VINDEX.[3] He rightly and reasonably explains the change of terminology from Augustus' *vindex* to Vespasian's *adsertor* by a desire to avoid a pun. 'The period of anarchy and civil war which Vespasian terminated had been started by a man of precisely that name who rebelled against Nero. The Romans being so addicted to plays on words, the name of Vindex must have given rise to many punning observations reminiscent of the phrase on Augustus' tetradrachms.'[4]

But that is not the whole story.[5] *Adsertor libertatis* is a technical term. The *adsertor libertatis* is the person who brings an action against someone who is, he claims, wrongfully holding a free man as a slave.[6] A peculiarity of the action involved, the *vindicatio in libertatem*, is that anyone could be the plaintiff, the *adsertor libertatis*. He need not have a financial interest in seeing the free man's liberty restored, or be a relative of his or even a citizen of the same state. This *adsertor libertatis* acted on his own initiative and was not appointed by the supposed slave. Indeed, at least in certain cases the *adsertor* could bring the action even against the wishes of the supposed slave. The supposed slave, of course, could not himself bring the

[1] Also at Tarraco, at an unknown mint in Gaul, and at Lugdunum: Mattingley, *Coins of the Roman Empire in the British Museum*, ii (London 1930), nos. 572, 781, 793, 805.

[2] Or PUBLIC.

[3] Mattingley, *Coins of the Roman Empire in the British Museum*, i (London, 1923), nos. 691, 692, 693.

[4] *Roman Imperial Money* (London, Edinburgh, etc., 1954), 187.

[5] We are not directly concerned here with the accuracy of Grant's claim that Vespasian is deliberately recalling Actium and *Aegyptus capta*.

[6] Cf. already, C. Kraay, 'The Coinage of Vindex and Galba, A.D. 68', *Numismatic Chronicle*, ix (1949), 129 ff., 140.

action.[7] Thus Vespasian's inscription implies two things. First, that Rome was previously being wrongfully held in slavery (and that he brought about her freedom). Secondly, that he had a *legal* right to act as he did to recover Rome's freedom. Vespasian, a man of obscure family none of whose members had held high office,[8] is concerned to stress the legitimacy of his occupation of the imperial throne. Though *adsertor* by itself is also used non-technically, there can be no doubt that here Vespasian is using *adsertor libertatis* as a technical term.

The inscription on Augustus' tetradrachm is a rather different matter. *Vindex libertatis* is not a technical term, though the word *vindex* itself has technical legal significance as well as being used non-technically. In law the *vindex* was a supporter of the defendant.[9] Since a slave could not be a party to a legal action and hence could not be a defendant, the implication here – if *vindex* is used technically – would be that the Roman people had not been enslaved though there was an assault upon its liberty, and that Augustus had defended this existing freedom rather than regained a lost freedom. This is also a natural way to understand the inscription even if *vindex* is to be taken non-technically. Outside the legal sphere, *vindex* often has a meaning such as 'avenger' but a common use is certainly as 'defender' or 'protector'. This sense of defender is nowhere more clear than in the combination *vindex libertatis*. One may refer to Cicero's *habeat sane populus tabellam quasi vindicem libertatis* (*De Leg*. iii. 39): and Livy's '*Provoco*' *inquit. audita vox una vindex libertatis* (iii. 56. 6).[10] But the passage from Livy warns us to be careful. The use of *provocatio* is seen as the first claim to a revival of liberty after a period of slavery. The inscription on Augustus' tetradrachm may also be imprecise and imply neither that Rome had remained free nor that Augustus was its defender rather than its *adsertor libertatis*. In fact, later, in the *Res Gestae* 1, Augustus does use language appropriate to an *adsertor libertatis*: *rem publicam dominatione factionis oppressam in libertatem vindicavi*.

[7] On all this see, e.g., G. Franciosi, *Il processo di libertà in diritto romano* (Naples, 1961), especially 136 ff.

[8] Suetonius, *Vesp*. 1.

[9] There was more than one kind of *vindex* – one intervened in the *legis actio per manus iniectionem*, another in the *in ius vocatio* – though we need not be more precise here. But cf. M. Kaser, *Das römische Zivilprozessrecht* (Munich, 1966), 49 ff., 99 ff., 165 f.

[10] Kraay, relying on Donatus on Ter. *Ad*. 194, claims that *vindex* and *adsertor* 'are equivalents in meaning': op. cit. 139 ff. But in technical usage this is not so (cf. Franciosi, op. cit. 11) and Vespasian's *adsertor libertatis* is certainly technical. Indeed, even in non-technical usage the words may be equivalents but are not necessarily so.

II

Property

7

Acquisition of Possession per Extraneam Personam

The thesis to be maintained is that shortly after the beginning of the Empire it was generally recognised by the jurists that one could acquire possession through one's *procurator omnium bonorum;* that this was then extended to tutors and curators; and that before the end of the classical period one could acquire possession trough any *extranea persona.* This development can be traced in the texts.

I hope that I have shown elsewhere [1]) that the rapprochement of *mandatum* and *procuratio* took place in classical law and that the texts show the development. Since there are more texts on that subject (and the thesis can therefore be more easily proved) and it has some bearing on the present question, it may be worth while summarising the arguments and conclusions. As regards the *procurator omnium bonorum*, the texts tell us that Celsus and Pomponius would give the *actio negotiorum gestorum* to or against him, and that they kept *mandatum* and *procuratio* clearly distinct. Africanus gives a choice of the *actio mandati* or *actio negotiorum gestorum.* Gaius allows a procurator to be appointed by mandate, and both Julian and Gaius permit a mandate to be *negotia gerere.* Paul will allow the former, but gives no sign of accepting the latter position. None of these three ever says that the *actio mandati* will lie against a general procurator (except Paul in the suspect D. 2.13.9. pr.), but Gaius and Paul might allow it against the *procurator ad litem.* Scaevola seems to adopt the same position as Julian, while Papinian and Ulpian have no hesitation in giving the *actio mandati* to or against the procurator. Such a progression on the face of the texts shows a historical development and the differing positions of the various jurists cannot be explained by supposing interpolations in the later texts. As for the *procurator unius rei*, we have one text of Scaevola, four of Paul and eight

1) *The Contract of Mandate in Roman Law*, Oxford 1961, pp. 36—60.

of Ulpian which recognise his existence, and this argues that the *procurator unius rei* was a late classical creation. Otherwise it is difficult to see why the compilers did not interpolate '*unius rei*' in the texts of other and earlier jurists.

The same historical approach will be adopted in the present article.

The earliest relevant text which we have is by Neratius (*7 Membran.*), D. 41.3.41:

> Si rem subreptam mihi procurator meus adprehendit, quamvis per procuratorem possessionem apisci nos iam fere conveniat, nihilo magis eam in potestatem meam redisse usuque capi posse existimandum est, quia contra statui captiosum erit.

Neratius tells us that if my procurator recovers property which had been stolen from me, then although in his time it was generally agreed that one could acquire possession through a procurator, none the less the property will not come under my control and will not be capable of usucapion. The text is generally regarded as genuine in substance [2], but Perozzi [3] and Bretone [4] both consider it interpolated and excise the part in which we are most interested, viz. *quamvis—conveniat*. The former gives no reason for his opinion beyond that from G. 2.95., he accepts that it was doubtful whether one could acquire possession through a procurator even in Gaius' time. The latter rightly declares that the text is concerned with the rule laid down by the *lex Atinia* forbidding *usucapio* of *res furtivae* until they are returned *in potestatem* of the person who was robbed. He says that this rule was the subject of interpretation by the jurists and *reversio* was understood as *reversio ad dominum*. This normally means, in his opinion, that the stolen object had to be again under the direct control of the *dominus* who had to be aware of its return, but there were some extensions. For example, Paul tells us (D. 41.3.4.7.) that

---

2) Albertario, *Possesso e quasi possesso*, Milan 1946 p. 120; Beseler, *Beiträge*, IV, p. 59 (who, however, holds interpolated *quia contra statui captiosum erit*); Lauria, *Possessiones*, I: *Età repubblicana*, Naples 1953, p. 113; Berneisen, *Per Liberam Personam*, 6 (3e série) RIDA 1959, p. 249 *et seq.* at pp. 255—256.

3) *Istituzioni di diritto romano*, 2nd ed., Rome 1928, I, p. 858, n. 2.

4) *Adquisitio per procuratorem?*, 1. Labeo 1955, pp. 280 *et seq.* at pp. 282—292.

Labeo held that there was *reversio* if something is stolen from my slave's *peculium*, which the slave recovers [5]), but Paul himself holds (D. 41.3.4.8.) that if my slave takes something of mine, then replaces it, it can be usucaped provided I did not know of the taking, since it has been returned to my *potestas;* if I did know of the taking it is essential that I also know that it has been returned. Likewise, Paul says (D. 41.3.4.11.) one must hold it sufficient in the case of a thing stolen from a pupil if his tutor knows that it has been restored to the house of the pupil, and if stolen from a lunatic that his curators know, and Julian believes (D. 47.2.57. (56).4.) that it is enough if it is returned to the *potestas* of the *tutor* or *curator furiosi* '*quia tutor domini loco habetur*'. The basis of *reversio*, says Bretone, is that the objective position before the theft is reestablished, and that the *dominus* can suffer no loss from the theft, and it is in connection with this requirement that the acquisition of possession of the *res furtiva* is considered sufficient or not. That is, he does not argue that *possessio* is always equal to *potestas*, but that where the *possessio* will give the *dominus* control there is *reversio in potestatem* [6]). Therefore, he says, acquisition of possession through a procurator, if it were recognised, must amount to *reversio in potestatem.* And accordingly he concludes that if in our text Neratius denied *reversio* in the case of *adprehensio* of the *res furtiva* by the *procurator*, he could not admit that generally one could acquire possession *per procuratorem.* Support for this conclusion he finds in G. 2.95.

But I do not think that Bretone has proved his case. First, although he takes into account the fact that possession does not always mean that *potestas* is also present and *vice versa*, and this does not necessarily affect his case adversely, D. 41.3.4.7. (Paul *54 ad ed.*) does show circumstances where the non-equivalence of *possessio* and *potestas* makes his proposition very doubtful.

---

5) This is what Bretone says, p. 286, but it is an oversimplification of the text. See *infra* pp. 24—25.

6) Other texts which he cites in his exposition are: D. 41.3.4.6; 41.3.49; 41.3.4. 21; 50.16.215; 41.3.4.10; 47.2.57(56).2; 41.3.4.11; 47.2.57(56).4; 41.4.7.3; 41.3.32. pr; 41.3.4.13; 47.2.85(84); 41.3.4.14; 41.2.15; and 41.2.4.18.

> Labeo quoque ait, si res peculiaris servi mei subrepta sit me ignorante, deinde eam nanctus sit, videri in potestatem meam redisse: commodius dicitur, etiamsi sciero, redisse eam in meam potestatem (nec enim sufficit, si eam rem, quam perdidit ignorante me, servus adprehendat): si modo in peculio eam esse volui: nam si nolui, tunc exigendum est, ut ego facultatem eius nactus sim.

The part which is important for us is from the beginning to '*redisse eam in meam potestatem*' [7]. Paul tells us that Labeo said if something belonging to the *peculium* of my slave is taken and I am unaware of this, and the slave then recovers it, it is regarded as having been returned to my *potestas*. Paul himself adds that it would be better to say that even if I knew of the theft, it had returned to my *potestas*. Thus, although generally a slave acquires possession *ex causa peculii* for his owner although the latter is unaware of the acquisition, Labeo would only allow the master to have *potestas* when the thing was returned, if he had been unaware of the theft. Otherwise, it would seem that he had to have knowledge of the return also. Therefore, Neratius in the more extreme case of the procurator (who, after all, is not in the *dominium* or *potestas* of his principal) might equally well have agreed that one could in general acquire possession through him, but not *potestas* for the purposes of the *lex Atinia*.

The second point against Bretone is that since he admits there was considerable interpretation of the meaning of the *lex Atinia* in this connection [8], it is of doubtful value to cite texts of Paul for showing the relation of *potestas* to *possessio* in the time of Neratius. D. 41.3.4.7. is a good example of the dangers inherent in this, since Paul's own view: '*etiamsi sciero, redisse eam in potestatem*', brings *potestas* much closer to *possessio* for this purpose

---

7) Beseler, *op. cit.*, IV, pp. 65—66, holds the texts interpolated from *commodius* to the end. He suggests that this is a paraphrase. Whether this part of the text is genuine, a paraphrase or a complete invention of the compilers will not affect the present argument, since the period of the wider view, whether late classical or Justinianic, is irrelevant. There is something wrong with at least (*nec enim — adprehendat*) since it contradicts what it is meant to justify. It may simply have been transposed in error and should come after '*nactus sim*'; Cf. Bretone, *loc. cit.*, n. 23.

8) *Op. cit.* p. 285. It should also be noted that if the text is interpolated it must be pre-Justinianic. Justinian could not have said '*iam fere conveniat*'.

than the earlier jurist Labeo ever did. And lastly, if the *procurator omnium bonorum* did not acquire possession for his principal there would have been no problem for Neratius, since it would have been obvious that acquisition of control by the procurator would not give his principal *potestas* for the purpose of the *lex Atinia* [9].)

Following the *communis opinio*, therefore, and taking the text as genuine, we can accept that by Neratius' time it was generally agreed that one could acquire possession through a procurator. The phrase '*iam fere conveniat*' suggests that there had been a dispute and this is borne out by the remark in Paul's Sentences 5.2.2. (which will be examined later) that '*utilitatis causa receptum est*' that one can acquire possession through a procurator. That phrase '*utilitatis causa receptum est*' always means, as an examination of the texts shows, that the rule was introduced by the jurists contrary to the existing principle. Accordingly, it is clear that in an earlier period one could not acquire possession through a procurator.

D. 41.1.53 (Modestinus *14 ad Quintum Mucium*):

> Ea quae civiliter adquiruntur per eos, qui in potestate nostra sunt, adquirimus, veluti stipulationem; quod naturaliter adquiritur, sicuti est possessio, per quemlibet volentibus nobis possidere adquirimus.

This text belongs not to Modestinus but Pomponius and is almost certainly correctly regarded as interpolated [10]). Beseler would rewrite the second half '*sicuti est possessio, etiam per procuratorem adquirimus*'. He rightly points out that '*volentibus nobis*' should

---

9) Another text of Neratius (*6 reg.*), D. 41.1.13. which says that if my procurator buys something for me '*ex mandato meo*', he acquires ownership for me even if I am unaware of the purchase, and that the same applies to a tutor's acquisition for his pupil, need not be dealt with in detail, since it is concerned with ownership and not possession. It is frequently held interpolated, but interpretations vary (cf. Index Itp.). It is, however, generally held that it allows the procurator to acquire for us; *e.g.* Beseler *op. cit.*, IV, p. 55 (who relates the rule to the fact that he was acting *ex mandato meo*); Albertario, *op. cit.*, p. 127 (who excises '*ex mandato meo*' as interpolated). On the other hand, the reference to the tutor is usually regarded as interpolated — see the works already cited in this note. If it is not, it may be some indication of extension at an early date.

10 Beseler, *op. cit.*, IV, p. 56; Berneisen, *op. cit.*, p. 279, and the authors she cites at n. 80.

be ‘*volentes*’, and this by itself is enough to cast the gravest doubts on the classicality of that part of the text. And of course, as it stands it is in conflict with the earlier text of Neratius and our third text in chronological order which comes from the Institutes of Gaius and is probably a little later.

> G. 2.95:
> Ex his apparet per liberos homines quoṣ neque iuri nostro subiectos habemus neque bona fide possidemus, item per alienos servos in quibus neque usumfructum habemus neque iustam possessionem, nulla ex causa nobis adquiri posse. et hoc est quod vulgo dicitur, per extraneam personam nobis adquiri non posse. tantum de possessione quaeritur an ⟨ ⟩ nobis adquiratur.

The fundamental question is what did Gaius write between *an* and *nobis*. The Verona Codex is illegible at this point and there are two alternatives suggested. The first is ⟨*per procuratorem*⟩, the second ⟨*per extraneam* (or *liberam*) *personam*⟩. In the Codex, after *an* can be read the letter *p* and the next letter is not at all clear — Studemund thought at first that it was another *p*[11]) but later suggested that it was an *s*[12]). The rest of the line (which could contain about 7 letters) is indecipherable. If the letter which can be imperfectly seen is *p* then the hypothesis of ‘*per procuratorem*’ (understanding the ordinary abbreviations used in the Codex) is virtually proved, if *s* it looks like the beginning of *personam* and one must suppose that ⟨*per extraneam*⟩ had been omitted. In the present state of the text, however, apart from counting spaces which seems to favour ‘*per procuratorem*[13]’, jurists have to decide the matter on external grounds. The majority[14], who favour ‘*per procuratorem*’, do so for the most part because they believe that

---

11) *Apographum*, Leipzig 1874, p. 76.

12) *Gai Institutiones*, edd. by Krüger and Studemund, 7th ed., Berlin 1923, p. xxviii.

13) *Cf.* Ferrini, *Manuale di Pandette*, 4th ed. by Grosso, Milan 1953, p. 249, n. 4.

14) E.g. Beseler, *op. cit.*, IV, p. 51; Albertario, *op. cit.*, pp. 125—126; Bretone, *op. cit.*, p. 281 and the jurists he cites at n. 8; Arangio-Ruiz, *Il Mandato in diritto romano*, Naples 1949, p. 50; Lauria, *op. cit.*, pp. 114—115; Meylan, *Per procuratorem possessio nobis adquiri potest*, Festschrift Lewald, pp. 105—106; De Zulueta, *The Institutes of Gaius*, I, Oxford 1946, p. 90; Ferrini, *loc. cit.*; Berneisen, *op. cit.*, p. 256, and David and Nelson ‘*Gai Institutionum Commentarii quattuor*’ Leiden 1960. (Text) p. 89; (Kommentar) pp. 310—311.

in Gaius' time there could be no question but that one could not acquire possession through an *extranea persona.* The others [15]) would say that since Neratius could write that it was generally agreed that one could acquire possession through a procurator, that question must have been settled by the time of Gaius who, therefore, must have been discussing the case of the *extranea persona.* Not only *a priori* reasoning and the number of spaces, but also Theophilus' Paraphrase supports the majority view. The Paraphrase, as is generally accepted, is based on a Greek translation of Gaius and only brought up to date by Justinian's Institutes. The passage with which we are concerned, 2.9.5., is a case where Justinian's Institutes are clearly only a subordinate source.

Ἐκ τῶν ἐφημένων οὖν φαίνεται, ὅτι δἰ ἐλευθέρων προσώπων, ἅτινα οὐκ ἔστιν ἡμῖν ὑπεξούσια οὐδὲ bona fide *δουλεύει ἡμῖν, ὁμοίως καί διὰ τῶν ἀλλοτρίων οἰκετῶν, ἐφ᾽ οἷς οὐδὲ* usúfructon *οὐδὲ* bona fide *ἔχομεν νομὴν, ἐξ οὐδεμίας αἰτίας προσπορίζεσθαι ἡμῖν τι δύναται καὶ τοῦτό ἐστι τὸ παρὰ πᾶσι λεγόμενον „δἰ ἐξωτικοῦ προσώπου μηδὲν προσπορίζεσθαι δύνασθαι" ἐξῃρημένου τοῦ λεχθησομένου θέματος. ἐὰν γὰρ πωλήσῃ τις ἐμοὶ κτῆσιν ἐν ἑτέρῳ διακειμένην τόπῳ, εἶτα οὐ δυνηθεὶς τοῖς τόποις ἐκείνοις ἐπιστῆναι πέμψω τὸν ἐμὸν* procurátora *καὶ τὴν νομὴν οὗτος παραλάβῃ, τῶν κτημάτων προσπορισθήσεταί μοι δἰ αὐτοῦ ἡ νομή. καὶ οὐ μόνον εἰ γινωσκόντων ἡμῶν τοῦτο συνέβη ἀλλὰ καὶ εἰ ἀγνοούντων ἐδόθη τι αὐτοῖς ἡμετέρῳ ὀνόματι, ἡ νομὴ ἡμῖν προσπορίζεται, ὡς βούλεται διάταξις Σεβήρου τοῦ βασιλέως* [16]).

---

[15]) *E.g.* Krüger and Studemund, *op. cit.*, p. 60; Kübler, *Gai Institutiones,* 7th ed. Leipzig 1935, pp. 75—76; Baviera, *Gai Institutionum commentarii quattuor,* in F.I. R.A., II, Florence 1940, p. 64.

[16]) Ex his itaque apparet per liberos homines, qui nostro iuri subiecti non sunt neque bona fide nobis serviunt, item per alienos servos, in quibus neque usumfructum neque bonae fidei possessionem habemus, nulla ex causa nobis adquiri posse. et hoc est quod vulgo dicitur per extraneam personam nihil adquiri posse: excepto casu quem nunc proponemus. si vendiderit quis mihi praedium alia regione positum, deinde cum illuc pervenire non possim, procuratorem meum miserim, qui possessionem praediorum suscipiat, adquiretur mihi per eundem possessio. quod non tantum scientibus nobis obvenit, sed etiam si ignorantibus nobis aliquid nostro nomine ipsis detur, possessio nobis quaeritur, sicut vult constitutio divi Severi... Ferrini's translation.

The mention of the constitution of Severus is only brought in, as it were, incidentally because it is related by Justinian in his Institutes, and it would seem better to take the preceding discussion of the acquisition of possession through a procurator as having been suggested by Gaius. This would seem to strengthen the probability that Gaius discussed whether one could acquire possession through a procurator and not through any *libera persona.*

The constitution just mentioned is our fourth text. C. 7.32.1 (*Impp. Severus et Antoninus AA. Attico*):

> Per liberam personam ignoranti quoque adquiri possessionem et, postquam scientia intervenerit, usucapionis condicionem inchoari posse tam ratione utilitatis quam iuris pridem receptum est. *PP. vi k. Dec. Dextro ii et Prisco conss.* [A.D. 196.]

The intention of this constitution seems, *prima facie*, to be to confirm what had been accepted by the jurists, namely, that one could acquire possession through a *libera persona.* But it has been suspected of interpolation, and is said to have referred originally only to the procurator. Albertario [17]) puts it side by side with J. 2.9.5.

> Ex his itaque apparet per liberos homines, quos neque iuri vestro subiectos habetis neque bona fide possidetis, item per alienos servos, in quibus neque usumfructum habetis neque iustam possessionem, nulla ex causa vobis adquiri posse: et hoc est quod dicitur, per extraneam personam nihil adquiri posse. excepto eo, quod per liberam personam veluti per procuratorem placet non solum scientibus, sed etiam ignorantibus vobis adquiri possessionem secundum divi Severi constitutionem et per hanc possessionem etiam dominium, si dominus fuit qui tradidit, vel usucapionem aut longi temporis praescriptionem, si dominus non sit.

---

[17]) *Op. cit.* p. 122. Cf. Beseler, *op. cit.*, IV, pp. 60—61; Berneisen, *op. cit.*, p. 263. Beseler and Albertario would also excise as interpolated at the end of the text [*tam*] . . . [*quam iuris*]. This may well be correct. If the decision could be reached on principle there would be no need to refer to *utilitas*. Justinian also uses *utilitatis causa* in a way alien to the classics in J. 2.4.2. and it is unlikely, *pace* Ferrini, *Opere*, II, p. 361, that this derives from Gaius. Another possibility is that the text is genuine, because the decision was reached on both *utilitas* and *ius*. It was accepted *utilitatis causa* that one could acquire possession through a free person, and as a matter of law that when one knew of the possession one could usucape. That is, *ratione utilitatis* refers to the acquisition of possession, *ratione iuris* to the usucapion.

From '*excepto eo*' to '*divi Severi constitutionem*', Justinian's text, it is argued, is derived from the constitution, and the reference to the procurator cannot easily be explained unless we assume that the constitution originally referred to him and not to any *extranea persona* [18]). The difficulty with this view, however, is that the compilers of the Institutes would take the text of the constitution (in so far as they did rely on it) not from any original source, but from Justinian's first Code of 529 A.D., which one would expect to have the same reading as that of the second Code. There is nothing whatever to suggest that Justinian innovated in the meantime. Moreover, the reference to the procurator could easily be a reminiscence from Gaius' Institutes which was certainly also used in the preparation of the passage. Accordingly, the demonstration of the text's interpolation is not convincing.

Paul has two important texts. D. 41.2.1.20.(*54 ad ed.*):

> Per procuratorem tutorem curatoremve possessio nobis adquiritur. cum autem suo nomine nacti fuerint possessionem, non cum ea mente, ut operam dumtaxat suam accommodarent, nobis non possunt adquirere. alioquin si dicamus per eos non adquiri nobis possessionem, qui nostro nomine accipiunt, futurum, ut neque is possideat cui res tradita sit, quia non habeat animum possidentis, neque is qui tradiderit, quoniam cesserit possessione.

This text has often been said to be interpolated, not only as to the first sentence in which we are interested, but more expecially as to '*cum autem — adquirere*' [19]). Apart from *a priori* views on the development of the acquisition of possession, three reasons are given for holding '*tutorem curatoremve*' interpolated. The first is that it is unbecoming that Paul should consider himself — or his listener or reader — (*nobis!*) a pupil, or insane or a minor [20]). That does not seem a serious objection. *Nobis*, when used in this

---

18) Albertario, *loc. cit.*

19) Cf. Index Itp.; Lauria, *op. cit.*, p. 115; Albertario, *op. cit.*, p. 126; Ferrini, *Pandette*, p. 250.n.4.

20) Albertario, *Lezioni di diritto romano*, Camerino 1912—1913, pp. 475—476; repeated with disapproval by Lewald 34 ZSS (1913), p. 453; Beseler, *op. cit.*, IV, p. 57. finds the argument conclusive for interpolation (although earlier he had not signalled that part of the text as compilatorial. *op. cit.*, III, p. 19.) Albertario in his later *Possesso e quasi possesso* does not refer to this argument.

way after a passive verb is not taken by the Romans to be personal. *Nobis possessio adquiritur* is the equivalent of the French '*on acquiert la possession*', and one would never in a relevant phrase take '*vous*', which '*on*' becomes when it is not the subject of the sentence as meaning the reader or listener personally. The second is that '*curatoremve*' is the work of the compilers because whenever one finds *curator* without reference to a determined type of *cura* the text is interpolated. The author of this view is Solazzi whose arguments I have not been able to see, but it is brought forward with approval by Albertario [21]). Without doubt some texts which merely say *curator* are interpolated, but it is going too far to raise this to a general rule, or even to hold that *curator* is, without anything more, suspicious. The examples in texts which are certainly classical do not leave much room for serious doubt [22]). Solazzi himself says elsewhere that the interpolation of '*tutorem curatoremve*' cannot be proved by arguments from internal evidence [23]). The third argument, which is produced by Albertario only, is that *tutorem* must also be interpolated because '*ut operam suam dumtaxat accommodarent*' is incomprehensible if it refers to the *tutor* as well as to the *procurator*. When this argument was first brought forward [24]), it was opposed by Lewald [25]) on the ground that its validity failed if one held with Gradenwitz [26]) that '*cum autem — adquirere*' was itself interpolated. And, indeed, better reasons have been produced for holding that this second part of the text is the work of the compilers [27]). Nevertheless, Albertario repeated his argument in 1946 without mentioning the doubts that the part of the text on which he relies is interpolated [28]). The *a posteriori*

---

21) *Op. cit.*, p. 126.

22) *E.g.* G. 4.99 (a very good text because it puts the powers of tutors and curators generally on a level just as in D. 41.2.1.20); 4.101; Ulp. Reg. XII.

23) *Sull' acquisto del possesso per mezzo di rappresentanti*, Scritti 1, pp. 295—360 at p. 319.

24) In the *Lezioni* above mentioned (n.20) at pp. 475—476.

25) *Loc. cit.*

26) *Interpolationen in den Pandekten*, Berlin 1887, p. 221.

27) *Cf.* Index Itp.

28) *Possesso e quasi possesso*, p. 126.

evidence, therefore, for doubting the classicality of the text is very slender. The text, in fact fits very well into the development which is referred to in what is probably the slightly earlier C. 7.32.1.

The second text of Paul (if we can believe that it gives his true opinion) is from the Sentences 5.2.2:

> Per liberas personas, quae in potestate nostra non sunt, adquiri nobis nihil potest. Sed per procuratorem adquiri nobis possessionem posse utilitatis causa receptum est. Absente autem domino comparata non aliter ei, quam si rata sit, quaeritur.

We are told that we can acquire nothing *per liberas personas*, and this is then qualified by saying that one can acquire possession through a *procurator*. From this it is argued that one cannot acquire possession through other *liberae personae* [29]). This is very plausible, but two points are worth remembering. First, there is nothing which tells that the work of Paul from which this derives was written after his book *54 ad edictum* or after the constitution of Severus. If it were written before, it might show a slightly earlier and narrow (even for its time?) interpretation. Secondly, as was stated at the beginning of this article, we can trace throughout the classical period a rapprochement of *mandatum* and *procuratio*. It cannot be discerned from the texts whether Paul would give the *actio mandati* against the *procurator*, but from P.S. 1.3.2. it is clear that he certainly recognised the *procurator unius rei* who is very close to the mandatary. It is possible that in our present text he would include *mandatarius* within the term *procurator* [30]). This argument, however, will not be insisted upon since it may be, even if he gave the *actio mandati* against the procurator, that he conceded that there were still differences between the *procurator* and the *mandatarius*.

---

29) Albertario *loc. cit.*; Beseler *op. cit.*, IV, pp. 51—52; *Juristische Miniaturen*, Leipzig 1929, p. 91; Solazzi, *op. cit.*, p. 301; Lauria, *op. cit.*, p. 116; Meylan, *op. cit.*, pp. 107—108.

30) This point is made by Buckland, *A Textbook of Roman Law*, 2nd ed., Cambridge 1932, p. 200. He also expresses his belief in a historical development of the acquisition of possession through others. *Cf.* his *The Main Institutions of Roman Private Law*, Cambridge 1931, p. 166.

Papinian has one text: D. 41.2.49.2.(*2 definit.*):

> Etsi possessio per procuratorem ignoranti quaeritur, usucapio vero scienti competit, tamen evictionis actio domino contra venditorem invito procuratore non datur, sed per actionem mandati ea cedere cogitur.

It is not at all surprising that in this text no mention is made of the tutor, curator or other free person. The acquisition of possession by the procurator is only mentioned by way of contrast with the main point of the text which is that there is no automatic transference of his actions to to the principal. To say '*etsi possessio per extraneam personam ignoranti quaeritur, usucapio vero scienti competit*' would be far less forceful, because apart from the tutor and curator the only free person who could acquire possession for another who could be unaware of this would be the mandatary, and it would happen less often in the case of the mandatary than in the case of the procurator that the principal would not know of the acquisition. Much more important, the tutor and curator would be included in the term *extranea persona* and since they are, naturally, in a special position, as regards the transference of contractual actions (which, as has been said, is the real subject of the text) it would have been wrong to bring them in [31]).

Complete proof, however, that in late classical law one did acquire possession through any *libera persona* is only obtained from an examination of the texts of Ulpian. D. 47.2.14.17 (29 ad Sab.):

> Si epistula, quam ego tibi misi, intercepta sit, quis furti actionem habeat? et primum quaerendum est, cuius sit epistula, utrum eius qui misit, an eius ad quem missa est? et si quidem dedi servo eius, statim ipsi quaesita est, cui misi: si vero procuratori, aeque (quia per liberam personam possessio quaeri potest) ipsius facta est, maxime, si eius interfuit eam habere. . . .

Most of this text, including the part not reproduced here, has, at one time or another, been held interpolated [32]). This applies, too,

---

[31]) Papinian is one of the two jurists who, as can be seen from this text and others (D. 17.1.55, 56.4; and 34.2.23) gives the *actio mandati* against the *procurator*. It may be that here, *procurator* does include the ordinary mandatary.

[32]) *Cf.* Index Itp.; Jolowicz, *Digest 47.2. De furtis*, Cambridge 1940, p. 19; Albertario, *op. cit.*, p. 123.

to the part in which we are mainly interested '(*quia per liberam personam possessio quaeri potest*)'. No reason is given for this other than the *a priori* one that one cannot acquire possession through a *libera persona*, or that, as Albertario says [33]), since one is dealing with a procurator the motivation ought to refer to him. The first of these need not be answered now, and for the second it is obvious that if, as here, a general motivation is given which covers the particular situation described, the motivation can hardly be regarded as suspect. The appreciation of this becomes clearer when one considers that it would have been impossible to say '*si vero liberae personae, aeque etc*' since if the *libera persona* had no connection with the addressee, he would, of course, not acquire possession for him. It was much neater for Ulpian to choose a particular example where the relationship was obvious, and then give the motivation in a general form where the relationship would be implied. Moreover, it was especially important to discuss the situation in this way since Ulpian was primarily concerned with ownership, and possession is only brought in in so far as it is relevant to the acquisition of ownership. The writer of the letter hands it to someone who is acting for the addressee, and the writer intends that property in the letter should pass to the addressee. It is held that ownership is transferred to the addressee because possession is acquired for him. Ownership is not transferred to the intermediary since there is no such intention either on his part or on that of the writer. For this situation, a close relationship (whether *procuratio*, *tutela*, *cura* or *mandatum*) between the intermediary and the addressee is necessarily required and it is essential to make this clear. This is a case, and there are, as we shall see, others, where the acquisition of ownership and possession have to be linked. D. 41.1.20.2 (Ulpian *29 ad Sab.*):

> Si ego et Titius rem emerimus eaque Titio et quasi meo procuratori tradita sit, puto mihi quoque quaesitum dominium, quia placet per liberam personam omnium rerum possessionem quaeri posse et per hanc dominium.

Once again Ulpian tells us one can acquire possession through a *libera persona*, but again '*liberam personam*' is regarded as an

---

33) *Loc. cit.*

interpolation for '*procuratorem*'. This change has given rise to at least two interpretations. The first is that it means that Titius was my *procurator omnium bonorum*, since the text would read '*quia placet per procuratorem omnium rerum possessionem quaeri posse*' and '*omnium rerum*' would have to be understood as attaching to '*procuratorem*' and not to '*possessionem*' [34]). This is an impossible construction of the text. First, if Ulpian had wanted to deal with acquisition through a *procurator omnium bonorum* he would have chosen a simpler situation, and if he had wanted to discuss a particular case where the *dominus* and the *procurator omnium bonorum* bought jointly, he would have made it clear at the beginning that Titius was the *procurator* of the *dominus* (and the first part of the text certainly looks genuine and has never been impugned). Secondly, if Titius were the *procurator omnium bonorum*, why say the *res* was delivered '*et quasi meo procuratori*'? And thirdly, why in such an obvious and well established case would Ulpian use '*puto*'? [35]) The second, put forward by Mitteis [36]) is that Titius is a mere *extranea persona*, but that he is regarded in the circumstances as if he were a *procurator*. That is, it is a particular attempt to get round the principle which, he said, remained until the time of Justinian that one can acquire possession through a *procurator* only, and not through other *liberae personae*. This is possible, and would explain the '*puto*', but attributes to the jurists, or at least Ulpian, too much casuistry. Another solution which would not be impossible is that the text from '*quia placet*' to the end is an interpolation. If this is correct, the text is evidence neither for the proposition that one can acquire possession through *procuratores* only, nor for the proposition that one can acquire possession through any *libera persona*. I submit, however, that not even that is the correct view and that the text is, in substance, genuine. Too little attention has been paid to the origins of the text. It comes from Ulpian book *29 ad Sabinum* and

---

34) Kniep, *Vacua Possessio*, p. 221 (not seen); Ferrini, *op. cit.*, p. 250 n. 2; *Cf.* De Zulueta, Digest 41.1.&2, Oxford 1950, p. 60.

35) Beseler's reconstruction of the text, *op. cit.*, IV, p. 55 has to face the same difficulty.

36) *Römisches Privatrecht*, Berlin 1908, pp. 212—213.

precisely from that part *de mancipatione et traditione rei venditae* [37]). It should be concerned, therefore, as *prima facie* it is, with a problem of ownership and not of possession, and this, I suggest, is the case. The references to ownership are not, as is usually thought [38]), interpolations. The situation is this. Titius who is just an *extranea persona* and I jointly buy a *res* — whether a *res mancipi* or *nec mancipi* is not clear. Titius receives delivery either by *mancipatio* or *traditio*, whichever is appropriate, both on his own behalf and on mine. To express the fact that he is also receiving on my behalf, Ulpian says '*et quasi meo procuratori*' and no further conclusions need or should be drawn from these words [39]). The question is then raised as to whether I am joint owner. The answer to this depends on the position of the other parties. Is the seller still part-owner despite the fact that there was a *mancipatio* or *traditio* with a *iusta causa*? Or is Titius sole owner although he received with the intention (and this was known to the transferor) that I was to be joint owner? The answer given in the text by Ulpian is that he thinks I am joint owner because it is settled that I can acquire possession of all things through a free person. '*Omnium rerum possessionem*' is stressed because Ulpian is concerned with the acquisition of ownership either of a *res mancipi* or a *res nec mancipi*. If the former, the argument is one can also acquire ownership of a *res mancipi* in this way in this particular situation because possession of all things is so acquired. If the latter, and this is by far the more probable, then *a fortiori* (even if Ulpian would not have allowed onc so to acquire ownership of a *res mancipi*) since one can acquire possession of all things one ought at least to be able to acquire ownership of *res nec mancipi* (i.e. the text would originally have ended '*et per hanc dominium rerum nec mancipi in a case such as this*'). It is this concern with the acquisition of ownership, not possession, which

---

37) Lenel, *Palingenesia*, II, 1123.

38) Cf. Index Itp.; Albertario, *op. cit*., p. 121.

39) It may well be that '*et quasi meo procuratori*' is an explanatory gloss. This would account for the rather odd form and their excision would facilitate the understanding of the text. I am indebted for this suggestion to Mr. A. M. Honoré, Rhodes Reader in Roman-Dutch Law in the University of Oxford.

accounts for Ulpian's '*puto*'. This is another example of a close relationship between ownership and possession [40]). It may be noticed that neither here nor in D. 47.2.14.17. is much discretion, if any, left to the agent.

D. 13.7.11.6 (Ulpian *28 ad ed.*):

> Per liberam autem personam pignoris obligatio nobis non adquiritur, adeo ut ne per procuratorem plerumque vel tutorem adquiratur: et ideo ipsi actione pigneraticia convenientur. sed nec mutat, quod constitutum est ab imperatore nostro posse per liberam personam possessionem adquiri: nam hoc eo pertinebit, ut possimus pignoris nobis obligati possessionem per procuratorem vel tutorem adprehendere, ipsam autem obligationem libera persona nobis non semper adquiret.

Again we are told that one acquires possession through a *libera persona*. Here again, the passage has been attacked many times as interpolated, but no sound *a posteriori* reasons are given for the proposition that it referred originally only to a *procurator* [41]). Solazzi here adopts a very cautious approach, and maintains that there are no internal traces of interpolation in the text, but that evidence for interpolation can be seen when one compares it with § 7.

> Sed si procurator meus vel tutor rem pignori dederit, ipse agere pigneraticia poterit: quod in procuratore ita procedit, si ei mandatum fuerit pignori dare.

Ipse in the singular seems, he says, an '*indice rivelatore*' that the genuine text did not mention the tutor [42]). This argument is absurd. '*Procurator*' and '*tutor*' are related by the disjunctive '*vel*', and are therefore naturally followed by the verb '*dederit*' in the singular (not denied by Solazzi). The following clause should be, as it is, on the same lines (otherwise there would be even greater evidence for interpolation) and so its verb is '*poterit*', of which

---

40) There would be routine alterations in the text due to Justinian's abolition of the categories of *res mancipi* and *res nec mancipi*.

41) *Cf. Index Itp.*; Albertario, *op. cit.*, pp. 126—127. As early as Cuiacius the interpolation of '*plerumque*' and '*semper*' was recognised.

42) *Op. cit.*, p. 321. His fear that his scruples to admit the interpolation may be regarded as excessive seems unjustified.

the subject, '*ipse*', must be, as it also is, in the singular. The reference to the *procurator* followed by that to the *tutor* is an indication of the way the rule had developed. The constitution referred to is, of course, that of Severus and Antoninus which has been dealt with already. D. 6.2.7.10 (Ulpian *16 ad ed.*):

> Si ego non emero, sed servus meus, habebo Publicianam. idem est et si procurator meus vel tutor vel curator vel quis alius negotium meum gerens emerit.

This text too has been said to be interpolated [43]), but Solazzi maintained that the interpolation had not been proved [44]). According to Albertario '*vel tutor vel curator vel quis alius negotium meum gerens*' looks like an interpolation, but Ulpian merely seems, quite properly, to be giving a list of persons purchase by whom will give the principal the right to the *actio Publiciana*. Albertario also says that '*vel curator*' without reference to a particular type of *cura* is compilatorial. This argument has been discussed in connection with D. 41.2.1.20 [45]) and does not seem justified. Once more the suggested signs of interpolation are very weak. On the other hand, the text is excellent evidence that there had been a historical development. At first one could acquire possession through one's slave only, then the rule was extended to the procurator, then to the tutor and curator and finally to *quis alius negotium meum gerens*. This last may be regarded as referring to anyone at all acting on one's behalf, not, as it is taken by Solazzi [46]), as concerning only a *negotiorum gestor* whose action has been ratified. If a *negotiorum gestor* had been specifically meant, one would have expected to find the plural, *negotia*, rather than the singular, *negotium*. D. 41.2.42.1 (Ulpian *4 regul.*):

> Procurator si quidem mandante domino rem emerit, protinus ille adquirit possessionem: quod si sua sponte emerit, non nisi ratam habuerit dominus emptionem.

---

43) *Cf. Index Itp.* Beseler, *op. cit.*, IV, p. 54; Albertario, *op. cit.*, p. 127.

44) *Op. cit.*, pp. 323—324.

45) *Supra*, p. 72.

46) *Loc. cit.*

The text is not usually discussed in this connection, but is by Beseler [47]) who would excise '*possessionem*', thus making the text deal with the acquisition of ownership. If this is correct, the text need not worry us as being contrary to the view of possession here put forward. The text as it stands, however, might be used to argue that, since it is concerned only with the *procurator*, one cannot acquire possession through other *liberae personae*. This argument, if it were produced, would be unjustified. This rule on authorisation of an act is not appropriate for a tutor or curator and so could not be expressed in general terms. Nor could it apply to the ordinary mandatary (i.e. appointed for one transaction) since he must in the nature of things have authorisation. Ulpian could say nothing but '*procurator*'.

C. 4. 27.1 (*Impp. Diocletianus et Maximianus AA. Marcello*):

> Excepta possessionis causa per liberam personam, quae alterius iuri non est subdita, nihil adquiri posse indubii iuris est. 1. Si igitur procurator non sibi, sed ei, cuius negotia administrabat, redintegratae rei vindicationem pactus est idque pactum etiam stipulatio insecuta est, nulla domino obligatio adquisita est. servis autem res traditae dominis adquiruntur. *D.k. Iul. ipsis iiii et iii AA. conss.* [290 A.D.]

Again it appears one can acquire possession, and only possession, through a *libera persona*. The procurator is mentioned in § 1 by way of example only and cannot be taken in any way as evidence that the constitution originally referred to him alone [48]).

C. 7.32.8 (*Impp. Diocletianus et Maximianus AA. et CC. Cyrillo*):

> Per procuratorem utilitatis causa possessionem et, si proprietas ab hac separari non possit, dominium etiam quaeri placuit. *PP. xviii k. Mart. Sirmi CC. conss.* [294 A.D.]

This text is generally held to be interpolated because it allows acquisition of ownership through a procurator and this was refused by the same Emperors in C. 4.27.1. which dates from only four years before. If this view is correct and '*et — etiam*' is excised,

---

47) *Op. cit.*, IV, p. 58. The text is generally held to have been interpolated by the compilers to restrict the powers of the procurator.

48) Beseler, *op. cit.*, IV, p. 60. holds '*liberam personam, quae alterius iuri non est subdidta*' an interpolation for '*procuratorem*'.

the constitution would seem to be very general and the reference to the procurator alone would seem to exclude even at this late date acquisition through others. But if the text is interpolated in this way, it is difficult to see why the rescript was ever needed and even survived since the rule that one could acquire possession through a procurator had been quite settled for a very long time. And in fact the text is genuine and deals with a very special case. The constitution expressly says one acquires possession through a procurator, and if ownership cannot be separated from possession, then one acquires ownership too. This formulation would be highly peculiar if it were an insertion intended to permit one to acquire generally even ownership through a procurator, but circumstances can be envisaged where such would be an exact formulation. It is well known and universally accepted that in classical law two persons could not have the same possession in a thing. Accordingly, when a procurator acquires possession for his principal, he does not have possession for himself. If, therefore, in any particular case, ownership is co-extensive with possession, who is owner? There are two possibilities. Either one says that ownership is not acquired for the principal, in which case possession too must be regarded as still being with the procurator. Or one says that since possession is acquired for the principal, he must also have acquired ownership. The latter is the solution preferred by Diocletian and Maximian. Nor is it difficult to imagine such a situation. For example, at my request and on my behalf my procurator has acquired a wild animal, either as a result of hunting or by purchase. Wild animals are only owned by anyone so long as he has possession. By the general rule, my procurator will have acquired possession for me, but will I also have acquired ownership? The question could be of great practical importance. For instance, if the wild animal did damage before it was delivered to me by the procurator, am I liable? It is a problem of this type to which the rescript must have returned an answer, and since it is concerned with a very particular case, doubtless concerning a procurator, the fact that it is not expressed in wider terms and does not refer to *extraneae personae* generally is not evidence that the rule permitting acquisition of possession through others was confined to the case of the procurator. Again we have a text where ownership and possession have to be closely linked.

These, then, are the texts. We have one by Neratius saying that it is generally agreed one can acquire possession through a procurator, and one by Pomponius (although ascribed to Modestinus) which tells us that one can acquire possession through anyone, but the text shows grave signs of interpolation. Then a text of Gaius almost certainly saying that it is questioned whether one can so acquire through a procurator, and a rescript of Severus and Antoninus relating that it is settled that one can acquire possession through any *libera persona*. A text by Paul tells us that possession can be acquired through a procurator, tutor or curator, and another that we acquire possession through a procurator, and there is one by Papinian on the same lines. Ulpian says in four texts that we can acquire possession through any free person, and in one that we can acquire through a procurator. Of these first four, one lists procurator, tutor, curator and *quis alius negotium meum gerens*, and another mentions the procurator and tutor. Lastly, we have two constitutions of Diocletian and Maximian, one maintaining that one can acquire possession through any *libera persona*, the other saying as much for the procurator. We have seen that the evidence adduced for substantive interpolation of the later texts is very flimsy. Four of the texts after the rescript of Antoninus and Severus mention the procurator only, but this is not inconsistent with there having been a wider development. One does not always want to state a proposition in the widest possible way. Indeed, in at least three out of the four cases one can give good reasons for the rule not being expressed more widely, and in two of these three it would have been impossible for reasons unconnected with the acquisition of possession to refer to others besides the procurator. Accordingly, the evidence for holding that the development to allow acquisition of possession through any *extranea persona* took place in classical law is very strong. Further, since one text mentions the procurator and tutor, another procurator, tutor and curator, and a third procurator, tutor, curator and anyone else, and all these are after the rescript of Antoninus and Severus, by which time the law was settled, it is a reasonable assumption that the development (which must have been quite rapid) progressed, before the rescript, in these stages [49]).

---

49) I am grateful to Professor David Daube of the University of Oxford and Professor J. A. C. Thomas of the University of Glasgow for very helpful criticism.

8

Acquisition of Possession and Usucapion per Servos et Filios

I. Acquisition of Possession

Some texts tell us that a master acquires possession *per servum* even unknowingly if the acquisition is *ex peculiari causa*, but that otherwise his knowledge is essential for the acquisition of possession. Others simply say, without any reference to *peculium*, that the master acquires possession *per servum*. The dominant modern view is that those texts which demand the knowledge of the master for acquisition of possession except where the taking is *ex peculiari causa* represent the classical law and that the other texts have suffered at the hands of the compilers,[1] but other jurists hold exactly the opposite.[2] The minority view seems to me to be certainly correct but it has not been altogether convincingly presented. The most unambiguous textual authority, D.41.2.23.2 and D.41.2.24, seems to have been strangely neglected and the text which provides the strongest support for the majority view, D.41.2.1.5, has not been adequately dealt with. Moreover, what seems to be the main general argument of Nicosia, who has dealt at greatest length with the subject, appears of doubtful value. He maintains [3] that *traditio* has its basis in possession and that it is impossible to acquire ownership by *traditio* without also acquiring possession, yet we know that, generally, *traditio* to a slave, even without the master's knowledge, gave the master ownership. But there is no evidence that it was ever regarded by the Romans as a principle that *traditio* had its basis in possession and it does not follow that because in the nature of things the transferee in the normal case acquires possession he must in all cases do so. Indeed, there is positive proof to the contrary. No one would deny that *traditio* directly to a pupil of whatever age and without any intervention by his tutor would give the pupil ownership.[4] But it is clear that at least some classical jurists, notably Paul, held that

1 *e.g.*, De Francisci, "Sull'acquisto del possesso per mezzo dello schiavo" (1907) Rend.Ist.Lomb., xl, p. 1002 *et seq.*; Buckland, *The Roman Law of Slavery* (Cambridge, 1908), p. 131, *A Textbook of Roman Law*, 2nd ed. (Cambridge, 1932), p. 200 *et seq.*; Albertario, *Corso di diritto romano: possesso e quasi possesso* (Milan, 1946), p. 113 *et seq.*; Amirante, *Captivitas e postliminium* (Naples, 1950), p. 143 *et seq.*

2 Beseler, *Beiträge zur Kritik der römischen Rechtsquellen*, IV (Tübingen, 1920), p. 61 *et seq.*; Schulz, *Classical Roman Law* (Oxford, 1951), p. 438; Nicosia, *L'acquisto del possesso mediante i "potestati subiecti"* (Milan, 1960), *passim.*

3 *Op. cit.*, chap. 4, pp. 115–136, especially from p. 117.

4 *Cf.* G.2.83.

traditio to an *infans* without his tutor's authority would not give him possession.[5]

> G.2.89: *Non solum autem proprietas per eos quos in potestate habemus adquiritur nobis, sed etiam possessio: cuius enim rei possessionem adepti fuerint, id nos possidere videmur; unde etiam per eos usucapio procedit.*[6]

G.2.86, 87, 88, 90, 91 and 92 are all concerned with automatic acquisition and it would be perverse to hold that § 89 in the middle of these was not.[7] We need not concern ourselves here with the exact meaning of *quos in potestate habemus*, that is, whether Gaius means those who are in our *familia* or only those who are under our direct control.

> D.41.2.15 (Gaius 26 ad ed. prov.): *Rem, quae nobis subrepta est, perinde intellegimur desinere possidere atque eam, quae vi nobis erepta est. sed si is qui in potestate nostra est, subripuerit, quamdiu apud ipsum sit res, tamdiu non amittimus possessionem, quia per huiusmodi personas adquiritur nobis possessio. et haec ratio est, quare videamur fugitivum possidere, quod is, quemadmodum aliarum rerum possessionem intervertere non potest, ita ne suam quidem potest.*

If we leave aside *et haec ratio* to the end which does not concern us at the moment, the only suspicion of the text is by Hägerström [8] who holds interpolated *quia per huiusmodi personas adquiritur nobis possessio*. He suggests that the clause is perhaps a gloss. His arguments, however, are not convincing. He considers that the reason is too narrow, that we also acquire possession through a procurator and through slaves bona fide possessed. But a reference to the procurator would have been absurd. The procurator is a free man through whom we can only acquire possession when he is acting on our behalf—which is certainly not the case when he steals from us. As for slaves bona fide possessed, apart from anything else, there is no special reason why they should have been mentioned. A text need not be written so as to include every possibility. It would have been different if the clause had said "because through such persons alone do we acquire possession." Thus, no good reason has been given for holding this part of the text interpolated and it is accepted as genuine even by Albertario.[9]

[5] *Cf.* D.41.2.1.3; *h.t.*32.2; C.7.32.3: Buckland, *Textbook*, p. 201; Kaser, *Das römische Privatrecht*, I (Munich, 1955), p. 332 and n. 13.

[6] This text is repeated in the Digest at 41.1.10.2.

[7] *Cf.* Beseler, *op. cit.*, IV p. 62.

[8] *Der römische Obligationsbegriff*, I (Uppsala, 1927), p. 178, n. 2 (at p. 179).

[9] *Studi di diritto romano*, II (Milan, 1941), p. 289. See also against Hägerström, Carcaterra (1938), A.G. cxx, p. 162 and n. 1; Nicosia, *op. cit.*, p. 376 and n. 64.

If the reason is Gaian, the text is excellent evidence that we acquire possession automatically through a slave, since otherwise it would be nonsense to use it to justify the particular proposition of the text.[10] That also means, of course, that acquisition of possession by the master without his knowledge was not restricted to cases *ex peculiari causa*. But one must accept the possibility of interpolation so that the text, highly persuasive as it must be, is not conclusive.

But conclusive is the testimony of D.41.2.23.2 (Iavolenus *1 epist.*):

> *Item quaero, si vinxero liberum hominem ita, ut eum possideam, an omnia, quae is possidebat, ego possideam per eum. respondit: si vinxeris hominem liberum, eum te possidere non puto: quod cum ita se habeat, multo minus per illum res eius a te possidebuntur: neque enim rerum natura recipit, ut per eum aliquid possidere possimus, quem civiliter in mea potestate non habeo.*

Apart from the deletion of the *is* following *quae*, which is suggested by Hägerström [11] (who takes it as *si*) and is unimportant, only *neque enim* to the end (which does not concern us here) is suspected of interpolation.[12] The text asks, if I bind a free man so that I possess him, do I possess through him all that he possessed? The answer given is that the free man is not possessed, *a fortiori* what he possessed is not possessed through him. This question could never even have been raised if one did not, in general, automatically acquire possession through persons in one's power. There can be no *peculium* here. Accordingly, the text is in itself the strongest possible proof that in classical law acquisition of possession *per servos* was not restricted to *ex peculiari causa* or where the *dominus* knew of the slave's taking. It could not be seriously argued that in the text Javolenus is considering acquisition of possession of those things alone which I knew the free man to possess. Apart from its inherent absurdity, that interpretation is ruled out by *omnia*.[13]

10 Of course, we are told in D.41.2.1.19 that if our slave takes control intending to acquire possession not for us but for Titius we do not acquire possession so that, if this represents classical law, the reason given in our text is not altogether logically valid. Nonetheless this is a point which need not spring to a jurist's mind unlike a restriction to acquisitions *ex peculiari causa*. But in any event, there is general agreement that the rule in D.41.2.1.19 is the result of interpolation: to Nicosia, *op. cit.*, p. 112, and the references he gives (n. 53) add Buckland, *Slavery*, p. 133 and n. 4.

11 *Op. cit.*, p. 199, n. 1, at p. 203.

12 See the authorities cited by Reggi, *Liber homo bona fide serviens* (Milan, 1958), p. 199, n. 193.

13 It might be maintained that, for the acquisition of possession, a distinction should be drawn between those things which a slave acquires during his

Another text of Javolenus which is, at the very least, highly pursuasive is D.41.2.24 (*14 epist.*).

> *Quod servus tuus ignorante te vi possidet, id tu non possides, quoniam is, qui in tua potestate est, ignoranti tibi non corporalem possessionem, sed iustam potest adquirere: sicut id, quod ex peculio ad eum pervenerit, possidet. nam tum per servum dominus quoque possidere dicitur, summa scilicet cum ratione, quia, quod ex iusta causa corporaliter a servo tenetur, id in peculio servi est et peculium, quod servus civiliter quidem possidere non posset, sed naturaliter tenet, dominus creditur possidere. quod vero ex maleficiis adprehenditur, id ad domini possessionem ideo non pertinet, quia nec peculii causam adprehendit.*

Various interpolations have been suggested but no view has won general acceptance.[14] However, it is probably fair to say that the references to the *peculium* are an addition.[15] If we could acquire possession unawares *ex peculiari causa* only, the question whether we acquired possession of something taken, without our knowledge, by our slave *vi* could never have arisen. This text, therefore, is also extremely strong evidence that there was generally automatic acquisition of possession of whatever a slave took. On the other hand, it might be argued that since this and the previous text are from Javolenus' *libri epistolarum* they are replies to questions raised by persons unskilled in the law, and which were inherently absurd. But it would then be impossible to explain why it was thought worthwhile to publish them in a work meant for lawyers.[16] Moreover, it would be an extraordinary coincidence if both of these texts resulted from the putting of absurd questions.

Further, it should be noticed that there are some texts concerned with the question of acquisition of possession through a slave in flight.[17] The decision given in these need not interest us here. It is enough to notice that the matter is discussed. None of these texts mention, or seem to be concerned with in any way, the *peculium*, and it would be perverse to suggest that that is what

servitude and those things which he possessed when he became a slave. If this is so, the text is no authority for the present proposition, but such a distinction is most unlikely. I am indebted for the point to Mr. Arthur Rogerson, Fellow of Jesus College, Oxford.

14 See Nicosia, *op. cit.*, p. 301 *et seq.* and the authorities he cites, p. 301, n. 3.

15 Apart from anything else, signs of interpolation begin only from *sicut id*; *cf.* the authorities cited in the preceding note.

16 It should be remembered that despite Celsus' strong language in D.28.1.27 the question raised by Domitius Labeo did have a legal point. Its fault was to be over-subtle: *cf.* Biondi, *Successione testamentaria* (2nd ed., Milan, 1955), p. 58, n. 1.

17 D.40.12.25.2; 41.2.1.14; *h.t.*50.1. For the point made in this paragraph, *cf.* Nicosia, *op. cit.*, p. 397 *et seq.*, especially at p. 484 *et seq.*

they are discussing, especially since D.15.1.48*pr*. (Paulus *17 ad Plaut.*) tells us that a runaway slave ceased to have *libera peculii administratio*. Again, there can be no question of the master's knowledge and this problem would never have existed if there had not normally been automatic acquisition of possession.

The inescapable conclusion to be drawn from the foregoing is that generally in classical law the taking of something by a slave without his master's knowledge automatically gave the master possession. That being fixed will be of great help when we now turn to the texts which seem more particularly concerned with acquisitions *ex peculiari causa*. It must by now be clear (and it will become even clearer) that, in general, those texts which demand that the acquisition be *ex peculiari causa* for the acquisition of possession by the master unaware of the taking are interpolated but we must not assume that acquisitions *ex peculiari causa* are always on a level with other acquisitions. There may, for instance, be differences in connection with *usucapio* or where the master lacks full capacity.[18]

> D.41.2.1.5 (Paulus 54 ad ed.): *Item adquirimus possessionem per servum aut filium, qui in potestate est, et quidem earum rerum, quas peculiariter tenent, etiam ignorantes, sicut Sabino et Cassio et Iuliano placuit, quia nostra voluntate intellegantur possidere, qui eis peculium habere permiserimus. igitur ex causa peculiari et infans et furiosus adquirunt possessionem et usucapiunt, et heres, si hereditarius servus emat.*

This is, to a great extent, the main text on which those jurists who maintain that in classical law one acquired possession unawares *per servum* only *ex peculiari causa* rely.[19] And it must be admitted that the reconstruction of Beseler [20] which is followed by Schulz [21] is unconvincing. They would delete as additions *earum rerum—tenent* and from *quia nostra voluntate* to the end.[22] If, however, Paul were saying something so obvious (from what has been said above) as that possession is acquired *per servos* even for masters unaware of the taking, he would have no reason to cite Sabinus, Cassius and Julian in support. But another reconstruction is plausible. The text may originally have run *Item adquirimus possessionem per servum aut filium, qui in potestate est, et quidem eas*

[18] Texts such as D.41.1.54.4 and 41.4.2.11 which on this point mention only usucapion are discussed *infra* p. 94 *et seq*.

[19] *e.g.*, De Francisci, *op. cit.*, p. 1002; Micolier, *Pécule et Capacité patrimoniale* (Lyons, 1932), p. 555 *et seq*.

[20] *Op. cit.*, p. 63.

[21] *Op. cit.*, p. 440.

[22] Nicosia's reconstruction is very similar but he changes, without excising, the last sentence: *op. cit.*, p. 211 *et seq*.

res, quas peculiariter tenent, etiam ignorantes usucapimus, sicut &c. That is, the text was making a distinction between acquisition of possession and the beginning of *usucapio*: the *dominus* or *pater* acquires possession *per servum aut filium* generally whenever the latter take control and no knowledge on the part of the principal is needed, whereas *usucapio* only follows on an acquisition *per servum aut filium* when the principal learns of the taking, except where the taking was *peculiariter* for then *usucapio* begins to run immediately. Probably complete proof that in classical law there was on this point a difference between acquisition of possession and the beginning of *usucapio* is impossible, but the texts, as we shall see later, do provide very considerable evidence that this was the position.

> D.41.2.4 (Ulpianus 67 ad ed.): *Quidquid filius peculiari nomine adprehenderit, id statim pater eius possidet, quamvis ignoret in sua potestate filium. amplius enim si filius ab alio tamquam servus possideatur, idem erit probandum.*

Beseler holds *peculiari nomine* interpolated, remarking reasonably enough that in both sets of circumstances it would be difficult for the son to have a *peculium* from his father.[23] Hägerström [24] denies this and gives as an example where there was a flaw in the form of the *emancipatio* and the father had allowed his son to keep the *peculium*. This is certainly a possibility but there is no sign that such a far-fetched possibility was in Ulpian's mind. It is even more difficult to imagine a likely case of a *filius bona fide serviens* who retained a *peculium* from his father. Micolier [25] produces another and perhaps even more convincing objection to *peculiari nomine* in the text. He points out that a *filius* who thought himself *sui juris* would acquire *suo nomine* [26] so that the expression *peculiari nomine adprehendere* would, in the circumstances, be incorrect. His solution, however, is to excise as interpolated all of the text from *quamvis*, so that the text, in his view, was originally concerned with acquisitions *peculiari nomine* by a *filius* who was aware that he was such. But that is very implausible. It involves holding that the compilers took a very small and not very important or original statement of Ulpian, added to it, and made it into a complete and original text in its own right. Since the Ulpianic " Urtext " on this interpretation was so very mediocre, it would

23 *Op. cit.*, p. 64; *cf.* Bonfante, *Corso di diritto romano* III *diritti reali* (Rome, 1933), p. 281; Schulz, *op. cit.*, p. 440; Nicosia, *op. cit.*, p. 272 *et seq.*

24 *Op. cit.*, p. 90, n. 3 at p. 104.

25 *Op. cit.*, p. 557, n. 48.

26 This is assuming—reasonably enough—that the *filius* is under the same misconception as the *pater*.

have been much more likely for the compilers simply to have added to it, or to one like it, in its context. Moreover, it means that one has to say that the compilers fairly deliberately added what is for all practical purposes nonsense while, if we take Beseler's view, *peculiari nomine* could have been added quite carelessly by compilers who were inserting it automatically wherever it seemed to them to be appropriate. The fact that virtual nonsense resulted could be more easily overlooked. Accordingly, even apart from our own initial investigations, Beseler's reconstruction is to be preferred. An objection raised to Beseler by Micolier [27] that, when the *filius* was *bona fide serviens* the possession of some acquisitions, *i.e.*, *ex re* and *ex operis*, would go to the supposed *dominus* is not serious. Obviously, the statement is not exact and does lack this qualification but this second case does very naturally flow from the first one discussed; and few of the readers of such an advanced work as Ulpian's *liber 67 ad edictum* were likely to be misled by the absence of the qualification.

> D.41.2.34.2 (Ulpianus 7 disp.): *Servus quoque meus ignoranti mihi adquiret possessionem. nam et servus alienus, ut Celsus scribit, sive a me sive a nemine possideatur, potest mihi adquirere possessionem, si nomine meo eam adipiscatur: quod et ipsum admittendum est.*

The first sentence of this text tells us that my slave acquires possession for me even without my knowledge. There is no reason to hold that an original restriction to acquisitions *ex peculiari causa* has been cut out. There is, however, something wrong with the second sentence. The text comes from Ulpian's book 7 of *disputationes*.[28] The connecting phrase *nam et* occurs in rhetorical texts where a decision has been given in a particular case and that decision is supported by the argument that the same decision has been given in a more extreme case.[29] That is the position here. But the second case is, in fact, so dependent upon the decision in the first that it could not even have been raised if the first had not been settled. So in the text as it stands *nam et* is inappropriate. This argument is also against Nicosia's reconstruction,[30] [*sive*] <*qui bona fide*> *a me* [*sive a nemine*]. Possibly, something intermediate has been excised but this suggestion can only be conjectural and no conclusions should be drawn from it. It would, however, account for the sentence which need not be interpolated

27 *Loc. cit.*
28 For rhetoric in such see Watson, "Two Studies in Textual History; 2. Tricks of Advocacy in the *libri disputationum*" infra, pp. 362 ff.
29 *Cf.* Watson, *op. cit.*, n. 34.
30 *Op. cit.*, p. 285.

except perhaps for *sive a me sive a nemine possideatur.*[31] Of course, whatever suspicions there may be of the second sentence should not affect the first.[32]

D.41.3.31.3 (Pomponius [33] *32 ad Sab.*): This text is dealt with later.[34]

> D.41.2.44.1 (Papinianus 23 quaest.): *Quaesitum est, cur ex peculii causa per servum ignorantibus possessio quaereretur. dixi utilitatis causa iure singulari receptum, ne cogerentur domini per momenta species et causas peculiorum inquirere. nec tamen eo pertinere speciem istam, ut animo videatur adquiri possessio: nam si non ex causa peculiari quaeratur aliquid, scientiam quidem domini esse necessariam, sed corpore servi quaeri possessionem.*

This text as it stands is nonsense.[35] The rule which it expresses, that is, that a *dominus ignorans* acquires possession *per servum ex peculii causa*, is clear enough, but the caution and explanation at the end are abominable. *Nec tamen eo pertinere speciem istam, ut animo videatur adquiri possessio*, seems incomprehensible since no one would doubt that there was *corpus*. Whatever doubt there was would be as to whether the *dominus* could be said to have the *animus possidendi*. The confusion becomes even greater with *nam si non ex causa peculiari quaeratur aliquid, scientiam quidem domini esse necessariam, sed corpore servi quaeri possessionem.* As de Zulueta says [36]: "Certainly the misunderstanding guarded against is absurd." This muddle is inexplicable on the assumption that the original point of the text was as it now stands. No glossator or compiler could have been so frankly stupid as to try to explain the point with *nec tamen*, etc. But the mess can be understood if we suppose that the point of the text has been changed and with it the explanation. It is always easier to make nonsense by altering a few words, some of them automatically, than by either writing a complete new account or by adding an explanation to an existing account.[37]

Thus, even some of the texts which are specifically concerned

31 For suggested interpolations, *cf. Index Itp.*, and the references given by Nicosia, *op. cit.*, p. 285 *et seq.* For the substance of this part of the text see Buckland, *Slavery*, p. 132 *et seq.*

32 The text is probably in some way concerned with a situation similar to that of § 1, *i.e.*, acquisition by an agent where the principal is under some mistake.

33 The MSS. have *Paulus*, but this must be a mistake.

34 *Infra*, p. 100.

35 *Cf. Index Itp.*

36 *Digest 41.1 & 2* (Oxford, 1950), p. 108.

37 For an attempt to reconstruct the text see Nicosia, *op. cit.*, p. 205. Another text, D.41.2.3.12, really adds nothing new.

with normal acquisitions by the slave do not restrict acquisition of possession by a master unaware of the taking to cases *ex peculiari causa*. And those which do can all be shown to be interpolated in the vital parts. If any doubt remains, three last points might be made. To begin with, most of the texts which are concerned with normal acquisitions require the taking to be *ex peculiari causa*; but those which deal with unusual cases, such as acquisition by the usufructuary or *bona fide possessor*, make no mention of such a requirement. This is precisely what one would expect if the compilers were responsible for the restriction: they would see most of the obvious cases, but miss a number of the others. On the other hand, it is not at all consistent with the idea that the compilers were widening the classical rule to cover all cases. Secondly, the question whether automatic acquisition of possession by the master *per servum* was restricted to cases *ex peculiari causa* or not would be an important one and if there were such a restriction one would expect it to have been mentioned by Gaius in his detailed account of acquisition through others in the Institutes 2.86–95. Gaius' silence is very strong evidence that one normally acquired possession automatically on any taking by the slave.[38] Admittedly, Justinian in the corresponding part of his Institutes, 2.9.3, also does not restrict the acquisition of possession to cases *ex peculiari causa* but this is almost certainly because he takes his account from Gaius. Lastly, there are three texts which tell us that we can acquire possession unawares through a procurator although we do not begin to usucape until we know of the taking. It is unlikely that one would be in a better position in respect of takings by a procurator than of takings by a slave.[39]

[38] *Cf.* Nicosia, *op. cit.*, p. 384 *et seq.* It might be argued against this that Gaius is concerned only with *per quas personas* and does not claim to give the rules of acquisition. But Gaius was concerned with automatic acquisition (*cf. supra*, p. 86) and if this were restricted to acquisitions *ex peculiari causa* he would be mentioning here what is at least in theory only the exceptional case and not the general rule.

[39] D.41.2.49.2 (Papinianus *2 definit.*); 41.3.47 (Paulus *3 ad Nerat.*); C.7.32.1 (A.D. 196). The first two, so far as relevant for us, never seem to have been held interpolated except that Frese would change in both *ignoranti to absenti*: *Studi Bonfante*, IV, p. 442, nn. 16, 17. As for the last, Albertario would excise *post scientia intervenerit*: *Corso cit.*, p. 122, but see Watson "Acquisition of Possession *per extraneam personam*" (1961), Tijd., xxix, p. 22 *et seq.* at p. 29 *et seq.* It might be argued against the general proposition of this part of this study that it is being alleged that Justinian was restricting the power to acquire possession *per servum* just when he was extending such a power to acquire *per liberam personam*. But in the article just cited it was maintained that the extensions were classical and not the work of Justinian. Moreover, it is generally admitted (*e.g.*, Bonfante, "Facoltà e decadenza del procuratore romano," *Studi giuridici varii*, III (Turin, 1926), p. 250 *et seq.*; Serrao, *Il Procurator* (Milan, 1947), *passim*) that in general Justinian restricted the powers of the procurator, and his restriction on acquisition of possession *per servum* may be another instance of the same tendency.

II. Usucapion

It may perhaps be worthwhile now to look at these texts which discuss the beginning of *usucapio* after a taking by a slave. The texts just mentioned which are concerned with the procurator show that in his case there was a difference in the acquisition of possession and the beginning of *usucapio*, so it would be unjustified just to assume that when the *dominus* acquires possession *per servum*, then at the same time he necessarily (unless the *res* is *furtiva* or there is some other flaw) begins to usucape. Cuias [40] in the sixteenth century and, more recently, Beseler [41] have maintained that here too *usucapio* begins only when the *dominus* learns of the taking except when the acquisition was *ex peculiari causa* when his knowledge is not necessary. Most recently, however, Nicosia [42] has maintained that whether the taking was *ex peculiari causa* or not the *dominus* begins to usucape from the moment of the slave's taking. It is suggested that although, as has been said, the evidence is not conclusive the texts are very much in favour of Cuias and Beseler.

The clearest text is D.41.4.2.11 (Paulus *54 ad ed.*).

> *Celsus scribit, si servus meus peculiari nomine apiscatur possessionem, id etiam ignorantem me usucapere: quod si non peculiari nomine, non nisi scientem me: et si vitiose coeperit possidere, meam vitiosam esse possessionem.*

In the text, Paul tells us that Celsus held that in the case of acquisitions *peculiari nomine* the *dominus* begins to usucape even unaware of the taking, while in the case of other acquisitions usucapion does not begin to run until the master knows of the taking. The text, however, is held interpolated by both Beseler [43] and Nicosia.[44] The former cuts out *id* and *quod-scientem me*. The text would then tell us simply that the *dominus* begins to usucape whatever his slave took *peculiari nomine* without his knowledge. His arguments are, first, that *quod-me* is very tortuous and disturbs the sequence of thought. It may be tortuous, but it is nonetheless the simplest way of saying what the text wants to say. On the other hand, it does seem to break the sequence of thought: *et si vitiose &c.* would follow much more neatly directly on *usucapere*. Secondly, he objects to the second *me* but even if grammatically it

40 *Cf.* the references given to his work by Nicosia, *op. cit.*, p. 2, n. 1.
41 *Op. cit.*, p. 61 *et seq.*
42 *Op. cit.*, *passim.* Another work on this subject, Fuentesca, *Possessio domino ignoranti* (1954) A.H.D.E., xxiv, p. 559 *et seq.* was not available, but see the summary in (1955), IURA, vi, p. 406.
43 *Op. cit.*, p. 67.
44 *Op. cit.*, p. 225.

is not strictly correct, which does not, in any event, seem to be the case, it is desirable to stress here that it is the principal who knows of the taking. Nicosia's treatment of the text is less happy. He inserts *cuius rei* after the first *si* and excises *peculiari nomine* and *quod-scientem me*, thus making the text say that the *dominus* begins to usucape anything of which, without his knowledge, his slave has taken possession. Nicosia agrees with Beseler that *id* is odd, saying that one cannot see to what it refers syntactically or logically, but his solution is to hold that *id* was in the original but that due to Justinianic alteration what it did refer to has been lost.[45] But it is difficult to see how the insertion of *peculiari nomine*, which he suggests, would demand the excision of *cuius rei* and if such had disappeared one would in any event have expected *eam* not *id*. Again, he says that *non nisi scientem me* is an impardonable error and the construction used should be an ablative absolute.[46] But the error would seem to be Nicosia's, the accusative is necessary here—*me* is the subject of the verb *usucapere* (understood in the context) in an accusative and infinitive construction. There seems no reason to prefer Nicosia's reconstruction to Beseler's, and even Beseler may be going too far.

> D.41.4.2.13 (Paulus 54 ad ed.): *Si servus bona fide emerit peculiari nomine, ego ubi primum cognovi sciam alienam, processuram usucapionem Celsus ait: initium enim possessionis sine vitio fuisse: sed si eo tempore quo emit, quamquam id bona fide faciat, ego alienam rem esse sciam, usu me non capturum.*

There have been very few suspicions of the genuineness of this text. The point of the text as it stands is that where a slave acquires a *res, peculiari nomine,* usucapion begins immediately. Hence, even if the *dominus* is aware, as soon as he knows of the acquisition, that the *res* belongs to another, *usucapio* continues since it began without a flaw. Here, too, *peculiari nomine* implies that *usucapio* does not begin in the case of other takings by a slave until the *dominus* knows of the taking. Nicosia[47] holds that *peculiari nomine* is an addition and adduces as evidence that *rem* must have been excised after *emerit* since *alienam* is in the text without a noun to refer to. But even if a *rem* has disappeared, which is by no means a necessary deduction, this is most likely to have been the result of carelessness in the transmission. It is not

45 The *id* may be genuine and nothing may have been cut out. Logically, there is no problem—the *id* quite clearly refers to the object acquired by the slave. And there is really no need for it to be related syntactically to anything.

46 *Op. cit.*, p. 226, n. 47.

47 *Op. cit.*, p. 230 *et seq.*; Perozzi, *Istituzioni di diritto romano*, I (2nd ed., Rome, 1928), p. 661, n. 1, also suggests that the text may have been altered.

easy to see why the compilers would deliberately have excised it. Even if one assumes that they did there is no reason to connect that with the presence in the text of *peculiari nomine.*

D.41.4.7.8 (Iulianus 44 dig.): *Liber homo, qui bona fide nobis servit, isdem modis ex re nostra adquirit nobis, quibus per servum nostrum adquirere solemus: quare sicut traditione, ita usucapione rem nostram faciemus interveniente libera persona, et si peculii nomine, quod nos sequi debet, emptio contracta fuerit, etiam ignorantes usucapiemus.*

This text has suffered from graver suspicions. Beseler, especially, would excise *sicut—et.*[48] His arguments for extensive interpolation, however, are not very strong. First, he feels that the logical reader misses, in connection with *faciemus* " under certain circumstances." But although one certainly would not always usucape, it would be absurd in every situation always to mention the other requirements or even that there were other requirements. Secondly, he thinks *faciemus* is odd since we are doing nothing. But why should *rem nostram faciemus* imply any activity on our part? Thirdly, *interveniente libera persona* should be, he says, *per liberam personam,* but the former is just as good Latin. Alternatively, if it is still thought odd, *interveniente libera persona* may simply be an explanatory gloss which has been intruded into the text. Bonfante [49] also thinks the construction here does not seem classical, but part at least of his objection is on the point that one is acquiring possession *per liberam personam* which he considers impossible in classical law. But even if that were the general rule [50] it would be irrelevant here since *libera persona* is referring to the *liber homo bona fide serviens* and certainly should not be taken as more general.[51] Fourthly, *et* is according to Beseler an illogical conjunction but we shall see in a moment that it is not. Nicosia goes further than Beseler and would excise *sicut—debet* and insert *si ab eo ex re nostra.*[52] The point of the text which is primarily concerned with usucapion [53] is that we acquire *ex re nostra* through a *liber homo bona fide serviens* in the same way as through one of our own slaves; and therefore we can usucape what he acquires; and if the acquisition is *peculiari nomine* (*quod nos sequi debet*) we usucape even unawares. *Et* is, thus, the correct and logical conjunction. One cannot argue as Beseler seems to [54] that *peculii nomine* is chosen as a concrete example of the general *ex re nostra.*

[48] *Op. cit.*, p. 68; (1925), Z.S.S., xlv, p. 451.
[49] *Op. cit.*, p. 276.
[50] For the contrary opinion, see Watson, *op. cit.*, p. 22 *et seq.*
[51] See also on this text the authors cited in Reggi, *op. cit.*, p. 410, n. 163.
[52] *Op. cit.*, p. 312 *et seq.*
[53] But *sicut traditione* is not on that account suspicious—the easier case is used to introduce the more difficult.
[54] Z.S.S. *cit.*

D.41.3.8*pr*. (Paulus 12 ad ed.): ***Labeo Neratius responderunt ea, quae servi peculiariter nancti sunt, usucapi posse, quia haec etiam ignorantes domini usucapiunt: idem Iulianus scribit.***

Ab infante quoque et furioso was regarded by Mommsen [55] as having dropped out of the text before *usucapi* and this emendation is generally accepted. Beseler,[56] however, was hesitant and suggested that perhaps *quia—usucapiunt* was a gloss. But there is an obstacle to this in that §1 runs on very smoothly if we accept Mommsen's reconstruction but not on Beseler's view. Accepting Mommsen's reconstruction, therefore, this text too tells us that without knowledge of the acquisition one usucapes what a slave acquires *peculiariter* and the structure of the text really excludes usucapion by a *dominus* unaware of other sorts of taking. Nicosia [57] would excise *peculiariter* for two reasons. First, because he believes that Paul allowed the *infans* and *furiosus* to acquire possession *per servum* without any restriction to the *peculium* and that, therefore, such a restriction here would be contrary to the thought of the jurist. But this is not a strong argument. Acquisition of possession is one thing, usucapion quite another, and, as we saw, in the case of takings by the procurator the rules in these two situations differed, so that it is quite unwarranted to state without any evidence that here the rules of acquisition of possession and of *usucapio* were the same. Secondly, he holds that the word *peculiariter* is itself suspicious though he admits that it is not interpolated in every text.[58] But it is impossible to show that *peculiariter* is generally an insertion (since it is the sort which would leave no trace) except by *a priori* reasoning so that this point does not materially assist Nicosia in an argument precisely on these substantive rules. Moreover, Pliny the Elder [59] and Quintilian [60] use *peculiariter* with the meaning " especially, particularly, peculiarly " and philologists whom I have consulted have all said that it is a most unlikely development that the word be used in that way at that time while it was not until much later that *peculiariter* with the meaning of " in connection with the *peculium* " really developed since the latter is so much closer to the meaning of the ultimate source of the adverb.

55 *Digesta Iustiniani Augusti*, II (Berlin, 1870) *ad h.l.*
56 *Beiträge*, IV, *cit.*, p. 66.
57 *Op. cit.*, p. 223 *et seq.*
58 *Op. cit.*, p. 224, pp. 212, n. 9 and 218, n. 24. He refers also to Lepri, *Saggi sulla terminologia e sulla nozione patrimonio in diritto romano* (Florence, 1942), p. 95, but Lepri gives no evidence either.
59 Hist.Nat. 25.2.3.7; 26.8.33.50.
60 Inst.Or. 1.2.16; 8.2.8; 11.3.130.

D.41.1.54.4 (Pomponius 31 ad Quintum Mucium): ***Quidquid tamen liber homo vel alienus quive bona fide nobis servit non adquirit nobis, id vel sibi liber vel alienus servus domino suo adquiret: excepto eo quod vix est, ut liber homo possidendo usucapere possit, quia nec possidere intellegitur, qui ipse possideretur. sed nec per servum alienum, quem nos bona fide possidemus, dominus peculiari nomine ignorans usucapere poterit, sicuti ne per fugitivum quidem, quem non possidet.***

In this text, *sed nec* to the end which is the only part with which we are concerned seems intended to show that a *dominus ignorans* cannot even usucape *peculiari nomine* through a slave whom he does not possess, and it is therefore prima facie evidence that so far as *usucapio* is concerned, acquisition by a slave *ex peculiari causa* for a *dominus ignorans* are on a different level from other acquisitions. But it may be interpolated. Nicosia [61] has already maintained that the whole reference to the *servus alienus* is interpolated because first, *h.t.* 54 from the *principium* up to this point was concerned solely with the *liber homo bona fide serviens* yet the *tamen* makes it appear that this *lex* is part of that discussion, secondly, there is something far wrong with the form of *alienus quive bona fide nobis servit*, and thirdly, that Pomponius himself in *h.t.*21*pr.* had different rules for the *liber homo bona fide serviens* and the *servus alienus*. Again, *excepto eo quod vix est* should introduce a solitary exception. It should not be followed by another.[62] These arguments, however, only tend to show that in the first part of the text, up to *possideretur*, the references to *servus alienus* are additions. There is no reason whatever why Pomponius should not, after considering the case of the *liber homo bona fide serviens*, also look at the case where the man was a *servus alienus*. And *sed nec* would not on this view be introducing a second exception but an entirely new case and so would be perfectly appropriate. It should, however, be noticed that *nec per*

61 *Op. cit.*, p. 170 *et seq.* *Peculiari nomine ignorans* itself is not necessarily suspicious in this context. Although in classical law the *peculium* was not automatically included in the sale of a slave (D.18.1.29 and 21.2.3) there are certainly cases where a slave is sold with his *peculium*, *e.g.*, D.12.1.31.1; 19.1.24.1.

62 *Excepto eo—possideretur* has itself been held interpolated. See the arguments of Nicosia, *op. cit.*, p. 174 *et seq.*, and the authorities, for and against, whom he cites, p. 174, nn. 31 and 32. Although the point is not very important here, it should be stated that the arguments for this interpolation are not very strong. They are (1) it looks like a marginal gloss; but so do almost all qualifications to a general principle; (2) *possideretur* shows a false sequence of tenses; certainly, but the mistake is so glaring (the *Vulgata* changes it to *possidetur*) that it can hardly have been made by a glossator or the compilers—rather, it should be attributed to a careless scribe; and (3) that the passage raises a doubt but does not settle it; but there is really no doubt—a clear exception is given to the general rule and the phrase *quod vix est* in fact emphasises the impossibility of any other decision.

servum alienum . . . dominus . . . usucapere poterit is odd, since the *dominus* would in fact be acquiring through a *servus proprius*. But it would be dangerous to maintain that this was proof of interpolation in this part also. The oddity is one of logic, not of language, and it would be almost as surprising if one of the compilers wrote this as if Pomponius did. It is the kind of thing which is not easy to write, but is difficult to spot once it is in the text. A more reasonable view, it seems to me, is that *alienum* was a gloss which has crept in due to a careless scribe.[63]

> D.41.3.47 (Paulus 3 ad Neratium): *Si emptam rem mihi procurator ignorante me meo nomine adprehenderit, quamvis possideam, eam non usucapiam, quia ut ignorantes usuceperimus, in peculiaribus tantum rebus receptum est.*

This says that if the procurator takes something in my name without my knowledge then, although I possess, I will not usucape since it is settled that only in the case of *res peculiares* do we usucape without knowing of the taking. There have been no real suspicions about the classicality of the first part of the text. But *quia* to the end with which we are primarily concerned here has been held interpolated on account of its form by Beseler [64] and Nicosia [65] but grammatically it is sound though admittedly a different word order would have been less clumsy. Nicosia also objects to it because it is presented as a reason for the previous decision but in substance it is not.[66] It is, I think, a reason all right, but Nicosia's very acute feeling that something is odd is justified. Rather, it seems that if it were established that we could usucape unawares only acquisitions *ex peculiari causa* then although one might say in a general way that we cannot usucape unawares through a procurator one could not really follow that with such a reason. No reason need be given at all, but it would be not only superfluous but also silly to justify the decision in the more extreme case by the established principle of the less extreme case. The reason is so overwhelmingly strong that it would make it appear pointless ever to have wondered about the case at all. Another explanation is plausible. The text comes from Paul's *liber tertius ad Neratium* and the texts in the *libri ad Neratium* are concerned less

63 Just as in the preceding note it is argued that *possideretur* is due to a careless scribe. Perhaps more likely, as Professor Daube has suggested to me, the state of the text is the result of the clumsy amalgamation of the two separate cases of the *liber homo bona fide serviens* and the *servus alienus*: *cf. infra*, p. 100, on D.41.3.31.3.

64 *Loc. cit.*

65 *Op. cit.*, p. 224.

66 He also seems to find something odd in *in peculiaribus rebus* but that construction is not objectionable.

with general propositions than with individual and difficult situations and one might expect such also to be the case here. Moreover, if the text were merely giving a general rule not only would *emptam* be superfluous but it would be surprising that it is given such an emphatic position in the text. The text was originally concerned with a particular situation where the principal bought a thing but did not take delivery of it and unknown to him his procurator did. In the circumstances it might well be argued that he usucaped from the moment of the procurator's taking since he did have such a very close connection with the particular thing. It would then be reasonable to decide this very difficult case in the negative using the argument give in *quia*, etc. The text, having been removed from its context, now appears much more general than it was.

> D.49.15.29 (Labeo 6 pithanon a Paulo epit.): *Si postliminio redisti, nihil, dum in hostium potestate fuisti, usucapere potuisti.* PAULUS: *immo si quid servus tuus peculii nomine, dum in eo statu esses, possederit, id eo quoque tempore usucapere poteris, quoniam eas res etiam inscientes usucapere solemus. et eo modo etiam hereditas nondum nato postumo aut nondum adita augeri per servum hereditarium solet.*

This text is worth quoting although it cannot be discussed properly in isolation from the other texts on *postliminium*. It is enough here to notice the reason for the decision, *quoniam eas res etiam inscientes usucapere solemus*. This is held interpolated by Beseler [67] and Nicosia [68] because *eas res* has no point of reference in the preceding part of the text. But no point of reference is needed. Just as Paul changing from the particular situation to the general principle behind it changes from *tu* to *nos*, so he changes from *quid* to *eas res*. This plural, too, marks the widening from the particular to the general.

> D.41.3.31.3 (Pomponius 32 ad Sab.): *Si servus meus vel filius peculiari vel etiam meo nomine quid tenet, ut ego per eum ignorans possideam vel etiam usucapiam: si is furere coeperit, donec in eadem causa res fuerit, intellegendum est et possessionem apud me remanere et usucapionem procedere, sicuti per dormientes quoque eos idem nobis contingeret. idemque in colono et inquilino, per quos possidemus, dicendum est.*

This text is prima facie an embarrassment. Beseler [69] who treats the text as genuine says " *vel etiam usucapiam* means ' and in given circumstances I also usucape.' Paul presupposes that his

67 *Op. cit.*, p. 70.
68 *Op. cit.*, p. 231 *et seq.*
69 *Op. cit.*, p. 66.

reader knows what the given circumstances are." But even if this is so, it is rather awkward that *peculiari vel etiam meo nomine* is balanced by *ignorans possideam vel etiam usucapiam.* One might have expected that even if there is no intentional balance the arrangement would have been the other way round. On the other hand, if one excises as an interpolation *vel etiam meo* [70] the text, although it would not be an obstacle to the view put forward here on *usucapio,* would go very much against the conclusions drawn as to the acquisition of possession *per servum* and these conclusions appear the more certain. Perhaps the explanation is a careless transposition by a pre-Justinianic scribe of *meo vel etiam peculiari nomine.* Transpositions are a common form of scribal error and the one suggested here would also get rid of the difficulty which some jurists have felt that *vel etiam* suggests a more extreme case and yet acquisitions *meo nomine* should be here the less difficult situation. Much more likely, however, the text as we have it is the result of clumsy amalgamation of two separate cases: the first where the acquisition was *ex peculiari causa,* the second where the acquisition was *meo nomine. Possessio* and *usucapio* would be allowed in the first, *possessio* alone in the second.[71] However, even if we take the text as it stands, it is not positive evidence that in classical law a *dominus ignorans* usucaped generally whatever a slave acquired possession of.[72]

Thus, the texts which we have examined all tell the same story (with perhaps the exception of D.41.3.31.3) and there are no texts which suggest the contrary. Admittedly, the form of the texts is not always perfect and one cannot altogether rule out the possibility that in all of them the reference to the *peculium* is an addition, but there is little evidence for alleging that it is. Above all, the unanimity of the texts is very much in favour of the view that they give the classical law—otherwise one must say that Justinian's compilers have shown here a far greater degree of skill and care than they usually do. One final point may be made. In the time of Justinian, the rules as to the acquisition of possession and the beginning of usucapion in this matter are the same. Likewise, according to Nicosia's view, although Justinian changed the classical law on this point, nonetheless in the classical period the rules as to acquisition of possession and the beginning of usucapion did again exactly coincide. But, as we have just seen, there is a large number of

70 *Cf.* the references given by Nicosia, *op. cit.*, p. 166 *et seq.*

71 I am grateful for this point to Professor Daube who tells me that he feels this is a "fairly clear case" of amalgamation. For examples of other such amalgamations see Daube (1959), Z.S.S., lxxvi, p. 249 *et seq.* (for D.43.16.17) and (1960), IURA, xi, p. 73 (for D.2.8.4.).

72 For a different explanation of the text see Nicosia, *loc. cit.*

texts which emphasise the time when *usucapio* begins and this fact strongly suggests that the texts have their origin in a period when the rules as to the beginning of possession and usucapion were in this case not the same.

III. Acquisition of Possession and Usucapion by an Infant

Although this study is concerned primarily with cases where the *dominus* or *pater* is a *civis* of full capacity and it is not intended to examine exhaustively situations where the principal is under some incapacity it is instructive to see how far the results can be checked with the texts concerned with cases where the principal is an *infans*.

D.41.2.1.5 (Paulus *54 ad ed.*): This has already been quoted.[73]

The last sentence *igitur ex causa peculiari et infans et furiosus adquirunt possessionem et usucapiunt, et heres, si hereditarius servus emat* alone concerns us here and it has been held interpolated in varying degrees.[74] Something would appear to be wrong with at least *et heres-emat* [75] since the immediately preceding part of the text is concerned with both acquisition of possession and usucapion and although some jurists seem to have held that the heir usucaped what the *servus hereditarius* acquired (*ex peculiari causa*?) [76] it is extremely unlikely that they would here also grant the heir possession since all other texts, impliedly or explicitly, say that there was no possession of *res hereditariae* until the heir took actual possession.[77] Few of the jurists who believe that there is something wrong with the rest of the sentence give reasons but Alibrandi [78] and Nicosia [79] who do call attention to the *igitur*. They say rightly that *igitur* weakens the reason given for the previous decision, *quia nostra voluntate intellegantur possidere, qui eis peculium habere permiserimus*. There can be no question of the *animus* or *voluntas* of the *infans*.[80] But I hesitate to accept on this ground that *igitur* to the end is an interpolation. Perhaps the *igitur* should not be pressed too hard. It is not unlikely that once it was accepted that a person of full capacity could usucape unawares whatever his slave acquired *ex peculiari causa* this rule would be extended to other cases even where the principal

73 *Supra*, p. 89.
74 To the references in the *Index Itp.* add Nicosia, *op. cit.*, p. 211 *et seq.*
75 Buckland, *Slavery*, p. 257 and n. 2 seems, *pace* Nicosia, *op. cit.*, p. 214, n. 15, to restrict his suspicion to this.
76 D.44.7.16; 41.3.44.3; but see 41.3.45.1.
77 D.41.2.23*pr.*; 41.2.30.5; 41.3.31.5; 41.3.40; 41.4.2.18; 41.4.6.2; 47.4.1.15.
78 *Opere*, I, p. 274 (not available to me).
79 *Op. cit.*, p. 214 et *seq.*
80 Who would even lack the capacity to grant a *peculium* so that the existence of such cannot be taken as a manifestation of his intention to possess whatever the slave acquires through it.

lacked full capacity and that the first case could be looked upon as justification for the others. This may well have been the connection in the jurist's mind—that is, when writing *igitur* he was still thinking of *et quidem—ignorantes*. If the reconstruction and interpretation given of the main part of the text [81] are accepted this will account for the *usucapiunt* in this part.[82]

D.41.2.32.2 (Paulus 15 ad Sab.): *Infans possidere recte potest, si tutore auctore coepit, nam iudicium infantis suppletur auctoritate tutoris: utilitatis enim causa hoc receptum est, nam alioquin nullus sensus est infantis accipiendi possessionem. pupillus tamen etiam sine tutoris auctoritate possessionem nancisci potest. item infans peculiari nomine per servum possidere potest.*

We are mainly interested in the last sentence which tells us that an *infans* can possess *peculiari nomine* through a slave. There are no internal signs of interpolation in this sentence but then, of course, one would not expect any even if *peculiari nomine* is an insertion as Beseler [83] and Nicosia [84] allege. The former gives no reason for his view though his *a priori* assumptions are clear but the latter says that Bonfante [85] recognises that the rest of the text is interpolated and that it is very surprising, therefore, that Bonfante in connection with Beseler's affirmation of the interpolation of *peculiari nomine* could say that there was no argument for or against. It is, he says, inexplicable that the compilers after having manipulated the text greatly to bring it into line with the new law would have retained in the last sentence a principle which Bonfante maintained was classical and in contrast with the compilers' views when it would have been relatively simple to eliminate *peculiari nomine*. But whatever the rights or wrongs of Bonfante's view as to Justinianic law, Nicosia's argument is really of little value to him on the main issue. Even if one were to accept that the rest of the text is heavily interpolated and that this last sentence does give the Justinianic position that does not show that *peculiari nomine* is an addition. There is nothing here to show that classical law was ever any different on this point from Justinian's law.[86] Moreover, *pace* Bonfante, it is unlikely that the first part of the text is interpolated. Bonfante has two arguments. First, he says that *auctoritas tutoris* was not created to supply the intention of the pupil when that was totally lacking. It is, of course, true that

81 *Supra*, pp. 89, 90.
82 Alternatively, *igitur-usucapiunt* if genuine may provide support for that reconstruction.
83 *Op. cit.*, p. 64; (1936) Z.S.S., lvi, p. 93.
84 *Op. cit.*, p. 221 *et seq.*
85 *Op. cit.*, p. 261.
86 Although he does not say so, Nicosia's main justification must—reasonably enough—be the evidence of other texts.

normally *auctoritas tutoris* applies only where the child is capable of intention but lacks judgment,[87] *i.e.*, where the child is *infantia maior*. But we know from Gaius' Institutes 2.80–84 that the tutor's authority was needed where the transaction might make the position of the pupil *infantia maior* worse but not where it could not have that effect. Now, it is perhaps just possible to think of situations where possession—as opposed to mere physical control—may harm the possessor, but these must be very rare. In almost all cases possession is an advantage. Ownership, too, may on rare occasions, but no doubt more often than possession, result in loss to the owner [88] yet we know from G.2.83 that ownership of all *res mancipi* and *nec mancipi* could be given to the pupil without *auctoritas tutoris*. Therefore, *a fortiori, auctoritas tutoris* should not be required for the acquisition of possession by a pupil *infantia maior*, although this is Bonfante's own conclusion.[89] It cannot here be adding judgment to the pupil's intention. Unless we accept Perozzi's view [90] that the requirement of *auctoritas tutoris* on this point is Justinianic and the references to it seem to be too deeply embedded in the texts for this to be acceptable [91] we must hold that the function of *tutoris auctoritas* here, whatever it was, was certainly different from its normal. And the function given in this text corresponds exactly to the opinion which seems to be Paul's own in D.41.2.1.3.[92] Bonfante also says that D.41.2.32.2 is against all of the theories on the acquisition of possession by an infant but this is only so if we assume, as few would be willing to do, that the classical jurists were all in agreement on this point.[93] Bonfante's second argument is that, as Albertario said, the text is badly constructed, that it speaks of the infant, then of the minor *infantia maior* and then again of the infant. But the text is in perfect order. It is concerned first with acquisition of possession by the pupil—*infans* and then *infantia maior*—*per se*, and then with acquisition of possession by the infant *per servum*.[94]

87 *Cf.* Buckland, *Textbook*, p. 157 *et seq.*; Kaser, *Privatrecht cit.*, I, p. 306; De Zulueta, *The Institutes of Gaius*, II (Oxford, 1953), p. 49.

88 Much less often than in modern law where there is no noxal surrender.

89 *Op. cit.*, p. 265.

90 *Op. cit.*, I, p. 860 *et seq.*

91 Note especially in D.41.2.1.3 *Ofilius quidem et Nerva filius etiam sine tutoris auctoritate possidere incipere posse pupillum aiunt. Cf.* D.41.2.1.5,11; 41.3.4.2.

92 D.41.2.1.3 is, however, itself often held interpolated and it is not in perfect order but this does not alter the fact that the rule finally attributed there to Paul is the same as in D.41.2.32.2. Interpolations could well be restricted to the first part of the text (as far as *incipiet possidere*). D.41.3.4.2 (Paulus *54 ad ed.*) is probably drawing the same distinction.

93 *Cf.* Kaser, *op. cit.*, p. 332 and n. 13.

94 There are no texts on the acquisition of possession *per servum* for a pupil *infantia maior* (except perhaps D.41.2.1.13) which suggests that such a pupil was in this connection in the same position as a full adult *civis*.

D.41.3.8*pr.* (Paulus *12 ad ed.*): This text which has already been quoted [95] tells us on Mommsen's reconstruction (which is generally accepted) that infants usucape whatever their slaves acquire through the *peculium*. But plausible as the reconstruction may be, it is nonetheless not independent evidence and should have no weight here.

These then are the texts directly in favour of the view that infants acquire possession *per servum* only *ex peculiari causa*. And it must be admitted that they are by no means conclusive.

There are also two main texts which lend support to the other view, namely that *infantes* acquire possession *per servum* generally.

> **D.41.3.28 (Pomponius 17 ad Sab.): *Si servo furiosi vel infantis res tradita sit, usu per eum eas personas capere posse constat.***

As Nicosia says,[96] in this text there is an unequivocable declaration of automatic acquisition of possession *per servum* and he equally rightly condemns De Francisci's [97] insertion of *peculii nomine* as a *petitio principii*. Nonetheless, it is extremely doubtful whether the text is any evidence that in classical law an *infans* acquired possession generally *per servum*. The text comes from Pomponius' 17th book on Sabinus and in that book he was concerned with *tutela*.[98] In that context it could have arisen in one of two ways. Either it was brought in to compare or contrast acquisition *tutore auctore* or *per tutorem* with acquisition *per servum*, or it is concerned with the situation where the slave takes possession *tutore auctore*.[99] If the former, the text is support for the view that an *infans* acquires possession *per servum* without restriction to the *peculium*, if the latter, it is irrelevant. Reference may be made to D.41.2.1.13 (Paulus *54 ad ed.*):

> ***Pupillus per servum sive puberem sive impuberem adquirit possessionem, si tutore auctore iusserit eum ire in possessionem.***

This tells us that if a pupil with the authority of his tutor sends a slave, whether above or below the age of puberty, into possession he will possess. Very little should be made of this text. *Tutore*

95 *Supra*, p. 97.
96 *Op. cit.*, p. 165.
97 *Op. cit.*, p. 1009; followed by Riccobono (1910) Z.S.S., xxxi, p. 358, n. 3; Albertario, *Studi cit.*, II, p. 235; Micolier, *op. cit.*, p. 569, n. 72 (at p. 570); Beseler (*Beiträge cit.*, IV, p. 66) says it is shortened or does not give a full account of the legal position. Bonfante (*op. cit.*, p. 283) inclines to accept the text as genuine holding that Pomponius belonged to the current who generalised the exception beyond the *peculium* at least for principals lacking capacity—but against that note the *constat*.
98 *Cf.* Lenel, *Palingenesia*, II, p. 124.
99 No conclusions should be drawn from the reference to the *furiosus* who is usually placed on a level with the *infans*. In the original context there may well have been a reference to the curator.

auctore is usually held to be an interpolation [1] and whether it is or not the fact that the pupil sent the slave into possession suggests that he must have been *infantia maior*. To return to D.41.3.28, it must be said that there is no evidence which points to one or other of the alternatives. In the circumstances it would be dangerous to use the text as an argument that an *infans* acquired possession generally *per servum* and without restriction to the *peculium*.[2]

> C.Th.8.12.2: Imp. Constantinus A. Aconio Catulino Proconsuli Africae. *Si quis in emancipatum minorem priusquam fari possit aut habere rei quae sibi donatur affectum, Italicum sive stipendiarium fundum crediderit conferendum, omne ius compleat instrumentis ante praemissis et inductione corporaliter impleta. Quod propter adtesationem fidei per eum servum, quem idoneum esse constiterit, transigi placuit, qui eo usque statu suo permanebit, donec is, cuius facultatibus cesserit, annos Laetoriae legis egressus legitimam compleverit aetatem, quo tunc demum, si eius integritas ac fides fuerit comprobata, si ita sederit possidentibus, libertatis praemium consequatur.* Dat. XII. Kal. Mai. Serdicae Sabino et Rufino Conss.[3]

This text has given birth to tremendous controversies [4] and perhaps the sole undisputed point is that acquisition of possession *per servum* is implied.[5] Nicosia [6] on the basis of the absolutely general *si quis* rightly rejects the view of Cuias and Gothofredus which is also followed by Solazzi that the situation concerns a donor who was the *pater* and at the same time the *tutor* of the emancipated minor. And, of course, there can be no question of a *peculium* here. Nevertheless, the text is no evidence whatever that in classical law *traditio* to a slave generally gave an *infans* possession. The researches of Levy [7] have shown that although in the

1 *Cf. Index Itp.*: the date of the Solazzi article referred to should be 1911; it now appears in his *Scritti di diritto romano*, I (Naples, 1955), p. 307: the reference to Buckland's *Textbook* should be p. 201, n. 3.

2 It seems very mysterious that this text, coming from a book *de tutelis*, should be excised and placed in its present context especially since as a general statement (as it now is) it is in disagreement with D.41.2.1.5 and *h.t.*32.2 both of which are from books more concerned with the subject in hand.

3 The date is uncertain but it is not before A.D. 316: see, most recently, Archi, *La donazione* (Milan, 1960), p. 234 *et seq.*

4 For a full bibliography, see Nicosia, *op. cit.*, p. 388 *et seq.*

5 It has been argued (*cf.* the references given by Nicosia, *op. cit.*, p. 390, n. 16) that, since recourse is had to this, the *infans* could not acquire possession *tutore auctore*. But this is not justified. Apart from anything else, the main reason for the particular procedure suggested in the constitution is not to acquire possession but to have someone responsible for the land until the child reaches majority, *i.e.*, 25.

6 *Op. cit.*, p. 390, n. 17.

7 *West Roman Vulgar Law: The Law of Property* (Philadelphia, 1951), p. 243 *et seq.*

fourth century there were still two procedures, "the one aimed at the reinstatement of the ejected party, the other set apart to the decision on the legal title" the former had undergone a transformation from the classical period. There were no longer any actions or interdicts for the retention of possession [8] but only for its recovery. And the sole matter apparently raised in these *interdicta* was whether the defendant had ejected the plaintiff, not whether the plaintiff was himself a *vitiosus possessor*.[9] Accordingly, for the possessory remedy it would seem now to be irrelevant that the plaintiff had what in classical law would have been regarded as *detentio* rather than *possessio*. The fact that he was ejected from physical control would seem to be enough.[10] Thus, in C.Th.8.12.2 the *infans* would have a remedy if his slave were ejected and this would be so whether or not the transaction would in classical law have been regarded as giving him *possessio*.[11]

The constitution is repeated in a shortened form in C.8.53.26 but probably should not be pressed as an expression of Justinian's attitude to the acquisition of possession *per servum* for an *infans* since it does not seem, prima facie, to be concerned with the acquisition of possession and it is in contradiction with D.41.2.1.5 and 41.2.32.2.

These then are the texts on the acquisition of possession *per servum* for an infant. Of the four, two require that the taking be *ex peculiari causa*, but the conjunction of one renders it suspect and in both the reference to the *peculium* could easily be an addition. The other two do not speak of a restriction to the *peculium*, but one of them may well be concerned with a totally different situation and the other throws no light on classical law. On balance, the evidence tends to suggest that an *infans* could possess and usucape only those acquisitions of his slaves made on account of the *peculium*, but the evidence is too ambiguous to admit of any firm conclusion. Nothing indicates that there were different rules for the acquisition of possession and usucapion.[12]

8 Levy, *op. cit.*, p. 263.
9 But see C.Th.4.23.1.
10 Of course, this does not mean that a person holding *alieno nomine* was regarded as possessing: *cf.* Levy, *op. cit.*, p. 62 *et seq.*
11 For the concept of possession in the Vulgar Law, see Levy, *op. cit.*, pp. 22–31. On this whole discussion, *cf.* Kaser, *Das römische Privatrecht*, II (München, 1959), p. 177 *et seq.*
12 I am indebted for very valuable criticism to Professor David Daube and Mr. J. K. B. M. Nicholas.

9

Acquisition of Ownership by Traditio to an Extraneus

SUMMARIUM. — Fontes de traditionibus extraneae personae factis inspiciuntur. Plerumque, tali traditione facta, dominium adquiritur, si haec persona extranea aut iussu aut scientia eius cui agitur accipit; sed si iniussu aut sine scientia illius accipit, dominium plerumque non adquiritur. Nihilominus plures diversitates sententiae non parvi momenti inveniuntur, quamquam lenem explicationem sequi non possumus.

The acquisition of ownership by *traditio* to an *extranea persona* has received remarkably little independent study [1]. Acquisition of possession *per extraneam personam* seems to have attracted most of the attention to itself and acquisition of ownership appears generally to be treated, without much interest, in its wake. But, of course, there are great differences between the two primarily because a *iusta causa* is needed for the acquisition of ownership by *traditio*.

Where an *extranea persona* takes on behalf of another, he may be acting as an agent or as an instrument. In the former case he will have initiative of his own, in the latter he will be following completely the precise instructions of his principal and there will be no real scope for initiative. In the present study it is hoped to show the extent to which one could acquire ownership by *traditio* [2] through an *extranea persona* where he is an instrument and also where he is an agent. It should be stated at the beginning that the texts do not show a doctrine developing steadily and consistently but display considerable divergence of view.

We have evidence first for the time of Servius.

D. 34, 2, 4 (Paul. 54 *ad ed.*): Cum quidam libertum suum in Asiam misisset ad purpuras emendas et testamento uxori suae lanam purpuream

---

1 Though see, e.g., VOCI, *Modi di acquisto della proprietà*, Milano 1952, 68ff.

2 Of course the principal will not acquire ownership of *res mancipi* which were mancipated to his free agent. *Mancipatio* will not be discussed here.

legasset, pertinere ad eam, si quam purpuram vivo eo libertus emisset, Servius respondit.

The text has excited very little discussion and is usually cited only as an instance of a *legatum quod eius* (scilicet, *uxoris*) *causa emptum paratumve esset* [3]. Ferrini [4], indeed, uses the text for the proposition that a *legatum rerum uxoris causa emptarum* was valid and effective even though the thing had not been handed to the woman: it would suffice that the thing was intended for her use. But there is no textual justification for regarding the situation as involving such a legacy. It is not said that the *libertus* was sent to buy the purple for the use of the wife and we are told that the legacy was of *lana purpurea*, not that it was of the *lana purpurea quae eius causa empta est, erit.* Moreover, there is nothing in the original context of Paul's 54th book on the Edict, which deals with *possessio* and *usucapio* [5], to indicate that it was a legacy of that type [6]. But if, as would appear, the legacy were simply of the testator's *lana purpurea*, only the purple wool which he owned at the time of his death would fall within the *legatum*. The legacy would not include wool to which he had a rightful claim but did not own [7]. Hence, too, the *vivo eo* of the text. Thus, it seems that in the last century of the Republic Servius at least held that the *patronus* would acquire ownership automatically and without knowledge of what his *libertus* received on his behalf when acting under his general instructions. The *libertus* would, of course, appear to be acting as an agent, not just as an instrument. His commission, so far as one can tell from the text, was to buy purple in Asia. The particular purple, so far as we can tell, was not nearer specified. In this aspect, as we shall see, the text shows a greater readiness to allow acquisition of ownership by the principal than probably appears again. In this the text is reminiscent of others which show that in other situations the requirements for acquisition of ownership were less stringent in the last century of the Republic than they were in classical law [8]. The text seems to be

---

[3] Voci, *Diritto ereditario romano*, 2, *parte speciale*[2], Milano 1963, 303 n. 181; Levy, *Iura*, 14 (1963), 17.

[4] *Opere*, 3, Milano 1929, 117 n. 1.

[5] Lenel, *Palingenesia Iuris Civilis*, 1 (reprinted Graz, 1960), 1069.

[6] Further, its inclusion in the title D. 34, 3 would not justify the conclusion that for the compilers it was a legacy of that type.

[7] Cf D. 34, 2, 34 pr (Pomponius 9 *ad Quintum Mucium*): Watson, *The Law of Obligations in the Later Roman Republic*, Oxford 1965, 107ff.

[8] For *traditio*; D. 18, 6, 1, 2, (Ulpian, 28 *ad Sab.*); *h. t.* 15 (14), 1 (Paul. 3 *epit. Alfeni*): cf Watson, *Obligations*, 59ff: cf D. 19, 1, 40 (Pomponius 31 *ad Quin-*

concerned with facts contained in a precise question put to the jurist Servius, and in this question the agent was his principal's *libertus*. There is no way in which we can really tell whether Servius would extend the rule to situations where the agent was not the *libertus* of the principal. The social bond between *libertus* and *patronus* was very strong and the *libertus* frequently continued to live in the house of the *patronus*[9]. In such circumstances, the *libertus* could be regarded as still a member of the patron's family and the acquisition of ownership through him might be allowed even though it would not generally be permitted *per extraneam personam*. Here it is worth mentioning that the earliest situation where acquisition of possession *per extraneam personam* was allowed was where the agent was a *procurator*. The usual explanation of this[10] is that in early times a Roman would most often appoint as his *procurator omnium bonorum* one of his freedmen, and that at that time *liberti* were less independent of their *patronus* than was later the case. In this text it should be noted – though the significance cannot be assessed – that the *libertus* is not further described as *procurator*.

A question which the text raises but does not seem to answer is whether the *patronus* has also acquired possession through his *libertus*. As has just been said, the earliest case of acquisition of possession *per extraneam personam* was *per procuratorem*. The earliest evidence we have even for this comes from Neratius who lived about a century and a half after Servius. He writes in D. 41, 3, 41 (7 *membran.*): ... *per procuratorem possessionem apisci iam fere conveniat*[11]; and Gaius, still later, treats acquisition of possession *per procuratorem* as an open question[12]. It may be suggested – reasonably enough – that where one acquires ownership by a *traditio* made to an *extranea persona* one must also have acquired possession through him, and that therefore in this case the *patronus* has also acquired possession through his *libertus*. But I would not wish utterly to exclude the possibility that for Servius

---

tum Mucium); cf Watson, *op. cit.* 61. For *occupatio*: D. 41, 1, 5, 1 (Gaius 2 *rer. cott.*); cf my forthcoming, *The Law of Property in the Later Roman Republic*, Oxford 1968, chapter 2.

[9] Cf now Watson, *The Law of Persons in the Later Roman Republic*, Oxford 1967, 226.

[10] Cf, e.g., Kaser, *Das Römische Privatrecht*, 1, München 1955, 227f.

[11] For the text see now Watson, *Acquisition of possession per extraneam personam*, supra, pp. 64 ff.

[12] G. 2, 95. For the reconstruction < *per procuratorem* > see now Watson, *op. cit.* 27f. Gaius tends to be rather out of date: cf Honoré, *Gaius*, Oxford 1962, 122ff.

there might be acquisition of ownership by a *traditio* to the *libertus* even though there was no acquisition of possession.

The second text is

> D. 41, 2, 51 (Iavolenus 5 *ex post. Labeonis*): Quarundam rerum animo possessionem apisci nos ait Labeo: veluti si acervum lignorum emero et eum venditor tollere me iusserit, simul atque custodiam posuissem, traditus mihi videtur. idem iuris esse vino vendito, cum universae amphorae vini simul essent. sed videamus, inquit, ne haec ipsa corporis traditio sit, quia nihil interest, utrum mihi an et cuilibet iusserim custodia tradatur. in eo puto hanc quaestionem consistere, an, etiamsi corpore acervus aut amphorae adprehensae non sunt, nihilo minus traditae videantur: nihil video interesse, utrum ipse acervum an mandato meo aliquis custodiat: utrubique animi quodam genere possessio erit aestimanda.

The substance of the text now seems generally to be accepted as genuine [13]. For both Labeo (*quia nihil interest, utrum mihi an et cuilibet iusserium custodia traditur*) and Javolenus (*nihil video interesse, utrum ipse acervum an mandato meo aliquis custodiat*) I become owner of something which I have bought when custody of it is delivered to someone acting under my instructions. The choice of words, *cuilibet* and *mandato meo aliquis,* shows that these two jurists would allow anyone to acquire ownership for the principal. It cannot be argued that they are thinking exclusively of the principal's slaves or sons *in potestate* or even of his *procuratores.* At the same time, this intermediary is nothing but an instrument. The contract of sale was made with the principal and the intermediary is taking custody of the thing on the express instructions of the principal. The situation in the text is such, however, that it does not by itself show that Labeo and Javolenus would exclude acquisition of ownership by the principal where the *extranea persona* was an agent.

Next we have two texts from Neratius.

> D. 41, 1, 13 pr (6 *reg.*): Si procurator rem mihi emerit ex mandato meo eique sit tradita meo nomine, dominium mihi, id est proprietas, adquiritur etiam ignoranti. 1. Et tutor pupilli pupillae similiter ut procurator emendo nomine pupilli pupillae proprietatem illis adquirit etam ignorantibus.

---

[13] Cf NICOSIA, *L'acquisto del possesso mediante i 'potestate subiecti'*. Milano, 1960, 104 n. 30. For a general account of the text see now WATSON, *Obligations,* 60. To what is said there, might be added that there is *traditio* even though the goods have not been removed from the land or building of the transferor. For Labeo and Javolenus this is part of the point of the discussion whether there was acquisition *corpore* here as well as *animo.*

In the *principium*, *id est proprietas* is generally regarded as a gloss. Apart from this, though, there have been numerous and various suggestions of interpolation [14]. Sometimes it is thought *ex mandato meo* should be deleted and/or *etiam ignoranti*. But there seems little reason to approach the text with extreme suspicion. It neither seems to be turning the classical *procurator* into the Justinianic *mandatarius* nor to be restricting cases where the *procurator* might buy to those where he has received specific instructions from his principal. The text is concerned only with the a c q u i s i t i o n o f o w n e r s h i p *per procuratorem*. It tells us that where a *procurator* acting under express instructions from his principal[15] to buy a specific thing does so, and the thing is delivered to him in the name of his principal, the principal acquires ownership though he is unaware of the delivery. In other words, where the *procurator* is a mere instrument following the precise instructions of his principal, the principal acquires ownership through him and he does not have to know of the taking by the *procurator*. This implies that for Neratius, where the *procurator* was acting as an agent, and bought without the express instructions of his principal he would not acquire ownership for his principal if the principal were unaware that the thing had been delivered to the *procurator*. This text is in harmony with three others which say that we can acquire possession unawares *per procuratorem* but we do not begin to usucape until we know of his taking [16]. The text is written in general terms and is not concerned with a particular situation, hence we can deduce from its precision that Neratius would not allow such acquisition through all *liberae personae*. In this his view is narrower than that of Labeo and Javolenus in D. 41, 2, 51. In the time of Neratius, *procuratio* and *man-*

---

14 Cf in addition to the references given in the *Index Itp.*, and by BRETONE, '*Adquisitio per procuratorem?*' in *Labeo*, 1 (1955), 280ff at 282 n. 13; FRESE, *Das Mandat in seiner Beziehung zur Prokuratur*, in *Studi Riccobono*, 4, 399ff at 410. For substantive genuineness cf NICOSIA, *Acquisto del possesso 'per procuratorem' e 'reversio in potestatem domini' delle 'res furtivae'*, in *Iura*, 11 (1960), 189ff at 194f.

15 VOCI, who regards the text as genuine in substance, takes *ex mandato meo* as referring to the general appointment of the *procurator* and not to express instructions for this purpose: *Modi*, 71f. Otherwise, he says, it would not accord with the fact that the principal can be *ignorans*. But there is no conflict. Obviously one can ask someone to buy something on one's behalf and then for some time be unaware that he had taken delivery.

16 D. 41, 3, 47 (Paul. 3 *ad Nerat.*); 41, 2, 49, 2 (Papinian. 2 *definit.*); C, 7, 32, 1.

datum had not yet fused [17]. But the text need not imply that the only *libera persona* through whom one can acquire is the *procurator*.

§ 1 is generally held to be completely interpolated or at least not to have referred to the *tutor* or to have denied that the *tutor* could acquire ownership for his pupils [18]. There are, in fact, two very good reasons for holding that the substance of the text cannot be genuine. First, in the *principium*, Neratius restricts acquisition of ownership *per procuratorem* to situations where the *procurator* is a mere instrument. The principal acquires ownership even unawares through his *procurator* when the latter has been given particular instructions to buy a specific thing and he does so and it is delivered to the *procurator* in the name of his principal. But it is difficult to believe that § 1 is thinking of acquisition of ownership *per tutorem* only where the latter was a mere instrument. In fact, the express *emendo nomine pupilli pupillae* of the text suggests that the other requirement which is not mentioned, namely that the *tutor* be acting under the pupil's instructions, was not contemplated. And if Neratius allows acquisition of ownership *per procuratorem* only where the *procurator* is a mere instrument, it is most unlikely that he would allow acquisition of ownership *per tutorem* where the *tutor* is acting as an agent. Secondly, it seems that in the time of Neratius the only extraneous person through whom one could acquire possession was the *procurator*. Only later did the *tutor* come to occupy the same position [19]. It is a priori unlikely that it was held that a pupil could acquire ownership through his *tutor* before it was accepted that a pupil could acquire possession through his *tutor*. The balance of probability is thus strongly against the text giving the view of Neratius.

A text which is not relevant to the problem but may appear to be is

> D. 41, 2, 1, 21 (Paul 54 *ad ed.*): Si iusserim venditorem procuratori rem tradere, cum ea in praesentia sit, videri mihi traditam Priscus ait, idemque esse, si nummos debitorem iusserim alii dare. non est enim corpore et tactu necesse adprehendere possessionem, sed etiam oculis et affectu ar-

---

[17] Cf Watson, *Contract of Mandate in Roman Law*, Oxford 1961, 36ff.

[18] Add to the references in the *Index Itp.* (where Beseler, Bonfante, Hägerström [and perhaps also Last and Grosso, whose works were not available to me], who are listed as having held the text genuine, regard it as completely compilatorial), Kaser, *Eigentum and Besitz im älteren römischen Recht*², Köln-Graz 1956, 312 n. 28. It is regarded as genuine in substance by Voci, *op. cit.* 79. Stein appears to treat it as genuine but without argument or discussion of literature: *Regulae iuris*, Edinburgh 1966, 80.

[19] Cf, e.g., Watson, *Acquisition of Possession*, and the references given there.

gumento esse eas res, quae propter magnitudinem ponderis moveri non possunt, ut columnas, nam pro traditis eas haberi, si in re praesenti consenserint: et vina tradita videri, cum claves cellae vinariae emptori traditae fuerint.

We are really concerned with the first two situations in the text. Priscus could be either Javolenus or Neratius[20]. The first situation (and, of course, the interpretation of the second depends on this) is often thought to be concerned with a *traditio* made to a *procurator* and hence with acquisition through him[21]. It would thus mean that for Priscus, since the *dominus* had to be present for *traditio* made to the *procurator* to transfer ownership to him, one could not acquire ownership *per procuratorem*. But the text is concerned with a very different matter, namely *traditio* to the principal[22]. The text as a whole is concerned with situations akin to *traditio longa manu*: where possession is taken not *corpore et tactu* but *oculis et affectu*. The first situation is this: The seller and buyer are in the presence of the goods – there is no sign that the buyer's *procurator* is also there[23] – and the seller apparently is ready to hand the thing over to the buyer. But the buyer instructs him to deliver it to his *procurator*. This counts as *traditio* to the buyer. The seller becomes a sort of custodian of the thing. When the seller eventually gives the thing to the *procurator* he is merely delivering up physical control of something which is already in the buyer's ownership. Likewise where the debtor and creditor are together and the debtor has the money ready to pay the debt. The creditor tells him to give the money to a third party. The coins at this point are regarded as being transferred to the creditor, and so it will be his money which in due course will be given to the third party. There will thus be a valid straightforward *mutuum* between the creditor and this third party.

The next text takes us to the time of Celsus.

D. 24, 1, 3, 12 (Ulpian 32 *ad Sab.*): Sed si debitorem suum ei (i.e. uxori) solvere iusserit (i.e. vir), hic quaeritur, an nummi fiant eius debitorque liberetur. Et Celsus libro quinto decimo digestorum scribit videndum esse, ne dici

---

20 BONFANTE thinks that he is probably Javolenus; *Corso di diritto romano*, 3, *Diritti reali* Roma, 1933, 298: VOCI that he is certainly Javolenus; *op. cit.* 77 n. 1: NICOSIA that he is probably Neratius; *op. cit.* 194 n. 24.

21 E.g., BESELER, *Beiträge zur Kritik der römischen Rechtsquellen*, 4, Tübingen 1920, 50 (hence he regards *procuratori* as an interpolation for *illi*); BONFANTE, *loc. cit.*; NICOSIA, *loc. cit.*

22 Cf OLIVECRONA, *Three Essays in Roman Law*, Copenhagen 1949, 71; VOCI, *op. cit.* 77.

23 Contra, VOCI, *loc. cit.*

possit et debitorem liberatum et nummos factos mariti, non uxoris: nam et si donatio iure civili non impediretur, eum rei gestae ordinem futurum, ut pecunina ad te a debitore tuo, deinde a te ad mulierem perveniret: nam celeritate coniungendarum inter se actionum unam actionem occultari, ceterum debito rem creditori dare, creditorem uxori, nec novum aut mirum esse, quod per alium accipias, te accipere: nam et si is, qui creditoris tui se procuratorem esse simulaverit, a debitore tuo iubente te pecuniam acceperit, et furti actionem to habere constat et ipsam pecunian tuam esse.

The text concerns a particular problem in connection with gifts between husband and wife which were, of course, generally void. The question is asked whether, if the creditor tells the debtor to pay the debt to his wife, the wife becomes owner of the coins and the debtor is released. Celsus' solution is that the coins have become the property of the husband. His argument is that even if the gift were not ineffective at civil law delivery by the debtor to the wife would first make the husband owner and ownership would then be transferred by the husband to the wife, though the speed with which the two acts were combined hides one of the acts. The genuineness of this approach of Celsus now seems to be beyond doubt [24]. Thus, for our purposes we can deduce – leaving aside the rest of the text for the moment – that where a husband instructs his debtor to hand over the money to his wife with the intention that ownership is to come to himself Celsus would hold that he does become owner through his wife. In these circumstances, the wife is acting as a mere instrument, not as an agent. Celsus then says that there is nothing new in *quod per alium accipias, te accipere.* For even if a person who pretends to be the *procurator* of your creditor receives, at your request, the money from your debtor, the money will be yours and you will have the *actio furti.* When this person on your instructions received the money from your debtor you acquired ownership through him though he was certainly not your *procurator*. He was, of course, being treated merely as an instrument. This text shows that for Celsus one can acquire ownership through anyone so long as that person is an instrument. The text does not throw any light on how far, if at all, Celsus would allow acquisition *per extraneam personam* where the intermediary was acting as an agent. Voci, however, thinks that the situation in the text is more limited and that one acquires ownership only when all three are present together [25]. He has three arguments. First, Celsus in describing the double passing of property says *celeri-*

---

[24] Cf H. J. Wolff, *Julian und die Celsinische 'Durchgangstheorie'*, in *Mélanges Meylan*, 1, 409ff and the references he given, p. 409 n. 1.

[25] *Op. cit.* 122ff.

tate coniungendarum inter se actionum unam occultari. This makes sense, says Voci, only if all three are present together. But the argument begs the question for if one can acquire ownership *per extraneam personam* then the absent husband can acquire through his wife and if his intention is that she should become owner there is no reason – apart from the rule that there can be no gift between husband and wife – why she should not at once acquire ownership by *traditio brevi manu* from her husband. She has sufficient physical control. Of course, Celsus' approach, the double passing of ownership, is very artificial but it is a sophisticated means to a practical end. To the particular question put to him he wants to answer that the debtor is released, but he does not want ownership of the coins to have gone to the wife. Hence he holds that if there had been no legal bar to the transaction there would have been two simultaneous transfers of property but, as it is, only the first of these has validity. Secondly, Voci says that Celsus gives the *actio furti* to the *creditor delegans* and yet he thinks that he cannot have acquired possession through the person who is not his *procurator* if he had not himself been present at the transfer of the money. And yet, he goes on, the plaintiff in the *actio furti* must have had either possession or detention. But in fact, for the *actio furti*, the owner did not have to have possession or detention. The most obvious instance concerns goods thrown overboard in a storm to lighten ship. There can be no doubt that the owner loses possession [26]. Yet a person who finds them and intends to keep them, and does not have the mistaken belief that they were abandoned, commits *furtum* [27, 28]. Moreover, *nam et si* to the end must not be attributed to Celsus. As the indicative *constat* shows, this part of the text is not in indirect speech. Thirdly, says Voci, we are told that the opinion of Julian in § 13 is *consequens* to that of Celsus in § 12 and we know that Julian did not accept double transfer in the absence of the *delegans*. But this is just not so. However we should interpret § 13 [29], there is nothing in the text which shows that Julian demanded the presence of the *delegans*.

For Julian himself we have two texts.

> D. 39, 5, 2, 6 (60 *dig.*): Sed si quis donaturus mihi pecuniam dederit alicui, ut ad me perferret, et ante mortuus erit quam ad me perferat, non fieri pecuniam dominii mei constat.

---

26 Cf D. 41, 2, 3, 13 (Paul. 54 *ad ed.*)

27 E.g., D. 47, 2, 43: 4-8, 10, 11 (Ulpian. 41 *ad Sab.*)

28 KASER appears to treat this aspect of our text as genuine without restricting it to situations where the parties were not present together: *Das Geld im römischen Sachenrecht*, in *Tijd.* 29 (1961), 170ff at 225 n. 187.

29 See most recently WOLFF, *op. cit.*

What concerns us here [30] is that obviously ownership was not passed to the donee when the donor gave the money to someone to take to the donee. But the text may only envisage circumstances where the donee was unaware of the delivery to the messenger and of the gift itself.

> D. 41, 1, 37, 6 (Iulian. 44 *dig.*): Si, cum mihi donare velles, iusserim te servo communi meo et Titii rem tradere isque hac mente acciperet, ut rem Titii faceret, nihil agetur: nam et si procuratori meo rem tradideris, ut meum faceres, is hac mente acceperit, ut suam faceret, nihil agetur. quod si servus communis hac mente acceperit, ut duorum dominorum faceret, in parte alterius domini nihil agetur.

In this text we are told that if you deliver a thing to my *procurator* with the intention that it should become mine, and he takes it intending to make it his own, the transaction is void. From the text it seems that we can conclude with Voci [31] that where the *procurator* took for his principal, the principal would become owner. Beseler, [32] however, suggests that we should understand *iussu meo* after *nam et si*. The argument for this must be the connection between this situation and the immediately preceding one of delivery to a common slave. But it is quite possible that Julian would hold that delivery made on behalf of the principal but without his knowledge to his *procurator* who does take on his behalf would be sufficient to give the principal ownership. Perhaps the best verdict here should be *non liquet* [33].

It is doubtful how much help is to be got from a text from Pomponius' 14th book *ad Quintum Mucium* [34].

> D. 41, 1, 53: Ea quae civiliter adquiruntur per eos, qui in potestate nostra sunt, adquirimus, veluti stipulationem: quod naturaliter adquiritur, sicuti est possessio, per quemlibet volentibus nobis possidere adquirimus.

The text would seem to have suffered at least some interpolation and though most suspicions are confined to the second part of the text [35] an older opinion at least [36] was that *stipulationem* was an insertion proba-

30 For the text in general see Biondi, *Successione testamentaria e donazione*², Milano 1955, 695; Voci, *op. cit.* 93 and 109.

31 *Op. cit.* 72.

32 *ZSS*, 44 (1924), 376: cf *Beiträge*, 4, 56.

33 For the *nam et si* of the text, see Watson, *Two Studies in Textual History*, infra, p. 378.

34 The Digest inscription has *Modestinus*, not *Pomponius*, but there is general agreement that this is an error: cf Berneisen, '*Per liberam personam*', in *RIDA*, 6 (1959), 249ff at 279, and the references she gives, n. 79: Watson, '*Acquisition of Possession*', supra, p. 67.

35 In addition to the *Index Itp.*, cf Berneisen, *op. cit.* 279ff; Watson, *op. cit.* 26f.

36 Cf the references given in the *Index Itp.*

bly for *mancipationem.* There is no need, though, to postulate the insertion of *stipulationem*: *civiliter* used in this way often simply refers to something being a matter of law, not of fact, and does not refer specifically to the civil law [37]. If we take the distinction drawn in the tevt as it stands then it can probably be argued that for Pomponius we can acquire ownership only through persons in our power since ownership is something which is acquired *civiliter* [38]. But there can be no way of knowing whether Pomponius' refusal to allow acquisition *per extraneam personam* would apply both where the *extraneus* was an agent and where he was an instrument, or only where he was an agent.

The next text is from Callistratus.

> D. 41, 1, 59 (2 *quaest.*): Res ex mandatu meo empta non prius mea fiet, quam si mihi tradiderit qui emit.

This text dates from after the rapprochement of *procuratio* and *mandatum* when the *actio mandati* began to be given against the *procurator* [39]. This, of course, does not necessarily mean that there were no differences between the mandatary and the *procurator* [40]. The term *is qui mandatum suscepit* would convey a very different picture to the Roman than would the term *procurator*. Thus, the text of Callistratus need not be thought of as including a *procurator*. The text tells us that a thing bought under my mandate does not become mine until it is delivered to me. Thus it would appear that Callistratus would not allow acquisition of ownership through a mandatary even where the mandatary was nothing but an instrument. In this Callistratus seems to be taking the same narrow view which, it was thought, could be deduced for Neratius from D. 41, 1, 13 pr [41]. Voci would take the text as referring originally to *res mancipi* [42] but there is no evidence for this and no argument other than an a priori one. A difficulty with the text is that, interpolated or not, it does not give the law of Justinian's own time [43].

---

37 Cf. WATSON, *The Form and Nature of 'acceptilatio' in classical Roman law*, infra, p. 208.

38 If the argument on the meaning of *civiliter* is correct, there is no reason to suggest that a distinction could be drawn between modes of acquisition which were *iuris civilis* and those which were *iuris gentium*.

39 Cf WATSON, *Mandate, loc. cit.*

40 Cf WATSON, *Acquisition of Possession*, 32.

41 *Supra*, p. 73 ff.

42 Cf, *op. cit.* 75f and 76 n. 1.

43 DE ZULUETA says that « in the time of Justinian one explanation of the present text would be simply the mandatarius' intention. »: *Digest 41.1 & 2*, Oxford 1950, 79. It is true that under necessity the text can be so harmonised but it is

C. 7, 32, 1 (*Impp. Severus et Antoninus AA. Attico*): Per liberam personam ignoranti quoque adquiri possessionem et, postquam scientia intervenerit, usucapionis condicionem inchoari posse tam ratione utilitatis quam iuris pridem receptum est. *PP. vi k. Dec. Dextro II et Prisco conns* [44].

The constitution, we learn, confirms what is said to have been already accepted and it tells us that a person begins to usucape when he learns that a free man has acquired possession for him. The constitution does not itself reveal whether it means that when the principal hears of the delivery he begins to usucape but that there can be no acquisition of ownership by *traditio* until the thing is delivered to him himself; or whether it means that in circumstances which are appropriate for *usucapio* but not for acquisition by *traditio*, *usucapio* will begin to run as soon as the principal hears of the delivery to the *libera persona*. Two other texts, D. 41, 3, 47 (Paul. 3 *ad Nerat.*) and D. 41, 2, 49, 2 (Papinian 2 *definit.*), which say that an *ignorans* acquires possession *per procuratorem*, but only begins to usucape when *sciens*, should not lead one to consider that the former is the more likely interpretation. Of these two texts, the first is in any event primarily concerned with the beginning of *usucapio* and it appears from D. 41, 1, 13 pr. [45] and D. 3, 5, 23 (24) [46] that both Neratius and Paul would hold that when the principal learnt of the delivery of a thing in his name to his *procurator* he would become owner as a result of the *traditio*. Again, the connection between *usucapio* and *possessio* is so close that it is natural to find texts which stress circumstances in which the moment of acquisition of possesion and the beginning of *uucapio* do not coincide. In view of the uncertainty of the interpretation of the text, it is perhaps best not to use it for any conclusions here even though, since *usucapio* as well as *traditio* requires a *iusta causa*, one would think that control sufficient to begin *usucapio* would be sufficient for *traditio*.

We come now to the text of Paul which has just been mentioned.

D. 3, 5, 23 (24) (24 *ad ed.*): Si ego hac mente pecuniam procuratori dem, ut ea ipsa creditoris fieret, proprietas quidem per procuratorem non adquiritur, potest tamen creditor etiam invito me ratum habendo pecuniam suam facere, quia procurator in accipiendo creditoris dumtaxat negotium gessit: et ideo creditoris ratihabitione liberor.

---

self-evident that the compilers were not thinking of the text as relating to situations where the mandatary's intention was to take things for himself.

44 For the substantive genuineness of this text see Watson, *op. cit.* 29 f. The text will be more fully examined in a future study, *The Relationship of Justinian's Institutes to the Code and Digest: Some Problems in Legal History.*

45 *Supra*, p. 119 ff.

46 *Infra*, p. 120 f.

For our present purposes the text says that money given by the debtor to the creditor's *procurator* with the intention that it should become the creditor's does not become his until he ratifies the transaction. Thus, there can be no acquisition of ownership unawares through a *procurator*. So Paul, too, it appears, would not allow acquisition of ownership through a *procurator* where the *procurator* is acting as an agent. The requirement of ratification shows what we could, in any event, have presumed, namely that where the principal has ownership when he learns of the *traditio* to the intermediary the principal has to be in favour of the transaction. Some jurists regard the substance of the text – so far as concerns us – as genuine [47]. Others think it interpolated because in classical law a *procurator* would be allowed to give a valid discharge for debts due to his principal [48]. Others think the *procurator* of the text is a *negotiorum gestor* for the same reason [49]. But the last two views are based on a priori argument and we have seen enough texts by this time to realise that on any general a priori grounds the presumption must be that Paul would demand the principal's knowledge before he would become owner after delivery to his *procurator*.

> D. 41, 1, 65 pr. (Labeo 6 *pith. a Paulo epit.*): Si epistulam tibi misero, non erit ea tua, antequam tibi reddita fuerit. PAULUS: immo contra: nam si miseris ad me tabellarium tuum et ego rescribendi causa litteras tibi misero, simul atque tabellario tuo tradidero, tuae fient. idem accidet in his litteris, quas tuae dumtaxat rei gratia misero, veluti si petieris a me, uti te alicui commendarem, et eas commendaticias tibi misero litteras.

In this, Paul seems to take rather a different view. To deal first with the text as far as *fient*. *Tabellarii* were usually slaves or freedman [50] and there is no reason to limit Paul's decision to cases where the *tabellarius* was a slave. Equally there is nothing to suggest that this decision should be restricted to cases where the *tabellarius* was told by his principal to bring back a reply. So Paul will allow the principal to acquire through a free *tabellarius* where the *tabellarius* takes a letter on his behalf without his knowledge and without his instructions. In

---

47 Cf, e.g., SOLAZZI, *Di alcuni punti controversi nella dottrina romana dell'acquisto del possesso per mezzo di rappresentanti*, now in *Scritti di diritto romano*, 1, Napoli 1955, 299 ff; BESELER, *op. cit.* 4, 52 f; MEYLAN, *Per procuratorem possessio nobis adquiri potest*, in *Festschrift Lewald*, 105 ff at 108 f.

48 E.g., BONFANTE, *Istituzioni di diritto romano*10, (reprinted, Torino 1957), 366; but he seems to hold this aspect of the text genuine, *Corso di diritto romano*, 2, 2, *La proprietà*, Roma 1928, 160 and n. 1; SERRAO, *Il procurator*, Milano 1947, 39.

49 VOCI, *op. cit.* 73.

50 Cf SCHROFF, *RE.* 4 A 1844ff.

the remainder of the text Paul seems to go further [51]. For there to be a proper point, the text must refer to letters handed to anyone at all – not just to your *tabellarius* – to take to you. It says that the same applies (that is, that ownership is transferred to you as soon as the letters are given to the intermediary) to letters solely in your interest, for instance, if I, at your request, send you a letter recommending you to someone. Thus, in the circumstances envisaged, Paul will allow acquisition of ownership by the principal, without knowledge, through an *extraneus* who is not acting under his instructions. Paul's two opinions in the text should not be extended beyond the particular circumstances set out. For reasons which will be given in respect of D. 47, 2, 14, 17, it is not unreasonable to treat letters, with regard to transfer of ownership, as exceptional.

There are three texts of Ulpian.

> D. 41, 1, 20, 2 (29 *ad Sab.*): Si ego et Titius rem emerimus eaque Titio et quasi meo procuratori tradita sit, puto mihi quoque quaesitum dominium, quia placet per liberam personam omnium rerum possessionem quaeri posse et per hanc dominium.

The text is concerned with a very particular situation [52]. *Omnium rerum possesio* is stressed because the text is concerned with the acquisition of ownership either of a *res mancipi* or of a *res nec mancipi*. Whichever it is cannot now be discovered but is of no great consequence to us here. If it were a *res nec mancipi*, the text will be allowing acquisition of ownership by *traditio* in particular circumstances, though it would not be extending this to acquisition of ownership of *res mancipi* by *mancipatio*. If it were a *res mancipi*, then a fortiori the text would show that *res nec mancipi* could be so acquired by *traditio*. But nothing will allow us to widen the scope of the decision to other situations. The situation is this: I and Titius buy something in common, and it is delivered to Titius who accepts both on his own behalf and on mine. This is the significance of the *et quasi meo procuratori* which should not be taken as meaning that Titius is my *procurator*. The question arises whether my share has been conveyed to me. Ulpian's reply is that he thinks it has. He gives as an argument for this: *quia placet per libe-*

---

51 This part of the text has been held interpolated by Arangio-Ruiz, *Responsibilità contrattuale in diritto romano* 2, Napoli 1958, 1.29 n. 1. He gives no specific arguments but his view is linked with his approach to D. 47, 2, 14, 17 which is quoted and discussed, *infra*, p. 204 f. De Zulueta also seems to have dobuts on the text: *op. cit.* 82.

52 Cf Watson, *Acquisition of Possession*, 34 ff.

ram personam omnium rerum possessionem quaeri posse et per hanc doninium <——>[53]. This argument is very instructive. It tells us first of all that Ulpian is not thinking of a situation where a *res mancipi* was mancipated to Titius who took on behalf of himself and me and I was aware of the transaction. That situation is so far removed from any possessory situation that a decision could not be justfied by an argument from possession. Nor can it be the analogous situation in *traditio* of a *res nec mancipi* because then we could not explain Ulpian's hesitant *puto*. Rather the situation concerns a case where I was unaware of the delivery and yet automatically become joint owner. Secondly, although on this view the argument is understandable, it is not a convincing argument. The real reason for the decision is that in practical terms any other decision would be absurd. We would have to hold either that despite his intention Titius became owner of the whole, or that the seller remains part-owner despite the *mancipatio* or the *traditio* with the *iusta causa*. Nothing in the text itself indicates whether or not when Titius took delivery he had instructions from me to that effect. But he cannot have been acting under my instructions, at least not if the thing were a *res nec mancipi*. The exceptional nature of the decision is shown by the *puto* and by the argument given for it, yet by this time there was such a body of opinion that you acquired ownership when someone acting under your instructions took delivery in your name that there could be no explanation for the hesitation or the strained argument. And we can more or less exclude the possibility that the situation envisaged is where Titius, acting under my instructions, took delivery by *mancipatio* of a *res mancipi*. The argument in the text, sophisticated on any interpretation, can hardly be thought to be of any persuasive force whatever for that situation. Further, there is nothing in the text to indicate that Titius was acting under my *iussum*. *Et quasi meo procuratori*[54] does not imply that Titius had instructions. In all probability the text should be taken as concerning an exceptional case where a person acquires ownership through a free person although the latter was not acting under his instructions and although the former did not know that the latter had obtained control of the thing. Of course, in this case, it was easier to accept the idea of acquisition of ownership *per liberam personam* in that the *ego* of the text had himself (along with Titius) bought the thing. There was an existing contract between the transferor and *ego*.

---

53 Cf WATSON, *op. cit.* 36.

54 Which may anyway be an explanatory gloss: cf WATSON, *op. cit.* 36 n. 39.

D. 47, 2, 14, 17 (Ulpian, 29 *ad Sab.*): Si epistula, quam ego tibi misi, intercepta sit, quis furti actionem habeat? et primum quaerendum est, cuius sit epistula, utrum eius qui misit, an eius ad quem missa est? et si quidem dedi servo eius, statim ipsi quaesita est, cui misi: si vero procuratori, aeque (quia per liberam personam possessio quaeri potest) ipsius facta est, maxime si eius interfuit eam habere. quod si ita misi epistulam, ut mihi remittatur, dominium meum manet, quia eius nolui amittere vel transferre dominium...

For what concerns us now, the text tells us that if a letter is handed to the *procurator* of the addressee, the addressee immediately becomes owner, especially if he had an interest in having it. Most of the text has been held interpolated at one time or another [55]. But in view of what has gone before in this study we are now in a better position to judge the main objections to its substance. These are that *si quidem* followed by *si vero* implies a contrast, yet the same decision is given; that the argument, *quia per liberam personam possessio quaeri potest*, does not justify the decision; that in view of the general nature of the decision, the qualification introduced by *maxime si* does not make sense [56] But the text comes from the same book of Ulpian as D. 41, 1, 20, 2 and the same considerations explain this text. Ulpian is faced with another exceptional situation where he wants ownership to be acquired through an intermediary although the principal does not know of the taking by the intermediary. The exceptional aspects of the situation are first that one does not usually think of a letter which is being sent in terms of ownership: When one is forced to, as here, it becomes easier to treat the situation in an unconventional way. Secondly a letter is peculiarly personal. Ulpian is well aware of the exceptional nature of the decision and this explains the form of the text. *Si quidem ... si vero* does imply a contrast, but not necessarily a contrast of decision. The great contrast for acquisition of ownership between delivery to a slave and delivery to a *libera persona* is implicit in the text and the *aeque* actually emphasises it, while at the same time stressing that the decisions will here be the same. The argument, *quia per liberam personam possessio quaeri potest*, is the same sophisticated reason which we saw in D. 41, 1, 20, 2. It is used because there is no better. The qualification introduced by *maxime si* is the result of Ulpian's hesitancy and uncertainty. But if *maxime si* is interpolated it proves the genuineness of the decision attributed to Ulpian. The com-

---

55 Cf *Index Itp.*; JOLOWICZ, *Digest 47.2. De furtis*, Cambridge 1940, 19 f; ALBERTARIO, *op. cit.* 123

56 For the argument about the change from *procurator* to *libera persona*, see now WATSON, *op. cit.* 33 f.

pilers could have no reason to be so hesitant about any ruling introduced by themselves. There is, I submit, no good reason for doubting the genuineness of the substance of this part of the text. An alternative interpretation of the text must also be reckoned with, namely that Ulpian is not treating the situation as exceptional but is trying to extend acquisition of ownership through a *libera persona* to all the situations where one could acquire possession *per liberam personam*. This view also could account for Ulpian's hesitation and for his use of the argument from acquisition of possession.

This alternative interpretation of D. 47, 2, 14, 17 may receive some support from

> D. 39, 5, 13 (Ulpian. 7 *disp.*): Qui mihi donatum volebat, servo communi meo et Titii rem tradidit: servus vel sic accepit quasi socio adquisiturus vel sic quasi mihi et socio: quaerebatur quid ageret. et placet, quamvis servus hac mente acceperit, ut socio meo vel mihi et socio adquirat, mihi tamen adquiri: nam et si procuratori meo hoc animo rem tradiderit, ut mihi adquirat, ille quasi sibi adquisiturus acceperit, nihil agit in sua persona, sed mihi adquirit.

The text has certainly been interpolated and there is wide agreement that, among others, *in sua persona, sed mihi adquirit* is an addition [57]. The text should give the same decision as Julian does in D. 41, 1, 37, 6, on which our text is obviously very dependent. And as with D. 41, 1, 37, 6, so here one can deduce that where the *procurator* took with the intention of making the thing his principal's, the principal would become owner at once. But this time there is no sign of a *iussum* to the common slave or to anyone else and so it cannot plausibly be argued that the text should be understood as concerning a *procurator* who took delivery on the instructions of his principal. So Ulpian here seems to allow acquisition of ownership *per procuratorem* where the principal has neither given instructions nor knows of the delivery.

We have two relevant constitutions from the Emperors Diocletian and Maximian.

> C. 4, 27, 1 (*Impp. Diocletianus et Maximianus AA. Marcello*): Excepta possessionis causa per liberam personam, quae alterius iuri non est subdita, nihil adquiri posse indubii iuris est. Si igitur procurator non sibi, sed ei, cuius negotia administrabat, redintegratae rei vindicationem pactus est idque pactum etiam stipulatio insecuta est, nulla domino obligatio adquisita est. servis autem res traditae dominis adquiruntur. *D. k. Iul. ipsis IIII et III AA. conss.* [290 A.D.].

---

[57] Cf *Index Itp.*

This begins by telling us that it is undoubtedly the legal position that apart from possession one can acquire nothing through a free person who is not subject to one's power. It goes on by saying that if a *procurator* makes certain particular arrangements not on his own behalf but on behalf of his principal no obligation is acquired by the principal. But, it ends, things delivered to slaves are acquired by their masters. Thus, the constitution, and especially the last sentence considered in its context, makes it abundantly plain that for these Emperors, one cannot acquire ownership *per liberam personam* or even *per procuratorem*. The constitution must mean, moreover, that even where the *procurator* or other *libera persona* is a mere instrument acting under instructions, or where the principal knows of the delivery to the *procurator* or other *libera persona*, no ownership is acquired by the principal. This emerges from the following facts. First, nothing at all is said about a *iussum* or *scientia* and so these are not regarded as relevant. And the existence of a *iussum* or *scientia* would not permit the acquisition of the *obligatio* through the *procurator* and it is the acquisition of this obligation which is the main concern of the rescript. Secondly, the contrast made with delivery to slaves would otherwise be nonsensical in its present form. If this last sentence is meant to point a difference between delivery to slaves and delivery to *liberae personae* where the intermediary is acting without instructions and without the knowledge of his principal it should have read something like *servis autem res traditae dominis ignorantibus adquiruntur*. It seems, therefore, that by this time the law on acquisition through free persons had entered a more restrictive phase.

> C. 7, 32, 8 (*Impp. Diocletianus et Maximianus AA. et CC. Cyrillo*): Per procuratorem utilitatis causa possessionem et, si proprietas ab hac separari non possit, dominium etiam quaeri placuit. *PP. xviii k. Mart. Sirmi CC. conss.* [294 A.D.].

This, which dates from four years after C. 4, 27, 1, concerns a very particular type of situation, namely where ownership cannot be separated from possession. In such situations, one can acquire possession *per procuratorem*, and even ownership [58]. Such situations are rare, but do occur, for instance in the case of *occupatio* of wild animals. The scope of the rescript should not be extended to situations where possession can be separated from ownership. Nothing is said of a *iussum* or *scientia* and probably one can presume that the principal will acquire without a *iussum* and without *scientia*.

---

[58] On this, and for the genuineness of the rescript, see WATSON, *op. cit.* 39 f.

Finally there is

> Inst. J. 2, 9, 5: Ex his itaque apparet per liberos homines, quos neque iuri vestro subiectos habetis neque bona fide possidetis, item per alienos servos, in quibus neque usum fructum habetis neque iustam possessionem, nulla ex causa vobis adquiri posse. et hoc est, quod dicitur per extraneam personam nihil adquiri posse: excepto eo, quod per liberam personam veluti per procuratorem placet non solum scientibus, sed etiam ignorantibus vobis adquiri possessionem secundum divi Severi constitutionem et per hanc possessionem etiam dominium, si dominus fuit qui tradidit, vel usucapionem aut longi temporis praescriptionem, si dominus non sit.

This is closely related to the constitution which appears in C. 7, 32, 1, whose substance it repeats though it is not directly taken from the constitution itself [59]. It tells us that possession is acquired through a *libera persona, non solum scientibus sed etiam ignorantibus*, and through this possession even *dominium* is acquired. But to judge from the texts from the Digest and Code which have been discussed this formulation is too wide for Justinian's law.

To sum up on the texts: The general position, both in classical and Justinianic law was that one could acquire ownership by *traditio* to an *extranea persona* only when that person was merely an instrument and not also when he was acting as an agent. When the principal had knowledge of delivery to an agent the position was of course the same as where the intermediary was an instrument. On this general position, however, there were variations. Thus, Neratius would allow acquisition through an *extranea persona* acting as an instrument where that person was the *procurator*: and possibly in some, but certainnly not in all other cases [60]. Callistratus, it seems, would not allow acquisition of ownership through a mandatary even where he was an instrument [61]. Diocletian and Maximian, the most restrictive of all, would not allow acquisition of ownership through any free person who was acting as an instruments [62]. These on the one hand. On the other hand, sometimes acquisition of ownership through a free agent was permitted. Thus, the same Diocletian and Maximian allow acquisition of possession *per procuratorem* and in the exceptional cases where possession and ownership cannot be separated they will even permit acquisition of

---

59 The relationship between the two texts will be examined in the study referred to, *supra*, p. 120 n. 44.

60 D. 41, 1, 13 pr.

61 D. 41, 1, 59.

62 C. 4, 27, 1.

ownership *per procuratorem*[63]. In another exceptional case, where two people buy something in common and it is delivered to one who takes on behalf of both but without the instructions or knowledge of that other, Ulpian rather hesitantly holds that the one who is being represented will acquire ownership of his share[64]. Moreover, where a letter is given to a *procurator* to take to his principal, Ulpian holds again that the principal will acquire ownership[65]. Methodologically this decision should probably be thought of as concerning another exceptional case but one cannot rule out the possibility that Ulpian was intending to extend the general rule of acquisition of ownership *per liberam personam* to all ordinary situations where the intermediary was a *procurator*. Another text of Ulpian[66] does in fact seem to suggest that he would in all ordinary situations allow acquisition of ownership *per procuratorem*. Paul would allow acquisition of ownership of a letter where it as handed to the *tabellarius* of the addressee, or where it was handed to any intermediary but was written solely in the interests of the addressee. Back in the Republic, Servius would allow a *patronus* to acquire ownership through his *libertus* who was acting as an agent under his principal's general instructions.

It was said at the beginning of this article that modern scholars have given this problem remarkably little independent study. The same would seem to be true of the Romans. The reason, I suspect, is that the legal position was thought to be obvious. It is this which probably explains the certainty with which both C. 7, 32, 1 (*pridem receptum est*) and C. 4, 27, 1 (*indubii iuris est*) declare that the law is settled and yet the two rescripts give different accounts of the state of the law. Thus, though Diocletian and Maximian take a very restrictive view of acquisition of ownership through a free person, they are not (necessarily) aware that their opinion is narrower than that accepted at an earlier time. Again, although much has been made here of the distinction between the intermediary as instrument and the intermediary as agent, the distinction itself does not appear in any of the sources. It might be imagined that the explanation of this is that the Romans used terms like *per procuratorem, per liberam personam* and so on, only where the intermediary was an agent. This would explain, it might be suggested, why Gaius can say in G. 2, 95, *et hoc est quod vulgo dicitur, per extra-*

---

63 C. 7, 32, 8.
64. D. 41, 1, 20, 2.
65 D. 34, 2, 4.
66 D. 39, 5, 13.

neam personam nobis adquiri non posse. Tantum de possessione quaeritur an p e r p r o c u r a t o r e m nobis adquiratur. There may be an element of truth in this but if so it is a very small element. There is quiete a number of texts which have *per* ... where the intermediary is nothing but an instrument. Thus, for instance, in D. 41, 2, 23, 2 (Iavolenus 1 *epist.*) which has *per illum* the question at issue is whether, if you bind a free man so that you possess him, you possess *per illum* everything which he possesses. Here no action or intention of the bound man is relevant. Again, there is D. 41, 2, 1, 13 (Paul. 54 *ad ed.*) which concerns acquisition of possession *per servum* who has been ordered to take possession. And there are texts, such as D. 41, 2, 30, 5 (Paul. 15 *ad Sab.*) and 41, 3, 31, 3 (Paul 32 *ad Sab.*) which are concerned with retention of posession *per colonum.* In these the *colonus* is an instrument in the sense in which the word is being used in this artcle. The real explanation for the absence of this distinction between agent and instrument – which is necessary in this context – is, I submit, the lack of interest in this topic. The distinction does appear in respect of contract where although we are told that we cannot acquire an obligation through an *extranea persona* other texts say that in the informal contracts we can make the contract *per nuntium* [67, 68].

---

[67] D. 17, 1, 1, 1 (Paul. 32 *ad ed.*); 17, 2, 4 (Modestinus 3 *reg.*); 18, 1, 1, 2 (Paul. 33 *ad ed.*).

[68] I have observed elsewhere [*The Acquisition of Young in the 'usufructus gregis'*, in *Iura*, 12 (1961) ; infra, pp. 137 f] that there is no evidence whatever that *constitutum possessorium* — accepting its existence in classical law — did anything more before the post-classical period than transfer possession. There is nothing in the conclusions of the present article which affects this point. It should not be thought that in that kind of situation the seller must be regarded simply as an *extranea persona* acting as an instrument for the buyer. For, just as easily, the seller in a sale uncomplicated by *constitutum possessorium* could have been regarded as an *extranea persona* acting as an instrument for the buyer, but this devolpment, as we know, did not occur. THOMAS' criticisms [*A Note on 'summissio'*; in *RIDA*, 11 (1964), 255 ff at 259 f] of the idea that *constitutum possessorium* may in classical law have transferred only possession seem to miss the mark: *a*). He has not shown, nor is it prima facie evident, that *constitutum possessorium* was a form of *traditio* or even connected with *traditio*; *b*). He says, '*Traditio* is essentially a transfer of possession accompanied by the intents to give and to receive ownership.' But accepting this for the sake of argument it does not help Thomas' case since in *traditio* the transfer of ownership and possession n e e d not coincide. As this article itself shows, especially in cases where *traditio* was made to an *extranea persona,* frequently possession but not ownership would be acquired at once by the principal. (I am, of course, not suggesting that *constitutum possessorium* was construed as a form of *traditio* to an *extranea persona.*).

10

The Acquisition of Young in the Usufructus Gregis

The main texts are:

D. 7. 1. 68 pr. (Ulpian 17 *ad Sab.*) *Vetus fuit quaestio, an partus ad fructuarium pertineret: sed Bruti sententia optinuit fructuarium in eo locum non habere: neque enim in fructu hominis homo esse potest. hac ratione nec usum fructum in eo fructuarius habebit. quid etiam si fuerit etiam partus usus fructus relictus, an habeat in eo usum fructum? et cum possit partus legari, poterit et usus fructus eius. 1. Fetus tamen pecorum Sabinus et Cassius opinati sunt ad fructuarium pertienere. 2. Plane si gregis vel armenti sit usus fructus legatus, debebit ex adgnatis gregem supplere, id est in locum capitum defunctorum.*

D. 7. 1. 69 (Pomponius 5 *ad Sab.*) *vel inutilium alia summittere, ut post substituta fiant propria fructuarii, ne lucro ea res cedat domino. et sicut substituta statim domini fiunt, ita priora quoque ex natura fructus desinunt eius esse: nam alioquin quod nascitur fructuarii est et cum substituit, desinit eius esse.*

D. 7. 1. 70 pr. (Ulpian 17 *ad Sab.*) *Quid ergo si non faciat nec suppleat? teneri eum proprietario Gaius Cassius scribit libro decimo iuris civilis. 1. Interim tamen, quamdiu summittantur et suppleantur capita quae demortua sunt, cuius sit fetus quaeritur. et Iulianus libro trecensimo quinto digestorum scribit pendere eorum dominium, ut, si summittantur, sint proprietarii, si non summittantur, fructuarii: quae sententia vera est. 2. Secundum quae si decesserit fetus, periculum erit fructuarii, non proprietarii, et necesse habebit alios fetus summittere, unde Gaius Cassius libro octavo scribit carnem fetus demortui ad fructuarium pertinere. 3. Sed quod dicitur debere eum summittere, totiens verum est, quotiens gregis vel armenti vel equitii, id est universitatis usus fructus legatus est: ceterum si singulorum capitum, nihil supplebit. 4. Item si forte eo tempore, quo fetus editi sunt, nihil fuit quod summitti deberet, nunc est post editionem: utrum ex his quae edentur summittere debebit, an ex his quae edita sunt, videndum est. puto autem verius ea, quae plena grege edita sunt, ad fructuarium pertinere, sed posteriorem gregis casum nocere debere fructuario. 5. Summittere autem facti est et Iulianus proprie dicit dispertire et dividere et divisionem quandam facere: quod dominium erit summissorum proprietarii.*

P. S. 3. 6. 20. *Gregis usufructu legato grege integro manente fetus ad usufructuarium pertinent, salvo eo, ut quidquid gregi deperierit, ex fetibus impleatur.*

From these texts and a sentence in D. 7. 1. 12. 5., (*Cum autem in pendenti est dominium* (*ut ipse Iulianus ait in fetu qui summittitur...* ([1])) it is concluded that two answers were given to the question who acquired the ownership of *fetus* in *usufructus gregis* ([2]). The first, given by Sabinus and Cassius, was that the *fetus* belong at birth to the usufructuary, but if to replace dead or useless members of the *grex* he makes *summissio* of any, ownership of these is automatically transfered to the *dominus* of the flock or herd. The conclusion as to the acquisition *ab initio* by the usufructuary is probably correct, but it is based on very flimsy foundations. Amirante ([3]) refers only to D. 7. 1. 68. 1., (although P. S. 3. 6. 20 is also relevant): *Fetus tamen pecorum Sabinus et Cassius opinati sunt ad fructuarium pertinere.* But *tamen* at the beginning of that sentence is inserted to alert us to the distinction between § 1 and the *principium*, where the case of the offspring of an *ancilla* is discussed. And the *principium* strongly suggests that for Ulpian the point at issue was the right to ownership rather than the acquisition of ownership. *Pertinere* is often used to mean that there is a right to something as well as ' to belong to '; for example, from the same book of Ulpian in D. 7. 1. 7. pr., we have *Usu fructu legato omnis fructus rei ad fructuarium pertinet,* although for ownership of

([1]) The text is given infra 134.

([2]) Amirante '*Ususfructus Gregis*' Studi Arangio-Ruiz 3. pp. 281 *et seq.*; Grosso *Usufrutto* Turin 1958 pp. 237-247; Buckland *A Textbook of Roman Law* 2nd ed. Cambridge 1932 p. 223.

([3]) Op. cit. p. 285.

the fruits *perceptio* as vell as the existence of the usufruct was required. Moreover, and this is perhaps more important, in § 1 Ulpian follows up his discussion of the acquisition of a child born to an *ancilla* with the rule as to acquisition of offspring where there is a usufruct of specific animals. It is only in § 2 that he goes on to deal with the case of a usufruct of a *grex*. This interpretation of D. 7. 1. 68. pr. and 1 is borne out by the continuance of the discussion by Ulpian in D. 7. 1. 70. 1. *Interim tamen, quamdiu summittantur et suppleantur capita quae demortua sunt, cuius sit fetus quaeritur* which suggests that until that point the exposition was on something other than the question 'who in actual fact is owner of *fetus* in *ususfructus gregis*?' which only here is being raised. Nevertheless some doctrine as to the acquisition of *fetus* in *ususfructus gregis* must have existed before Julian and it is most reasonable to assume that they went to the usufructuary who, however, was in this respect under certain obligations to the *dominus gregis*.

The second answer to the question was given, it is said, by Julian who here, as elsewhere, introduced pendency. According to Julian, ownership was in suspense, and if there were *summissio* of the *fetus* then it belonged to the *dominus gregis* from the time of birth, and if there were not (or it became impossible) it belonged to the *fructuarius* from the same time. That this view of Julian's was accepted by Justinian is clear from D. 7. 1. 70. 1. (*quae sententia vera est*) and J. 2. 1. 38.

> J. 2. 1. 38. *Sed si gregis usum fructum quis habeat, in locum demortuorum capitum ex fetu fructuarius summittere debet, ut et Iuliano visum est, et in vinearum demortuarum vel arborum locum alias debet substituere. rcete enim colere debet et quasi bonus pater familias uti debet.*

Almost certainly too, it was accepted by later classical jurists, since as was submitted above, it appears that Ulpian in D. 7. 1. 68. pr. was considering not the acquisition of ownership, but the right to ownership, and so no later contrary view has come down to us ([4]).

But taking these two answers as representing classical opinion, we are faced with the problem why Julian considered it desirable to introduce a new viewpoint. Certainly his position is not free from practical difficulties, ([5]) especially where the *fetus* was stolen before *summssio*.

> D. 7. 1. 12. 5 (Ulpian 17 *ad Sab.*) *Iulianus libro trigesimo quinto digestorum tractat, si fur decerpserit vel desecuerit fructus maturos pendentes, cui condictione teneatur, domino*

([4]) It is suggested by Amirante (*op. cit.* p. 287, n. 16) that *quae sententia vera est* may be a Justinianic interpolation. There is no evidence for his.

([5]) Buckland *op. cit.* p. 223 says the rule 'does not look convenient'.

fundi an fructuario? et putat, quoniam fructus non fiunt fructuarii, nisi ab eo percipiantur, licet ab alio terra separentur, magis proprietario condictionem competere, fructuario autem furti actionem, quoniam interfuit eius fructus non esse ablatos. Marcellus autem movetur eo, quod, si postea fructus istos nactus fuerit fructuarius, fortassis fiant eius: nam si fiunt, qua ratione hoc evenit? nisi ea, ut interim fierent proprietarii mox adprehensi fructuarii efficientur, exemplo rei sub condicione legatae, quae interim heredis est, existente autem condicione ad legatarium transit. verum est enim condictionem competere proprietario. cum autem in pendenti est dominium (ut ipse Iulianus ait in fetu qui summittitur et in eo quod servus fructuarius per traditionem accepit nondum quidem pretio soluto, sed tamen ab eo satisfacto), dicendum est condictionem pendere magisque in pendenti esse dominium.

None of the suggested interpolations affects the value of the text for our purposes ([6]). We are told that where, on Julian's view, ownership is in suspense, so likewise is the *condictio furtiva*. Since *summissio* requires a physical act, (which consists in branding the sheep or something similar) ([7]) and is not simply a question of intention, it cannot be carried out when the *fetus* is not in the hands of the usufructuary ([8]), and so the *condictio* will continue to be un available. What applies to the *condictio furtiva* must also apply to the *vindicatio* — for example, if offspring of a flock in wihch there is a usufruct were accidentally mixed with the flock of a neighbour who sold his *grex*, neither the usufructuary nor the *dominus gregis* could have a *vindicatio* or indeed any other action (such as the *actio Publiciana*) against the purchaser.

Such difficulties would not exist on the rule which is supposed to have been adopted by Sabinus and Cassius. There, before *summissio*, the usufructuary was owner and had right to both *condictio* and *vindicatio*. Nor can any practical improvements be found to have resulted from Julian's innovations. Thus, if the *fetus* died before *summissio*, both on Julian's view and what is said to be that of Sabinus and Cassius, the loss fell on the usufructuary, and if the *fetus* died after *summissio* the loss, again in both cases, was on the *dominus* but the usufructuary had a duty to replace. Amirante ([9]) says that there is no one who does not see that Julian was attempting to protect the *dominus vis-a-vis* the fructuary: that pendency created a real bond on the

([6]) Cf. *Index Itp.*

([7]) Cf. Amirante *op. cit.* p. 284.

([8]) If the *fetus* is killed or dies while in another's hands, ownership of it would pass to the usufructuary (since *summissio* has become impossible) But this would not usually help the usufructuary much.

([9]) *Op. cit.* p. 294 n. 29.

fetus so that the usufructuary could not take any so long as the *grex* was incomplete. But it is difficult to see how the *dominus* was better protected *vis-a-vis* the fructuary. There is no reason to believe, and no-one has ever alleged, that the ownership of *fetus* born when the *grex* was incomplete automatically went to the *dominus gregis*. Protection of the *dominus gregis* would normally be by the action on the *cautio fructuaria* ([10]) or by a praetorian action ([11]), and where the usufructuary behaved wrongfully these actions would be available equally where the *dominus gregis* had a right to be made owner of the *fetus*, and where he was not owner of the *fetus* but could be made so retroactively by an act of the usufructuary. Nor is likely (although there is no direct evidence) that either before or after Julian's innovation the *dominus gregis* could bring an *actio furti* where the usufructuary acted contrary to the right to ownership of the *dominus*. In neither situation could he allege that he was owner of the *fetus* nor was he a possessor or *detentor* ([12]).

Julian's doctrine, therefore, seems a retrograde step so far as practical utility is concerned, and at the most it might be argued that it is an improvement in theory. Even this, however, does not hold water. Where would the improvement lie? It could only be on the point that on the older view it is alleged that *summissio* automatically transferred ownership from the usufructuary to the *dominus gregis*, and yet in theory ownership should only be transferred where there is physical delivery. But once it had been accepted by Sabinus and Cassius — a century before Julian — that in this case ownership was transferred without actual delivery, the rule would have been worked into the system as were other exceptions such as *traditio brevi manu* and there would be little justification for altering it simply because it was an exception. Moreover, even where it might be appropriate in theory, pendency was not always introduced in other fields where in practice it was not beneficial, or at least where it was positively detrimental, as it was here ([13]).

So on the common view, Julian's innovation had not only practical considerations against it, but also it would not lead to any theoreti-

([10]) D. 7. 9. At least as early as Julian it was available in all types of usufruct, no matter how constituted; D. 7. 1. 13. *pr.*

([11]) For the nature of this action see Lenel *Edictum Perpetuum* 3rd ed. Leipsig 1927 pp. 368-369. To his references add Grosso *op. cit.* pp. 274-277.

([12]) Cf. Jolowicz *Digest XLVII. 2. De Furtis* Cambridge 1940, p. XXX.

([13]) Cf. *pendens* in *postliminium*. Captivity suspended *patriapotestas*, terminated marriage which did not revive on return, and ended *tutela* which, however, revived, but was not retroactive. Julian seems to have introduced the concept of *pendens* into the acquisition of *legatum per vindicationem*; D. 30. 86. 2 (Julian 34 *dig.*) cf. Amirante ' In tema di acquisto del legato *per vindicationem* ' 3 IVRA (1952) pp. 249-253. This certainly makes the theoretical position neater and there is no evidence that it improved the position of the *heres vis-a-vis* the *legatarius* or vice versa. In any event it would not adversely affect the actions available against a third party.

cal improvements. Yet there must have been good reason for the innovation, and I submit that the common view as to the position before Julian is incorrect and that *summissio* did not automatically transfer ownership to the *dominus gregis*.

The only text which might be used to argue that ownership was so transferred is D. 7.1.69. But this text, as it stands, cannot be completely the work of Pomponius and it is emended by Mommsen, and various Romanists have suggested interpolations ([14]). Lenel's reconstruction ([15]) is that most commonly accepted. ([16]) He excises *ex natura fructus* and *et cum substituit desinit eius esse*. That the ownership of the useless sheep goes to the usufructuary *ex natura fructus* is, he says obyiously not true and it conflicts with the following *nam quod nascitur fructuarii est*, and the closing words (*et cum &c*) are added by someone who did not understand what immediately preceded. ([17]) This seems the best explanation of the construction of this part of the text. Thus, so far as acquisition of ownership of the *fetus* is concerned, the text tells us only the following; a) when *summissio* is made, ownership of the *fetus* goes to the *dominus gregis*; b) apart from the case of *inutilia capita* only what is born (or, no doubt, produced) goes to the usufructuary. Nothing in the text tells us when the usufructuary acquires such ownership, i. e. whether at birth or when it is definitely incorporated among his own animals. Nor is anything said about the automatic transference of ownership from the usufructuary to the *dominus gregis* on *summissio*. The text on Lenel's reconstruction, therefore, throws no light on the question of ownership before *summissio*. Accordingly, Pomponius may be expressing the same view as Julian, i. e., pendency. Admittedly, Pomponius' book 5 *ad Sabinum* must have been written before Julian's book 33 *digestorum* ([18]) but this is no obstacle to holding that he expressed the same view. Two explanations are possible. First, Julian's view as to pendency of ownership of the *fetus* was known even before he wrote his book 35. After all, Julian was passionately interested in pendency and may have adverted to this case to illustrate some earlier point. Secondly, and this I consider more

---

([14]) Cf. *Index Itp.* For post-classical work on Pomponius *Ad Sabinum*, cf. Schulz *History of Roman Legal Science* Oxford 1953 pp. 211-212; Wieacker *Textstufen klassischer Juristen* Göttingen 1960 329-330.

([15]) Lenel 39 ZSS (1918) pp. 161-162.

([16]) Cf. Amirante *loc. cit.* p. 286.

([17]) Pendency is a subtle concept and was often not understood by the post-classics: *cf. Gai Fragm. Augustodun.* 1. 22; *Epit. Gai* 1. 6. 2; *P. S.* 2. 25. 1. Amirante *op. cit.* argues from these that the theory of 'pendenza' developed on the trunk of the old theory of extinction without completely supplanting it in classical law. But this is unjustified. All the classical texts accept pendency and these post-classical texts are — as indeed appears clearly from them — an unintentional corruption of the theory.

([18]) Cf. Krüger *Geschichte der Quellen und Litteratur des römischen Rechts* 2nd ed. Munich 1912 p. 191 n. 6.

likely, pendency may have been accepted here even shortly before Julian, but his interest in it, and emphasis on it may well have caused later jurists to refer to him for this point. Two cases may be given to illustrate this. *Postliminium* we know existed in the Republic ([19]) and it must inevitably have affected the status of the *filii* of the captive. But the earliest text which we have which discusses the status of the children is D. 49. 15. 22. 2 ([20]) which comes from Julian's book 62 *digestorum*, and it says that the status of the children is in suspense. There is no good reason for saying that this rule was introduced by Julian even though he may have stressed it. Again, a popular question is for whom ownership is acquired when a slave is bought by and delivered to a *servus usufructuarius* who has not yet paid the price. The answer given in all the texts ([21]) is that ownership is in suspense until the price is paid, for if payment is made *ex re fructuarii*, he will become owner, if not the *dominus* of the *servus fructuarius* will. This decision is usually referred to Julian ([22]) and we have no text which goes further back. Clearly, Julian was very interested in this point which was seized by others. But there is no reason for holding that there was some other rule before Julian — indeed it is difficult to see what other rule there could have been — or that Julian was innovating.

It is also difficult to see on what principle ownership would be transferred automatically by *summissio*, since physical delivery which is normally required is lacking here. It might be argued that there were two specific grounds on which transfer here could be based, namely, *constitutum possessorium* ([23]) and the unity of the *grex*.

So far as *constitutum possessorium* is concerned, three arguments can be adduced for holding that it was not effective in this field. First, there is no evidence whatever that *constitutum possessorium* (accepting, as we must, its existence in classical law) ([24]) ever did more before the post-classical period than transfer possession. All the relevant texts in the Digest refer to possession alone ([25]), although constitutions in the

---

([19]) Cicero *Topica* 8. 37.

([20]) The text is not perfect, but despite Beseler, 45 ZSS (1925) p. 210, it does show pendency of status. Cf. works cited in *Index Itp.* and Amirante *op. cit.* p. 56 and n. 7.

([21]) D. 7. 1. 25. 1 and D. 7. 1. 12. 5 (Ulpian - refers to Julian); 21. 1. 43. 10. (Paul); 41. 1 43. 2 (Gaius); 45. 3. 18. 3 (Papinian, but Julian is cited in the text on another point).

([22]) Cf. Grosso *op. cit.* pp. 232-233.

([23]) The argument would be that the usufructuary by *summissio* transferred ownership of the *fetus* but retained them under his control by virtue of his usufruct. The idea that transfer of ownership here was by *constitutum possessorium* goes back as far as Donellus *Commentarii de iure civili* X. 13. § 25; *cf.* Glück *Pandekten* I. 41-42 (1887) pp. 443-445.

([24]) Cf. Buckland 'Le Constitut possessoire, *animus et corpus*' 4 RHD (1925) pp. 355 *et seq.*; Voci *Modi di Acquisto della Proprietà* Milan 1952 pp. 118-121.

([25]) D. 41. 2. 18 pr.; h. t. 19 pr.; h. t. 21. 3; D. 6. 1. 77; cf. D. 43. 26. 6. 3; h. t. 22 pr.

Codex Theodosianus ([26]) and Codex Iustinianus ([27]) dating from the 5th and 6th centuries A. D. show that by that time ownership too was transferred. It has to be admitted, however, that the Digest texts are concerned with *res mancipi* (or in the case of D. 6. 1. 77 with *fundus provincialis* ([28]) which could not be owned) so that ownership would not be transferred by *constitutum possessorium* even if ownership of *res nec mancipi* would be so transferred ([29]). Nevertheless, it is significant that we have no text from the classical period which says that *constitutum possessorium* transferred ownership since such a transfer would surely have been helpful in a number of situations. Moreover, if such classical texts had existed, one would have expected some trace of them to survve since they would give Justinian's own law. The main reason for holding that *constitutum possessorium* transferred ownership is that it is regarded as the converse of *traditio brevi manu* ([30]) which certainly did. But this is unjustified, since there are a number of important differences. To begin with, *traditio brevi manu* is a much easier case. There the object is in fact under the control of the acquirer, not, as in the *case of constitutum possessorium,* still in the hands of the transferor. Then *traditio brevi manu* is primarily concerned with *res nec mancipi* ([31]), *constitutum possessorium* primarily with *res mancipi.* And most important of all, *traditio brevi manu* is mainly concerned with the transfer of ownership, *constitutum possessorium* with the transfer of possession. No such relationship between *traditio brevi manu* and *constitutum possessorium* is hinted at in the texts.

Secondly, even if *constitutum possessorium* did transfer ownership of *res nec mancipi,* it certainly did not in the case of *res mancipi* ([32]), so that it could not operate on *summissio* to transfer the *fetus* where the *grex* consisted of cattle, mules or horses ([33]). This would create great difficulties on what is regarded as the view of Sabinus and Cassius and would mean that the value of *summissio* varied according to the nature of the flock. And if it be objected that it was doubted whether

---

([26]) C. Th. 8. 12. 8 (415 A. D.); 8. 12. 9 (417 A. D.) = C. 8. 53. 28. Perhaps the change which is being alleged sprang from the general slackness regarding the difference between ownership and possession in post-classical times. Cf. Levy *West Roman Vulgar Law; The Law of Property* Philadelphia 1951, *passim,* but especially pp. 19-34.

([27]) C. 8. 53. 35. 5 (530 A. D.).

([28]) Voci *op. cit.* p. 120 explains this by saying that the natural ambit of *constitutum possessorium* was immovebles. But there is little reason for this on the assumption that it tansferred ownership: cf. C. 8. 53. 35. It is perhaps an odd point for Voci to make since elsewhere (p. 118) he stresses the connexion with *traditio brevi manu,* whose natural ambit was very much *res mobiles.*

([29]) Lenel *Palingenesia* 2 515 and n. 5.

([30]) E. g. Buckland *Textbook* p. 227; Voci *op. cit.* p. 118.

([31]) The main texts are D. 41. 1. 9. 5; 6. 2. 9. 1, 2; 15. 1. 8; 21. 2. 62 pr.

([32]) Cf. Voci *op. cit.* p. 120.

([33]) For *ususfructus gregis* of such animals, see D. 7. 68. 2; and h. t. 70. 3.

such animals were *res mancipi* from birth or only from the time they were broken in, it should be remembered that it was precisely the Sabinians who took the former view ([34]). If the first argument against the concept of *constitutum possessorium* being used in this filed is incorrect, it could be maintained that it was because *summissio* did not transfer ownership of young cattle, mules and horses that the doctrine of *pendens* was introduced in this connexion.

Thirdly it is difficult to see how *summissio* could in any event be interpreted as a form of *constitutum possessorium*. To begin with, the *summissio* is not normally made as a result of a contract. And again, any agreement in *usufructus gregis* as to *summissio* is in respect of *res futurae* which are not even specified by number.

The other ground on which it might be argued that *summissio* was effective to transfer ownership automatically is that a *grex* was regarded as a unit, a *corpus ex distantibus* ([35]) and that *summissio* by having the *fetus* marked with the distinguishing features of the particular *grex*, enabled them to be recovered along with the other animals in the flock or herd by the *vindicatio gregis* at the end of the usufruct, so that they were indeed owned by the *dominus gregis*.

But there are a number of objections to this argument.

To begin with, the idea of a flock as a *corpus ex distantibus* has limited legal significance and applies in only a few situations. First, where ownership of a *grex* is alleged, the plaintiff need not allege ownership of each individual animal, but can bring a *vindicatio* of the flock or herd ([36]). The reason for this rule is clearly cônvenience. And again, if a testator leaves a legacy of a *grex*, the legatee receives any additions made to the *grex* after the will ([37]). This, obviously, is in order to carry out the wishes of the testator. But, in other situations, *e. g. usucapio*, the important unit is the individual, not the *grex*. Usucapion of the particular animal must be shown, and it is not enough that it is part of the *grex* owned by the plaintiff ([38]). Branding or other means of marking the animal as part of the flock would not, *ipso facto*, transfer ownership. So, in our case, if the *fetus* of which *summissio* had been made were separated from the *grex*, whether sold by the usufructuary or retained by him, since a *vindicatio gregis* would be inappropriate the fact that the *fetus* had been treated as part of the flock would not, of itself, give the *dominus gregis* right to a *vindicatio*. And in practice, where there was a dispute between the *dominus* and the usufructuary or his heir this would normally be the situation. Where

---

([34]) G. 2.15.

([35]) D. 6.1.23.5; 41.3.30; J. 2.20.18. Cf. Bonfante *Corso di Diritto Romano* 2. *La Proprietà* sezione 1. pp. 108-130.

([36]) G. 4.17; D. 6.1.1.3; h. t. 2; h. t. 3 pr.; h. t. 23.5; h. t. 56; 44.2.21.1.

([37]) D. 22.1.39; 30.21; J. 2.20.18. Also. where a *grex* is given as a *pignus*, offspring become part of the pledge, D. 20.1.13 pr.

([38]) D. 41.3.30.2; cf. D. 6.1.2; h. t. 23.5.

the usufructuary had made *summissio* and his heir failed to return the *grex* and was sued by a *vindicatio*, he was scarcely likely to bring into issue the question of transfer of ownership of *fetus summissi* which, at the least, he was under a duty to deliver.

Secondly. if the *fetus summissi* could be recovered by the *vindicatio gregis* this would be the result of a technical rule of procedure. At the most, ownership would be transferred at the time of vindication, not of *summissio*.

Thirdly, the *vindicatio gregis* where successful does not give the plaintiff ownership of animals included in the flock but which belonged to another. It is also possible that by the *vindicatio* he did not even obtain control of these animals which did not belong to him. There are two texts. D. 6. 1. 1. 3 (Ulpian 16 *ad ed.*)... *Sed enim gregem sufficiet ipsum nostrum esse, licet singula capita nostra non sint*: *grex enim, non singula corpora vindicabuntur*. This is ambiguous. It could mean that the plaintiff recovers all the animals since the *vindicatio* covers the *grex* generally without reference to the particular animals. On the other hand, it could also mean that the *vindicatio gregis* would still be available even though not all of the animals were the plaintiff's, but those which were not his would not be recovered. Thus one would translate 'For the flock, not the individual animals (i. e. belonging to another - understood from the context) will be vindicated'. This interpretation however, will not be insisted upon. More important is D. 6. 1. 23. 5 (Paul 2 *ad ed.*)... *Ideoque posse me gregem vindicare, quamvis aries tuus sit immixtus, sed et te arietem vindicare posse...* ([39]). This, too, is ambiguous. It could either mean something similar to the second alternative suggested above, *i. e.* the *aries* was not recovered by the *vindicatio*, or that although it was, it could be vindicated from the *dominus gregis* by the true owner. In either eventuality, the *vindicatio gregis* did not give the *dominus* ownership of an animal which belonged to another.

From the above it appears that although a *grex* was treated in some ways as a unit, incorporation of an animal into the *grex* did not, of itself, give ownership of the animal to the *dominus gregis*. Hence, *summissio* could not operate on this account to transfer ownership automatically.

A variation on this second ground could also be propounded. A *grex*, it could be argued, is a unit. Therefore, when the *usufructuarius* adds the *fetus* to the *grex* by *summissio* they become part of the unit and are incorporated into it by *accessio*. But this is impossible. Apart from anything else, on this basis there would be no distinction between animals added by *summissio* and those added by other means by any third party without the knowledge of the *dominus gregis*.

([39]) This part is not affected by the interpolations which are suspected in the text. Cf. *Index Itp.*

It might also be argued that *summissio* transferred ownership in its own right just as in some cases *fructuum separatio* did. But against that it must be remenbered that, unlike *fructuum separatio*, this would be a transfer of ownership *inter vivos* of things which had previously a completely independent existence. In *fructuum separatio* before separation the fruits did not exist as separate entities. And, further, on this view, *summissio* to be satisfactory would have to transfer ownership of *res mancipi* without delivery, not to say without *mancipatio*. It would thus be much more extreme than *constitutum possessorium*.

Perhaps at this stage it would be as well to summarise what little certainty there is.

1. Pendency which was accepted in this connexion at least by Julian and later jurists gives less satisfactory results in practice than what is said to have been the earlier view of Sabinus and Cassius.

2. D. 7. 1. 68. 1 from which is deduced the view of Sabinus and Cassius is irrelevant.

3. The only text which is earlier than Julian's book 35 *Digestorum* is D. 7. 1. 69 which is ambiguous and may be giving the same view which is expressed by Julian.

4. Automatic transference of ownership from the usufructuary to the *dominus gregis* could not be effected by *constitutum possessorium* or as a result of the concept of the unity of the flock. If *summissio* effected such automatic transference in its own right, it would be the most extreme example of *inter vivos* transfer witout delivery known to classical law.

Therefore, since there is no textual authority for automatic transfer of ownership from the usufructuary to the *dominus gregis* ([40]), since it is extremely difficult to see how this could be effected (especially in the case of *res mancipi*), and since the view which was accepted at least from the time of Julian would work much less well in practice and would be a retrograde step, we must hold that before Julian *summissio* did not transfer ownership from the usufructuary to the *dominus gregis*.

I suggest that there are two possibilities. First, that the pre-Julian position was vague, shadowy and uncertain. There would be few disputes on the question which could to a great extent be ignored by the jurists. Nonetheless, the concept of pendency, here as well as elsewhere,

---

([40]) D. 7.1.70. 4 is no evidence for automatic transference when ownership had vested in the usufructuary. The text is ambiguous and the most natural interpretation is that once ownership has vested in the usufructuary he cannot transfer ownership by *summissio*, but losses in the flock must be made up from future births, or by pecuniary payaments (or *traditio* of the *fetus* born earlier) at the end of the usufruct. If he had been able to transfer ownership by *summissio*, one would have expected in view of the direct phrasing of the question, to be told that although he were owner of the *fetus* he could make up for future losses by *summissio* of those already born.

was in the air, and that is what Pomponius was expressing in his text. Julian's great merit on this understanding is not to have invented the concept, but to have clarified and developed it. It may be that he did not, in general, substitute pendency for some earlier standard doctrine. This may be why although texts on pendency usually go back to Julian we do not normally find later jurists saying 'X and Y maintain this, but Julian rightly says... '. There was in fact no earlier conflicting doctrine — the law was simply left very cloudy.

Secondly, and this I think preferable, if one feels that pendency must have replaced some earlier conflicting doctrine, the position may have been that before this time *fetus* in a *usufructus gregis* went at birth to the usufructuary who was under a duty to make *summissio* of some of them to make up for losses in the flock. *Summissio,* however could not and did not make the *fetus* the property of the *dominus gregis.* It was simply a practical way of keeping up the strength of the flock, and of showing that it was so kept up. Ownership was transferred at the end of the usufruct when the *grex* was returned to the owner. During the continuance of the usufruct ownership of the *fetus summissi* remained with the usufructuary who thus had the *vindicatio* and the *condictio furtiva.* The *domnus gregis* was protected only by the *cautio usufructuaria* and the praetorian action. These would not always be sufficient safeguards. For instance, if the usufructuary went bankrupt, the *fetus summissi* (being his property) could be seized by his creditors. Again in the case of a long usufruct, it would sometimes happen that all of the animals which originally formed the *grex* died or were slaughtered. If the *fetus* all belonged to the usufructuary, the usufruct would either end then, before the time fixed, or only continue as the result of the fictional notion of the *grex* as a unit separate from the sum of the animals forming it. Hence the introduction of pendency was a valuable innovation, even although it was not completely satisfactory in all cases. The innovation may have been due to Julian and his view be known to Pomponius even before he wrote his 35 *digestorum.* Alternatively, perhaps someone writing slightly earlier — maybe Pomponius himself — should be given credit for introducing pendency here, but the idea was taken up and made fully acceptable by Julian ([41]). It is unlikely that Ulpian would know that Pomponius 5 *ad Sabinum* was written before Julian 35 *digestorum* and he could well attribute the new doctrine to the latter who had written a lot about pendency in various situations.

([41]) Julian's teacher Javolenus in other situations shows considerable interest and skill in pendency: D. 5.1.35; 23.3.80; 24.1.20; 45.1.106; 12.1.36: only the last seems to have been held interpolated in this respect; cf. *Index Itp.*

11

Cicero, ad Fam. 7.5.3

About April, 54 B. C., Cicero wrote to Caesar in Gaul recommending to him his friend, the jurist C. Trebatius Testa. The letter ends:

> *Hunc, mi Caesar, sic velim omni tua comitate complectare ut omnia quae per me possis adduci ut in meos conferre velis in unum hunc conferas. De quo tibi homine haec spondeo non illo vetere verbo meo, quod cum ad te de Milone scripsissem, iure lusisti, sed more Romano quo modo homines non inepti loquuntur, probiorem hominem, meliorem virum, pudentiorem esse neminem. Accedit etiam, quod familiam ducit in iure civili, singulari memoria, summa scientia. Huic ego neque tribunatum neque praefecturam neque ullius benefici certum nomen peto, benevolentiam tuam et liberalitatem peto, neque impedio quo minus, si tibi ita placuerit, etiam hisce eum ornes gloriolae insignibus: totum denique hominen tibi ita trado, de manu, ut aiunt, in manum tuam istam et victoria et fide praestantem. Simus enim putidiusculi quamquam*[1] *per te vix licet, verum, ut video, licebit. Cura ut valeas et me, ut amas, ama.*

I should like to suggest that *totum denique hominem tibi ita trado, de manu, ut aiunt, in manum tuam istam et victoria et fide praestantem* may be a complex legal joke.

De manu, ut aiunt, in manum tuam presents a number of curious features. First, *ut aiunt* gives a sort of mock solemnity to the clause. Secondly, the same words should imply that *de manu in manum* was a common phrase – a cliché perhaps, or a catch phrase, or a standardized expression such as one might find in a legal situation. But although Plautus, Tri. 902, has *E manibus dedit mi ipse in manus,* there is no real indication that it was a common expression,[2] whether a cliché or a catch phrase, and there is no sign of such a clause appearing as a standard form in any branch of law. Thirdly, *ut aiunt* inevitably brings to mind Cicero's earlier *De quo tibi homine haec spondeo non illo vetere verbo meo, quod cum ad te de Milone scripsissem, iure lusisti.* Caesar had teased Cicero for using a cliché or standard phrase (*illo vetere verbo*) when recommending Milo. Cicero is now falling again into that fault, or at least is claiming that he is, deliberately and with humorous intent, telling Caesar that *de manu in manum* is a cliché or standardized expression. Fourthly, the humorous aspect of this

[1] The commonly accepted emendation of the editions for the *quam* of the mss.

[2] Cf. Tyrrell and Purser, The Correspondence of Cicero, II, 2nd edit. (Dublin, 1906), p. 132.

part of the sentence consorts ill with what is normally taken as the straight and extravagant flattery of *et victoria et fide praestantem.*[1]

It would not be too fanciful, I think, to see in *de manu in manum* a humorous reference to *mancipatio*, the formal mode of transfer of certain kinds of important property including slaves,[2] where the transferee had to take in his hand the object to be transferred.[3] The Romans, indeed, derived the term *mancipatio* from 'taking by the hand'.[4] The mock solemnity which has already been noted would then have a particular point. Again, although a clause *de manu in manum* does not appear in the *mancipatio* ceremony, *ut aiunt* would now have the function of calling Caesar's attention to the fact that Cicero is using *de manu in manum* not just casually but deliberately and whith a particular intent. He wants to emphasise that there is more here than the surface meaning. And a legal joke would be especially appropriate since Trebatius was – and is so described by Cicero–a leading jurist: *familiam ducit in iure civili, singulari memoria, summa scientia.* If it can be accepted that there is here a joking reference to *mancipatio*, then *et victoria et fide praestantem* –"(a hand) as distinguished for its victories as for its loyality"– may be continuing the joke with two punning references. The flattery would still be there, but overlaid with humour to make it less noisome and more in keeping with the rest of the passage.

The first pun could be contained in the word *victoria* which would be used to mean not only 'victory' but also a small copper coin (on which the goddess Victoria appeared). It was an essential part of the *mancipatio* ceremony that the transferee struck a pair of scales held by a citizen termed a *libripens* with a piece of *aes*.[5] Normally a small coin would be used. One might think of Plautus, Truc. 274f. The slave, Truculentus, asks the slave-girl, Astaphium:

mancupion qui accipias, gestas tecum ahenos anulos?
pignus da ni ligneae haec sint quas habes Victorias.

Astaphium has finger rings or earrings of bronze or copper (*ahenos anulos*) and Truculentus asks if she wears them so as to be able to claim things by *mancipatio*. The rings are made out of coins which bear the figure of the goddess Victoria and Plautus calls the coins simply '*Victoriae*'. The point in his joking wager that the coins are made of wood is both that the coins are forgeries and of no value and that, since they are not of *aes*, they cannot be used for *mancipatio*. It is, of course, only reasonable to suggest that Cicero could be making a pun in his letter if there was a strong likelihood of Caesar seeing the point, and I submit that there was such a likelihood. There were several issues of

[1] Cf. Tyrrell and Purser, loc. cit.; Williams, Cicero, Letters to his Friends, II (Loeb Classical Library, London, New York, 1928), p. 26; Constans, Cicéron, Correspondance, III (Paris, 1936), p. 59. The last writes: «Cf. le même éloge de César développé, neuf ans plus tard, dans le Pro Deiotoro, 3, 8: *istam, inquam, dexteram non in bellis neque in proeliis quam in promissis et fide firmiorem.*» Of course, the circumstances of that speech demand a more serious treatment than Cicero accords his request in the present letter.

[2] Presumably this is what Williams is referring to in his comment; "A legal phrase, equivalent to the more usual *per manus.*": op. cit., p. 25.

[3] Gaius, Inst. 1. 121.

[4] Varro, de ling. lat. 6. 85; Gaius, Inst. 1. 121.

[5] Gaius, Inst. 1. 119.

copper coins bearing the goddess Victoria between 90 and 86 B. C.[1] New issues of copper coins were rare after 84 B. C., and after 81 B. C. until Cicero's letter there was none at all in the Roman world except for one from Sicily[2] and one from Agrigentum.[3] Thus, a large proportion of the copper coins in circulation in 54 B. C. would portray Victoria.[4] Moreover, Cicero's pun might even have been suggested by the Plautus' passage and for that very reason he might have expected Caesar to notice it. Plautus' plays were widely read at this time.

The other pun would lie in the word *fide*. Cicero would be referring not only to Caesar's good faith in general but also recalling a clause which apparently contained the word *fides* and formed part of a *mancipatio* performed *fiduciae causa*.[5] In this kind of *mancipatio*, the ownership of the thing was transferred with the understanding that the transferee would eventually reconvey the thing to the transferor. It was used either as a form of real security when, of course, it put the creditor into a very strong position, or where it was felt for some reason, usually political, that the thing would be safer if it were owned by a friend for the time being.[6] In the *mancipatio fiduciae causa* it seems that the transferee claimed that the thing was transferred to him and to his *fides et fiducia*.[7] The institution was common enough for it to be jokingly referred to by Plautus.[8] Tri. 117 is perhaps especially significant. A free-born youth was entrusted by his father to the case of a friend, and of the youth it is said *mandatus est fide et fiduciae*. There is the same kind of pun here[9] as is being suggested for the Cicero passage. One free person entrusted to another is spoken of as if he were a slave or other thing mancipated *fiduciae causa*.

Simus enim putidiusculi quamquam per te vix licet, verum, ut video, licebit is capable of more than one interpretation. It may be that Cicero is excusing himself for his request that Caesar should become Trebatius' protector, but it may equally be that it refers only to the preceding sentence from *totum*.[10] If the latter, and the relevant part of the preceding sentence is to be understood as I have suggested, then the present sentence will mean something like: "Excuse this affectation of mine although it is scarcely permissible in addressing you [i. e., who have already taken me to task for my *vetus verbum* when I wrote to you on behalf of Milo] yet, as I see, you will permit it." *Putidiusculus* means 'rather tiresome', 'slightly silly' or 'rather affected'.

1 See Sydenham, The Coinage of the Roman Republic, revised by Haines, edited by Forrer and Hersh (London, 1952), issues nos. 677 (90–89 B. C., rev.); 682 (90–89 B. C., rev.); 690g (89–88 B. C., obv.); 701a (88 B. C., rev.); 715 (86 B. C., rev.); 715a (86 B. C., rev.); 716 (86 B. C., rev.).

2 Sydenham, op. cit., no. 923.

3 Sydenham, op. cit., no. 924.

4 Some of the issues with Victoria seem to have been large: Sydenham, op. cit., issues nos. 677; 701a; 715; 715a; 716.

5 Cf. Watson, The Law of Obligations in the Later Roman Republic (Oxford, 1965), pp. 172ff.

6 Cf. Boethius, ad top. Ciceronis, 10.

7 Cf. Watson, loc. cit.

8 Most clearly in Epid. 697–9: cf. Watson, op. cit., p. 172.

9 Cf. Watson, op. cit., p. 174.

10 For both interpretations see Tyrrell and Purser, loc. cit.

12

Towards a New Hypothesis of the Legis Action Sacramento in Rem

According to Gaius (1), the form of the *legis actio sacramento in rem* was as follows :

A. *Hunc ego hominem ex iure quiritium meum esse aio secundum suam causam. Sicut dixi, ecce tibi vindictam imposui.* (As he said this he *festucam imponebat*).

B. (*Eadem dicebat et faciebat*).
Praetor. *Mittite ambo hominem.*

A. *Postulo anne dicas qua ex causa vindicaveris.*

B. *Ius feci, sicut vindictam imposui.*

A. *Quando tu iniuria vindicavisti, quingenario* (or *quinquagenario*) *sacramento te provoco.*

B. *Et ego te.*

A & B to the witnesses. *Testes estote.*

It is, I think, universally accepted first that both parties to the action were put on a level, that the right and title of both of them was in issue and that it was not enough for the defendant to base his case on the weakness of the plaintiff's claim (2), and secondly

(1) G. 4. 16.

(2) Cf. e.g., Bethmann-Hollweg, *Der römische Zivilprozess* 1 (Bonn, 1864), p. 132; Lévy-Bruhl, *Recherches sur les actions de la loi* (Paris, 1960), pp. 37 ff.; Kaser, *Das römische Zivilprozessrecht* (Munich, 1966), p. 71. Lévy-Bruhl says (p. 49) very significantly for this article : " Il est, en effet, tout à fait singulier — et inattendu — de voir les deux plaideurs placés exactement sur le même rang dans un procès en revendication. La situation est radicalement différente pour chacun d'eux puisque Secundus possède la chose, alors que Primus, qui la réclame, ne la possède pas. Or, de cette possession, qui est cependant d'une importance capitale, il n'est

that in the schema as set out above, A represents the plaintiff, i.e., the one who did not have control of the slave (or other thing claimed) before the start of the *actio,* B the defendant (3). I should like to suggest that a different hypothesis for the *legis actio,* in which both these opinions are false, is possible and more satisfactory.

When one looks at the form of words one sees that, if both parties are regarded as being on a level, there is a surprising lack of symmetry in at least one respect. This is that only one of the parties is asked to explain why he has made his claim. Rather, one might have expected :

A. *Postulo anne dicas qua ex causa vindicaveris.*

B. *Ius feci, sicut vindictam imposui. Postulo anne dicas qua ex causa vindicaveris.*

A. *Ius feci, sicut vindictam imposui. Quando tu iniuria vindicavisti &c.*

If we accept the standard view, this lop-sidedness is all the more remarkable because the only person asked to explain why he made his claim is B, that is, the defendant. One would not expect that in an action disputing ownership the one person who is asked to justify his claim — on whom ostensibly the onus is being placed — is the defendant, the person who (usually, at least) had had physical control of the disputed slave (or other thing) (4). This part of the form would make much more sense if A were the defendant, B the plaintiff. In the circumstances it

absolument pas fait état dans la marche du procès. Tout se passe comme si les deux parties se disputaient la propriété d'une *res nullius*. Il n'y a, à proprement parler, ni demandeur ni défendeur ».

(3) Cf. e.g., BETHMANN-HOLLWEG, *op. cit.*, p. 130; WENGER, *Institutionen des römischen Zivilprozessrechts* (Munich, 1925), p. 121 n. 16; LÉVY-BRUHL, *op. cit.*, p. 37; KASER, *op. cit.*, p. 69; PUGLIESE, *Il processo civile romano I, le legis actiones* (Rome, 1962), pp. 39 and 276. Pugliese thinks that the plantiff carried or led *in ius* the thing claimed : " l'attore portava o conduceva *in ius* la cosa di cui si trattava " (p. 39) ; " L'attore, che aveva prima portato o condotto *in ius* la cosa " (p. 276).

(4) It is appropriate to recall the sentences of LÉVY-BRUHL quoted, *supra*, p. 2 n. 2.

would be instructive to examine the *legis actio* on the hypothesis that A is the defendant, B the plaintiff. It is not hostile to this hypothesis that Gaius uses the words *qui vindicabat* of A ([5]) because he uses that verb of the conduct of both parties ([6]).

***

A. *Hunc ego hominem ex iure quiritium meum esse aio secundum suam causam. Sicut dixi, ecce tibi vindictam imposui.* (As he says this he *festucam imponebat*).

Proceedings begin by the person who had physical control of the slave, the defendant, maintaining that he is the owner. Though this is an unusual start to litigation it is convenient here. The defendant has been made to come before the praetor, the plaintiff's claim will certainly be forthcoming, and it is reasonable to begin by having the defendant's ownership expressly maintained against the forthcoming challenge to it. More important, this declaration helps to set the scene in that the defendant shows his position of power by placing his *festuca* on the slave and keeping it there ([7]). The purpose of the opening declaration and this behaviour is to show the 'Machtlage'. In a formalized process for ownership in which both parties make identical declarations or claims — in itself a very unusual procedure — it would not be surprising if the first assertion is that of the defendant declaratory of the apparent state of affairs, the second the plaintiff's challenge to it. It would be much more surprising if the form were that the plaintiff made a formal claim that the slave was his, and the sole response of the defendant was weakly to declare in the same words that the slave was his.

B. (*Eadem dicebat et faciebat*).

The plaintiff makes his claim and challenges the defendant's title by placing the *festuca* on the slave.

(5) G. 4. 16.
(6) G. 4. 16.
(7) Argued from the praetor's *mittite ambo hominem*. This is not conclusive since the words may be used in a symbolic, not factual, way.

Praetor. *Mittite ambo hominem.*

A. *Postulo anne dicas qua ex causa vindicaveris.*

The defendant demands that the plaintiff explain why he has made his claim.

B. *Ius feci, sicut vindictam imposui.*

The plaintiff declares that he has acted properly (8).

A. *Quando tu iniuria vindicavisti, quingenario* (or *quinquagenario*) *sacramento te provoco.*

The defendant challenges the plaintiff in a *sacramentum* of 50 or 500 *asses* because he claimed without right. It may be raised as an objection to the present hypothesis that, since the *sacramenta* are essential for the furtherance of the process, it should not be the defendant but the plaintiff (who wants the case to go on) who takes the initiative in issuing the challenge. But once the dispute has come before the magistrate, it is as much in the interest of the defendant as of the plaintiff that either the case proceeds to the *apud iudicem* stage or that the adversary withdraws (9). The sum involved in the *sacramenta* was large — 50 *asses* for cases of less than 1,000 *asses*, 500 *asses* for cases of more than 1,000 *asses* — and the *sacramenta* must often have had a dampening effect on litigation (10). It is quite natural, therefore, for the first challenge to be issued by the defendant, the person who had had control of the thing, since, inter alia, it would act as a deterrent to a rash claimant. One must remember here the number of provisions which existed even in classical law with the purpose of discouraging unnecessary litigation, some of which operated against a vexatious defendant, others against a vexatious plaintiff (11). It is also no objection to this hypothesis that in the very different procedure of *legis actio sacramento in*

(8) Further precision is not necessary here. For difficulties with this reply see, e.g., KASER, *op. cit.*, pp. 71 ff.

(9) For the *addictio* of the praetor in the *legis actiones* see now KASER, *op. cit.*, pp. 28 f. and the references he gives.

(10) Cf. e.g., KELLY, *Roman Litigation* (Oxford, 1966), pp. 81 ff.

(11) Cf. G. 4. 171-182.

personam the first challenge is issued by the plaintiff. The underlying social reality is more significant for a form than a supposed parallel with a different form would be. Since in both actions a challenge is issued by both parties the difference in form is not all that great.

B. *Et ego te.*

The plaintiff also challenges the defendant in a *sacramentum.* The interpretation of this part is of the greatest importance. This *sacramentum* may be a counter-*sacramentum* relating to the veracity of the plaintiff's own claim or one relating to the defendant's opening declaration or claim. The latter possibility seems to be universally accepted ([12]), but it is probably the less plausible. *Et ego te* seems too remote to be a challenge to the fundamental opening declaration of the defendant — B has not even declared that A had vindicated *iniuria* — and it is more appropriate as a formalised reply to the immediately preceding challenge. Moreover, if there are two separate challenges, each in respect of a different declaration, there is no express acceptance of either challenge. It is instructive to compare the challenge in this *actio in rem* with the challenge in the later *formula per sponsionem* ([13]). There the challenge comes from the plaintiff ; here, it is alleged, from the defendant. But both concern the same matter, namely, the accuracy of the plaintiff's claim. There the challenge is to pay a sum if the plaintiff's case is just ; here if the plaintiff's case is unjust.

It might be suggested that since there are two *vindicationes* and two *sacramenta,* each *sacramentum* should relate to the veracity of one of the *vindicationes.* But this is not, I think, a separate objection in its own right. If, as on the general view, both parties and hence both *vindicationes* are on a level, then each *sacramentum* should refer to a separate *vindicatio.* But if,

(12) Though of course, in the sense of the standard view this opening declaration which is being challenged is that of the plaintiff. If A is the plaintiff there is really no choice but to regard *et ego te* as a challenge to his opening declaration.

(13) Cf. G. 4. 93.

as I have been suggesting, the *vindicationes* are not on a level, but the first is the declaration of the apparent state of affairs and the second is the challenge to it, then it is perfectly reasonable that both *sacramenta* concern the veracity or otherwise of the challenge.

***

If it is plausible to maintain that A is the defendant and B the plaintiff and that *et ego te* is a counter-challenge relating to the truth of the plaintiff's claim, then the *legis actio* takes on a completely new aspect. The parties are no longer on an equal footing. It is the plaintiff alone who has to prove his claim. If he fails, the defendant retains the slave. In this respect there would be no difference between the *legis actio sacramento in rem* and the later formulary *vindicatio* (14).

Other points should be brought forward for consideration. And first a possible objection to the hypothesis should be looked at. According to Gaius' Institutes, 4, 16, after the procedure for the *legis actio* already outlined, the praetor declared *vindiciae* in favour of one of the parties (*secundum alterum eorum*), that is, he gave him interim possession and ordered sureties to be given to his opponent for the thing and its profits. In the formulary *vindicatio,* as we know from Gaius' Institutes, 4. 89, interim possession was given to the defendant — unless, of course, a *sequester* was appointed. Now it might be thought that the praetor's behaviour in the *legis actio* means that the parties are being put on a level and shows that neither can properly be regarded as plantiff or defendant, and hence that the title of both parties must be in issue. But such an argument would be of very doubtful weight. There is no way of telling the praetor's practice on this matter. It may have been that the practice was to award interim possession to the defendant except in cases where this seemed unsuitable. Indeed, any other procedure would be surprising.

(14) It will have been noticed that the hypothesis brought forward here is against the widely accepted concept of " relative ownership ". Further difficulties for that concept are discussed in Chapter 4 of the writer's forthcoming book, *The Law of Property in the Later Roman Republic.*

Thus, for instance, Kaser, himself (15), sees in the fact that the thing does not simply remain with the defendant evidence that he was suspected of theft. In this connection, an important difference between the defendant in the formulary *vindicatio* and the defendant in the *legis actio* in early law should be observed. The formulary *vindicatio* would frequently be preceded by a possessory interdict which would determine who ought to have possession and hence who was to be the defendant in the ensuing *vindicatio*. In that system, accordingly, it is natural that, unless a *sequester* be appointed, possession remains with the defendant during the action. But in early law there could be no interdict preceding the *legis actio* and, so far as we can tell from Gaius' account, there was no specific investigation in this connection by the praetor before he declared *vindiciae* in favour of one of the parties (16). In these circumstances it is reasonable, even though the defendant is in a more favourable position than the plaintiff in respect of the outcome of the *legis actio,* that the praetor may exercise discretion in awarding interim possession to either party.

The existence of *in iure cessio,* an institution based on and imitating the *legis actio sacramento in rem,* can provide no argument either for or against the present hypothesis. According to the main source for its form, G. 2. 24, the transferee, holding the object in the presence of the magistrate, says : *Hunc ego hominem ex iure quiritium meum esse aio*. The magistrate asks the transferor whether he makes a counter-claim, and he either replies in the negative or keeps silent. The magistrate then makes *addictio* to the person who had vindicated. On the traditional view, the person who is in fact the transferee is regarded as being in the position of a plaintiff, on my hypothesis he is to be thought of rather like a defendant. Nothing in the institution itself nor in G. 2. 24 should be thought of as favouring one view or the other. Technically, *in iure cessio* is not a conveyance and the person who is really the transferee is treated as if he always had been owner.

(15) *Op. cit.*, p. 73 n. 44. But LÉVY-BRUHL, most recently *op. cit.* pp. 178 ff., thinks that the praetor always gave interim possession to the party who had control at the beginning of the action.

(16) Cf. KASER, *loc. cit.*

It makes, if anything, slightly better sense if he is thought of as being in the position of a defendant whose title to ownership is first challenged, but the challenge is then dropped.

But considerable support for the present hypothesis is to be found in Cicero's account of *manum conserere* (17), the procedure adopted in a *legis actio sacramento in rem* where the object of the dispute was an immoveable or could not easily be moved.

> *pro Murena,* 12. 26. Cum hoc fieri bellissime posset : 'Fundus Sabinus meus est.' 'Immo meus', deinde iudicium, noluerunt. 'FUNDUS', inquit, 'QUI EST IN AGRO, QUI SABINUS VOCATUR.' Satis verbose ; cedo quid postea ? 'EUM EGO EX IURE QUIRITIUM MEUM ESSE AIO.' Quid tum ? 'INDE IBI EGO TE EX IURE MANUM CONSERTUM VOCO.' Quid huic tam loquaciter litigioso responderet ille, unde petebatur, non habebat. Transit idem iuris consultus tibicinis Latini modo. 'UNDE TU ME', inquit, 'EX IURE MANUM CONSERTUM VOCASTI, INDE IBI EGO TE REVOCO.' Praetor interea ne pulchrum se ac beatum putaret atque aliquid ipse sua sponte loqueretur, ei quoque carmen compositum est cum ceteris rebus absurdum, tum vero in illo : 'SUIS UTRISQUE SUPERSTITIBUS PRAESENTIBUS ISTAM VIAM DICO ; ITE VIAM.' Praesto aderat sapiens ille, qui inire viam doceret. 'REDITE VIAM.' Eodem duce redibant. Haec iam tum apud illos barbatos ridicula, credo, videbantur, homines, cum recte atque in loco constitissent, iuberi abire, ut, unde abissent, eodem statim redirent. Isdem ineptiis fucata sunt illa omnia : 'QUANDO TE IN IURE CONSPICIO' et haec [sed] : 'ANNE TU DICIS, QUA EX CAUSA VINDICAVERIS ?' Quae dum erant occulta, necessario ab eis, qui ea tenebant, petebantur ; postea vero pervulgata, atque in manibus iactata et excussa inanissima prudentiae reperta sunt, fraudis autem et stultitiae plenissima.

(17) For *manum conserere* see also Gellius, *N.A.*, 20. 10. 1-10 ; Verro, *de ling. lat.*, 6. 64 ; Festus, *s.v. conserere manu* ; Probus, 4. 4 ; cf., most recently, KASER, *op. cit.*, pp. 70 and 74 f., and the references he gives.

According to Cicero — if we can take him as being accurate — proceedings began by one party saying something like :

> *Eum fundum, qui est in agro, qui Sabinus vocatur, ego ex iure quiritium meum esse aio. Inde ibi ego te ex iure manum consertum voco.*

The other replied :

> *Unde tu me ex iure manum consertum vocasti, inde ibi ego te revoco.*

If Cicero is accurate, in this modified form of the *legis actio sacramento in rem* only one party expressly claims that the estate is his *ex iure quiritium.* The probability is that Cicero has not omitted the vindication of the other party since the point he is making — in a playful way — is the unnecessary and ridiculous verbosity and complexity of the law. It would not suit his purpose at all to miss out anything which would make the procedure seem even more formalized and comic. If only one party expressly vindicates, that party must be the plantiff ([18]). That the person who utters the words *Inde ibi ego te ex iure manum consertum voco* is the plaintiff is shown moreover by the words *unde petatur* used in respect of the other party. On my view, the defendant's initial assertion declaratory of the apparent state of affairs has been dropped. On the traditional view, the defendant's counterclaim to the plaintiff's vindication has been dropped. Though it should not be over-stressed, if the parties are treated as being on an equal footing, it would be surprising that the defendant does not here make a counter-vindication. The omission of the defendant's *ex iure quiritium meum esse aio* becomes more significant when it is considered in conjunction with a subsequent part of the procedure. Later one party says :

> *Quando te in iure conspicio (postulo ?)* ([19]) *anne tu dicas qua ex causa vindicaveris.*

On the traditional view this challenge must be uttered by the plaintiff ([20]), on my view by the defendant. If Cicero is accurate

(18) Cf. Kaser, *op. cit.*, p. 74.

(19) Cf. Kaser, *op. cit.*, p. 75.

(20) Cf. Kaser, *loc. cit.*

in his account of the earrlier part of the proceedings, one person alone expressly vindicated and that person can only have been the plaintiff. Hence the person who challenges the vindication must be the defendant. Moreover, whether or not Cicero is accurate in his account of the earlier part of the proceedings and even if there were two vindications, it would be only reasonable to think that the words *Quando te in iure conspicio &c* would be uttered by that party who summoned the other back *in ius* with the words ... *inde ibi ego te revoco,* that is, likewise, by the defendant.

If one feels that, contrary to his interest, Cicero has missed out from his account a formal claim *ex iure quiritium meum esse aio,* one must ask what position that claim would have had in the proceedings. It would be extremely implausible to suggest that it occurred between the vindication reported by Cicero and the *Inde ibi ego te ex iure manum consertum voco.* The tenor of Cicero's words indicates that nothing came between these sentences. Hence the most likely place for the other claim — if there was one at all, which is improbable — is before the claim which Cicero records. And if this is so, then this first claim can only be uttered by the defendant, since Cicero's words *unde petatur* show that the immediately preceding part of the ritual was uttered by the plaintiff.

***

It would be unwise not to stress the difficulties for the hypothesis which has been suggested. It has to be frankly admitted that explanations have had to be found for two unusual features, namely that the defendant speaks first, and also that he issues the first challenge to a *sacramentum* which is necessary for the furtherance of the action (and that in the *legis actio sacramento in personam* the first challenge comes from the plaintiff). But the obstacles here, I think, are less than those to the prevailing hypothesis according to which the defendant in reply to the plaintiff's claim to be owner merely makes an identical claim ; where it is the plantiff and the plantiff alone who demands that the defendant explain why he has claimed the thing ; and where, perhaps most surprising of all, in an action for ownership the legal claims of the plaintiff and defendant are treated as being on a level, despite the latter's physical control of the thing when proceedings begin. And the sole really helpful textual evidence, Cicero, *pro Murena,* 12. 26, is very much in favour of the hypothesis which is being proposed and is equally against the dominant view.

III

Succession

13

D.28.5.35.(44): an Unprincipled Decision on a Will

D.28.5.45 (44) (Alfenus *5 dig.*) is a text of quite exceptional interest:

> Pater familias testamento duos heredes instituerat: eos monumentum facere iusserat in diebus certis: deinde ita scripserat: 'qui eorum non ita fecerit, omnes exheredes sunto': alter heres hereditatem praetermiserat, reliquus heres consulebat, cum ipse monumentum exstruxisset, numquid minus heres esset ob eam rem, quod coheres eius hereditatem non adisset. respondit neminem ex alterius facto hereditati neque alligari neque exheredari posse, sed uti quisque condicionem implesset, quamvis nemo adisset praeterea, tamen eum heredem esse.

I

Any proper discussion of the text must begin with Pernice's brilliant exegesis (*1*). He pointed to what in his opinion were grave difficulties in the text as we have it: a *modus* was imposed by the testator on the heir but Servius (or Alfenus) treats it as a condition (2); again, he says, disinhersion of the *heres scriptus* in the same will was not permitted (3); and the express *exheredatio* of an *extraneus* is odd. The text, as Pernice observes, with its *adire* and *praetermittere hereditatem* makes it difficult to think of a *suus heres* (4). He suggests that the text would make best sense if the testator had imposed a *cretio*: this would explain the *certi dies*, the *praetermittere,* and the *exheredatio* which must ensue at the *cretio* (5). He proposes a wording for the institution something like this: *'Titius et Maevius heredes*

(*1*) *Labeo,* III.i (reprinted, Aalen, 1963), pp. 43f: followed by Lévy-Bruhl, "Etude sur la *cretio*' *NRHDF* xxxviii (1914) pp. 153ff at pp. 182. Buckland, '*Cretio* and connected topics' *Tijd.* iii (1922) pp. 239ff at pp. 263f; De Sarlo, *Alfeno Varo e i suoi Digesta* (*Milan,* 1940), pp. 13ff; cf. also Schindler, *Justinians Haltung zur Klassik* (Cologne, Graz, 1966), p. 174 n. 29.

(2) A *modus* has the same content as a condition but the validity of the provision to which it is attached is not dependent upon it.

(*3*) Pernice refers to D.28.2.13.1 and 28.4.1.4.: op. cit., p. 43 n. 4: but see *infra.*

(*4*) Buckland, op. cit. p. 264 and n. 5 thinks it not impossible that the heirs were *sui heredes.* It should be observed, though, that there is nothing at all in the text to suggest that they were. *Paterfamilias* is often used of a testator with no implication that the heirs are *sui*: cf. e.g., G.2.144 [In three of the four texts in Gaius' *Institutes* where the word *paterfamilias* occurs it is used simply to indicate a person who was *sui iuris* and does not suggest he had persons in his *potestas*—the other texts are: 3.83; 4.77 and 3.154a.]; D.30.6; 30.96pr. 32.102.1.

(*5*) Cf. e.g., G.2.165, 174.

sunto, cerniteque in diebus cc. proximis, in quibus monumentum mihi a vobis fieri iubeo; (*si*) *qui vestrum non ita creverit, omnes exheredes estote.*' This would explain, he says, why the talk is always of a condition, and why the emphasis in the decision is not on the duty imposed but on the *adire,* that is the *cretio.* The main reason for the interpolation of the text would be, of course, that *cretio* had disappeared by Justinian's time and references to it had to be excised. This reconstruction looks extremely attractive and prima facie is convincing but nonetheless it must be quite wrong.

To the problem put to the jurist, Servius (or Alfenus), we have the reply, *respondit neminem ex alterius facto hereditati neque alligari neque exheredari posse: sed uti quisque condicionem implesset, quamvis nemo adisset praeterea, tamen eum heredem esse.* Solazzi (6) has suggested an interpolation in this part of the text because a Republican jurist should have written *neque hereditati alligari neque exheredari posse,* and he considers that the possibility of a scribal error should be excluded. But the oddity in the text concerns the sense as much as the grammar and Solazzi does not complain how thse blame for this is to be placed on the compilers and not on the Republican jurist. The oddity in the text as it stands is the tautology of *hereditati exheredari* and the dative depending on *exheredari.* But the solecism does not seem all that great when one takes into account the separation of *hereditati* from *exheredari* by *neque alligari neque* and the fact that *hereditati* is mainly dependent upon *alligari.* Certainly the passage is not written in as exact a form as it should be, but there is not enough to justify holding that it was not so written by Alfenus. But then we have to ask ourselves why Servius (or Alfenus) bothered to say that no one can be bound to an inheritance by the behaviour of another, as well as giving the main decision—for the questioner—that no one can be disinherited by the behaviour of another. There must be some point to *neminem ex alterius facto hereditati . . . alligari . . . posse* and this cannot lie solely in a perverted attempt to have the main decision accepted (7). The *responsum,* after all, was apparently given to the *coheres,* not to a judge or fellow jurist. The only explanation is that Servius (or Alfenus) felt it desirable to observe that the *alter heres* who *hereditatem praetermiserat* did not become heir as a result of the behaviour of the *coheres.* But if formal *cretio* had been demanded from both by the testator in the will no one could ever have wondered whether the *alter heres* was bound to the *hereditas* if the *coheres* had alone made *cretio* (8). The position is different if the sole condition imposed upon the institution was that the two heirs should build a sepulchral monument. Only one single act was

(6) *IURA* iii (1952), p. 26.
(7) But see *infra.*
(8) And certainly it would be rather absurd for the jurist to say this to the heir who had made *cretio.*

involved—not two separate acts as would be the case for two *cretiones*—so one might wonder about the position of the *alter heres* if the *coheres* performed that act all alone. Thus, despite Pernice, the will could not have demanded *cretio* from the two *heredes scripti*. This brings us also to the first important conclusion from the text. The idea that the *alter heres* might actually be heir as the result of the monument being built could never have occurred—however slightly—to the jurist if something more than the performance of the condition imposed in the will was demanded for that result. Hence at that time, in order to become entitled to the *hereditas* there can have been no need for an actual *cretio*, and it must have been enough that one acted as if one were heir. Thus, as early as Servius (or Alfenus) *pro herede gestio* was recognised. There seems no other evidence for its existence before the Empire (9).

We are thus forced to reconsider Pernice's arguments for the alteration of the substance of the text. His reconstruction seems totally unnecessary. If *'Titius et Maevius heredes sunto, cernitique in diebus cc. proximis, in quibus monumentum mihi a vobis fieri iubeo; (si) qui vestrum non ita creverit, omnes exheredes estote'* would escape the difficulties listed by him then so would: *'Titius et Maevius heredes sunto, eosque in diebus cc. proximis monumentum mihi facere iubeo; (si) qui eorum non ita fecerit omnes exheredes sunto'*. If the former involves a *conditio* and not a *modus*, then so does the latter: if in the former there is no later *exheredatio* in the same will of the *heredes*, then neither is there in the latter (*10*). And this is surely the right approach (*11*). That we are told that the *alter heres hereditatem praetermiserat* and *hereditatem non adisset* should not be taken

(9) Cf. Buckland, *A Textbook of Roman Law*, 3rd edition by Stein (Cambridge, 1963), p. 313: "In the Empire *cretio* was not necessary unless expressly required by the will, but it probably was in the time of Cicero." In support he observes (n. 3) that "Cicero never mentions *pro herede gestio*." Cf. also his '*Cretio* and connected topics' *Tijd*. cit., pp. 249f.

(*10*) Though I do not wish to lay too much stress on this, the texts cited by Pernice (see *supra*) in this connexion for the proposition that an *heres scriptus* could not be disinherited in the same will do not seem to bear the weight which he has to put upon them. Neither has anything to do with disinheritance upon condition. They do show that, if in the same will, you have a clause which purports to deprive him of the inheritance, the second clause will be rejected. This may simply be a rule for solving contradictions, and be due to *favor testamenti*. It is noticeable that it is applied less rigorously if there is a substitute who takes if the institution fails.

(*11*) Cf. e.g. G. 2.174: *Interdum duos pluresve gradus heredum facimus, hoc modo: L. Titius heres esto cernitoque in diebus centum proximis quibus scies poterisque. Quodni ita creveris. exheres esto. Tum mevius heres esto cernitoque in diebus centum et reliqua, et deinceps in quantum velimus substituere possumus*: cf. G.2.165. That the condition and the *exheredatio* attached to the institution occur in the sentence immediately following the institution is obviously not considered objectionable. Basically I can see no difference between this formulation and that in D.28.5.45(44) and do not understand why some writers [e.g., Fein-Glück, *Commentario alle Pandette, libro* xxix, *parte secunda* (Milan, 1909), p. 75 and n. 98] regard our text as the only one which allows legal effect to the disinhersion of the heir in the same will: cf. Buckland, *Tijd.*, cit., p.264 n.5.

where the heirs are *extranei* if it is attached to a failure of the condition to imply that the duty of making *cretio* was imposed: the phrases are perfectly consistent with the idea that he simply took no steps to have himself established in the *hereditas*. And the express clause of *exheredatio* if the condition is not fulfilled is wholly reasonable even on the *institutio* (*12, 13*).

It is quite natural for the stress in the text as we have it to be that the *alter heres* did not want the *hereditas* rather than that he did not fulfil the condition. The heir who did perform would put his question to the jurist in the way he did to express his indignation and disgust that he might forfeit his inheritance because the *alter heres* did not want to be heir. It is more forceful to say "Surely I am not less the heir because the other heir passed over the inheritance?" than to have "Surely I am not less the heir because the other heir did not help to fulfil the condition?" The stress once established in the question would remain in the decision. Again, to say he passed over the inheritance implies in fact that he did not fulfil the condition, and it is at the same time much more indicative of the frame of mind of this *alter heres*. It even simplifies the discussion since one can ignore the possible situation that the *alter heres* did not get round to fulfilling the condition and yet does not want to forfeit the inheritance: what would the situation be in such a case, especially if he were prepared to contribute to the cost of the monument?

The main interest of the text, though, lies in the decision which is completely unexpected. How could the jurist decide that the *heres scriptus* who built the monument was entitled to the *hereditas* when the will expressly stated that if any one did not build both were to be disinherited? But first the kind of provision in the will must be distinguished from two other kinds of provision with which it is sometimes linked. To begin with, it is not the same (*14*) as a condition which requires for its fulfilment the co-operation of a third party who refuses: for instance, "if you adopt Titius", and Titius refuses to be

(*12*) Buckland, who was concerned with the *exheredatio* clause attached to the requirement for *cretio* in wills says: "The application of the notion of *exheredatio* (*exheres esto*) to one who is not a *suus heres*, indeed is not a *heres* at all, but only a potential *heres*, looks anomalous. It has been explained in many ways. In the absence of evidence nothing more than conjecture is possible. The most probable view seems to be that it is part of the illogical juggling by which a true testamentary *heres* was constructed under the *mancipatio familiae*. As we know, the logic of the early lawyers was more ingenious than convincing": *Tijd.* cit. p. 252.

(*13*) Pernice's reconstruction would also to some extent have involved us in a possible difficulty which is now avoided. There could be no *aditio* while a condition was outstanding: cf. Buckland, *Textbook* cit. pp. 298f, and see the texts he cites, p. 299 n. 1. How then could one heir alone make *cretio* if the will expressly declared that neither could be heir unless both were? Any difficulty disappears if the need for *cretio* did not exist. There could be *pro herede gestio* by one who later asks if the condition had been satisfied.

(*14*) *Pace* Gothofredus referring to C.6.46.6(7).

adopted (*15*). Apart from anything else, in conditions such as these the third party's failure to co-operate is not envisaged or at least is not expressly provided for, so that there is greater scope for interpreting the intention, or the presumed intention, of the testator. In D.28.5.45(44) the testator expressly provided that if one of the *heredes scripti* failed to build the monument neither could be heir. Again this provision is not the same as those which simply impose a duty *coniunctim* and state that if it is not performed the provision is to fail: for instance, "if they build a monument" (*16, 17*). The problem in these is whether if one person has performed (his part) the condition is to be accepted as satisfied by him even though the other has not performed. Again apart even from other considerations, there is considerable scope for interpreting the testator's intention. But in D.28.5.45(44) the testator expressly states that both must perform the condition or neither will be heir. So far as I am aware, in fact, there is no other text with a provision parallel to that in D.28.5.45(44), and modern jurists do not seem to have paid much attention to the decision.

A glance at a different text will show just how extreme Servius' or Alfenus' decision is.

> D.28.5.29 (Pomponius 5 ad Sab.). Hoc articulo 'quisque' omnes significantur: et ideo Labeo scribit, si ita scriptum sit: 'Titius et Seius quanta quisque eorum ex parte heredem me habuerit scriptum, heres mihi esto', nisi omnes habeant scriptum heredem testatorem, neutrum heredem esse posse, quoniam ad omnium factum sermo refertur: in quo puto testatoris mentem respiciendam. sed humanius est eum quidem, qui testatorem suum heredem scripserit, in tantam partem ei heredem fore, qui autem eum non scripserit nec ad hereditatem eius admitti.

The extent to which the text is interpolated or is not interpolated need not concern us. The significant thing is that the decision which seemed obvious to the jurists was that neither was to be heir unless both were. That one alone might be heir was accepted only because it was *humanius*. Yet in that institution there was more room for argument since there was no express *exheredatio* of both if one failed to institute the testator as heir. That text also shows how inexact is the reply of D.28.5.45(44) that no person can be disinherited by the

(*15*) Cf., e.g., D.28.7.3 (Paul *1 ad Sab.*); 28.7.11 (Iulianus *29 dig.*) 35.1.14 Pomponius *8 ad Sab*).

(*16*) Though Schindler seems to ignore the distinction: op cit., pp. 167ff and p. 174 n. 29.

(*17*) Cf., e.g., D.35.1.112pr., 2 (Pomponius *12 epist.*); 40.4.13.2 (Ulpian *5 disp.*); 40.7.13.2 (Iulianus *43 dig.*). See also D.28.5.29 (Pomponius *5 ad Sab.*), quoted *infra*, and D. 40.4.13. pr. (Ulpian *5 disp.*). If in this last text *nisi aliud expresserit testator* is an interpolation the clause would have been added only for the sake of completeness and not because Ulpian—who was concerned with the situation where there was no relevant express clause—was of a different opinion: contra, De Sarlo, op. cit., p. 17.

behaviour of another. So far as we know there never was a time when it was even argued that a condition on an institution of an *heres extraneus* was valid only if it were in the power of the *heres scriptus* to perform: certainly, D.28.1.25 (Iavolenus *5 post. Labeonis*) would seem to show that neither Servius nor Alfenus would subscribe to such a view (*18*).

But the *responsum* of D.28.5.45(44), inexact though it is, is highly significant. Its very general and abstract nature shows that the respondent is not arguing from the intention or presumed intention of the testator. This must mean that he cannot. Also, it shows that there was nothing particular in the situation which would on legal grounds justify the decision there but not in general. Again, it indicates that the respondent did not feel that his opinion would carry weight if he declared it to be an exception based on the equity of the situation. And further, since he does not expressly say anything about the *omnes exheredes sunto* clause—which is the overwhelming obstacle to his view—he is in effect tacitly admitting that the validity of that clause cannot be attacked.

If the foregoing is correct the text takes on special significance. Servius or Alfenus is caught giving a decision which is contrary to legal principle and which cannot be defended, juridically, as an exception to the rule. There are no reasons for thinking he has just made a mistake, and we have evidence that the state of the law was known to him. At the same time the jurist must feel that there are no factors which would persuade enough other people to reach his decision on grounds of equity. No argument can convincingly be produced to show that the jurist decided the way he did because of personal ties with the questioner.

The situation and the decision must be re-examined in the light of this conclusion. A testator institutes two *extranei* as his heirs and he orders them to build a sepulchral monument for him within a certain time: if either fails to build both are to be disinherited. The wording of the provision is unambiguous and the testator's intention is certain. One of the *heredes scripti* omits the *hereditas,* the other builds the monument by himself. Clearly now the law of wills demands that neither be heir. But there are equitable reasons for allowing the person who built to take the hereditas. He more than fulfilled the condition put upon him—he also performed the obligation put on the other *heres scriptus*. Servius (or Alfenus) wishes him to be heir and gives his decision accordingly. He can only have been swayed by the equity of the situation (*19*), but he is not prepared to argue on that: a strong indication that here *aequitas* could not be expected to prevail over *ius.* He has to argue, therefore, from principle but one which does not

(*18*) For a full discussion of this whole point see *infra.*
(*19*) A desire to find that the will could operate, *favore testamenti,* would never have been enough to explain, or justify, the decision.

exist and so he replies in a manner which is not altogether straightforward. First, what is really the argument for the decision—no one can be bound to an inheritance or disinherited by the behaviour of another—is presented not as an argument but as the decision. Secondly, the main part of the decision—no one can be disinherited by another's behaviour—is preceded by a different point—no one can be bound to an inheritance by another's behaviour—which has relevance to the situation but none whatsoever to the main decision. Its real function is to appear to be the converse of the main decision: if it is true, which it is, that no one can be bound to an inheritance by another's behaviour, then it is also true, which it is not, that no one can be disinherited by another's behaviour. It is, to that extent, a red herring. Thirdly, the main part of the decision is expressed as a very general proposition of law. This makes it more difficult to display its inaccuracy. Contrary cases might be treated as exceptions which were perhaps not thought of as falling within the principle. Cases which seem to accord with the principle can be treated as proving its existence. It is not surprising that, as mentioned earlier, the situation in D.28.5.45 (44) is at times linked with situations which are basically different. Indeed, the last part of the text, *sed uti quisque condicionem implesset, quamvis nemo adisset praeterea tamen eum heredem esse,* is probably intended to make one think of situations such as those which occur in D.35.1.112 pr. (20) where presumably Servius (or Alfenus) would hold that the one who performed would always become heir. Fourthly, this categorical and extremely wide mode of giving the decision makes it less obvious that the jurist is concealing the real obstacle to his view, the *omnes exheredes sunto clause.* It is precisely the disingenuous nature of the *responsum* which best shows the difficulties in the decision.

D.28.5.45(44) is not the only text in which Servius—assuming that the *responsum* goes back to him—gives a decision contrary to the intention of the testator. He does the same in D.35.1.40.3 (Iavolenus *2 ex post. Labeonis*).

> Dominus servo aureos quinque legaverat: 'heres meus Sticho servo meo, quem testamento liberum esse iussi, aureos quinque, quos in tabulis debeo, dato'. nihil servo legatum esse Namusa Servium respondisse scribit, quia dominus servo nihil debere potuisset: ego puto secundum mentem testatoris naturale magis quam civile debitum spectandum esse, et eo iure utimur.

A master freed a slave by will and left him a legacy of "the five *aurei* which I owe him according to my account books". Servius held that no legacy was given to the slave because a master can owe his slave nothing. But, of course, there could be no doubt as to the testator's intention, and Servius' decision was completely contrary to it. Still in this case Servius was in a stronger position because he

(20) Cf. *supra.*

could rely strictly on the wording of the will, which he obviously could not do in D.28.5.45(44). The two texts taken together are very instructive for Servius' social and moral outlook. Clearly he was unsympathetic to the slave in D.35.1.40.3 being given the legacy, and so he interpreted the will against the testator's intention (21). Equally clearly in D.28.5.45(44) he wanted the *heres scriptus* who had done what he could to fulfil the condition and had no doubt spent money in the process to be heir and so, for a very different reason, he interpreted the will against the testator's intention (22).

II

Up to this point I have excluded from the discussion Buckland's theory of the early history of conditional institution which is, however, also important for D.28.5.45(44). I think Buckland's view can be shown to be implausible but a more detailed examination is required than would have been appropriate in the first part of this note.

Buckland thought that the early history of conditional institution was obscure, and he says: "The most probable story seems to be that it was unknown to the Comitial will, and, for long, to the Mancipatory will, appearing first, by a somewhat uncertain mode of evolution, about the close of the Republic. The first conditions, or quasi conditions, would be such as must necessarily be satisfied by the time when the will operated. The next would be those depending only on the will of the *heres,* such as could be satisfied at once, involving no delay in *aditio.* These seem to have been admitted in or shortly after, the time of Cicero. Those involving delay were not admitted, or, at any rate, were not treated as conditions till the Empire, and then became common. It is clear that conditions were earlier and more prominent in legacy" (23). Later he summed up the theoretical arguments: "It is not clear how they (i.e., conditions on institution) came to be allowed at all in what must have been a typical *actus legitimus.* The fact that the Praetor's remission produced civil effects suggests that the Praetor may have been the first agent in introducing them" (24). If Buckland is right, then the *responsum* in D.28.5.45(44) may be perfectly straightforward, and it may indeed have been the

(21) Cf. most recently on the text, Watson, 'Morality, Slavery and the Jurists in the Later Roman Republic' *Legal Origins and Legal Change*, chapter 24, at p 269. The writer observes that, of the 139 texts on legacies which go back to Republican decisions, D.35.1.40.3 is the only one which shows a decision contrary to the testator's clear intention. The very different reason for the decision in D.28.4.45(44) is added support for the writer's main proposition that D.35.1.40.3 shows Servius acting unfairly towards a slave. [The *aureos* of the text is, of course, an interpolation for some other monetary unit.]

(22) From D.33.10.7.2 (Celsus *19 dig.*) we know that Servius was of the opinion that in interpreting a will the testator's intention should be taken into account: cf. Watson, op. cit, p. 296.

(23) *Tijd.*, cit., p. 257.

(24) *Textbook*, cit., p. 299.

law at the time that a person could not be disinherited by the behaviour of another.

The arguments for and against Buckland's position will be considered in two stages: first the main theoretical arguments; secondly arguments from the texts.

(i) Let us first look at the arguments about *institutio heredis* being an *actus legitimus.* "That *institutio heredis*" he says, "was thought of as an *actus legitimus* is shown by the strict rules surviving in classical law, as to the forms admissible. '*Heres esto*' was the proper form, though '*heredem esse iubeo*' was allowed." But in the first place, *legatum per vindicationem* and *legatum per damnationem* had just as strict rules about the proper form (25) and Buckland at the very least would admit that conditions on legacies were earlier than the period we are concerned with. So even if at one time conditions were not possible on an *institutio* this in itself would be a rather weak argument for holding that the position was basically unchanged as late as the first century B.C. Again, *substitutio* seems to be nothing other than a *conditional institutio* where the condition is outside the power of this subsequent heir. Indeed, in *substitutio vulgaris* where the *institutus* is an *extraneus* who eventually accepts the inheritance, the subsequent heir is excluded by the *factum* of another. Even Buckland does not seem to deny that *substitutio* is ancient (26), and he tries to circumvent this obstacle in another way. He says (27): "But *substitutio,* however ancient, is not essentially a conditional *institutio.* The objection to a condition in *institutio* is that it suspends by an express provision the operation of an *actus legitimus. Substitutio* does not do this: there is no moment, so far as the document is concerned, in which it is not open for an heir to enter at once. The entry is not held up. The language of the texts does not suggest that it was regarded as a condition." But this looks very much like special pleading. *Substitutio* quite clearly is conditional *institutio,* and that *institutio* is definitely suspended by the condition. Moreover, even if one can regard *substitutio* as differing from some other conditional *institutiones,* if it remains a suspensive condition at all, it still takes away all the force (28) from the argument about *institutio* being an *actus legitimus* and hence, of necessity, unconditional. On the ordinary understanding of *actus legitimus,* no proper conditions of any kind should be possible. Also, I am not sure that it is meaningful to say

(25) G.2.199, 201. On the use of these forms see my forthcoming *The Law of Succession in the Later Roman Republic,* Chapter 9.

(26) Cf. e.g., for *substitutio vulgaris*: D 28.1.25 (Iavolenus *5 ex post. Labeonis*), referring to Servius; 28.6.39.2 (Iavolenus *1 ex post.* Labeonis) referring to Ofilius and Cascellius. For *substitutio pupillaris* it is enough to refer to the famous *causa Curiana* of 93-91 B.C.: cf. e.g., Cicero, *Brutus,* 52-53.194-198; *de orat.* 1.39.180; *de inven.* 2.42.122. Presumably this case is also proof of the existence at the time of *substitutio vulgaris.*

(27) *Tijd.* cit., p. 244.

(28) After the recognition of *substituto.*

"The objection to a condition in *institutio* is that it suspends by an express provision the operation of an *actus legtimus.*" The idea that an *actus legitimus* cannot have a condition seems to be that when it is 'made' it must take effect fully and at once (29). But when is the *institutio* 'made' in this sense? If it is an *actus legitimus* and like the others, it cannot be 'made' when the will is written since none of the provisions can take effect before the testator dies, nor can it be when the testator dies since an *heres extraneus* does not become heir until he accepts. Thus, if *institutio heredis* is an *actus legitimus* and is like the others, then it is 'made' only when the heir accepts. Hence, even if *institutio heredis* is an *actus legitimus* this is no reason for refusing to allow conditions which have to be fulfilled before the *institutio* is 'made'. Buckland, indeed, has to say that *institutio* "differed fundamentally" from other *actus legitimi* in that it does not operate at once. "This state of affairs", he declares, "is one of the factors facilitating the introduction of ordinary conditions (30). But how are we to reconcile this with his later statement that *institutio* "must have been a typical *actus legitimus*" (31)?

Moreover we are nowhere told in the sources that *institutio heredis* was an an *actus legitimus.* Actually, the meaning of that term is not itself clear. It occurs only in one text, D.50.17.77 (Papinian *28 quaest.*) and its use may not be technical: in the context the term may mean no more than 'a legal institution which cannot be made subject to a condition' and have no wider significance (32).

Secondly, Buckland's argument, "The fact that the Praetor's remission produced civil effects suggests that the Praetor may have been the first agent in introducing them [i.e. conditions]" (33), is not convincing. The remission in question (34) is the remission of the *condicio iurisiurandi.* Elsewhere he expands; "It has been shown by Pernice that the praetor's *remissio* of *condicio iurisiurandi* had full civil law effect. The introduction of this *remissio* seems to coincide roughly in time with the recognition of ordinary conditions and it is not easy to see how the *remissio* should have had this effect if conditions were fully valid at civil law" (35). But in D.28.7.28 (Papinian *13 quaest.*) we find Servius concerned with an ordinary condition (36) and this is earlier than the edict *de condicione iurisiurandi* (37).

(29) Thus, D.50.17.77 (Papinian *28 quaest.*) describes *tutoris datio* as an *actus legitimus* but a testator could appoint a tutor conditionally by will: D.26.2.8.2 (Ulpian *24 ad Sab.*); cf. Buckland, *Textbook* cit., p. 144. What is meant is that no one can be tutor under a condition.
(30) *Tijd.*, cit., p. 256.
(31) *Textbook*, cit., p. 299.
(32) Cf. Watson, 'The form and nature of *acceptilatio* in classical Roman Law', *RIDA* viii (1961), p. 391ff at p. 405. *Legitimi* in D.50.17.77 may also be an interpolation: cf. *Index Itp.*
(33) *Textbook*, cit., p. 299.
(34) See the *Textbook*, loc. cit., and the cross-reference in n. 12 to n. 6.
(35) *Tijd.*, cit., p. 267.
(36) Cf. *infra.*

Buckland's arguments raise very sharply—and do not resolve—the problem of how conditions, if they were introduced by the praetor, came to have civil law effect. He himself admits "*Condicio* in *institutio,* as we know it, is a civil law institution. It is discussed mainly in treatises on the civil law" (38). The difficulty, created by his theory, is even greater than the problem he is trying to solve.

Accordingly, it seems that the theoretical justifications for Buckland's view are not persuasive.

(ii) The texts, or lack of texts, do not really provide Buckland with more support (39).

Plautus, he observes, has nothing about conditional *institutio* (40). But this is not significant. Plautus, in fact, has very few texts on succession at all. For instance, there seems to be only one of any kind on legacy (41).

More importance is attached by Buckland to Cicero: "The writings of Cicero are full of allusions to *hereditas,* but few have any significance for the present question and they seem to show that he did not know of ordinary conditions on institutions" (42). Buckland seems to have two points in mind here: first, the texts show situations in which conditional institution would have been appropriate but in which some other method of achieving the object was employed; secondly, no text actually shows a conditional institution. It would appear that he attaches most importance to *de off.* 3.24. 93.

> Quid? si qui sapiens rogatus sit ab eo, qui eum heredem faciat, cum ei testamento sestertium milies relinquatur, ut, ante quam hereditatem adeat, luce palam in foro saltet, idque se facturum promiserit, quod aliter heredem eum scripturus ille non esset, faciat, quod promiserit, necne? Promisisse nollem et id arbitror fuisse gravitatis; quoniam promisit, si saltare in foro turpe ducet, honestius mentietur, si ex hereditate nihil ceperit, quam si ceperit, nisi forte eam pecuniam in rei publicae magnum aliquod tempus contulerit, ut vel saltare, cum patriae consulturus sit, turpe non sit.

He rightly points out that no condition is involved in the will and states: "The passage shows how at that time, testators secured that their *heredes* should do something in the future, not by a condition

(37) Cf. Pernice, op. cit., pp. 50f. A condition might be remitted by the praetor before the introduction of the edict: cf. Cicero, *in Verrem* 2.1.47.123, 124; and *infra.* But it is not known whether this had a civil law effect.
(38) *Tijd.* cit., p. 267.
(39) It must be observed, in fairness to Buckland, that he did not hold that the texts proved the evolution suggested by him, only that they "unquestionably give strong support": *Tijd.* cit., p. 258.
(40) *Tijd.*, cit., p. 261 n. 6.
(41) *As.* 306.
(42) *Tijd.*, cit., pp. 258f.

involving suspension of *aditio*" (43). But this rather wide claim is not justified by the text. What Cicero was concerned with here, as 3.24.92 and 3.25.94 show, was situations in which it might be questioned whether a promise should be kept. Hence §93 could not reasonably have concerned a conditional institution (44). Moreover the situation described is particularly suitable for Cicero's purpose. A bad promise has been made and the promisor will receive a reward on account of it whether he actually fulfils it or not. What ought he to do? A neater situation for the point is hard to envisage. The promisee has to be dead—or a more complicated situation has to be invented—to allow the promisor to be in the situation where he has not yet received the reward for his performance, yet able to get it without actually performing. The example could have been chosen even if it was quite unreal in practice. At the very least, the example can not be generalised as showing how testators secured that their heirs do something in the future.

> *in Verrem* 2.1.47.123. Superbia vero quae fuerit, quis ignorat? quem ad modum iste tenuissimum quemque contempserit, despexerit, liberum esse numquam duxerit? P. Trebonius viros bonos et honestos conplures fecit heredes; in iis fecit suum libertum. Is A. Trebonium fratrem habuerat proscriptum. Ei cum cautum vellet, scripsit, ut heredes iurarent se curaturos, ut ex sua cuiusque parte ne minus dimidium ad A. Trebonium illum proscriptum perveniret. Libertus iurat; ceteri heredes adeunt ad Verrem, docent non oportere se id iurare facturos esse, quod contra legem Corneliam esset, quae proscriptum iuvari vetaret; inpetrant, ut ne iurent; dat his possessionem. Id ego non reprehendo; etenim erat iniquum homini proscripto egenti de fraternis bonis quicquam dari. Libertus, nisi ex testamento patroni iurasset, scelus se facturum arbitrabatur; 124 itaque ei Verres possessionem hereditatis negat se daturum, ne posset patronum suum proscriptum iuvare, simul ut esset poena, quod alterius patroni testamento optemperasset. Das possessionem ei, qui non iuravit; concedo; praetorium est. Adimis tu ei, qui iuravit; quo exemplo? Proscriptum iuvat; lex est, poena est. Quid ad eum, qui ius dicit? utrum reprehendis, quod patronum iuvabat eum, qui [tum] in miseriis erat, an quod alterius patroni mortui voluntatem conservabat, a quo summum beneficium acceperat? utrum horum reprehendis? Et hoc tum de sella vir optimus dixit: dixit: 'Equiti Romano tam locupleti libertinus homo sit heres?' O modestum ordinem, quod illinc vivus surrexit!

Buckland comments: "The merits of the case do not concern us. So far as appears this was not *condicio* but direct *iussum*, perhaps

(43) *Tijd.*, cit., p. 259.
(44) Nor even a *iussum* in the will! Cf. *infra*.

independent of the *institutio* and enforceable in one of the several ways applied to such things. Probably it was one of the requirements of the *cretio* clause operating as a condition. The form '*iussit*' does not exclude a true condition, and it may have been: '*T. heres esto si juraverit se curaturum* (etc.) *cernitoque in diebus*' (etc.). This is less probable, but if it is the true interpretation then this earliest type of condition which is quite potestative and involves no delay was recognised in Cicero's time as it certainly was not long after" (45). But there is no "*iussum*" *or* "*iussit*" mentioned in the text, and no reason to assume *iussum* rather than conditional *institutio* (46). Incidentally, most of the several ways referred to by Buckland of enforcing the *iussum* seem to date from the Empire (47).

*Ad Att.*7.8.3. does talk about *iuberi* but Buckland himself does not exclude the possibility of a condition on the *institutio* (48).

Thus, these Ciceronian texts do not convincingly show that where conditional institution would have been appropriate, some other method of achieving the object was used. Indeed, even if it could be proved that conditional *institutio* did not appear in any text of Cicero, the fact would have doubtful significance. A number of Ciceronian texts concerns legacies but none shows a conditional legacy, though conditions on legacies were certainly admitted long before Cicero. Actually, it would not be surprising if *iussum* frequently appeared in place of a condition on an *institutio* even if the latter was possible. There are various reasons—such as *sacra, usucapio lucrativa*—why in practice a testator would not wish *aditio* to be long delayed.

The remaining texts are from the Digest. The important ones for us, apart from D.28.5.45(44) itself, are D.35.1.6.1 (Pomponius *3 ad Sab.*) and 28.7.28 (Papinian *13 quaest.*).

In D.35.1.6.1. we have: *sed Servius respondit, cum ita esset scriptum 'si filia et mater mea vivent' altera iam mortua, non defici condicione* (49). For Buckland (50), and indeed other modern scholars (51), this situation does not involve a true condition since it does not depend upon a future and uncertain event: the *institutio* is valid or not according to a situation existing when the will was opened. The distinction between the two kinds of case is real and important but it should be noticed that Servius appears to treat the situation in D.35.1.6.1 as involving a *condicio* of some kind. And

(45) *Tijd.*, cit., p. 260.
(46) Certainly not from the separation in the text of the *institutio* and the direction to make the *iusiurandum*. This is due to the need to tell us about the proscribed brother. The construction of the passage is very neat.
(47) *cf.* Pernice op. cit. pp. 36ff, whom Buckland himself cites.
(48) *Tijd.*, op. cit., p. 261. Buckland also refers to other texts which are not really instructive either for his proposition or the contrary one: *ad Att.* 11.15.4; *in Verrem* 2.2.14.36; 2.1.10.27; 2.2.8.22.
(49) Cf. D.28.5.46(45) (Alfenus *2 dig. a Paulo epit.*).
(50) *Tijd.*, cit., p. 262; *Textbook*, cit., p. 297.
(51) Cf. e.g.., Kaser, *Das römische Privatrecht* I (Munich, 1955), p. 219.

moreover, Roman jurists who draw a distinction between the two kinds of case (52) nonetheless call both *condiciones.* Thus in what is the most important text, D.28.3.16 (Pomponius *2 ad Quintum Mucium*) Pomponius can write: *multum autem interest, qualis condicio posita fuerit: nam aut in praeteritum concepta ponitur aut in praesens aut in futurum.* How clearly different kinds of *condicio* were distinguished in early law is unknown. One might hesitate, therefore, to say that though in the time of Servius, an institution '*si filia et mater mea vivent*', was valid this is no indication that 'true' conditions were possible.

D.28.7.28 tells us: *argumentoque est, quod apud Servium quoque relatum est: quendam enim refert ita heredem institutum, si in Capitolium ascenderit, quod si non ascendisset, legatum ei datum, eumque antequam ascenderet mortem obisse: de quo respondit Servius condicionem morte defecisse ideoque moriente eo legati diem cessisse.* Buckland comments: "This seems to express a true condition, but it is one which can be performed at once, dependent only on the will of the *heres.* On that view it is the earliest recorded instance of such a condition but it is at least possible since it comes from a jurist as late as Papinian, that Servius is translated into the language of another age" (53). And we should remember his: "The first conditions, or quasi-conditions, would be such as must necessarily be satisfied by the time when the will operated. The next would be those depending only on the will of the *heres,* such as could be satisfied at once, involving no delay in *aditio.* These seem to have been admitted in or shortly after, the time of Cicero. Those involving delay were not admitted, or, at any rate, were not treated as conditions till the Empire, and then became common" (54). This time Buckland is really too narrow. The significant thing about D.28.7.28 is surely that the condition certainly need not be performed at once and that delay is permitted. Note that the text has *antequam ascenderet,* not *antequam ascendere posset.*

Buckland does not make much of D.28.5.45(44) where he follows Pernice's reconstruction (55).

The absence of Digest texts for the Republic and even rather later showing a conditional institution dependent upon a future event outside the power of the heir cannot in itself be treated as significant. There are numerous other, even more important, aspects of law which

(52) And between their effects.
(53) *Tijd.,* cit., pp. 262f.
(54) *Tijd.,* cit., p. 257.
(55) *Tijd.,* cit., pp. 263ff. Buckland refers to a number of other texts but these do not seem very significant for either point of view: D.35.1.80 (*Scaevola 8 quaest.*); 35.1.27 (Alfenus Varus *5 dig.*); 50.16.202 (Alfenus Varus *2 dig.*); 28.5.70 (Proculus *2 epist.*);)28.6.39pr (Iavolenus *1 ex post. Labeonis*) [The procedure suggested by the jurists in this text is the neatest possible and certainly preferable to a conditional *institutio* of the *extraneus*]; 28.7.20pr., 1 (Labeo 2 *post. a Iavoleno epit.*); 35.1.39.1 (Iavolenus *1 ex post. Labeonis*); 50.16.217. pr. (Iavolenus *1 ex post Labeonis*).

are not evidenced in the Digest for the Republic yet whose existence is undeniable (56). Nor is it strange that earlier evidence exists for what Buckland considers to be not true conditions and also for true conditions dependent solely upon the heir. These are in practice much commoner situations. A quick glance at Digest Title 35.1 will confirm this. True statistical accuracy cannot be expected but if all the texts in the Title which quote the actual words of a condition, whether it is valid or not, and whether it is on *institutio,* legacy or manumission, are analysed, the following picture seems to emerge: there are 51 certain and 4 possible cases involving a true condition dependent upon the beneficiary; 13 certain and 8 possible cases involving what for Buckland and others is not a true condition; only 6 certain and 6 possible cases involving a true condition independent of the behaviour of the beneficiary. Hence this last situation is relatively uncommon. Buckland seems to have drawn legal conclusions from his observations without noticing that the picture in the texts reflects social behaviour, rather than any necessary or even plausible existing state of the law.

Thus, if we leave aside D.28.5.45.(44) for the moment, it seems that Buckland's view of the early history of conditional institution receives no practical support from the sources and is not confirmed by his theoretical arguments. Indeed, the early existence of *substitutio* would seem to provide very strong evidence that Buckland's thesis cannot stand.

D.28.4.45(44) which at first sight seems in line with Buckland's theory is too fragile to support by itself the weight of that theory. The *responsum* would still be too wide: *neminem ex alterius facto . . . exheredari posse* would still not be accurate because an *extraneus institutus* would exclude the *substitutus* from the *hereditas.* But if the text does not prove Buckland's theory then in the circumstances it follows that the theory cannot be used to explain the text. We are forced back to the conclusions reached in the first part of the note (56).

(56) For instance, no Digest text mentions for the Republic the edict *de bonorum possessione secundum tabulas* but its extreme importance is brought out in the lay sources, e.g., Cicero, *in Verrem,* 2.1.44.114; *top.*4.18.

I am grateful to a number of friends for their criticism; especially to Mr. John L. Barton, Mr. Robin Seager, Professor Reuven Yaron, Dr. A. M. Honoré and Dr. Geoffrey MacCormack.

IV

Contract

Arra in the Law of Justinian

So much has been written in recent years on *arra* in Justinian's law that one hesitates to add to it (1). But there is, I submit, a solution to the problem raised by the texts which is simpler than any so far suggested, and which gives a satisfactory result.

The texts at the heart of the matter are C. 4. 21. 17. and J. 3. 23. pr. The former is generally — but not universally — admitted to be the earlier (with which *communis opinio* I agree) (2), and gives rise to no great problem. The constitution enacts in its *principium* that with regard to certain specified contracts, including sale and *arrarum datio,* if the parties have agreed that the contract be put in writing, then the contract will be of no effect until the writing has been properly completed i.e. reduced to its final form and confirmed by the subscription of the parties (3), and where it is being drawn up by a notary completed by him and finally released to the parties. A draft in the handwriting of one or both of the parties, we are told, will not enough. § 2 enacts that where *arra* is given, whether with writing or without, in respect of the making of

(1) See, for example, Thomas, « Arra in Sale in Justinian Law », 24 Tijd. 253 (and the references given therein) ; « Arra Reagitata », 1956, *Butterworths South African Law Review* 60 ; « A Postscript on Arra », *Jura* 10 (1959) ; D'Ors, « Las Arras en la Compraventa Justinianea », *Jura* 6 (1955) 149 ; « 'Arra Reagitata ' sive in scriptis sive sine scriptis », *Jura* 9 (1958) 78. Schuster, « Die Funktion der ' Arrha ' by Justinian », *Labeo* 5 (1959), p. 26, came to notice too late for consideration.

(2) Contra D'Ors, *loc. cit.*

(3) De Zulueta is surely wrong (' The Roman Law of Sale ', Oxford, 1945, p. 22) when he says that this constitution laid down that *subscriptio* is required of documents made *per alium* but not of autographs of the parties. Possibly J. 3. 23. pr. relaxed the provision where the writing was autograph of the parties, but this does not necessarily follow from the wording of the text.

a sale, then, if the person who promised to sell repudiates the sale he will be compelled to pay double the value of the *arra*, if the person who promised to buy withdraws from the purchase he will forfeit the *arra* he has given. In this part of the constitution *sive in scriptis sive sine scriptis* refers to the giving of *arra* (4).

The difficulty lies in the interpretation of J. 3. 23. pr. The passage reads :

> Emptio et venditio contrahitur, simulatque de pretio convenerit, quamvis nondum pretium numeratum sit ac ne arra quidem data fuerit. nam quod arrae nomine datur, argumentum est emptionis et venditionis contractae. sed haec quidem de emptionibus et venditionibus, quae sine scriptura consistunt, optinere oportet : nam nihil a nobis in huiusmodi venditionibus innovatum est. in his autem quae scriptura conficiuntur non aliter perfectam esse emptionem et venditionem constituimus, nisi et instrumenta emptionis fuerint conscripta vel manu propria contrahentium, vel ab alio quidem scripta, a contrahente autem subscripta et, si per tabellionem fiunt, nisi et completiones acceperint et fuerint partibus absoluta. donec enim aliquid ex his deest, et paenitentiae locus est et potest emptor vel venditor sine poena recedere ab emptione. ita tamen impune recedere eis concedimus, nisi iam arrarum nomine aliquid fuerit datum : hoc etenim subsecuto, sive in scriptis sive sine scriptis venditio celebrata est, is qui recusat adimplere contractum, si quidem emptor est, perdit quod dedit, si vero venditor, duplum restituere compellitur, licet nihil super arris expressum est.

From the beginning to *innovatum est,* the text deals with unwritten sales and Justinian categorically states that he has made no change in the law relating to them. From there to *fuerit datum* he is concerned with sales which are to be put into writing. He declares, first, that such an *emptio venditio* is not *perfecta* until the agreement has been put into writing and the formalities demanded by C. 4. 21. 17. completed ; secondly, that

(4) Cf. Thomas, 24 Tijd., pp. 263-267.

so long as anything in the formalities is lacking, either party may withdraw without penalty ; thirdly, than he can only so withdraw without penalty where no *arra* has been given. At this stage one could expect Justinian to explain what happens in cases of sale to be put into writing where *arra* is given and one party withdraws before the formalities are completed. And that, I suggest, is what he does do. This view is supported by the words *hoc etenim subsecuto* which clearly link the sentence in which they occur with what precedes. The words which cause all the difficulty, *sive in scriptis sive sine scriptis venditio celebrata est,* should be translated « Whether the sale (scil. which has to be put into writing with other attendant formalities) was agreed upon in writing (i.e. but which lacks the other formalities) or without writing ». In other words, the parties have agreed on the terms of the sale but have declared it should be put in writing, and at the time of the withdrawal either there is no writing or there is writing which does not meet all the requirements laid down in C. 4. 21. 17. and repeated in this *lex*. On this interpretation, the Institutes' passage would be in complete harmony with the Code, and would also be entirely self-consistent. It is most unlikely that, in this passage, the compilers after declaring they had not altered the classical law of unwritten sale, would have surreptitiously introduced a new rule (which is not mentioned at all in the Digest) or could have allowed what is on any other interpretation, so blatant a mistake, even if it did give the *de facto* position (5). A view which involves holding (a) that we have suddenly moved to a general discussion of *arra* in sale, (b) that Justinian is altering, deliberately or accidentally, the law of unwritten sale, and (c) that carelessly he has left out *celebranda* after *in scriptis,* needs too many conjectures to be readily acceptable.

Of course, the interpretation which is here put forward involves holding that to some extent the words *sive in scriptis sive sine scriptis venditio celebrata est* repeat what has gone before, but it is not surprising that Justinian should emphasise his own legal reforms ; moreover, the passage is wholly com-

(5) Cf. Thomas, *loc. cit.*

pilatorial and we see from his Paraphrase that Theophilus at least was not averse to repetition. This present view, however, can only hope to win support if it can be shown, first, that the words *in scriptis* in this text may mean « in writing, but where the other formalities are lacking », and secondly, that *venditio* may be used where the sale is not perfect.

For the first of these points we have the evidence of C. 4. 38. 15. 1. which is another of the constitutions of Justinian.

> Quam decidentes censemus, cum huiusmodi conventio super venditione procedat 'quanti ille aestimaverit', sub hac condicione stare vendiitonem, ut, si quidem ipse qui nominatus est pretium definierit, omnimodo secundum eius aestimationem et pretia persolvi et venditionem ad effectum pervenire, sive in scriptis sive sine scriptis contractus celebretur, scilicet si huiusmodi pactum, cum in scriptis fuerit redactum, secundum nostrae legis definitionem per omnia completum et absolutum sit.

Clearly, then, in view of the qualification at the end (*cum in scriptis fuerit redactum etc.*) the fact that the contract is now *in scriptis* does not mean that all the requirements have been met, and accordingly, such a contract *in scriptis* may still be *imperfecta* and of no avail. In this text, the first use of the words *in scriptis* (in the phrase *sive in scriptis sive sine scriptis*) and the second use of these words (in the phrase *cum in scriptis fuerit redactum*) correspond respectively to the use of *scriptura* and *in scriptis* in J. 3. 23. pr.

As for the second point, it is not uncommon to find *emptio* or *venditio* used where the sale is not yet in existence or is void. An example of *emptio* being used in this way is, in fact, found in the very passage of Justinian's Institutes with which we are concerned. The sentence runs : *Donec enim aliquid ex his deest, et paenitentiae locus est et potest emptor vel venditor sine poena recedere ab emptione.* It will suffice to give one other example, viz. D. 18. 1. 36 (Ulpian 43 *ad edictum*) :

> Cum in venditione quis pretium rei ponit donationis causa non exacturus, non videtur vendere.

In a similar way, one uses *emptor* and *venditor, emere* and *vendere,* where there is no sale (6). Although it is perhaps not technically accurate, it is convenient.

Likewise, there is no difficulty in the use of *celebrata est.* *Celebrare* takes its colour from the noun to which it relates, and if *venditio* means « imperfect sale » or « agreement for sale » *sive in scriptis... venditio celebrata est* would mean « whether the agreement for sale (or « sale not yet perfected ») was made in writing... ». It does not follow from the use of a past tense of *celebrare* that the agreement etc. to which it relates is valid ; e.g. on the giving of security in law suits, J. 4. 11. 7.

In conclusion, one can say that Justinian has not innovated on *arra* in the Institutes ; that he retains the classical law for unwritten sales, and follows his own constitution in the Code for sales to be put into writing. Confusion has arisen as a result of his careless use of words, but his choice is not unreasonable or indeed unprecedented, and the meaning was probably clear to his contemporaries (7).

(6) E.g. D. 18. 1. 34. 3 ; h.t. 35. 1 ; h.t. 16. pr. ; h.t. 41. 1.

(7) There is nothing in Theophilus or the Basilica which militates against this solution.

15

Apochatum Pro Uncis Duabus

Two of the Transylvanian sale triptychs contain the clause *apochatum pro uncis duabus*. The beginning of each reads :

> Dasius Breucus emit mancipioque accepit puerum Apalaustum, sive is quo alio nomine est, n(atione) Grecum, apocatum pro uncis duabus, ⳨ DC de Bellico Alexandri, f(ide) r(ogato) M. Vibio Longo (1).
>
> Cl. Iulianus mil. leg. XIII g(eminae) Ↄ (2) Cl. Mari, emit mancipioque accepit mulierem nomine Theudotem, sive ea quo alio nomine est, n(atione) Creticam, apochatam pro uncis duabus, ⳨ quadringentis viginti de Cl(audio) Phileto f(ide) a(ccepto) Alexandro Antipatri (3).

The first document dates from 142 A.D., the second from 160 A.D. What meaning is to be attributed to *apocatum* (or *apochatam*) *pro uncis duabus,* literally "receipted for two ounces" ? Mommsen conjectured (4) that it meant that the seller gave the buyer the receipt which was given to him by the person who had sold to him, and that two ounces of gold was the actual price which he had paid. This suggestion was shown to be very improbable by Bruns (5) who pointed out that it would mean that two slaves of very different value (600 and 420 *denarii*) had by a strange coincidence previously been sold for exactly the same amount. Bruns' line of criticism was followed by

(1) Bruns, *Fontes Iuris Romani Antiqui,* 7th edit. (Tübingen, 1909), no. 130.

(2) *I.e., centuria.*

(3) Bruns, *op. cit.*, no. 132.

(4) *Corpus Inscriptionum Latinarum* III (Berlin, 1873), p. 941 nn. 2, 3.

(5) *Fontes cit.* 3rd edit. (Tübingen, 1876), p. 185 n. 5 at p. 186.

Appleton (6) who also made the point that there was no reason at that time and place for sales to have been made for an actual weight of gold rather than for a sum of coined money, and that it would be intolerable for commerce if the seller gave the buyer the receipt for his own purchase, thus showing not only what he had paid but also the amount of his profit. Bruns suggested (7) that since the word *apochare* is concerned with the estimation of tax in *C.Th.* 11.2.1.2, it should be understood here as meaning something similar. But there seems no reason why one should restrict the use of the very rare word *apochare* to situations concerned with the collection of taxes (8). Appleton suggested that *unciae* should be understood as ounces of copper and that, therefore, two *unciae* was four *as* ; that this minimal sum had a connexion with *mancipatio uno nummo* ; that *apochatum* referred to a receipt for a previous transaction ; and that the clause was used to show that the seller had acquired title by purchase. Not, he goes on, that in fact the previous sale had been carried through by a *mancipatio uno nummo*, but this fictitious sum is used so that the buyer will remain unaware of the seller's profit (9). This very ingenious solution, however, will just not do. Firstly, it is unlikely that such information — although the buyer might well want to know how the seller got hold of the slave — would be recorded in the written document of sale, and certainly not in such a prominent place. Secondly, if such information were to be recorded, it would be more to the point to state who the transferor to the seller was, rather than the purely fictitious price paid by the seller. Thirdly, what would the value to the buyer of the receipt for the fictitious price be, assuming that the receipt were given him ? If it were intended to enable him to sue as a sort of *procurator in rem*

(6) " La clause '*apochatum pro uncis duabus*' et l'histoire de l'*as* sextantaire ", *Studi Scialoja* II (Milan, 1905), p. 503ff.

(7) *Loc. cit.*

(8) Cf. Appleton, *op. cit.*, p. 511.

(9) Followed by Kübler, xxvi *ZSS* (1905), p. 536ff ; Arangio-Ruiz, *Fontes Iuris Romani Antejustiniani III Negotia* (Florence, 1943), p. 285 n. 2 : cf. Meylan, xxi-xxii *Revue des Etudes latines* (1943-44), p. 34f.

suam the transferor to the seller, it would appear to allow him to recover four *unciae* by the *actio auctoritatis.* Fourthly, if the point is that the buyer should know that the seller had an *auctor,* this does not need a receipt — especially one which virtually does away with all the value of *auctoritas.* Fifthly, so far as we can tell, there is no implication in *apochatum* of a *mancipatio,* so the clause would not have any value as showing that the seller stated that he had received the slave by *mancipatio.* In general, Appleton's suggestion makes it appear that the parties to the sale resorted to an unnecessarily complicated manœuvre when a simple statement that the seller had bought the slave and that he had been mancipated to him by Maevius would have been more satisfactory. However, in favour of Appleton's explanation of *unciae* as referring to copper there is the fact that from an early time *unciae* had the transferred meaning of a 'trifle', something of very little value ([10]).

The real explanation, I suggest, is that *apochatum pro uncis duabus,* 'receipted for two *unciae*', refers to the present *mancipatio,* not to a previous one, and that the point of the clause is to limit the *actio auctoritatis* to four *unciae,* a negligible sum.

Although the point is not always made in the textbooks ([11]), it would, I imagine be generally accepted that since the *actio auctoritatis* was inherent in the *mancipatio,* then, considering the formal nature of that institution, it could not be excluded by agreement between the parties ([12]). That, of course, is why

(10) Cf. Plautus, *Rudens* l. 913. Appleton and Meylan also point out that the use of the word *unciae* rather than the denomination of a coin suggests that the clause has a long history. Copper, too, is especially appropriate if the clause is referring to *mancipatio.*

(11) It is, however, by Girard, *Mélanges de droit romain* II (Paris, 1923), p. 22ff : cf. Buckland, *Textbook of Roman Law* 2nd edit. (Cambridge, 1932), p. 489 n. 6 ; Bonfante, *Corso di diritto romano* II *La proprieta,* 2 (Rome, 1928), p. 144 ; De Zulueta, *The Roman Law of Sale* (Oxford, 1945), p. 43 ; Donatuti, *Lo Statulibero* (Milan, 1940), p. 120.

(12) Thus, when Varro (*de re rust.* 2.10.5) discusses the purchase of a slave it is only in cases where there is no *mancipatio* that he says the buyer should take a *stipulatio duplae* or, if it is so agreed, a *stipulatio*

the parties, when they wished to exclude the transferor's liability to the *actio auctoritatis*, had recourse to *mancipatio uno nummo*, thus restricting the operation of the *actio auctoritatis* to *duo nummi*. Similarly, some device had to be found to limit the effectiveness of the *actio auctoritatis* when the buyer insisted on *mancipatio* but the seller wished to restrict his liability to simple damages. Such a device was, I submit, indeed found and consisted of *mancipatio* being made *uno nummo* (or *duabus uncis*) followed by the seller giving a stipulation promising single damages if the buyer were evicted from whole or part of the slave. This device, I suggest, is shown in full operation in the document of sale of a female slave the relevant part of which is quoted above. It tells us that the female slave was bought and mancipated at a figure stated to be two *unciae*, the price paid being 420 *denarii*. The document then goes on to say that if the buyer is evicted from whole or part of the slave the seller has stipulated to pay him his interest ([13]). The seller also acknowledges receipt of the 420 *denarii*. This explanation accounts not only for the inclusion of *apochatam pro uncis duabus* in the document but also for its prominent position. *Apochatam* is used rather loosely to mean " stated to have been received for... ", *i.e.*, it refers to an oral, not a written statement of receipt. There may well also be a written receipt given by the buyer to the seller showing that the *mancipatio* was for the minimal sum.

Support for this explanation may be found in a comparison with the opening clauses of a document attesting a *mancipatio fiduciae causa* dating from 61 A.D. and which was found at Pompeii ([14]).

> Poppaea Prisci liberta Note iuravit pueros Simplicem et Petrinum, sive ea mancipia alis nominib[*us*] sunt, sua esse

simplae. The implication is that where there was a *mancipatio*, the seller's liability is automatic and cannot be changed or excluded by agreement. *P.S.* 2.17.1-3 suggests that this was still the position when that work was written.

(13) The clause is quoted *infra* p. 189.

(14) Bruns, *op. cit.* 7th edit., no. 134 ; Arangio-Ruiz, *op. cit.*, p. 291ff.

> seque possidere, neque ea mancipia ... ali ulli obligata esse neque sibi cum ulo com[*munia*] esse, eaque mancipia singula sestertis nu[*mmis sin*]gulis Dicidia Margaris emit ob seste[*rtios* ... *ct*] mancipio accepit de Poppea Prisc[*i liberta Note*].

Line 34 of the document enables us to fill in the gap after *seste*[*rtios* as *LD*. These clauses say that the transferee bought the slaves *sestertis nummis singulis* on account of 450 sesterces and received them in *mancipatio* — the same order as in the Transylvanian triptych is preserved ; first the statement of the fictitious price mentioned in the *mancipatio,* then the actual consideration.

The other triptych quoted, that for the *mancipatio* of the slave boy, also accords with this explanation of *apochatum pro uncis duabus*. It must, of course, be pointed out that here the stipulation against eviction is giving a warranty for double damages, but in the interior part of the triptych, *duplam* is written in above the line ([15]). The original omission of *duplam* is better explained as the result of following a style for a document giving a warranty for simple damages, than simply as a scribal omission of the word. The original form of the clause, *t*(*antam*) *p*(*ecuniam*) *p*(*robam*) *r*(*ecte*) *d*(*ari*) *f*(*ide*) *r*(*ogavit*) *Dasius Breucus,* is the same as that in the other two Transylvanian triptychs for *mancipationes* with stipulations for single damages : *tantam pecuniam probam recte dari f*(*ide*) *r*(*ogavit*) *Cl. Iulianus* in the sale of a female slave dealt with above ; *t*(*antam*) *p*(*ecuniam*) *r*(*ecte*) *d*(*ari*) *f*(*ide*) *r*(*ogavit*) *Andueia Batonis* in the sale of half of a house ([16]). But even with the insertion of *duplam* it is significantly different from that of the slave girl ([17]) in which a warranty for double damages is given : *<tan>tam pecuni<a>m et alterum tantum dari, fide rogavit Maximus Batonis*. Thus, either *duplam* was omitted accidentally

(15) Mommsen, *op. cit.*, p. 940f ; Bruns, *op. cit.*, p. 329 n. 5 and p. 429 : not shown by Arangio-Ruiz in his edition of the text.

(16) Bruns, *op. cit.*, no. 133.

(17) Bruns, *op. cit.*, no. 131.

— and against the intention of the parties — by a scribe who slavishly followed a style for a document containing a warranty for single damages in the event of eviction, or the document was deliberately drafted in this way by a seller who was then forced by the buyer to give a warranty for double damages. In either event, the document was modelled on a style which gave a warranty in the case of eviction for single damages only and it is suggested that *apocatum pro uncis duabus* owes its existence here to that fact ([18]). This also explains why here, as in those for single damages, the unit of damages chosen is the *interesse* unlike that for double where the unit is the price.

Against this interpretation of *apochatum pro uncis duabus* may be urged the use of *empta sportellaria* in the mancipatory document of the little slave girl which has been already mentioned ([19]). The opening clauses run :

> Maximus Batonis puellam nomine Passiam, sive ea quo alio nomine est, annorum circiter p(lus) m(inus) sex, empta sportellaria, emit mancipioque accepit de Dasio Verzonis, Pirusta ex Kavieretio, X ducentis quinque.

There have been a number of interpretations of *empta sportellaria* — *sportellaria* being a word otherwise unknown — but the only one which may affect us adversely is that of Mommsen ([20]) which has had a considerable following ([21]). Mommsen says that perhaps the girl had been sold to the vendor with her mother and that no price had been reckoned for her but she was included in the sale of the mother as a sort of accessory. It should be noted that Mommsen offered this suggestion because he thought the phrase corresponded to *apochatum pro uncis*

(18) That styles were used in the drawing up of the Transylvanian triptychs is evident from *partemve quam ex eo* in l. 9 of Bruns, *op. cit.*, no. 131 instead of *partemve quam ex ea*. The error is found in both the interior and exterior writing of the triptych and results from the use of a style which gave the masculine : cf. Mommsen, *op. cit.*, p. 923 ; Bruns, *op. cit.*, p. 330 n. 7.

(19) Bruns, *op. cit.*, no. 131.

(20) *Op. cit.*, p. 937 n. 2.

(21) *E.g.*, Arangio-Ruiz, *op. cit.*, p. 284 n. 1.

duabus (22) and it is also for this reason that it was accepted by others (23). Thus, if on other grounds the idea that *apochatum pro uncis duabus* refers to a receipt for a previous transaction is regarded as being very improbable, Mommsen's interpretation of *empta sportellaria* can hardly be used to bolster it. There are, moreover, very strong arguments against Mommsen's interpretation of *empta sportellaria*. First, as he himself says, there is no evidence that the word *sportella* was ever used to mean an accesory. Secondly, even a baby slave is potentially too valuable to be treated as a mere accessory. Even if the main object wanted were the mother slave and only one price in consideration of the whole transaction were mentionned there would still have to be *mancipatio* both of her and of the little girl and any mancipatory document would refer to both the mother and the daughter as having been bought and mancipated in return for the price. Thirdly, so far as I am aware, of the deminutives of *sporta* (a plaited basket) only *sportula*, not also *sportella*, was used in the transferred sense of 'a gift'. Fourthly, even assuming *sportella* might be used to mean a gift, *empta sportellaria*, " bought as a gift " is rather a contradiction in terms.

Mention should also be made here of the Transylvanian triptych for the sale and *mancipatio* of half of a house (24), which contains a warranty for simple damages but has nothing corresponding to *apochatum pro uncis duabus*. This would be against our interpretation of that clause only if it could lead one to think that the parties could directly exclude liability to the *actio auctoritatis*. There is no evidence elsewhere that they could — and all the indications lead to the contrary opinion (25) — and this document can hardly be relied upon for this purpose since the *mancipatio* is in connexion with provincial land which did not have the *ius Italici* (26). Thus, the *mancipatio* was invalid

(22) *Loc. cit.*

(23) Cf. Arangio-Ruiz, *loc. cit.*

(24) Bruns, *op. cit.*, no. 133.

(25) Cf. *supra*, p. 250.

(26) Arangio-Ruiz, *op. cit.*, p. 289.

and so in any event there could be no possibility of the *actio auctoritatis.* Doubt could arise only if the document followed exactly and without the change of any clause a style relating to Italic land and there is nothing to lead us to that conclusion. Even if it did so derive from such a style there could be grave doubt as to the legal accurary of the original.

16

The Form and Nature of Acceptilatio in Classical Roman Law

1. *ACCEPTUM HABERE* AND *ACCEPTUM FACERE.*

Until recently, it would seem to have been agreed among Romanists that in early classical Roman law only one form of words, namely « *Habesne acceptum ? habeo* » was permitted for a valid *acceptilatio*, but that by the time of Ulpian a second form (and no more), namely « *Acceptum facis ? facio* » had been accepted (1). Indeed, that this was the position is accepted without discussion by Mr. Nicholas in a very thorough article on the form of the stipulation (2). Mr. Nicholas' main goal is to show that in classical law *stipulatio* was a formal act and required to be made in one of six possible forms. In support of this, he stresses the importance of formal words in ritual acts in Roman law and after dealing with other acts which require formal words he goes on (3) :

> « More important, however, is the parallel, already mentioned, of *acceptilatio*. For this is intimately connected with the stipulation, of which it is, indeed, the *contrarius actus*. For *acceptilatio* Gaius admits only one formula which is given also by Ulpian in the Digest, with the addition that a second is also admissible... The form of *acceptilatio* was apparently never altered by legislation for Justinian in the Institutes reproduces Gaius, with Papinian's addition as to Greek. »

(1) *E.g.* Solazzi, 'L'Estinzione dell'Obligazione nel diritto romano' 1, 2nd ed., Naples 1935, p. 247 ; De Zulueta, 'The Institutes of Gaius' 2, Oxford 1953, p. 189.

(2) 'The Stipulation in Roman Law', 1953, L.Q.R. p. 63 *et seq.*

(3) *Op. cit.*, p. 69.

Perhaps the case of *acceptilatio* is even more fundamental for Mr. Nicholas than he himself admits, since it, alone of the institutions mentioned by him in support of his argument that the stipulation required formal words is, like stipulation, without doubt *iuris gentium* (4). This is an important point. It is one thing to show that in the *ius civile* there are ritual acts with formal words, quite another to show that ritual acts with formal words occur also in that part of Roman law which was open to peregrines. After all, the main purpose of the introduction of the *ius gentium* was to facilitate foreign trade and to protect *peregrini* and it is accepted that this is best accomplished by making the law as simple as possible (5).

But the contrary opinion, that *acceptilatio* did not require formal words, is suggested, to my knowledge, by Dr. Winkler

(4) Contra Solazzi : see *infra* pp. 207-9.

(5) The other institutions which Mr. Nicholas names are : *mancipatio, in iure cessio*, institution of an *heres*, appointment of *tutor testamentarius, exheredatio, cretio*, the creation of the various types of legacy, appointment of a *cognitor*, and the creation of *dos* by *dotis dictio*. Of these all except the last two are certainly ritual acts and *iuris civilis*. Probably a peregrine could appoint a *cognitor*, but how formal the institution was and whether ritual words were required is doubtful. C. 4.93 tells us that the *cognitor* was substitued for the dominus « *cum... certis et quasi solemnibus verbis* », while Ulpian in F.V. 318 has « *Non tamen sic putat certis verbis cognitorem dari debere, ut si quid fuisset adiectum vel detractum, non valeat datio, ut in legis actionibus* ». Nothing more may be meant than that a certain form of words was customary, as is commonly the case in court proceedings. Moreover, even if the institution were a semi-ritual act, it would not affect the present argument to any great extent since the words would be spoken in the presence of a judicial officer who would correct any error at once, and so a peregrine would be adequately protected. The evidence that *dotis dictio* required formal words is even weaker (Gai Epit. 2.9.3,4 ; C.Th. 3.13.4 ; G. 3.95 ; Lib. Sing. Reg. 6.1.2 ; D. 23.3.25 ; h.t. 44.1 ; h.t. 46.1). Buckland, who like others, maintains that *dotis dictio* was ritual has to use very sophisticated and unconvincing arguments to make it fit into his obviously correct concept of ritual acts ; « Ritual Acts and Formal Words », Festschrift Koschaker 1, p. 16 *et seq.* at pp. 24-25. Nor is it clear that a peregrine could create *dos* by *dotis dictio*. The only person who could make *dotis dictio* who might in practice (if it were permitted) be a peregrine would be the bride's debtor.

alone, in an article in which she attacks Mr. Nicholas' thesis ([6]). She submits that it is at least possible to hold this opposite view and that Gaius in a short treatment of *acceptilatio* need only, for teaching purposes, give one example of how it was carried out and that the fuller treatment in the Digest shows *acceptilationes* were in the form of question and answer but no more, as is seen from D. 46.4.6,7. Moreover, she says, the use of Greek does not appear to be restricted to particular forms. These arguments, however, are rather weak and do not take into account the construction of D. 46.4.7, which probably more than any other factor has inclined modern jurists to hold that *acceptilatio* required formal words.

> D. 46.4.7 (Ulpian *50 ad Sab.*) Sane et sic acceptilatio fieri potest : 'accepta facis decem ?' ille respondit 'facio'.

Dr. Winkler asks rhetorically why this form should be permitted for *acceptilatio* but others excluded ([7]). But this does not take us very far since the text by its insistence that this form could be used is very good evidence that it had once, and probably recently, been excluded. And, on the general view, the reason for the exclusion of this form would be that hitherto only one form « *habesne acceptum ? habeo* » had been recognised. Ulpian now admits, it would be argued, a second form, but no more. On this point, Dr. Winkler does not seem to make any impression on Mr. Nicholas' case.

However, despite the foregoing, it will be maintained in the present note, 1) that there is a vast difference in the meaning of *acceptum facere* and *acceptum habere*, 2) that it was because of his meaning, not its form, that « *accepta facis decem ? facio* » did not make a valid *acceptilatio* until perhaps as late as Ulpian, 3) that its acceptance at that time is very good evidence that *acceptilatio* did not need formal words, and 4) that other evidence is available tending to the same conclusion.

(6) « Gaius 3.92 », 5, R.I.D.A. (3rd ser.), 1958, p. 603 *et seq.*, especially pp. 619-620.

(7) *Op. cit.*, p. 620, n. 56.

To take *acceptum facere* first. There can be not the slightest doubt that in legal Latin the expression is technical and means always « To make an *acceptilatio* ». Excluding for the moment D. 46.4.7 which is the text in which we are interested, there are 47 juristic texts which use *acceptum facere* in that sense and not one which can bear any other meaning (8). It therefore seems a safe assumption that in D. 46.4.7 the only meaning which can be given to « *Accepta facis decem ? facio* » is « Do you make *acceptilatio* of the ten ? » « I do ». Pliny the Younger also uses the term in that way.

> Ep. 4.2. Ad quod te ne verbis magis quam rebus horter, quidquid mihi pater tuus debuit, acceptum tibi fieri iubeo.

Perhaps because *acceptum facere* had among lawyers acquired a technical meaning it is found nowhere else in lay Latin except in Pliny the Elder who, however, does use is differently (9).

But the texts, lay and legal, show that *acceptum habere* had a very different meaning.

> Livy 6.9.12. Sutrio recepto restituoque sociis Nepete exercitus ductus, quod per deditionem acceptum iam totum Etrusci habebant.

Here « *acceptum... habebant* » means simply « they had received ». So *acceptum habere* would mean « to have received ».

The only other non-legal texts which we have use *acceptum habere* in the same way.

(8) It would be pointless to give examples which would prove only that *acceptum facere* could be so used (which no one doubts) and it would take too much space to quote all the texts. Here, however, is a list of the texts. Labeo ; D. 28.7.20 pr. ; 46.3.91 ; 46.4.23 : Javolenus ; 12.4.10 ; 19.2.21 ; 24.3.66.6 : Celsus ; 46.3.71.2 : Julian ; 18.4.19 ; 18.5.5 pr. ; 23.3.49 ; 30.81.5 ; 30.82.5 ; 30.84.7 ; 34.3.10 ; 39.5.2.3 ; 45.1.56.8 ; 46.7.14 pr. : Pomponius ; 46.3.80 ; 46.4.10 : Africanus ; 39.6.24 : Gaius ; 4.2.10.1 ; 46.4.22 ; G. 3.171, 172,215 : Venuleius ; D. 42.8.25 pr. ; 46.4.21 : Florentinus ; 46.4.18.1 : Ulpian ; 4.2.9.7 ; 4.2.14 pr., 3,9 ; 17.1.10.13 ; 23.3.36 ; 32.3 pr. ; 42.8.10.14 ; 44.4.7.1 ; 46.4.8.3,4 ; 46.4.13.6,9,10,12 : Paul 23.4.12.2 : 46.3.10 ; 46.4.11.1 : J. 3.29.1.

(9) Hist. Nat. 8.61 ; 28.10 ; 34.139,142.

Curtius 4.1.18. Admiratus Hephaestion magnitudinem animi spernentis, quod alii per ignes ferrumque peterent, « Vos quidem macte virtute » inquit « estote, qui primi intellexistis, quanto maius esset regnum fastidire quam accipere. Ceterum date aliquem regiae stirpis, qui meminerit a vobis acceptum habere se regnum ».

Vulg. Tob. 12.5. Et vocantes eum, pater scilicet, et filius, tulerunt eum in partem : et rogare coeperunt ut dignaretur dimidiam partem omnium, quae attulerant, acceptam habere.

The legal texts tell the same story. Never do we find *acceptum habere* used to signify that an *acceptilatio* has taken place, but the phrase always gives or expresses the words used in the making of the *acceptilatio.*

G. 3.169. I*tem* per acceptilationem tollitur obligatio. acceptilatio autem est velut imaginaria solutio. quod enim ex verborum obligatione tibi debeam, id si velis mihi remittere, poterit sic fieri, ut patiaris haec verba me dicere : QUOD EGO TIBI PROMISI, HABESNE ACCEPTUM ? et tu respondeas : HABEO.

D. 46.4.15. (Pomponius *27 ad Sab.*) Si is qui Stichum promisit ita interroget : 'quod Stichum promisi, Stichum et Pamphilum habesne acceptos ?'. puto recte accepto latum et pro supervacuo Pamphili mentionem factam, quemadmodum si is qui decem promisit ita interroget : 'quod tibi decem promisi, viginti habesne accepta ?', etiam decem nomine erit liberatus.

D. 46.4.6. (Ulpian *47 ad Sab.*) Pluribus stipulationibus factis si promissor ita accepto rogasset : 'quod ego tibi promisi, habesne acceptum ?', si quidem apparet, quid actum est, id solum per acceptilationem sublatum est : si non apparet, omnes stipulationes solutae sunt : ......

D. 46.4.9. (Paul *12 ad Sab.*) Pars stipulationis accepto fieri potest non tantum, si sic dicat : 'ex nummis decem, quos tibi promisi, quinque habesne acceptos ?' sed et si sic : 'quod ego tibi promisi, id pro parte dimidia habesne acceptum ?'.

The relevant formula is given by Florentinus (*8 Inst.*) in D. 46.4.18.1 and shows the same usage.

> « Quod Numerius Negidius Aulo Agerio promisit spopondit, id haberetne a se acceptum, Numerius Negidius Aulum Agerium rogavit, Aulus Agerius Numerio Negidio acceptum fecit. »

Nowhere do the respective meanings of *habere acceptum* and *facere acceptum* appear more clearly. « *Id haberetne a se acceptum ... rogavit* » can only mean « He asked if he had received it from him ». A translation such as « He asked if he had made *acceptilatio* from him » would be absurd. Apart from other considerations, it is excluded by the words « *a se* ». On the other hand « *acceptum fecit* » can mean only « he made *acceptilatio* ». It is quite impossible to translate it as « he accepted it », firstly because in fact he received nothing, and secondly, if it were meant to express the words used by Aulus Agerius in reply to Numerius Negidius it would be dependent on a verb such as '*ait*' and be in the subjunctive.

Accordingly, legal as well as lay usage shows that *acceptum habere* always meant « to have received », never « to make *acceptilatio* ». If it could have borne the latter meaning we would, without debt, have found texts where the expression was used to indicate that *acceptilatio* had taken place. And this interpretation of the meaning is borne out by the history of *acceptilatio. Acceptilatio* was the *contrarius actus* of the *stipulatio* and originally mere performance did not release the debtor. *Acceptilatio* at that time accompanied the payment and was necessary for the extinction of the debt. The words, therefore, testified to a real payment. And considering the archaic nature of « *acceptum habesne ? habeo* » there can be little doubt that this form goes back to that period, where it must have meant « Have you received ? » « I have ».

Thus, to sum up so far : « *acceptum facere* » means « to make an *acceptilatio* » : and « *acceptum habere* » means « to have received ».

There is therefore, a great difference between the meanings of the phrases « *Accepta habes decem ? habeo* » and « *Accepta facis decem ? facio* ». In the first, on the face of it there had been a payment, in the second clearly there has been no payment. And I submit that it was because the latter showed that no payment had been made that it was so long excluded from acting as a release. As in stipulation the words used rather than the intent of the parties were of primary importance. While in « *acceptum habesne ? habeo* » it did not affect the validity of the release that there had been no payment but merely a pretence of such of which everyone was aware, a failure to pretend vitiated the release. Where the law recognises and acts on a fiction in the dealings of individuals, the truth shoud not appear *ex facie* the words or writs which form the basis of the fiction. Therefore, Gaius tells us right at the beginning of his account of *acceptilatio* in the Institutes 3.169 that it was a sort of imaginary payment. Even in modern law where a fiction is recognised, the true position must not appear *ex facie*. Scotland provides a good example of this.

Under Scots law, it is theoretically impossible to transfer land in security, although often it would be useful to do so. Scottish conveyancers have therefore devised a way round the prohibition. The normal document (called a Disposition) which transfers land and which must be registered begins : « I, A.B., in consideration of the sum of £ —, of which I acknowledge the receipt do hereby sell and dispone to C.D. heritably and irredeemably all and whole that plot of ground... ». Where, however, C.D. makes an advance to A.B. and wants the property to be transferred to him as security, the Disposition runs : « I, A.B., in consideration of certain good and onerous causes and considerations do hereby sell and dispose to C.D. heritably and irredeemably all and whole that plot of ground... ». The Disposition is then registered and the debtor is protected by another document which relates the true state of affairs but is not registered. Every Scottish law student and practitioner knows that when he sees « for certain good and onerous causes and considerations » he is dealing with a security although the document purports otherwise. Indeed, even the Inland Revenue authorities do not demand the stamp duty which would be payable on an out and out transfer. Nevertheless, the general knowledge of the true intent of the parties, which is contrary to the law, does not affect the validity of the transfer. If, however, the parties with the same intention allowed it to appear on the face of the deed which was to be registered, they would achieve nothing. Thus, a Disposition beginning : « I, A.B., in consideration of an advance of £ — of which I acknowledge the receipt do hereby dispone to C.D. all and whole that plot of ground... » would be refused registration.

Moreover, the extension permitting « *facisne acceptum ? facio* » to constitute a valid *acceptilatio* is very strong evidence that *acceptilatio* did not require formal words in classical law. The difference in meaning from the form « *habesne acceptum ? habeo* » is too great for it to be accepted as the first alternative. Rather, an alternative form, having approximately the same meaning, *e.g.* « *dedine ? dedisti* » would have been introduced. The acceptance of « *acceptum facisne ? facio* » shows not a relaxation of form but that the concept of *acceptilatio* was undergoing considerable modification by the time of Ulpian and that its fictitious nature was ceasing to have any importance ([10]). The retention of « *habesne acceptum ? habeo* » as the main form would be due to legal conservatism.

There are also other arguments that *acceptilatio* was informal.

First, Greek was allowed provided the *acceptilatio* were made as it would have been if Latin had been used.

> D. 46.4.8.4 (Ulpian *48 ad Sab.*) ... et ideo puto et Graece posse acceptum fieri, dummodo sic fiat, ut in Latinis verbis solet : ἔχεις λαβὼν δηνάρια τοσα ; ἔχω λαβών.

Ulpian, not Papinian as Nicholas says ([11]), tells us he thinks Greek can be used, and he gives a form of *acceptilatio* in Greek. It would be straining commonsense to assert that this form were

(10) « *Sane et sic* » in D. 46.4.7 make it probable that the modification was generally accepted in the time of Ulpian and that he was not responsible. For the breakdown of the fiction of performance see *infra*, pp. 407 *et seq.*

(11) *Op. cit.*, p. 69.

the only one possible because it alone is given here since we know that Ulpian himself would, at the very least, allow two forms in Latin. And the very fact that Greek was permitted is a strong argument against the view that *acceptilatio* required formal words. Where ritual words are needed, translations are not usually permitted. Thus there is not the slightest evidence that Greek was ever allowed in *mancipatio* and *in iure cessio* and there is a very strong presumption against its use, while we know that a mancipatory will could not be written in Greek until 439 A.D. ([12]).

Secondly, since Justinian's Institutes reproduce Gaius with the addition as to Greek, and there was, so far as we know, no legislation, Mr. Nicholas holds ([13]) that *acceptilatio* remained formal in the time of Justinian. This is forced upon him because it would be illogical to hold that Gaius' account showed that *acceptilatio* was formal, while the same account in Justinian dealt with informal release. But it is most unlikely that *acceptilatio* was formal in the time of Justinian. If it were, it would be the sole remaining ritual act which required formal words. It is much more probable that Justinian is giving merely an example and at that the most common ([14]). And if one holds that *acceptilatio* were informal in the time of Justinian, then there is no evidence whatever that Gaius took any other view.

2. *CONTRARIUS ACTUS.*

The complex nature of *acceptilatio* in classical law derives from two factors : first, it began as the *contrarius actus* of the stipulation, but sometime during the Republic ceased to be so ; secondly, thereupon, it continued to act as a release under the fiction that the obligation had been performed.

(12) C. 6.23.21.6. The same argument also weighs against the view that *stipulatio* required formal words.

(13) *Loc. cit.*

(14) Again remember legal conservation. In the case of stipulation, the oldest form « *Spondesne ? spondeo* » occurs several times more frequently than all the other examples added together.

From its original connection with *stipulatio* it retains during classical and Justinianic law a number of rules, none of which ever seems to have been greatly weakened.

The first of these is that there can be no conditional *acceptilatio* (15). Naturally if the original scope of *acceptilatio* was to terminate a verbal obligation when there had been performance and to provide evidence of this, no *dies* or *condicio* could be possible. Likewise, of course, this would mean that orginally there could be no such thing as a partial *acceptilatio*. And we have evidence that this was the case, although in this respect *acceptilatio* does show signs of development.

> G. 3.172. Item, quod debetur, pro parte recte solvitur ; an autem in partem acceptilatio fieri possit, quaesitum *est*.

So, in the time of Gaius, an attempt was being made to permit a partial *acceptilatio* but this had not yet prevailed. But other texts show that eventually the innovation was completely accepted (16).

> D. 46.4.10. (Pomponius *26 ad Sab.*) Sed et si non numerata pecunia, sed certum corpus, veluti homo in stipulationem deductus est, potest ex parte acceptilatio fieri : quo modo et uni ex heredibus acceptum fieri potest.
>
> D. 46.4.13.1. (Ulpian *50 ad Sab.*) Si id, quod in stipulationem deductum est, divisionem non recipiat, acceptilatio in partem nullius erit momenti, ut puta si servitus fuit praedii rustici vel urbani ......
>
> D. 46.4.9 (Paul *12 ad Sab.*) This is quoted *supra* p. 395.

The second such rule is that only verbal obligations can be so extinguished. Any other obligation had first to be turned into a stipulation.

> G. 3.170. Quo genere, ut diximus, *toll*untur *illae obligationes* quae *in verbis consistunt,* non etiam ceterae. consen-

(15) D. 46.4.4 (Pomponius *9 ad Sab.*) ; h.t. 5 (Ulpian *34 ad Sab.*).

(16) D. 46.4.17 (Julian *54 dig.*) is probably interpolated. *Cf.* Solazzi, *op. cit.*, p. 25, Index Itp.

> taneum visum est verbis factam obligationem posse aliis verbis dissolvi. sed id quod ex alia causa debeatur potest in stipulationem deduci et per acceptilationem *dissolvi*.

This rule remained unchanged in the law of Justinian ([17]).

The third rule which *acceptilatio* owes to its origins is that just as there could be no *stipulatio alteri*, so one could not make *acceptilatio* on behalf of a person not in one's *potestas*. But whereas in the case of stipulation there was some relaxation in the law of Justinian ([18]) there is no sign of any in *acceptilatio*.

> D. 46.4.3. (Paul *4 ad Sab.*) Per procuratorem nec liberari nec liberare quisquam acceptilatione sine mandato potest.

There is general agreement that *sine mandato* is a Justinianic interpolation ([19]), and the interpolation is clearly shown by a text of Ulpian (*50 ad Sab.*).

> D. 46.4.13.10. Tutor, curator furiosi acceptum ferre non potuit, nec procurator quidem potest facere acceptum : sed hi omnes debent novare (possunt enim) et sic accepto facere. ne his quidem accepto fieri potest, sed novatione facta poterunt liberari per acceptilationem. nam et in absentium persona hoc remedio uti solemus : stipulamur ab aliquo id novandi causa, quod nobis absens debet, et ita accepto liberamus, a quo stipulati sumus : ita fiet, ut absens novatione, praesens acceptilatione liberetur.

Solazzi argues correctly ([20]) that the former of these texts does not in Justinianic law free the procurator from the necessity of proceeding to an *acceptilatio* by way of *novatio*. *Sine mandato* has been added by Tribonian who demands that the procurator should have a special mandate before he has the power to make *novatio*. It is one example of the Justinianic restrictions on the powers of the procurator.

(17) D. 46.4.8.3 (Ulpian *48 ad Sab.*) ; J. 3.29.1.
(18) *E.g.* D. 45.1.38.22 ; J. 3.19.19,20.
(19) *Cf.* Index Itp. ; SERRAO, 'Il Procurator', Milan 1947, p. 36.
(20) *Op. cit.*, p. 251.

> D. 46.4.8.4. (Ulpian *48 ad Sab.*) Filius familias promittendo patrem civiliter non obligat, sed se obligat : propter quod accepto rogare filius familias potest, ut se liberet, quia ipse obligatus est, pater autem acceptum rogando nihil agit, cum non sit ipse obligatus, sed filius. idem erit et in servo dicendum : nam et servus accepto liberari potest, et tolluntur etiam honorariae obligationes, si quae sunt adversus dominum. quia hoc iure utimur, ut iuris gentium sit acceptilatio : ...... ([21])

This text shows the full force of the doctrine. Where a *filiusfamilias* enters into a contract he himself is fully liable ([22]), but the *paterfamilias* is not unless (and only on the extent that) one of the *actiones adiecticiae qualitatis* is available. Thus, the liability of the *pater* is purely subordinate and differs therefore from the liability of a *fideiussor*. Since the *pater* is not subject to the *potestas* of the *filius,* he cannot, we are told, make a valid *acceptilatio* to release a debt incurred by his *filius*. The text then goes on to say that the same applies where a slave is liable under a stipulation, although here, of course, there is only a *naturalis obligatio*. But when the slave himself is released by *acceptilatio* this wipes out even the master's praetorian obligations. Conversely, just as one could acquire through the stipulation of a slave in whom one had a usufruct ([23]) so an *acceptilatio* could be made to a *servus fructuarius* which would release the usufructuary.

> D. 7.1.23 pr. (Ulpian *17 ad Sab.*) Sed sicuti stipulando fructuario adquirit, ita etiam paciscendo eum adquirere exceptionem Iulianus libro trigensimo ([24]) digestorum scribit. idemque et si acceptum rogaverit, liberationem ei parere.

(21) '*Civiliter*' would seem to be interpolated ; *cf.* Index Itp. ; for other suggested interpolations, see *infra*, pp. 208 f.

(22) *Cf.* Solazzi, 'Sulla Capacità del *filius familias* di stare in giudizio', Scritti 1, pp. 1 *et seq.*

(23) *E.g.* G. 2.91 ; D. 7.1.24.

(24) It should read 35. *Cf.* F.V. 72.i. ; D. 2.14.55.

Again, there is the rule that a slave cannot release his master's debtor by *acceptilatio* even at his owner's request.

> D. 46.4.22 (Gaius *3 de verborum obligationibus*) Servus nec iussu domini acceptum facere potest.

This stems from the ancient principle that a slave can do nothing to injure his master (25). Just as originally the slave could make a valid stipulation the benefits of which would accrue to his master while he could not bind his master by stipulation (26), so he could release his master by making an *acceptilatio* on his behalf (27) but could not release his master's debtor. Solazzi denies this reason (28), and says that the slave's incapacity is purely on the ground of form. The reply « *Habeo acceptum* », he says, to be effective, must come from the creditor. But why, from the point of view of form, should it ? A payment of a debt due to the master, if made to the slave with the master's consent would, of course, like such a payment to anyone else, release the debtor. Therefore, considering *acceptilatio* from the point of view of form, there is no reason why a slave's acknowledgement that he has received the sum due to his master should not likewise effect the release.

What is perhaps a slightly more conjectural instance of the influence that *stipulatio* continued to have over *acceptilatio* is in G. 3.171.

> Quamvis *autem fiat acceptilatio* imaginaria solutione, tamen mulier sine tutore auctore acceptilationem facere non potest, cum alioquin solvi ei sine tutore auctore possit.

Almost nothing is known of the rights and duties of the *tutor mulieris* in early law, but Bonfante tells us that the history of

(25) This, the common formulation, is rather too wide : *cf.* Buckland, « The Roman Law of Slavery », Cambridge 1907, p. 163.

(26) The better view would also seem to be that while a slave could receive by *mancipatio* he could not so deliver : *cf.* Mitteis, « Römisches Privatrecht », Leipzig 1908, p. 208 and n. 16 ; *contra*, Buckland, *op. cit.*, p. 159.

(27) *Cf.* D. 46.4.8.1,2 ; 11 pr. ; 1,2,3.

(28) « L'Estinzione » *cit.*, p. 250.

tutela mulieris is the history of its dissolution (29). Accepting Bonfante's view (and few would quarrel with it), perhaps the rules expressed in Gaius' text developed in the following way. Clearly the motive behind *tutela mulieris* was to protect the woman's property for the benefit of the person who would become heir on her death and this person would normally himself be the tutor. Accordingly, the woman was not allowed to do anything which might diminish her patrimony without her tutor's consent. Therefore, without his authority she could not release a verbal obligation i.e. by *acceptilatio*. Probably, like a pupil in classical law (30), she could receive payment of a debt and the money became hers although the debtor was not released. But eventually with the breakdown of the requirement of *contrarius actus* and the weakening of the position of the *tutor mulieris* it was admitted that payment to her, without her tutor's consent of a debt due under stipulation released the debtor without any further ado. At the same time however, she was not allowed to grant *acceptilatio* since it, being now a fictitious payment would result in a definite loss to her patrimony. And this rule, as a result of Roman conservation, was not altered in classical law (31).

Perhaps some of the foregoing will seem self-apparent, but it is nevertheless important to remember that many of the rules of *acceptilatio* have their origin in its connection with stipulation. Otherwise it is only too easy to draw false conclusions as to the nature of *acceptilatio*.

(29) « Corso di diritto romano » 1. Diritto di Famiglia. Rome 1925, p. 409.

(30) *Cf.* G. 2.84.

(31) De Zulueta, *op. cit.* 2 p. 189 attributes it to *acceptilatio* being originally an *actus legitimus*. But on the ground of formalism it is difficult to see why the act of a woman should be invalid unless accompanied by the tutor's consent which, strictly speaking, is not part of the act. In respect of the disabilities of women a distinction should be drawn between cases where the woman lacks capacity, even with the consent of the tutor, and cases where she can act provided she has such authority e.g. *acceptilatio, mancipatio* or in making a will. In the latter category all the acts are such as could either result in a loss to her patrimony or at least weaken the right of the *tutor legitimus* to it.

The awareness that *acceptilatio* had been the *contrarius actus* of *stipulatio* would seem to have been blurred as early as Gaius otherwise it is difficult to account for his weak reason for *acceptilatio* being available to release verbal obligations only (32). And for later jurists matters were made even more complicated by Papinian including it among *actus legitimi* « *qui non recipiunt diem vel condicionem* » (33). The meaning of *actus legitimus,* which occurs only in this text is doubtful. It may signify nothing more than 'a legal institution which cannot be made subject to a condition' ; and indeed, *legitimi* may even be an interpolation (34). But *actus legitimi* are now, without any real evidence, taken to mean solemn transactions originating in the old *mos maiorum* and so false conclusions about the original nature of *acceptilatio* are drawn (35). It is of course true that *acceptilatio* could not be conditional but this, as we have seen, was because it was, to begin with, a release from a verbal obligation. This also explains why a partial *acceptilatio* was at first impossible although it would be difficult to account for this on the ground that it was a formal act in the law.

Probably Solazzi (36) more than anyone else was led astray by failing to give proper weight to the importance of the original purpose of *acceptilatio.* For instance, basing himself to a great extent on the texts cited above in this connection, he maintains that even in classical law *acceptilatio* was not *iuris gentium.* The steps in his argument are as follows. First, he says that D. 46.3.107 (Pomponius *2 enchiriddi*) of which he quotes part only, denies that *acceptilatio* was *iuris gentium.*

(32) G. 3.170. *Cf. supra,* p. 400. *Cf.* Pomponius D. 46.3.80.

(33) D. 50.17.77.

(34) *Cf.* Index Itp.

(35) *E.g.* ARANGIO-RUIZ, 'Istituzioni di diritto romani', 14th. ed., Naples, p. 86 ; BUCKLAND, 'Textbook of Roman Law', 2nd ed., Cambridge, 1932, p. 180, n. 1. Even a shrewd observer like De Zulueta could write « Like *stipulatio* it was *iuris gentium,* but it retained characteristics that show it to have once been an *actus legitimus* », *loc. cit.* This does not even agree with Pomponius who says that it is an *actus legitimus.* Perhaps like stipulation *acceptilatio* was at the beginning restricted to one form, but this need not make it a very formal act. *Cf. supra,* p. 202, n. 31.

(36) « L'Estinzione » *cit.,* pp. 247 *et seq.*

Verborum obligatio aut naturaliter resolvitur aut civiliter : naturaliter veluti solutione aut cum res in stipulationem deducta sine culpa promissoris in rebus humanis esse desiit : civiliter veluti acceptilatione vel cum in eandem personam ius stipulantis promitentisque devenit.

But the contrast is not as he would have it between release by matter of fact and release by operation of the *ius civile*. If it were, since Pomponius is contrasting all the *genera* of release of a verbal obligation (this follows from « *Verborum obligatio aut naturaliter resolvitur aut civiliter* ») we would have to hold that stipulation could not be released by any praetorian mode, which would be odd in the case of a *iuris gentium* obligation. Especially, we should have to hold that *confusio* of a verbal obligation is also *iuris civilis* ([37]). Here *civiliter* means not « by operation of the *ius civile* » but, as elsewhere, simply « by operation of law » ([38]).

He then turns to D. 46.4.8.4 ([39]) in which he admits that *civiliter* is interpolated ([40]). He then declares that the text is also interpolated from « *idem erit et in servo dicendum* » because if for the slave the same principles operated as for the son of whom it is said that he can make an *acceptilatio* « *quia ipse obligatus est* » neither the slave nor his master could make an *acceptilatio*. What he is really saying is that although *civiliter* is interpolated, the son can release himself by *acceptilatio* because he is bound *iure civile*, whereas his *pater* cannot since he is only liable *iure gentium*, and therefore since the slave is not liable *iure civili* he cannot release himself by *acceptilatio*.

(37) Accordingly so concluded by SOLAZZI, *op. cit.*, p. 279. On the same page n. 1 he declares that the distinction drawn by Pomponius between extinction *naturaliter* and *civiliter* is valid not only for *verborum obligatio* but for all obligations. Yet elsewhere he admits that there could be *compensatio* even of *naturales obligationes* at least in the *actiones bonae fidei*. « La Compenzatione nel diritto romano », 2nd ed., Naples 1950, p. 7.

(38) *Civiliter* is also used to signify that an *obligatio* is simply actionable as opposed to a natural obligation. *Cf.* D. 41.1.53 ; 41.2.24 ; 44.7.14 ; 45.1.1.2 ; 46.2.1.1 (where « *an honoraria* » is a gloss : *cf.* Index Itp.).

(39) Quoted *supra*, p. 204.

(40) « L'Estinzione » *cit.*, p. 248, n. 1.

But we have seen that the reason for the rule in both cases is that the primary debtor is the son or slave while the obligation of the *pater* or *dominus* is purely subsidiary and since the latter, naturally, are not in the *potestas* of the former they cannot release them by *acceptilatio*. There are no traces of interpolation in the text (41).

3. THE BREAKDOWN OF THE FICTION.

The second great factor in the nature of *acceptilatio* was its character as a fictional payment. When it ceased to be required as the *contrarius actus* of a verbal obligation which had been fulfilled it found this new function. No doubt for some time after it was no longer essential to release a stipulation (42) it would still be used where payment had been made and would retain all the characteristics it had when it was required, but eventually would be used only where there had been no performance. Probably, at this point it would be a complete fiction. Not much later, however, the jurists would begin to destroy its fictional character bit by bit. A fiction of this type cannot retain its purety long. When this process began we cannot say, nor can we trace its history to any great extent. Indeed, although in some cases we can show a change in juristic attitude between early and late classical law, in those cases in which we might expect the fiction to break down quickest we have no early authority.

Perhaps the first attacks on the fiction would be in the spheres of release in fraud of creditors and of donations between husband and wife.

(41) The order of the text at the end may be disarranged : *cf.* Index Itp. ; but this is not necessarily so. *Honorariae obligationes* and not *honorariae actiones* should not in itself be suspicious in the time of Ulpian, since *obligatio* often by then did refer to a praetorian obligation : *cf.* SEGRÈ, *Studi Bonfante* 3, p. 601, who, however, on p. 599 holds that there is a post-classical and Byzantine tendency to use *obligationes honorariae*. See the works cited by him *op. cit.*, p. 599, n. 291.

(42) When this was cannot be stated, but it was certainly during the Republic. Cf. LÉVY-BRUHL, 'Le deuxième chapitre de la loi Aquilia'. R.I.D.A. (3rd Ser.), 5, 1958, p. 507 *et seq.*

For the former, however, we have only the testimony of Ulpian.

> D. 42.8.1.2. (Ulpian *66 ad ed.*) Ait ergo praetor 'quae fraudationis causa gesta erunt'. haec verba generalia sunt et continent in se omnem omnino in fraudem factam vel alienationem vel quemcumque contractum. quodcumque igitur fraudis causa factum est, videtur his verbis revocari, qualecumque fuerit : nam late ista verba patent. sive ergo rem alienavit sive acceptilatione vel pacto aliquem liberavit.

> D. 42.8.10.14. (Ulpian *63 ad ed.*) Si, cum mulier fraudandorum creditorum consilium inisset, marito suo eidemque debitori in fraudem creditorum acceptum debitum fecerit dotis constituendae causa, locum habet haec actio et per hanc omnis pecunia, quam maritus debuerat, exigitur nec mulier de dote habet actionem (43) ......

Both texts have been interpolated but not in any way which would diminish their value for us (44). They both show quite clearly that it is accepted by Ulpian at least that the court will take notice of the fact that really there has been no payment.

For the breakdown of the fiction in *donatio inter virum et uxorem* we have evidence as early as Julian.

> D. 24.1.5.1. (Ulpian *32 ad Sab.*) Si maritus duos reos habeat Titium et mulierem et mulieri accepto tulerit donationis causa, neuter liberatur, quia acceptilatio non valet : et haec Iulianus libro septimo decimo digestorum scribit. plane si mihi proponas Titio acceptum latum, ipse quidem liberabitur, mulier vero manebit obligata (45).

But although for neither of the above situations have we evidence that the fiction broke down early, we have such evidence in other cases.

> D. 28.7.20 pr. (Labeo *2 post. a Iavoleno epit.*) Mulier, quae viro suo ex dote promissam pecuniam debebat, virum here-

(43) *Cf.* D. 18.4.2.5.
(44) *Cf.* Index Itp.
(45) *Cf.* D. 24.1.32.23.

> dem ita instituerat, si eam pecuniam quam doti promisisset, neque petisset neque exegisset. puto, si vir denuntiasset ceteris heredibus per se non stare, quo minus acceptum faceret id quod ex dote sibi deberetur, statim eum heredem futurum. quod si solus heres institutus esset in tali condicione, nihilo minus puto statim eum heredem futurum, quia ἀδύνατος condicio pro non scripto accipienda est.

Thus, were a wife constitued a dowry by *dotis dictio* (46) which was never paid and left her husband her heir on condition that he neither sued for nor exacted the dowry, it was held as early as Labeo (or perhaps Javolenus) that if the husband were prepared to make *acceptilatio* to his co-heirs he would become heir immediately. This relaxation of the fiction might have become necessary as the only way in which the husband could take his share of the inheritance. A *pactum de non petendo* might not at first have been sufficient, although it was later (47), since the husband would still have the right to sue for the dowry although his co-heirs could meet him with an *exceptio*. A declaration by the husband that it was not due to him that *acceptilatio* was not made, though it could have only the force of a pact may have been permitted on the facts either because the co-heirs had not entered the inheritance or because they refused to make *acceptilatio* (47). This relaxation of the fiction is the one for which we have the earliest proof in the texts.

Javolenus is also responsible for giving us proof of the disintegration of the fiction in another field.

> D. 12.4.10 (*Iavolenus primo ex Plautio*) Si mulier ei cui nuptura erat cum dotem dare vellet, pecuniam quae sibi debebatur acceptam fecit neque nuptiae insecutae sunt, recte ab eo pecunia condicetur, quia nihil interest, utrum ex numeratione pecunia ad eum sine causa an per acceptilationem pervenerit.

A woman by way of dowry releases by *acceptilatio* a debt owed to her by her future husband. The marriage does not take place

(46) *Cf.* Index Itp.
(47) *Cf.* D. 35.1.7.1.

and we are told that the woman has a *condictio* for the recovery of the sum, which could never have been the case if the *acceptilatio* were regarded as a true payment by the man for which the woman released him. Nevertheless, the *acceptilatio* extinguished the verbal obligation, otherwise Javolenus could not have said « *quia nihil interest, utrum ex numeratione pecunia ad eum sine causa an per acceptilationem pervenerit* » (48).

The cases so far dealt with, although probably among the earliest, are unsatisfactory for us to the extent that they do not show any signs of development and might suggest that in classical law *acceptilatio* had lost all traces of its former position as a fiction. But that this was not the case is shown by other situations.

> D. 46.4.23. (Labeo *5 pithanon a Paulo epit.*) Si ego tibi acceptum feci, nihilo magis ego a te liberatus sum. PAULUS : immo cum locatio conductio, emptio venditio conventione facta est et nondum res intercessit, utrimque per acceptilationem, tametsi ab alterutra parte dumtaxat intercessit, liberantur obligatione.

Labeo tells us that if I release you by *acceptilatio,* I am not in any way released from my obligation to you. Obviously, he is thinking of obligations under a bilateral contract (49) and where neither party has performed his part of the agreement. Where there is such a bilateral, consensual contract (50) which is unperformed a release by one party would normally terminate the contract (51), but Labeo holds fast to the fiction that *acceptilatio*

(48) In D. 23.3.43, Ulpian tells us that in the same situation Scaevola, with whom he agrees, held that the *acceptilatio* was void and that the original obligation remained. But the text may be interpolated : *cf.* Beseler, 45 ZSS (1925), 489 ; Amelotti, « La *Donatio Mortis Causa* in diritto romano », Milan 1953, pp. 180-181.

(49) No one would suggest that if I am your debtor under a stipulation and I am left a legacy by a testator to whom you are heir, *acceptilatio* of the *stipulatio,* without anything further, would have any effect on the legacy.

(50) The contract must be consensual because only such can exist where both parties have still to perform their part of the agreement.

(51) *Cf. e.g.* D. 18.1.72 ; Duff, ' Studies in the Roman Law of Sale dedicated to De Zulueta ', ed. by Daube, Oxford 1959, pp. 69-70.

is a payment of what is owed (52) and so the releasing party is not himself freed from his obligation. Paul, however, in the case of sale and hire, which are the situations in which this would normally operate holds that the releasing party is himself freed. For him, in this respect, *acceptilatio* is nothing but a release where there has been no performance. When the view accepted by Paul became current can be more closely dated since we have a text of Julian (*15 dig.*) putting forward the same opinion.

> D. 18.5.5 pr. Cum emptor venditori vel emptori venditor acceptum faciat, voluntas utriusque ostenditur id agentis, ut a negotio discedatur et perinde habeatur, ac si convenisset inter eos, ut neuter ab altero quicquam peteret, sed ut evidentius appareat, acceptilatio in hac causa non sua natura, sed potestate conventionis valet.

Both of these texts are widely held interpolated as to form (53), but one might have thought it difficult to dispute their substance. But this too, has been done. Perozzi held that the substance of the latter was interpolated by Justinian since in classical law *acceptilatio* had no effect on obligations other than verbal or literal (54). And this seems also to have been the opinion of Beseler who would reconstruct the text as follows : '*Cum emptor venditori vel emptori venditor acceptum facit, nihil agitur*' (55). But apart from the fact that that side of the contract which is to be the object of the *acceptilatio* might well have been turned into a verbal obligation by an Aquilian stipulation and this has been omitted for reasons of brevity (as is certainly the case in the situation discussed by Labeo in D. 46.4.23 or the *acceptilatio* could never have wiped out the obligation of one party), both Perozzi and Beseler ignore the important point that the consensual contract is still *integer* (56).

(52) There must have been a *stipulatio Aquiliana* although it is not mentioned.

(53) *Cf.* Index Itp.

(54) ' Istituzioni di diritto romano ', 2nd ed., Rome 1928, p. 403, n. 1.

(55) 47 ZSS (1927), p. 358.

(56) *Cf.* Riccobono, ' Studi Bonfante ' 1, p. 155.

Where a consensual contract is *integer* and the parties change one of the essential terms, the old contract is wiped out and a new one rises in its stead ([57]), and where one side of the obligation is waived the contract is terminated and no new one takes its place. Hence, in an *integer* consensual contract even an invalid *acceptilatio* could have the effect of destroying the contract completely, provided one recognised that that *acceptilatio* was a mode of release without performance ([58]). Solazzi, in his turn, holds that both texts are interpolated as to substance ([59]). He gives the additional reason for his view that *acceptilatio* by the buyer of the seller attests that he has received the object. How, he asks, could such a declaration release the buyer from the obligation to pay the price. But this argument would be valid only if *acceptilatio* had always retained its pure character as a fictitious payment whereas it is abundantly clear that during the classical period this was lost step by step. Moreover, Solazzi fails to ask himself one fundamental question. D. 46.4.23 is a text of Labeo *5 pithamon* epitomised by Paul, and on Solazzi's view one must hold that the whole substance of the section supposed to represent the view of Paul is interpolated. But Paul must have held an opinion differing from that of Labeo or he would not have bothered to discuss the point. And it is difficult to see what this could have been other than that given in the text.

We can also trace the disintegration of the fiction in the history of *legatum liberationis*. *Legatum liberationis* is not early ([60]), but in classical law it could be made in two main ways ; either by *legatum sinendi modo* or by *legatum per damnationem*. The earliest reference to a *legatum liberationis per damnationem,* which is the form in which we are interested is in a text of Pomponius (*6 ad Sab.*).

(57) *Cf. supra*, p. 212, n. 51.

(58) This is surely what is meant by '*sed ut evidentius etc*' whether or not it is an interpolation.

(59) *Op. cit.*, pp. 268-270.

(60) The earliest reference is to Nerva and Atilicinus in D. 34.3.16 : *cf.* BIONDI, 'Successione Testamentaria', 2nd ed., Milan 1955, pp. 455 *et seq.*

> D. 34.3.2 pr. Heredem, damnatum a fideiussore non petere a reo petere posse, sed a reo petere vetitum, si a fideiussore petat, reo ex testamento teneri Celsus putat.

Here we are told that Celsus held that if a *legatum liberationis* were left *per damnationem* to a guarantor, the heir could not sue him but he could sue the principal debtor ; but where the *legatum liberationis* was to the principal debtor and the heir sued the guarantor, the principal debtor would have an *actio ex testamento* against the heir, *i.e.* because he would be liable to the *fideiussor* on an *actio mandati*. From this text, it would seem that in Celsus' view, if the legatee were sued he had an *exceptio doli mali* (61), and if the *fideiussor* were sued successfully when the legacy was to the principal debtor, the latter had an *actio ex testamento* for the amount of the debt.

But other jurists from the time of Julian took a different approach (62).

> D. 34.3.5 pr. (Ulpian *23 ad Sab.*) Si quis reum habeat et fideiussorem et reo liberationem leget, Iulianus ibidem scripsit reum per acceptilationem liberandum : alioquin si fideiussorem coeperit convenire, alia ratione reus convenitur... 1. Quod si fideiussori sit liberatio legata, sine dubio, ut et Iuliano scribit, pacto erit fideiussor liberandus...

Thus, Ulpian tells us that Julian held that where a *legatum liberationis* is left to the principal debtor he must be released by *acceptilatio,* but where the *legatum* is to the *fideiussor* only, he is to be released by pact. It might, however, be argued that the situations in the two texts are fundamentally different in

(61) It is impossible for '*petere non potest*' here to mean 'he cannot bring the action' because the *legatum* does not extinguish the debt since otherwise the heir could not bring the action against the other debtor. This is confirmed by § 1 where we are told that Celsus likewise held that the heir of the heir cannot sue and this point would never have been raised if the legacy extinguished the debt. For the *exceptio*, *cf.* D. 39.6.28 ; 44.4.17.1 ; 34.3.20 pr. ; 44.4.8 pr., 1.

(62) It is best to leave D. 44.4.8 pr., 1 (Paul *6 ad Plaut.*) out of account since it is not clear, first, how far the decision shows any innovation and secondly, how far the decision is due to Plautius or Paul.

that in the former the legacy was expressed *'damnas esto non petere'*, in the latter *'damnas esto liberare'* ; and that therefore the second stronger form required positive action by the heir, and this accounts for the two contrasting decisions. But that the form in which the *legatum liberationis* was expressed did not affect Julian's decision is shown by another text from the same book of Ulpian.

> D. 34.3.7.1. Si is qui stipulatus Stichum aut decem damnaverit heredem Stichum non petere, legatum valere constat : sed quid contineat, videamus. et Iulianus scribit actionem ex testamento in hoc esse videri, ut debitor accepto liberetur : quae res utique debitorem et in decem liberabit, quia acceptilatio solutioni comparatur, et quemadmodum, si Stichum solvisset, debitor liberaretur, ita et acceptilatione Stichi liberari.

Here the legacy, as in D. 34.3.2 pr. is expressed *'damnas esto non petere'* yet Julian says that *acceptilatio* must be made. This text brings out a vital point which is not clear in D. 34.3.5 pr., namely, that the *actio ex testamento* lies to compel the heir to free the debtor by *acceptilatio*. This is obviously a big advance from the time of Celsus where it would seem that the debtor had only the right to an *exceptio* if sued or an *actio ex testamento* where the debt was paid. It shows a complete breakdown of the fiction that *acceptilatio* was a release on performance when a creditor who is under an obligation not to accept the debt can be judicially ordered to release the debtor by *acceptilatio* ([63]).

Also probably not very early is the relaxation which permits an *acceptilatio* which is made *mortis causa* to be treated in all respects as a *donatio mortis causa* ; hence it may be revoked if the donor recovers and it is treated as part of the inheritance for the purposes of the *lex Falcidia*. Since the earliest texts we have are one from Africanus ([64]) and two from Gaius ([65]) in

(63) For other texts on *acceptilatio* in this connection see D. 34.3.3.3 ; h.t. 10 ; h.t. 29 ; 38.2.50.6 ; 35.2.82 ; C. 6.42.17 ; J. 2.20.13.

(64) D. 39.6.24.

(65) D. 39.6.31.1,4.

one of which he refers with approval to Julian, it is possible that the breakdown of the fiction here does not go back beyond that last jurist (66).

Thus, throughout the classical period, *acceptilatio* lost one by one the features it had had as a release on performance and which it should have retained so long as it was a fictitious payment (67). Eventually, indeed, it could be shown *ex facie* the *acceptilatio* that there had been no performance. But perhaps even in Justinian's law one rule remained which showed that *acceptilatio* had once been release on performance or at least, a fiction of such. It is generally agreed (68) rightly, that where there was *acceptilatio* of a conditional debt, the *acceptilatio* did not take effect unless and until the condition were realised. In this it resembles *novatio* of a conditional obligation. The texts do not really tell us much about the practical effects of this rule, but drawing an analogy from *novatio* it is argued that if the debtor died or were deported, *pendente condicione,* his heir or other successor would be liable for the debt (69). This, however, does not really explain the rule. The reason for it cannot be that the creditor wishes to release the debtor, but not, if he dies or is deported, his successor. If this were the creditor's intention, it would be both much simpler and more effective for him to do nothing and if the condition were fulfilled during the debtor's lifetime, simply to neglect exacting the debt for the time being. Nor can the reason be the maxim sometimes cited in connection with *novatio* of a conditional obligation « *inelegans est obligationem ad heredis persona incipere* » since *accepti-*

(66) Other texts are D. 39.6.35.6 (Paul) ; 35.2.82 (Ulpian). *Cf.* Amelotti, *op. cit.*, pp. 179-187 ; Simonius, 'Die *Donatio mortis causa* im klassischen römischen Recht', Basle 1958, pp. 270-272.

(67) There are a few other texts not discussed above which show to a greater or less extent that the fiction was breaking down in a particular field ; D. 46.3.71.2 ; 46.3.10 ; 32.3 pr. ; 46.3.71.2 ; 12.4.4.

(68) *E.g.* Boháček, 'Annali Palermo' 11 (1924), pp. 379-384 ; Solazzi, *op. cit.*, p. 253 ; Bonifacio, 'La Novazione nel diritto romano', Naples 1950, pp. 80-81 : The texts are D. 46.3.16 ; 46.4.12 ; 46.4.21.

(69) Boháček, *op. cit.*, p. 381.

latio operated to extinguish an obligation and, if it took effect at once would, of course, terminate the obligation during the lifetime of the parties. The only text which discusses the consequences of the rule shows how absurd they could be.

> D. 46.4.13.6. (Ulpian *50 ad Sab.*) Si Stichum aut decem sub condicione stipulatus Stichum acceptum fecerit et pendente condicione Stichus decesserit, decem in obligatione manebunt, perinde ac si acceptilatio interposita non fuisset.

Here the intention of the parties would seem clearly to have been to wipe out the obligation. I suggest that the rule dates back to the time when *acceptilatio* was a real payment. If then the debt were paid and *acceptilatio* made, *pendente condicione*, the debtor would be given a *condictio* against the creditor on account of *indebiti solutio* ([70]). And the rule remained even after *acceptilatio* ceased in other respects to be a fiction, perhaps because the reason for the rule, which can never have been very important, was not obvious.

(70) *Cf.* D. 12.6.16,17.18, *etc.*

17

D.12.1.32 and Delegatio

D. 12, 1, 32 (Celsus libro quinto [sexto - Lenel] *digestorum*): Si et me et Titium mutuam pecuniam rogaveris et ego meum debitorem tibi promittere iusserim, tu stipulatus sis, cum putares eum Titii debitorem esse, an mihi obligeris? subsisto, si quidem nullum negotium mecum contraxisti: sed propius est, ut obligari te existimem, non quia pecuniam tibi credidi (hoc enim nisi inter consentientes fieri non potest): sed quia pecunia mea quae ad te pervenit, eam mihi a te reddi bonum et aequum est.

Since the celebrated short article by Rabel « In tema di delegazione »[1], D. 12, 1, 32 is usually thought to show that in the delegatory stipulation there need be no express mention of the previous obligation[2]. Recently, too, Feenstra has gone further and argued that if in *delegatio* one can use a stipulation 'sans renvoi' it must be concluded that a novation without a 'clause de renvoi' is possible[3]. And, indeed, it seems difficult to quarrel with Feenstra's reasoning. I would like to suggest, however, (*a*) that it is not clear that D. 12, 1, 32 is concerned with a valid *delegatio* or with a *delegatio* which would have been valid but for the error; (*b*) that it is by no means certain even that *delegatio* was intended by the parties; and (*c*) that, therefore, the text is not evidence that *delegatio* could be made without a 'clause de renvoi' and hence it is not evidence for the possibility of a *novatio* without a 'clause de renvoi'.

First, it must be conceded that in the stipulation made between the debtor and the new borrower there was no reference to the preceding obligation otherwise the

---

1 *Scritti Ferrini* (*beatificazione*), 4 (Milano, 1949), p. 218 f.

2 Cf. Kaser, *Das römische Privatrecht*, 1 (Munich, 1955), p. 544 n. 22; 2 (Munich, 1959), p. 326 n. 12; Endemann, *Der Begriff der Delegatio im klassischen römischen Recht* (Marburg, 1959), p. 53; Feenstra, *L'effet extinctif de la novation*, in *Tijd.* 29 (1961), p. 397 ff. at p. 410 and n. 31; review of Endemann *op. cit.* in *Tijd.* 29 (1961), p. 507 ff. at p. 509 n. 8.

3 *L'effet, cit.*, p. 410 f.

new borrower could not have thought that the promissor was Titius' debtor and not, as he was, my debtor. But apart from that, what does the text tell us? It tells us, first, that the *stipulatio* is valid – *sed quia pecunia mea etc.* – and, secondly, that I can no longer successfully sue the debtor on the original debt – again *sed quia pecunia mea etc.* Nothing is expressly said in the text about *delegatio*, valid or invalid.

The validity of the stipulation throws no light on the question of the existence of a *delegatio*. The stipulation is valid simply because one party promised a sum of money to the other. Not even the error which we are told about affected this. Whether there had been no *delegatio*, whether there had been *delegatio* intended and it was valid, whether there had been *delegatio* intended and it was void, in all these cases the *stipulatio* would still be valid.

Nor does the fact that *ego* can no longer recover the debt from the original debtor show the existence of *delegatio* or even of attempted *delegatio*. If there had been *delegatio*, the original debt would have been extinguished *ipso iure*. But if there was no *delegatio*, it is inconceivable that, given the validity of the *stipulatio* between the debtor and the new borrower, the creditor would be able to sue the old debtor successfully. Even if strictly the old obligation still survived, the creditor would be rebutted by the *exceptio doli* [4]. This is surely true whether there was an attempt at *delegatio* which was unsuccessful either because of the error or because of a flaw in the form *i. e.*, because of the absence of a 'clause de renvoi' in the stipulation, or whether there was no attempt at *delegatio* but the *stipulatio* was understood as being in place of payment to the creditor [5]. Hence, whether there was *delegatio* or not, the creditor would be unable to recover from the debtor on the old obligation. The text does not even indicate whether the old obligation was extinguished, was merely no longer enforceable or whether the action on it could be rebutted by an *exceptio*. No information on this point can be gained from *sed pecunia mea etc.* [6]. The clause cannot be taken literally. My money has not come to you – there has been no such change of ownership. It expression only the practical effect that you are entitled to a sum of money from my debtor, which was due to me, and I can no longer recover it from my debtor.

Thus, we cannot deduce from the legal points which can be extracted from the text that there was a *delegatio*, valid of invalid. It might, however, be sug-

---

[4] Assuming that the original obligation were *stricti iuris*. If it were *bonae fidei* the defence would be inherent.

[5] The availability of an *exceptio doli* to the debtor will surely be conceded even though the mention of the *exceptio* in D. 36, 2, 4 is probably interpolated: to the references in the *Index Itp.* add KASER, *op. cit.* 2, p. 326 n. 12; BONIFACIO, *La novazione in diritto romano*, 2nd edit. (Napoli, 1959), p. 124 n. 4.

[6] Which, in any event, is not in perfect form: cf. RABEL, *op. cit.* p. 218.

gested that the text implies that this was a method which was commonly used to transfer a debt and that, at least in the absence of an error of the kind found in the text, it must have counted as *delegatio*. Such a suggestion would be without weight. First, the text is concerned with a particular case whether hypothetical or real and so the circumstances of it need not be common. Secondly, the interest of the case for Celsus is the question whether the creditor has a *condictio* against the stipulator where there was an error of the kind outlined in the text. But for such an error to come about there could be no reference in the stipulation to the previous obligation. Hence, if this is a hypothetical case, a situation would have been invented in which there was no 'clause de renvoi' in the stipulation. Since the point which is of interest to Celsus remains unchanged whether there was or was not *delegatio*, it would have been irrelevant to him whether the omission of a 'clause de renvoi' in the stipulation had any effect upon the validity of *delegatio*. Likewise if this were an actual case. Even if the parties had intended *delegatio*, the *delegatio* might have been void because of the lack of a 'clause de renvoi' in the stipulation and this would not effect the point which is of interest to Celsus. Moreover, it can be argued that even if it were common to transfer a debt in this way without a 'clause de renvoi' in the stipulation this might have been done deliberately in order to avoid *delegatio*. *Delegatio*, like *novatio* of which it is a form, had its drawbacks especially in that if the delegatory stipulation is void the old obligation may monetheless be wiped out [7]. This might induce a careful creditor to try some other and safer method of transfer. If there was no *delegatio* and for some reason the new stipulation was void, the probability is that the old creditor would be able to recover from the debtor, while if there was no *delegatio* and the new stipulation was valid, the debtor would be protected from the old creditor by the *exceptio doli* in the case of a *stricti iuris* obligation and *ipso iure* in the case of a *bonae fidei* obligation. The new stipulator, too, might prefer a *stipulatio* without a 'clause de renvoi' if this meant there was no *delegatio*, since there could then be no danger of his right failing because of some fault in the old obligation [8].

Thus, to conclude. Not only is there no evidence that in D. 12, 1, 32 we have a case of *delegatio* but there is no strong reason to believe that *delegatio* was even intended. The text, therefore, does not show that there could be *delegatio* without a 'clause de renvoi' [9] and so it does not imply that there could be *novatio* without a 'clause de renvoi'.

---

[7] C. 3, 176.

[8] Cf. DAUBE, *ZSS*, 66 (1948), p. 101 (on D. 16, 1, 17 pr.).

[9] And no other text shows that it could: cf. FEENSTRA, review of Endemann *cit.* p. 509 n. 8.

18

Iusiurandum in Litem in the Bonae Fidei Iudicia

According to the texts, *iusiurandum in litem* was possible in the following actions [1]: *actiones in rem* [2] (specifically mentioned or clearly intended are *vindicatio* [3], *vindicatio pignoris* [4], *vindicatio servitutis* [5], *petitio hereditatis* [6], *actio ad exhibendum* [7]) *bonae fidei iudicia* [8] (expressly mentioned being at least the *actio tutelae* [9]), *actio depositi* [10], *actio commodati* [11], *actio rei uxoriae* [12], *actio rerum amotarum* [13], *actio furti* [14], *actio de dolo* [15], *actio quod metus causa* [16], and *actio Fabiana* [17]. Also mentioned is *actio stricti iudicii* [18] but terms of this sort are Justinianic. *Iusiurandum in litem* had two different functions. It could be given in an attempt to find the true loss which the plaintiff had suffered; or it could be given, no doubt usually at an unrealistically high figure, to persuade the defendant to perform a particular obligation rather than suffer condemnation. Schulz [19] denies that the idea of *iusiurandum in litem* was to compel the defendant to make specific restitution by threatening him with an assessment made by the plaintiff who might overvalue. He suggests that modern historians underrate Roman *fides* and piety — an average Roman, he thinks, would not easily forswear himself. The idea, he claims,

---

1) Omitting the question of interdicts.
2) D. 6,1,46; 12,3,2; 12,3,5pr; C. 3,32,21. 3) D. 12,3,2.
4) D. 20,1,16,3. 5) D. 8,5,7. 6) D. 5,3,25,10.
7) D. 10,4,5,2; 12,3,2; 12,3,5,pr; 49,1,28,1. 8) D. 12,3,5 pr; 13,6,3,2.
9) D. 12,3,4pr; 26,7,7pr; 27,7,4pr; C. 5,53,1; 5,53,2; 5,53,5.
10) D. 5,1,64pr; 12,3,3; 16,3,1,26. 11) D. 5,1,64pr;; 13,6,3,2.
12) D. 24,3,25,1. 13) D. 25,2,8,1; 25,2,9. 14) D. 12,3,9.
15) D. 4,3,18pr; 16) D. 4,3,18pr; 17) D. 38,5,5,1.
18) D. 12,3,5,4. This text (and D. 12,3,6) are discussed, *infra* p. 224, n. 22.
19) *Classical Roman Law* (Oxford, 1951), p. 370.

was an expedient designed to hasten condemnation as it spared the judge a lengthy and wearisome task. But, on that explanation, *iusiurandum in litem* would be equally appropriate where there was *dolus* and where there was only *culpa*. Yet the texts all tell the same story, namely that *iusiurandum in litem* was only permitted where there was *dolus* or *contumacia* [20]). Where there is only *culpa*, the *iudex* makes the *aestimatio*. This is explicable only if *iusiurandum in litem* is regarded as some sort of punishment for, or at least as unfavourable to, the defendant. Indeed, some texts more or less say that the *aestimatio* of the plaintiff will be greater than this *interesse* or that the defendant is being punished [21]). Of the actions mentioned above, the *actio furti* is the only one in which the purpose of the *iusiurandum in litem* can never be to compel the return of the *res* but must always be for a true estimate of the value of the stolen object [22]). The *actio furti* is purely

---

20) D. 5,1,64pr; 6,1,68; 6,1,71; 12,3,2; 12,3,4,4; 12,3,5,3; 12,3,8. Interpolations in one sense or another have often been signalled in the texts, but there is wide agreement that the *iusiurandum in litem* was given only if there was *dolus*, not just *culpa*: for suggested interpolations of the texts see *Index Itp.*, and the references given to the texts by Chiazzese, *Jusiurandum in litem* (Milan, 1958) and Provera, *Contributi allo studio del iusiurandum in litem* (Turin, 1953).

21) D. 5,1,64pr; 6,1,68; 12,3,2; 12,3,8. The relevant passages are usually held interpolated; cf references in n. 22. It is not intended to discuss the question at length here but it should be noted that the main argument in favour of interpolation is very weak. This is (Chiazzese, *op. cit.* pp. 193ff; Provera, *op. cit.* pp. 14ff) that in these texts a distinction is drawn between *quanti ea res erit* and *quanti in litem actor iuraverit*, the latter being regarded as a greater amount. Yet the *iusiurandum* is for the *interesse* of the *actor*, hence, it is said, the distinction cannot have been made by the classical jurists with their strong adherence to the diction of the *formulae*. But granted that logically such a distinction ought not to have been made, nevertheless if it were admitted that in practice the *actor* did swear for more than his interest, nothing is more natural than to use such language. It is the neatest possible way of making the point found in the texts, and it is crediting the classical jurists with little sense to say that they would not use it. The fact that the *iusiurandum in litem* was not available where there was only *culpa*, its function to compel performance and this present distinction are all bound up together.

22) Unless the heavily interpolated (cf Marchi, *Il giuramento in lite e la stima della cosa perita nei giudizi di stretto diritto*, Studi Scialoja I (Milan, 1905), pp. 167ff; Levy, *Zur Lehre von den sog. actiones arbitrariae*, ZSS (1915) pp. 1ff at p. 68

penal and a reipersecutory action *vindicatio* or *condictio furtiva* — can always be brought in addition.

It is generally held, however, that despite the texts there was no *iusiurandum in litem* in the *bonae fidei iudicia* [23]). The purpose of the present paper is to show that the arguments put forward for this proposition are weak and unconvincing.

Firstly, it is said (by Levy and Betti) that *iusiurandum in litem* conflicts with *ex fide bona* in the *formula.* Betti says that the condemnation ought to be in the hands of the judge. But I do not find it easy to see where the conflict between *iusiurandum in litem* and *ex fide bona* lies. If it is meant that it does not conform to good faith to compel a defendant to give something up or do something against his will, this does not seem a real objection. It must be remembered that according to the texts *iusiurandum in litem*, which is permissible at the discretion of the judge [24]), will be given only if there is *dolus* on the part of the defendant. On occasion it will seem that what the plaintiff really ought to have is performance — as for instance where he has bought for sentimental reasons something belonging to his grandfather

---

n. 1; Chiazzese, *op. cit.*, p. 191) D. 12,3,5,4 has a classical basis and is taken in conjunction with D. 12,3,6. The action there is a *condictio certae rei* arising from a stipulation for a slave Stichus who has died. Thus, on the facts of the case, performance is impossible and what is wanted from the *iusiurandum* can only be a true estimate of the plaintiff's loss. And D. 12,3,6 which in its present context is closely linked with D. 12,3,5,4 has simply, *alias, si stipulatu vel ex testamento agatur, non solet in litem iurari.*

23) E.g., Levy, *op. cit.* pp. 67f and 68 n. 2; Betti, *Studi sulla litis aestimatio* I (Pavia, 1915), p. 57 n. 86; Chiazzese, *op. cit.* pp. 3 f; Medicus, *Id quod interest* (Cologne, Graz, 1962), pp. 183f; *contra*, to a limited extent, Provera, *op. cit.* pp. 51ff. If I am not mistaken, the main conclusions of this present article were also at one time held by Betti: *La litis aestimatio in rapporto al tempo nelle varie specie di azioni e di giudizî* (programma del corso di diritto romano tenuto nell' Università di Camerino, 1918—1919), p. 17. But the nature of that work forbade the giving of arguments, and he now appears to have reverted to his position of 1915: *Istituzioni di diritto romano* I, 2nd edt. (Padua, 1947), p. 297 n. 69 at p. 298.

24) Therefore, contrary to Betti, the measuring of damages by *iusiurandum in litem* is not a limitation on the powers of the *iudex*: and cf. D. 12,3,5,1 and 2.

and the defendant refuses to deliver — and only then, one may assume, will the *iudex* allow *iusiurandum in litem*. Or the idea may be that by *iusiurandum in litem* the plaintiff might overvalue his claim and so get more than his interest and that this is contrary to the concept of good faith. But we must remember that the defendant will be able to escape this *condemnatio* by delivering the *res* etc. Again, some texts make it clear that on occasion the *condemnatio* in *quidquid . . . dare facere oportet ex fide bona* would give the plaintiff less than his loss [25]), so similarly at times — if only where the defendant was fraudulent — the defendant might be condemned in more than the plaintiff's loss. Above all, we must not forget that in some cases this condemnation allowed a plaintiff to sue successfully where he had suffered no loss. For instance, *mandata aliena gratia* are always treated as completely valid — unlike *stipulationes alteri* — and they are distinguished from *mandata mea et aliena gratia*. If the *actio mandati* always required an interest in the plaintiff one would not have expected to be told without qualification that *mandata aliena gratia* are valid nor might one have expected them to be distinguished from *mandata mea et aliena* [26]). Equally significant is D. 19,1,13,30 (Ulpian 32 *ad ed.*):

> Si venditor habitationem exceperit, ut inquilino liceat habitare, vel colono ut perfrui liceat ad certum tempus, magis esse Servius putabat ex vendito esse actionem: denique Tubero ait, si iste colonus damnum dederit, emptorem ex empto agentem cogere posse venditorem, ut ex locato cum colono experiatur, ut quidquid fuerit consecutus, emptori reddat.

As Mayer-Maly says [27]), it is impossible to doubt the genuineness of the text's substance. We are interested in the second of the two situations in the text. A sale has been made with a condition

---

[25]) *E.g.*, D. 19,1,43—45; *cf* Medicus *op. cit.* p. 81ff; D. 19,1,13pr. and 1; *cf* Medicus *op. cit.* p. 128ff and p. 126 n. 5.

[26]) *Cf* Watson, *Contract of Mandate in Roman Law* (Oxford, 1961) p. 115ff. The question is not expressly considered by Medicus who, however, does deal with D. 3,5,27(28); *op. cit.* p. 190f.

[27]) *Locatio conductio* (Vienna, 1956) p. 55f: *cf* Medicus *op. cit.* p. 171 n. 2.

that a *colonus* of the seller should remain in occupation. The *colonus* damages the property and Tubero says that the buyer can bring an *actio ex empto* against the seller to compel him to sue the *colonus* by the *actio ex locato* and to restore to the buyer whatever he obtains. In both the *actio ex empto* and the *actio ex locato* the *condemnatio* will be *quidquid . . . dare facere oportet ex fide bona*. But what interest has the seller in the *actio ex locato*? He no longer is the owner of the property and cannot suffer loss directly by the damage. Nor can one really say that his interest is the extent of the loss caused to the buyer which the buyer can recover from him by the *actio ex empto*. The *actio ex empto* is only available because the seller has the *actio ex locato*. Any attempt to base the *condemnatio* in both actions on the plaintiff's *interesse* would result in a vicious circle [28]). Of course, it is obviously convenient — and in accordance with good faith — that these two actions should be available; hence, no doubt the *actio ex locato* where the plaintiff had no *interesse* [29]). But if it is admitted that at times *bonae fidei* actions could be brought where the plaintiff had no interest, it becomes difficult to argue that *iusiuranda in litem* would be totally excluded from the *bonae fidei iudicia* because they might give the plaintiff more than his loss.

---

28) There is not the slightest indication in the text that Tubero was concerned with a special clause in the contract of sale to make the seller liable for any damage done by the *colonus*.

29) This second part of the text is also of interest in another way. The *actio ex empto* is brought, we are told, to compel the seller to sue the *colonus* and hand over to the buyer whatever he recovered. Of course, the seller could not suffer condemnation to do such a thing, pecuniary condemnations alone being allowed. Nevertheless, the action must have been brought with the intention that the seller be compelled to sue and no doubt this was achieved by facing him with a choice either of suffering pecuniary condemnation or of giving a *cautio* that he would sue the *colonus* and hand over the proceeds to the buyer. To achieve the latter the alternative must have been made less attractive (since he could otherwise suffer condemnation and then himself sue the *colonus* and keep what he recovered) and *iusiurandum in litem* may well have been the means to this end. Cf Watson *The Law of Obligations in the Later Roman Republic* (Oxford, 1965) pp. 51ff.

Secondly, Levy says that if Marcian in D.12,3,5pr had wanted to give a complete list of actions in which *iusiurandum in litem* was possible he would also have mentioned the *actio rerum amotarum, actio quod metus, actio de dolo, actio de recepto* [30]) and the *actio Fabiana.* D. 12,3,5 pr (Marcian 4 *reg.*) runs:

> In actionibus in rem et in ad exhibendum et in bonae fidei iudiciis in litem iuratur.

Levy's argument would seem to be that the reference here to the *bonae fidei iudicia* can only be justified if Marcian is giving a list of the actions in which *iusiurandum in litem* is permitted. And that if Marcian had been giving such a list, it would, of necessity, have been exhaustive. But this argument does not take account of the nature of the work — the fourth book of Marcian's *Regulae* — from which the text comes. *Libri regularum* are intended for elementary education and seem to differ from *Institutiones* only in that they have no closely knit plan of presentation and that the individual legal rules which are given follow one another without any attempt to link them together in a logical fashion [31]). But in students' elementary textbooks one expects lists of all sorts to be given and one is not surprised if the list is not exhaustive, a general picture is all that the author need give [32]).

Thirdly, Levy sees in this text (and also in D. 13,6,3,2) [33]) the generalising tendency of the compilers. But if the text has been altered by Justinian's compilers with the intention of generalising the classical position, it is difficult to see why *h.t.* 5,4 and *h.t.* 6 are allowed to say in effect that it is possible in the *actio ex*

---

30) *The actio de recepto* has not been mentioned before and it is not intended to go into it. It is probable both that the *formula* had a restitutory clause and that *iusiurandum in litem* was permitted but the evidence for neither the one nor the other is very clear: cf Lenel *op. cit.* p. 135 and n. 1; Levy *op. cit.* p. 27.

31) Cf Krüger *Geschichte der Quellen und Litteratur des römischen Rechts,* 2nd edit. (Munich, 1912) p. 141.

32) Thus, the list of *bonae fidei iudicia* in G. 4,62 is not complete.

33) Cf *infra* p. 233 f.

stipulatu and *actio ex testamento* to have *iusiurandum in litem*, but only rarely [34]).

Fourthly, Levy says that actions were excluded from *iusiurandum in litem* which were not fitted either in general or in particular cases to give restitution [35]). But even he does not hold interpolated D. 12,3,5,3 [36]):

> Sed in his omnibus ob dolum solum in litem iuratur, non etiam ob culpam: haec enim iudex aestimat.

This tells us that there is no *iusiurandum in litem* if there is merely *culpa*. In that case the *iudex* makes the *aestimatio*. In other words, *iusiurandum in litem* is not automatic in the actions where it is allowed. Thus, the fact that it would not always be appropriate in a *bonae fidei iudicium* is no evidence that it was never allowed.

Fifthly, there are no texts on sale or hire which give *iusiurandum in litem* — the same is true also of partnership and mandate — yet, it is said, it would often have been useful and hence it cannot have been permitted [37]). Related to this argument is the one that the texts which allow *iusiurandum in litem* in the *actio commodati* and the *actio depositi* are concerned with the *actiones in factum* of these contracts. But if *iusiurandum in litem* was not automatic but was allowed where it was thought appropriate, we must ask ourselves in which circumstances the Romans would allow it in a *bonae fidei iudicium*. No doubt, through the centuries practical rules were worked out by the judges, though these would not be mentioned by the jurists. Perhaps it would be instructive to look at a modern system which allows condemnation to be for the performance of an obligation. Scottish law „favours a

---

34) For these two texts cf *supra*, p. 225 n. 22.

35) For Levy this is a conclusion rather than an argument.

36) So far as I am aware the only suggestions of interpolation are by Betti (*op. cit.* p. 57) who would excise *in his omnibus* which would not seem to affect us; and by Krüger (*Supplementum ad Digesta*) who hesitatingly suggests *h.t.* 5,1—3 are Justinianic — this view apparently being based on Levy's conclusion.

37) Medicus *op. cit.* p. 184.

claim for specific performance and there is a presumption in Scots law that an obligation is enforceable by such a decree, if there be no reason in equity to refuse it" [38]). Nonetheless, there are a number of standard exceptions. Walker says [39]): „Contracts will in general not be specifically enforced where performance is impossible, where the compulsory performance would involve an intimate relationship, as of service or agency or partnership, contracts requiring supervision, contracts of sale where there is no *pretium affectionis*, where exceptional hardship would be involved, and where the court decides in its discretion that damages are appropriate in the circumstances". *Pretium affectionis* means that the plaintiff really wants the particular object of the sale; there is none if an exact equivalent can easily be obtained elsewhere. These exceptions to the general rule were not laid down in any statute but have developed over the years by judgements concerned with what was fair and practicable. Similarly, I suggest, in Rome. The judges over the years developed the feeling that in many actions under *bonae fidei iudicia* money damages only — not performance — was appropriate and so there would be no place for *iusiurandum in litem* to compel delivery or performance. To judge from Scotland (and this does harmonise with the Roman texts) this would, generally speaking, be so in the case of the *actio pro socio*, the *actio mandati* and the *actio locati* where the hire was of services. In the case of sale, normally *iusiurandum in litem* to compel delivery would be allowed only in the comparatively rare case where the buyer particularly wanted the object of sale and pecuniary damages would not be satisfactory [40]). In *depositum*, *commodatum* and *locatio rei*, *iusiurandum in litem* would however be permissible to recover the plaintiff's own property. Moreover, it is difficult to concede much force to the argument on the lack of texts specifically on sale and hire — which, of course, are covered by the reference

---

38) Walker, *Law of Damages in Scotland* (Edinburgh, 1955) p. 480.

39) *Op. cit.*, p. 481.

40) It would also be appropriate in the situations in the texts cited *supra* n. 29.

to the *bonae fidei iudicia* — since all in all there are very few texts which do mention *iusiurandum in litem*, and a large proportion of these merely lists situations where *iusiurandum in litem* is possible. Thus, for instance, we have only one, or possibly two, texts which mention *iusiurandum in litem* in connexion with the *actio furti*. The explanation of this lack of texts is that *iusiurandum in litem* is a procedural matter, not a question of substantive law, and the jurists were generally interested only in the latter.

At this stage we must deal with D. 19,2,48,1 (Marcellus 8 *dig.*):

> Qui servum conductum vel aliam rem non immobilem non restituit, quanti in litem iuratum fuerit damnabitur.

The dominant modern opinion is that this text although it appears in the Digest title *locati conducti* was concerned originally with the *actio furti* [41]). The arguments for this are that in book 8 of his Digest Marcellus did deal, *inter alia*, with *furtum*, but not with *locatio* [42]), and more recently that the words *non immobilem* which for a long time have rightly been regarded as a gloss must have been inserted by someone who was thinking of the *actio furti* because they are meaningless for the *actio locati* [43]). But on examination neither of these arguments appears as strong as it does at first sight, and there are objections to holding that the text was concerned with the *actio furti*. To take the first argument. An inspection of the remains of the writings of Marcellus shows that he was rather fond of drawing parallels etc. so that a number of texts deal with topics which were not part of the subject with which he was immediately concerned. Indeed the very *principium* of our text shows that. The *principium* and § 1 in their original context were not linked together [44]) but the former came from

---

41) Cf Medicus *op. cit.* p. 183f and the references he gives: *contra*, but without strong arguments, Provera *op. cit.* p. 51ff; Amirante *BIDR* 61 (1959) p. 115 n. 3 at p. 116.

42) Cf references given by Medicus, *loc. cit.*

43) Medicus *op. cit.* p. 184.

44) Lenel *Palingenesia* I 607; *contra*, Provera, *op. cit.* p. 52.

Marcellus' discussion of the *actio tutelae*. Yet the *principium* is concerned with the *actio locati*, not with the relationship between tutor and pupil, although it was probably an argument or a parallel adduced for some point connected with this relationship. Similarly, it should not be too lightly assumed that § 1 must have been directly concerned with the *actio furti*. Secondly, Medicus' argument from *non immobilem*. If Medicus is right, the gloss is very silly, though harmless, since it was completely established that there could be theft only of moveables. Another solution is possible, namely that the glossator was thinking of tacit relocation which did apply only to land [45]). His intention, then, would be to emphasise that tacit relocation did not apply to chattels. Against the text having been originally concerned with the *actio furti* are these points. First, one would have to postulate further alteration of the text — and there is no sign of this — this time by the compilers since the condemnation would be for double the amount of the *iusiurandum in litem*. Secondly, and this is far more important, it is difficult to see why there would be *iusiurandum in litem* here at all [46]). In the *actio furti*, the function of the oath is to give a true estimate of the plaintiff's loss, not to compel the defendant to performance. But in a case where the *conductor* refuses to restore the *res* to the *locator* its true value will normally be fairly apparent to the *iudex*, so that a *iusiurandum in litem* would not be necessary. On the other hand, if the action concerned is the *actio ex locato* we would have a case where the point of the oath is to compel the defendant to return the plaintiff's own thing. And the texts on the *actio depositi*, *actio commodati*, *actio rei uxoriae* and *actio rerum amotarum* tend to show that *iusiurandum in litem* was regarded as especially appropriate where the

---

45) See Mayer-Maly *op. cit.* p. 219 n. 20. Of course, the lease would not continue if the lessor were opposed to its continuance but if he were silent for a time the lessee no doubt would be protected and the lease would be regarded as continuing for a year.

46) Unless *iusiurandum in litem* was compulsory in the *actio furti* and there is no evidence for that.

object of the action was to secure that the plaintiff recovered his own property, The same applies to the *vindicatio*.

Sixthly, there is the argument mentioned above that the texts on *depositum* and *commodatum* refer to the *actio in factum* and not to the *actio in ius*. To take *depositum* first. There are two texts — both from Ulpian 30 *ad edictum* — D. 12,3,3 and 16,3,1, 26. There is no indication in the substance of either as to whether it is concerned with the *actio in factum* or the *actio in ius*. Levy, concerned with D. 16,3,1,26, says it is the former [47]) and Kaser says it probably is [48]). But Lenel, concerned with the structure of Ulpian's book 30 *ad edictum*, thought at one time that, of D. 16,3,1, §§ 1—19 were concerned with the *formula in factum*, §§ 20—26 probably with the *formula in ius* [49]). Later he changed his mind rather, holding that §§ 1—19 still dealt with the *formula in factum*, §§ 20—26 with the *officium iudicis* but that it could not be determined which *formula* lay at the root of the discussion, §§ 27 to the end and *h.t.* 3 with a free discussion of deposit not dependant upon any *formula* [50]). Lenel rightly links D. 12,3,3 with D. 16,3,1,26 so that it is not independent evidence. On Lenel's later view, however, if one cannot see to which *formula* the texts on *officium iudicis* refer the explanation probably is that they are of a general nature; if so, *iusiurandum in litem* would be permitted in both the *actio in ius* and the *actio in factum*. But the proper verdict from the internal evidence of the texts and their context must be *non liquet*. There is one text on *commodatum*, D. 13,6,3,2 (Ulpian 28 *ad ed.*):

> In hac actione sicut in ceteris bonae fidei iudiciis similiter in litem iurabitur; et rei iudicandae tempus, quanti res sit, observatur, quamvis in stricti litis constestatae tempus spectetur.

This text was concerned with the *actio in factum* [51]) as *quanti*

---

47) *Op. cit.* p. 75.

48) *Quanti ea res est* (Munich, 1935) p. 71.

49) *Op. cit.* II 613f.

50) *Edictum cit.* p. 289.

51) Lenel *op. cit.* p. 253.

res sit shows. Hence, as is generally agreed, *sicut . . . iudiciis* is interpolated. But the duplication of the words which suggest a comparison, *sicut* and *similiter*, one of which must be an accidental survival, shows that *sicut in ceteris bonae fidei iudiciis* is one comparison substituted for another. Lenel plausibly suggests [52]) *in hac re similiter ac si in ius concepta formula agatur* etc. This would have been excised by the compilers along with all the other texts which mentioned the existence of two actions here and in deposit. In any event, since *sicut . . . iudiciis* was really replacing an unwanted comparison, the clause is no evidence whatever that Justinian was innovating in the case of *iusiurandum in litem* in the *bonae fidei iudicia.* The fact remains, however, that it is certain there could be *iusiurandum in litem* in the *actio in factum* in *commodatum* and there is no evidence for it in the *actio in ius*; while it certainly existed for *depositum* but the evidence available does not point to one action rather than to the other.

There is, however, one *bonae fidei iudicium*, the *actio tutelae*, which did not have a *formula in factum* and in which there is not the slightest doubt that *iusiurandum in litem* was permitted. This is attested in D. 12,3,4 pr.; 26,7,7 pr; 27,7,4 pr; C. 5,53,1; 5,53,2 pr; 5,53,4 pr; and 5,53,5 [53]). Although there are suspicions of interpolation, the references to *iusiurandum in litem* remain [54]). Chiazzese, however, held [55]) that the *iusiurandum in litem* was incompatible with the classical *iudicium tutelae*, the *iusiurandum* not being allowed in any *formula* devoid of a *clausula arbitraria*, and that it was allowed in the *iudicium tutelae* only by way of innovation by the classical Emperors and that they introduced it solely for failure to produce an inventory. That scholar's death, unfortunately, has prevented us from receiving his arguments for

---

52) *Loc. cit.* n. 2.

53) A further text concerned with *tutela*, D. 12,3,8 (Marcian 8 *dig.*) does not mention the action and may have been concerned with the *vindicatio*: Chiazzese *op. cit.* p. 273ff; *contra*, Provera, *op. cit.* p 57ff.

54) See the references given by Provera *op. cit.* p. 57ff.

55) *Op. cit.* p. 275.

this proposition. But the texts do not seem to give a great deal of support to his view.

C. 5,53,1:

> *Impp. Severus et Antoninus AA. Asclepiodoto.* Adversus heredem tutoris ad transferendam tutelam iudicem accipiens tempore litis ad puberem instrumenta pertinentia restitui desiderabis. quod si dolo non exhibeantur, in litem iurandi tibi facultas erit, modo si quondam pupillo debitam adfectionem ad vincula quoque religionis extendere volueris. *PP. k. Aug. Geta II cons.* [205 A.D.].

The text is not quite in perfect order and it has been suggested that *quondam* has been inserted by the compilers to make the text refer to the *curator* [56]). Presumably, then, *puberem* was originally *impuberem*. However, this may be, the text seems to be concerned with the *actio tutelae* and it says that if the heirs of a tutor do not produce the *instrumenta* and this is the result of *dolus* on their part the plaintiff may give the *iusiurandum in litem*. One cannot, however, assume that the Emperors are innovating. The language is very matter of fact and completely appropriate to a statement of the existing law. The rescript, moreover, is concerned with a *tutela* of the addressee and there is no reason to assume that he is anything other than a private citizen especially since high officials were excused from *tutelae*. Further, the *iusiurandum* is to compel production of *instrumenta*. But one should not equate *instrumenta* with *inventarium*. *Instrumenta* covers all of the documents relevant to the case. There seems to be no text in which *instrumenta* can definitely be said to be used as a synonym for *inventarium*. On the other hand, there are a number where the word is obviously used with the wider meaning — sometimes almost in distinction to the inventory — for instance, in D. 26,7,5,6 (Ulpian 35 *ad ed.*) . . . *si nondum rationes redditae nec ad causam instrumenta pertinentia*, and C. 5,53,4 . . . *tutor enim inventarium ceteraque instrumenta si non proferat . . .*

---

56) Cf Provera *op. cit.* p. 59 n. 90, following, it would appear, Solazzi *La minore età nel diritto romano* (Rome, 1912) pp. 58 n. 1 and 213 n. 1, which was not available to the present writer.

C. 5,53,2:

Imp. Antoninus A. Severo. Is, qui rationes tutelae seu curae reposcit, invitus in litem iurare compelli non potest. sed volens ita demum audiendus est, si heres per longam successionem tutoris instrumenta pupillaria dolo [dolo *del. Mommsen*] circumveniendi pupilli gratia exhibere non vult. 1. Sin vero neque dolus neque lata culpa neque fraus heredis convincetur, omissa iurisiurandi facultate iudex de veritate cognoscet, quae etiam argumentis liquidis investigari potest. *PP. xi k. Oct. duobus Aspris conss.* [212 A.D.].

Again there have been suggestions of interpolation of the *principium* [57]) (which is what we are mainly concerned with) but no one excises the reference to *iusiurandum in litem* in *tutela.* Indeed the text since it is concerned solely with the oath would have to be a complete fabrication — which is impossible — before that view could be maintained. This time the main point is the production of accounts (*rationes*) though *instrumenta pupillaria* are also mentioned. Here, however, there can be no question of Imperial innovation if only because the rescript, of A.D. 212, is on the same point and gives the same law as the rescript just examined which dates from 205 A.D. The tone of the two rescripts is also the same.

C. 5,53,4pr:

Imp. Gordianus A. Muciano. Alio iure est tutor, alio heres eius. tutor enim inventarium ceteraque instrumenta si non proferat, in litem iusiurandum adversus se potest admittere: at enim heres eius ita demum, si reperta in hereditate dolo malo non exhibeat. 1 . . . *PP. vii k. Oct. Pio et Pontiano conss.* [238 A.D.].

Again the action at the base of the rescript is for the production of accounts and other relevant documents. Once more, there is no question of innovation here [58]).

C. 5,53,5:

Impp. Diocletianus et Maximianus AA. et CC. Artemidoro. Licet adversus heredes ob non factum inventarium iusiurandum in actione tutelae praeter-

---

57) Cf Solazzi *SDHI* 24 (1958) p. 44ff and the references he gives.

58) On the question of interpolation see Provera *op. cit.* p. 60 and n. 92.

mitti placuerit, iudicem tamen velut ex dolo tutoris aliis indiciis instructum adversus eos ferre sententiam convenit. *S. viii k. Ian. Nicomediae CC.. conss.* [294 A.D.].

In an action against the heirs, *iusiurandum in litem* is not allowed when no inventory had been made.

The following points emerge from the examination of the texts of the Code. First, *iusiurandum in litem* is permitted only where there is *dolus* on the part of the defendant, yet we know that in developed classical law at least, the *actio tutelae* also lay for *culpa* [59]). Secondly, the multiplicity of rescripts is not the result of repeated innovations by the Emperors since the three later rescripts hardly take one any further than the first does. That there are as many as four rescripts can only be due to this being a continuously recurring problem in practice. Thirdly, there is no evidence at all in the rescripts of any innovation by the Emperors. The three later ones certainly do not innovate, so the earliest one which is similar in form and substance equally may be giving existing law. Fourthly, the *iusiurandum in litem* was used not only to compel the production of accounts, but of all documents. A wider scope — at least in theory — cannot be excluded. The actions concerned are all against the heirs of the tutor, and the only performance which could conceivably be exacted is the production of documents. Even in the case of the tutor himself one would not expect *iusiurandum in litem* to be used to compel any other kind of performance [60]).

The three Digest texts are all from Ulpian.

D. 26,7,7pr (35 *ad ed.*):

Tutor, qui repertorium non fecit, quod vulgo inventarium appellatur, dolo fecisse videtur, nisi forte aliqua necessaria et iustissima causa allegari possit, cur id factum non sit. si quis igitur dolo inventarium non fecerit, in ea condicione est, ut teneatur in id quod pupilli interest, quod ex iureiurando in litem aestimatur. nihil itaque gerere ante inventarium factum eum oportet, nisi id quod dilationem nec modicam exspectare possit.

---

59) Cf Kaser *Privatrecht* I *cit.* p. 310 and the texts and references he gives, n. 30.

60) As the example of Scots law, *supra* p. 229, would suggest.

This text has been held interpolated and is reconstructed to say simply that failure to produce an inventory makes a tutor liable [61]). None of the suggested interpolations, however, affects us. The text tells us that if the tutor is sued for failure to produce an inventory, he is liable in *id quod pupilli interest* which is to be estimated by *iusiurandum in litem.* Nothing in the texts suggests that this is a revolutionary decision or that it derives from Imperial rescripts.

D. 12,3,4pr. (36 *ad ed.*):

> Videamus in tutelari causa quis iurare et adversus quem possit. et quidem ipse pupillus, si impubes est, non potest: hoc enim saepissime rescriptum est. sed nec tutorem cogendum vel matrem pupilli admittendam, etsi parata esset iurare, divi fratres rescripserunt: grave enim videbatur et ignorantes et invitos tutores sub alieni compendii emolumento etiam periurium anceps subire. curatores quoque pupilli vel adulescentis non esse cogendos in litem iurare rescriptis imperatoris nostri et divi patris eius continetur. si tamen tantam affectionem pupillo suo vel adulescenti tutores vel curatores praestare volunt, auctoritas iuris non refragabitur, quin iudicio, quod inter ipsos acceptum est, finis eiusmodi possit adhiberi. non enim ad suam utilitatem iurisiurandi referenda aestimatio est, sed ad domini, cuius nomine tutelae ratio postulatur. adulescens vero si velit iurare potest.

This text, too, is frequently held interpolated but again for us the basic point that *iusiurandum in litem* is allowed in the *actio tutelae* does not seem disputed [62]). Moreover, the rest of D. 12,3,4 is concerned with *iusiurandum in litem* and Ulpian's book 36 *ad edictum* is concerned with the *actio tutelae.* Nothing in the text restricts the use of *iusiurandum in litem* to the production of an inventory but this is not significant because the point of the text is who may give or be compelled to give a *iusiurandum in litem.* Imperial rescripts certainly are prominent in the text but these lay down circumstances in which the *iusiurandum in litem* will not be allowed or cannot be compelled. The basic picture in the text is that there was a right to *iusiurandum in litem* but the

---

61) To the *Index Itp.* add Provera, *op. cit.* p. 62 and the authors he cites, n. 94.

62) Cf *Index Itp.* and *Supplementum.*

circumstances in which it was appropriate were defined by the Emperors. Nothing suggests that *iusiurandum in litem* in the *actio tutelae* was an Imperial innovation.

D. 27,7, 4pr. 36 *ad ed.:*

> Cum ostendimus heredem quoque tutelae iudicio posse conveniri, videndum, an etiam proprius eius dolus vel propria administratio veniat in iudicium. et exstat Servii sententia existimantis, si post mortem tutoris heres eius negotia pupilli gerere perseveraverit aut in arca tutoris pupilli pecuniam invenerit et consumpserit vel eam pecuniam quam tutor stipulatus fuerat exegerit, tutelae iudicio eum teneri suo nomine: nam cum permittatur adversus heredem ex proprio dolo iurari in litem, apparet eum iudicio tutelae teneri ex dolo proprio [63]).

The point of the text is this. The heir of a tutor, says Ulpian, can be summoned in an *actio tutelae*, but can his own fraud be brought into issue in this action? And he says there is an opinion of Servius that if the heir does act he will be liable *suo nomine* in an *actio tutelae* because, since the *iusiurandum in litem* is available against the heir for his own *dolus*, it appears that in the *actio tutelae* he is liable for his own *dolus*. The text must be regarded as a whole. The argument used to justify the decision is of supreme importance because it does not in fact justify it. The distinction (and the text shows there must be one) between the heir's liability for *dolus*, *suo nomine*, and the availability of the *iusiurandum in litem* is that the latter is given by the plaintiff to compel the heir to produce accounts and other documents left by the tutor and which the heir has deliberately not produced. In other words the *iusiurandum in litem* is for failure to do something which he, in his capacity as heir, is responsible for doing; whereas Servius and Ulpian are making the heir liable for his own positive acts which as the text shows need not necessarily have anything to do with his quality as heir. The argument is either stupid or very clever — in the latter case a deliberate sophisticated attempt to

---

63) For suggested interpolations, see *Index Itp.* and Lauria Studi Riccobono III p. 300 n. 72.

extend a remedy where no good legal argument exists for the extension which, however, is very useful and practical since it saves the plaintiff the trouble of suing by two distinct actions. The skill with which the reference to *iusiurandum in litem* is managed is in favour of the view that the jurist knew what he was about. At the same time, such an argument is hardly likely to be Justinianic — the procedural difficulty would hardly have interested the compilers enough for them to use so much sophistry. Moreover, the form of the text requires an argument or at least something more than „there exists an opinion of Servius who thinks an action lies." Further, however, a sophistical argument of this type proves that the jurist is trying to innovate; otherwise he would not bother with an argument at all if he could find no better. De Robertis has suggested that the action which Servius gave was the *actio utilis* [64]). This is extremely unlikely since the very form of the text is against it. The text opens by Ulpian saying that the tutor's heir can be sued by the *actio tutelae* and asking whether his own fraud *veniat in iudicium*, *i.e.*, can be raised in this action. It is scarcely an answer to say that Servius gave an opinion that an *actio utilis* lay [65]). The argument for the decision, moreover, can only have reference to the direct *actio tutelae*. A final question in this text is whether the argument is to be attributed to Ulpian or Servius. If to Servius, then of course *iusiurandum in litem* in the *actio tutelae* would date back to the Republic. Provera, however, maintains it is Ulpian's but he produces no argument [66]). If it is thought to be Ulpianic because the verb *apparet* is in the indicative — suggestive of direct speech — then we must remember that Magdelain has already correctly maintained [67])

---

[64]) *De eo qui pro tutore negotia gessit*, Annali Bari 15 (1958) p. 65ff at p. 96 n. 121.

[65]) Nothing indicates that anything has been cut out between the decision and the argument. The present writer regrets that he had not access to two other works by De Robertis, *La responsabilità del tutore nel diritto giustinianeo* (Bari, 1954); and *La protutela in diritto romano* (Bari, 1956).

[66]) *Op. cit.* p. 61.

[67]) *Les actions civiles* (Paris, 1954) p. 9.

that the use of the indicative is perfectly compatible with indirect speech and constitutes a peculiarity of the style of Ulpian. No proof that it is the work of one or the other jurist would seem possible, but the balance of probability would appear to be in favour of Servius. To begin with, in most cases a reason given for a reported decision is attributable to the author of the decision. Secondly, especially where there is an innovation, one would except an argument to be given by the person proposing the new view. Thirdly, Ulpian would be unlikely to add a very sophistical reason for a decision which went so far back as Servius. In any event, in this text there is no indication of innovation by the Emperors.

Thus the texts on *iusiurandum in litem* in the *actio tutelae*. Its use seems to have been restricted in practice to compelling the defendant to produce documents — not just accounts — relating to the *tutela*, and this is precisely the scope which a comparison with Scots law would lead us to think appropriate. There is not the slightest indication anywhere that *iusiurandum in litem* here was an innovation of the Emperors and there is a strong suggestion that it goes back beyond Servius. The conclusions on *tutela* are of considerable general importance because the fact that there could definitely be *iusiurandum in litem* takes away all the force from the arguments to the effect that *iusiurandum in litem* was inappropriate in the *bonae fidei iudicia*. This, indeed, concludes the examination of the texts on the *bonae fidei iudicia* and it is hoped that it has been shown that there is little reason for the belief that *iusiurandum in litem* was impossible in these actions.

19

Drunkenness in Roman Law

Drunkenness appears in a prominent rôle in most legal systems, both in actual rules of positive law and in particular cases noted for their human interest. Instances may be chosen at random. Thus, in the Scots case of Johnston v. Brown[1] an irregular marriage was set aside on Mary Brown's plea "that at the time when she declared an irregular marriage before a Justice of the Peace, and for the three days thereafter during which she cohabited with Johnston, she was incapable, by reason of stupefaction occasioned by intoxication, of giving a rational consent, or of understanding what she did." In the English law of larceny the intention to deprive the owner permanently of the thing must be present at the time the offence is committed. In Ruse v. Read,[2] Read took a bicycle when he was too drunk to form any intention in respect of it. The following day, not knowing what to do with the bicycle, he dispatched it by rail to York. It was held there was no larceny when he took the bicycle, but larceny was committed when he dispatched it. *Voet* tells us that in the Rhineland, drunkenness is so common especially in inns and eating houses, that sales made in the country in taverns are not valid unless confirmed by the lapse of twenty-four hours, and in the meantime either party has the right to withdraw, though forfeiting earnest money and token.[3] Very recently, the case of S. v. Johnson[4] in South Africa confirmed that voluntary intoxication, where there is no disease of the mind such as *delirium tremens*, is no defence in respect of an offence committed during the drunkenness. And in the Ancient World, Pittacus, dictator of Mitylene from around 589 to 579 B.C., is said to have enacted that if men commit an offence while drunk the penalty is to be greater than if they had been sober. This law was introduced, we are told, on the ground of expediency because more men are insolent when drunk than when sober.[5] Aristotle[6] shows he is aware that inebriation can be regarded as a mitigating factor.

---

1 1823. 2. S. 437.
2 [1949] 1 K. B. 377; [1949] 1 All E. R. 398.
3 Commentarius ad Pandectas, lib. 18, tit. 1, 4.
4 1969 (1) S. A. 201 (A. D.) The case contains full citation of the Roman-Dutch authorities.
5 *Aristotle,* Politics, 1274 b, 19—23.
6 Loc. cit.

But at Rome matters are strikingly different. In the legal sources there are not more than six texts which relate in any way to intoxication, conduct influenced by alcohol, habitual drunkenness or heavy drinking, and of these only two or three seem to concern acts done while drunk. Probably to these six texts should be added a seventh from Aulus Gellius, where he records a passage of Ateius Capito which seems to involve drunken behaviour.

This absence of texts cannot be explained by any scarcity of alcohol. Admittedly the Romans did not know the process of distillation, but wine was plentiful and cheap.[7] Indeed a cursory glance at the Digest title 18.1 might suggest that wine was one of the commonest objects of commerce. Nor is the explanation that the Romans were particularly sober. In Plautus, we meet, for instance, the old woman desperate for a drink,[8] and the totally inebriated Callidamates[9] and Pseudolus[10]. Terence's characters may appear more restrained but they are not more abstemious.[11] The Roman custom of appointing at dinners a *magister bibendi* whose commands for drinking had to be obeyed[12] guaranteed frequent intoxication. Drunken *Lucius* thrust his sword through three wineskins in the belief that they were thieves breaking into his host's house.[13] And so on.

The seven legal texts should be looked at more closely, in their approximate historical order.[14]

1. Aulus Gellius, Noctes Atticae 4, 14. Gellius came across a decree of the tribunes in Ateius Capito's ninth book of *coniectanea* headed *de iudiciis publicis*. A curule aedile, Aulus Hostilius Mancinus — who is probably the legate of 149 B.C.[15]—summoned the prostitute, Manilia, before the people because at night he had been struck by a stone from her apartment. He showed the wound caused by the stone. Manilia appealed to the tribunes of the plebs and declared that Mancinus, *comessator*, had come to her house, that it was not to her advantage to admit him, and that he was driven away by stones when he tried to break in. The tribunes decreed that the aedile had lawfully been driven away from the place where it was not proper for him to come with a garland round his head. Accordingly the tribunes intervened to prevent the aedile bringing an action before the people.

---

7 Cf. *Marquardt,* Das Privatleben der Römer, reprinted 1964, 443 ff.
8 Curc. 96 ff.
9 Most. 313 ff.
10 Pseud. 1246 ff.
11 See Eun. 727 ff.; Ad. 589 ff.
12 Cf. *Marquardt,* Privatleben, 331 ff.
13 *Apuleius,* Meta. 2. 32; 3. 5—9.
14 To be determined not on the basis of the date when the text was written, but of the date of the information relevant to us in the text.
15 Cf. *Broughton,* The Magistrates of the Roman Republic I, 1951, 460 n. 5.

Now it is not expressly said, but can reasonably be implied, from the word *comessator* for instance, that Hostilius Mancinus had had too much to drink. But it should be noticed that the tribunes' decree was not based on that point. They declared he was rightly driven from a place where it was not proper for him to come with a garland round his head; not, where it was not proper for him to come while drunk. The case involved criminal proceedings, not civil litigation; and the defendant based her plea not on any incapacity of her own but on the conduct of the aedile. Moreover, to judge from the tenor of the passage, the stress of the plea was on the aedile's attempt to break in, not on his drunkenness. Nothing suggests that the aedile's alcoholic consumption was legally relevant in any way.[16]

2. Call. D. 48, 3, 12 pr. (lib. 5 de cogn.). Callistratus tells us of a rescript of the Emperor Hadrian to the legate of Aquitania. A soldier who set a prisoner free or knowingly allowed matters to be such that the prisoner could escape should be put to death.[17] But if the escape occurred *per vinum aut desidiam custodis* the guard is to be flogged and *in deteriorem militiam dari*. If the soldier lost the prisoner by chance he is not to be punished.

This time, too, private law is not in issue, but military law or military discipline. It is doubtful whether Hadrian is referring to intoxication when he says *per vinum*; more probably he is thinking of the situation where a guard becomes drowsy after a few glasses of wine. The rescript sets out the action to be taken when a prisoner escapes, due to a guard's deliberate misconduct or negligence, or as a result of more accident. The guard's drowsiness through wine is equated with his laziness. Over-indulgence (in the circumstances) in wine is clearly not put in a separate category, and it makes no difference to the result. It is one form of negligence.[18]

3. Ulp. D. 21, 1, 4, 2 (lib. 1 ad ed. aed. cur.). The text is concerned with determining the defects in a slave which count as a *vitium*[19] under the aedilician Edict and hence have to be declared by the seller, or else give the buyer the right to redhibition. Pomponius, says Ulpian, declared that certain jurists held that *aleatores et vinarii* were not covered by the

[16] On the text see *Mommsen*, Römisches Strafrecht, reprinted 1955, 465 n. 1; *Düll*, Zur Frage der Provokation im römischen Zivilprozeß, ZSS 56, 1936, 1 ff. at 6.

[17] *Animadvertere* is a common euphemism for „to put to death".

[18] § 38 of the *Leges Militares* appended to the *Ecloga* discusses negligent letting escape but does not mention drunkenness. The *Rufus* named in the heading cannot be further identified: cf. above all *von Lingenthal*, Wissenschaft und Recht für das Heer vom 6. bis zum Anfang des 10. Jahrhunderts, Byzantinische Zeitschrift 3, 1894, 437 ff. at 455 ff. For a rather more positive approach, see now *Brand*, Roman Military Law, 1968, 138 f.

[19] Specifically *vitium*, not *morbus*.

Edict. This opinion is in harmony with the general principle that only physical defects have to be disclosed by the seller.[20] This and D. 21, 1, 25, 5, which we will look at shortly, are apparently the only texts in ancient Latin which use *vinarius* of a man who drinks. Whether the word should be translated as 'a man fond of wine' or as 'a habitual drunkard' is not too clear.

4. Ulp. D. 21, 1, 25, 6 (lib. ad ed. aed. cur.) concerns another clause of the aedilician Edict, namely that a buyer who is returning a defective slave has to make good to the seller if the slave has been made worse in some respect. Ulpian observes that 'made worse' refers not only to the body but also to *animi vitia*, for instance if in imitation of his fellow slaves this one is an *aleator forte vel vinarius vel erro evasit.*[21] This clause was interpreted more widely than that involved in D. 21, 1, 4, 2.[22]

5. Arr. Men. D. 49, 16, 6, 7 (lib. 3 de re militari) needs to be quoted together with the preceding *lex*:

6. *Si quis commilitonem vulneravit, si quidem lapide, militia reicitur, si gladio capital admittit.*

7. *Qui se vulneravit vel alias mortem sibi conscivit, imperator Hadrianus rescripsit, ut modus eius rei statutus sit, ut, si impatientia doloris aut taedio vitae aut morbo aut furore aut pudore mori maluit, non animadvertatur in eum, sed ignominia mittatur, si nihil tale praetendat, capite puniatur. per vinum aut lasciviam lapsis capitalis poena remittenda est et militiae mutatio irroganda.*

The citation of Hadrian's rescript ends at *puniatur*, and *per vinum* to the end was no part of it as the use of the indicative, *remittenda est*, shows. *Mommsen* thinks that the text is not in perfect form and that *per vinum* to the end was misplaced by a scribe in copying and should appear after *capital admittit.*[23] But this is most unlikely since *per vinum etc.* shows no sign of the distinction of injuring with a stone or wounding with a sword which is so important in § 6.[24] *Levy*, in his turn, suggests that *per vinum etc.* may be a gloss.[25] He finds it surprising that in the preceding part of the text, much less serious offences are punished by ignominious dismissal (*ignominia mittatur*), which he considers a much heavier penalty. He also says that *militiae mutatio* as a contrast to *capitalis poena* is amazingly light, and that the plural *lapsis* harmonises only with difficulty with the singulars between which it stands. But these arguments do not seem very strong. It is very understandable in

20 Cf. D. 21, 1, 1, 7; 21, 1, 4, 4.
21 Corruptions suggested in the text do not concern us: cf. Index Itp.
22 Cf. Ulp. D. 21, 1, 23 pr. (lib. 1 ad ed. aed. cur.).
23 Digesta Iustiniani Augusti II, reprinted 1963, 895 n. 4.
24 For other objects to *Mommsen's* reconstruction see *Levy*, Die römische Kapitalstrafe, now in Gesammelte Schriften II, 1963, 325 ff. at p. 362.
25 Loc. cit.

military terms that deliberate self-wounding—even when regarded as excusable—should lead to ignominious dismissal. The act may be repeated and it is bad for the morale of the troops. On the other hand, self-wounding as a result of too much wine or horseplay is a cause for laughter among the others, does not affect morale, and should not be regarded too seriously. In contrast to the death penalty for deliberate and inexcusable self-injury, *militiae mutatio*, for drunken self-wounding does not appear unexpectedly light. Switches from singular to plural and so on are common in legal writing and not suspicious.[26] In fact the whole of this fragment from Arrius Menander can provide other examples. The present switches are not important: Arrius reverts to the plural after the singular of Hadrian's rescript, and § 8 concerns a totally different situation.

There is no strong reason, therefore, to think either that *per vinum etc.* is not in its proper place or is a gloss. Several points about the sentence beginning *per vinum* then become important for us. Firstly, the question of the effect of alcoholic consumption is again raised in a context of military law, not of private law. Secondly, it is considered by Arrius Menander, and does not go back to the rescript of Hadrian. Thirdly, it is striking that the situation discussed is self-injury, not the more important one of wounding another. Fourthly, self-wounding *per vinum* is put on a level with self-wounding as a result of horse-play, that is, it is again being treated as a form of negligence. Hence, total intoxication is probably not what is under consideration.[27]

6. Marci. D. 48,19,11,2 (lib. 2 de publicis iudiciis). Marcian says that an injury may be caused *aut proposito aut impetu aut casu*, "with premeditation, on the spur of the moment, by chance" and to illustrate injury *impetu* he has *cum per ebrietatem ad manus aut ad ferrum venitur*. Perhaps not surprisingly the text has been little discussed.[28] For the text does not tell us what legal consequences flow from the distinctions he draws; what Marcian means by *delinquitur impetu* is not too clear, and the word *impetus* with a meaning like this occurs nowhere else in the legal sources; and we have no other information on the effect of drunkenness on the commission of a crime. We cannot tell for certain whether Marcian is thinking of drunkenness so extreme that the wrongdoer could form no intention or merely such that he did not consider the consequences of his act; not can we conclusively determine whether the drunkenness operates to exclude liability or simply mitigates the penalty. Probably, though, Marcian is thinking of a drunkard who did not pause to consider the consequences of his act and the intoxication acts

---

[26] Numerous instances can be found in Gaius' Institutes.

[27] § 45 of the Leges Militares is a generalised version of this text.

[28] Though see *Mommsen*, Strafrecht, 626 and n. 3.

to mitigate the punishment.[29] The text is, of course, concerned with criminal, not civil, liability.

7. C. Th. 3, 16, 1. The Emperor Constantine declares in 331 A.D. that it is settled that a woman, on account of her own wicked desires, is not allowed to divorce her husband for a frivolous reason such as that he is a drunkard (*ebriosus*), a gambler or a woman-chaser.[30]

Several striking points emerge from this brief analysis of the seven texts. First, of the seven, two concern criminal law and two military law. This is a remarkably high proportion when one considers how little prominence is given to criminal and military law in the legal sources as a whole.[31] Secondly, of the small number relating to private law, not one concerns the drunk man's ability to consent or form an intention. Yet one might have expected drunkenness to be discussed in the context of the *animus furandi, iniuria*, and agreement in the *bonae fidei* contracts, especially sale. This absence of information is highlighted when we glance at the works of jurists of a later age who had to rely on Roman authorities for their legal propositions. Thus, *Voet*[32] declares that drunkenness bars agreement in sale. He cites three Roman texts in support: D. 48, 19, 11, 2, which we already know about; Inst. 2, 11, 1 which is to the effect that, since a military will can be made without the ordinary formalities being observed, care has to be taken to confirm that the dead soldier had spoken with the intention of making a will; and Paul. D. 50, 17, 48 (lib. 35 ad ed.) which says that whatever is done or said in a fit of temper is not finally settled unless the intention is shown by perseverance, "and so a wife who returns in a short time is not regarded as having divorced her husband."[33] None of these texts is at all relevant, and one must sympathise with *Voet* who could find no better authority. Thirdly, even the texts on military and criminal law are sparing in their information on drunkenness and intention. Fourthly, intoxication or partiality to alcohol appears more prominently in later texts.

From the nature of these seven texts and the absence of any others the following conclusions can be drawn:

A. Originally, and for a very long time, intoxication was legally irrelevant. Hence the absence of authority before late classical law, the surprising lack of emphasis on *Mancinus*' drunkenness in Aulus Gellius Noctes Atticae 4.14, and the absence of any mention of drunkenness in

[29] This also seems the opinion of *Mommsen*, loc. cit.

[30] Generally on the text see now *Yaron*, De divortio varia, TR 32, 1964, 533 ff. at pp. 542 ff.

[31] Even though drunkenness is much more common in crimes and military offences than in contract or delict.

[32] ad Pandectas, lib. 18, tit. 1, 4.

[33] The *lex gemina*, D. 24, 2, 3, has a rather different version.

the reported facts of any case. It is, in fact, very noticeable that in connection with, say, actions under the *lex Aquilia* it is never said that one of the parties was inebriated.[34]

B. Consideration of the effect of alcohol on behaviour came in gradually in classical law in military and—perhaps slightly later—criminal law. It is unlikely to be a mere coincidence that in all three texts relevant to this point, Hadrian's rescript in D. 48, 3, 12 pr., Arrius Menander's opinion in D. 49, 16, 6, 7 and Marcian's discussion in D. 48, 19, 11, 2, a distinction is being drawn between at least deliberate wrongdoing and negligent or unpremeditated wrongful behaviour. The point is being made that a wrong following upon too much alcohol is less serious than deliberate wrongdoing. Insobriety need not have been so treated, of course, hence the significance of the self-wounding in D. 49, 16, 6, 7. It is easier to regard inebriated self-injury as less serious than deliberate self-wounding, than it is to see the drunken wounding of another as of lesser gravity than a premeditated assault.[35, 36]

C. In private law intoxication was never considered to bar agreement to a contract, consent to a marriage, formation of an *animus furandi*, and so on. The evidence for this is not just the total absence of any texts in private law on the effect of alcohol on intention—though that would be enough—but also the existence of three texts on legal aspects of habitual drunkenness. This raises sharply the question of the precise meaning of *consensus* and *animus*.

D. Even in military and criminal law intoxication as a relevant factor in determining the seriousness of an offence made little impact. Hence, in two of our three texts, D. 48, 3, 12 pr. and D. 49, 16, 6, 7, conduct influenced by alcohol is treated simply as one form of negligence; hence in D. 49, 16, 6, 7 the easy case of self-wounding, not the more difficult case of injury to another, illustrated the idea that some degree of intoxication may operate as a mitigating factor; hence, the general lack of precision in even such a late text as D. 48, 19, 11, 2.[37]

---

[34] One might feel, though, that in Alf. D. 9, 2, 52, 1 (lib. 2 dig.) the taker of the lantern is not treated as a thief because the removal was rather a drunken prank.

[35] And there is no text on a drunken attack an another.

[36] Nothing significant for drunkenness in military law can be found in *Müller,* Die Strafjustiz im römischen Heere, Neue Jahrbücher für das klassische Altertum, 17, 1906, 55 ff.; *Sander,* Die römische Militärstrafe, Rheinisches Museum für Philologie, 103, 1960, 289 ff.; *Brand,* Roman Military Law.

[37] Perhaps the significant point is not so much the vagueness of this text as the absence of any text more precise.

V

Delict

20

Personal Injuries in the XII Tables

The provisions on injuries less than death to humans which are contained in the Twelve Tables present some of the most fascinating and intractable problems in legal history. Three clauses have come down to us – at least in a modernised version – from this archaic Roman code of the 5th century B.C. Modern commentators place them in Table VIII, as follows:

> 2. Si membrum rup ⟨s⟩ it, ni cum eo pacit, talio esto. 3. Manu fustive si os fregit libero, CCC, si servo, CL poenam subito. 4. Si iniuriam faxsit, viginti quinque poenae sunto[1].

A standard translation[2] would be:

> 2. If person has maimed another's limb, let there be retaliation in kind unless he makes agreement for composition with him. 3. If he has broken or bruised freeman's bone with hand or club, he shall undergo penalty of 300 pieces; if slave's, 150. 4. If he has done simple harm [to another], penalties shall be 25 pieces.

These provisions stand at the beginning of the development of both the Roman law of damage to animate property (as set out in the later *lex Aquilia*) and of the delict *iniuria* which covered deliberate assault and defamation, particularly to a free person. But what was the original scope and meaning of the provisions? What is the distinction between *membrum rumpere* (apparently, "to break a part of the body") and *os frangere* (literally, "to break a bone")? Why is the compensation fixed for the latter to be three hundred pieces of copper[3] if a free man is injured, 150 if the injured party is a slave, whereas for *membrum rumpere*, unless the parties agree on a composition, retaliation is appropriate? Does *membrum rumpere* concern more serious injuries than *os frangere*? Does one or other of these clauses represent a survival from a more primitive age? Do *membrum rumpere* and *os fractum* together cover all serious but non-fatal injuries to the human body? What was the injury provided for in Tab. VIII.4, for which such a relatively small penalty as 25 pieces of copper was considered appropriate? More questions still are raised by the provisions but this paper will attempt in the first place to deal with those already enumerated. Other issues will be discussed as they arise.

Inevitably the provisions have been much discussed and numerous solutions proposed to the problems. It is neither necessary nor appropriate to list here

1. For this reconstruction of the clauses see the apparatus in C. G. Bruns, *Fontes Iuris Romani Antiqui*, 7th edit. by O. Gradenwitz (Tübingen 1909), pp. 29f.
2. That of E. H. Warmington, *Remains of Old Latin*, 3 (Loeb Classical Library, London–Cambridge, Mass, 1938), p. 477.
3. The XII Tables were promulgated long before coined money was introduced at Rome.

all the solutions which have been suggested, but the account of F. de Zulueta[4] is instructive and can set the scene:

> We have here an admirable illustration of the evolution of delictual obligation: in the gravest case composition for vengeance is still voluntary, in the others there is a tariff of fixed penalties, but not yet estimation according to the case. Adequate commentary belongs to comparative law. An obvious problem is the meaning of *membrum ruptum* and its distinction from *os fractum.* One view is that *membrum ruptum* meant amputation of a limb, a mutilation; but if so, a serious wound which neither severed a limb nor broke a bone carried no higher penalty than a punch with the fist – 25 *asses.* This objection leads to the supposition that a clause dealing with bloody wounding has been lost; but the loss is improbable. Perhaps the most popular view is that *membrum ruptum* meant a permanent disablement of some part of the body; thus if a bone was broken it would depend on the ulterior consequences whether *talio* or 300–150 *asses* should be the penalty. The conjecture may be ventured that the distinction lay in the nature of the act rather than in the result: *membrum ruptum* was wounding with a cutting weapon – a sword, dagger, or knife – which would be an act of private war deserving of *talio*, whereas a blow with a stick or the fist was simple *iniuria*, carrying a *poena* of 25 *asses*, but multiplied by 12 or 6 when a bone was broken.

The problem is, of course, the scarcity of surrounding information. It is not enough to produce answers which are sensible or even historically appropriate; one must also make them plausible. It is hoped that the approach taken in this paper may render some of the conclusions persuasive, though not all of the views expressed are by any means new.

Mention has already been made of the *lex Aquilia*. D.9.2.27.5 (Ulpian *18 ad ed.*) reports the wording of the third chapter as follows:

> Tertio autem capite ait eadem lex Aquilia: "Ceterarum rerum, praeter hominem et pecudem occisos, si quis alteri damnum faxit, quod usserit fregerit ruperit iniuria, quanti ea res erit in diebus triginta proximis, tantum aes domino dare damnas esto".
>
> Now in the third chapter the *Lex Aquilia* goes on to say: "In respect of all other things, besides slaves or cattle killed, if anyone does damage to another by wrongfully burning, breaking or breaking off, whatever the matter in issue shall turn out to be worth in the next thirty days, so much let him be condemned to pay to the owner"[5].

It is widely accepted that the original wording of the *lex* began only at *Si quis alteri* "If anyone" and that what precedes is a later addition[6]. The origi-

4. *The Institutes of Gaius* 2 (Oxford 1953), p. 217: see also D. V. Simon, *Begriff und Tatbestand der Iniuria im altrömischen Recht*, ZSS 82 (1965), pp. 132ff. at pp. 163ff.; P. B. H. Birks, *The Early History of Iniuria*, T.v.R. 37 (1969), pp. 163ff.; H. F. Jolowicz and B. Nicholas, *Historical Introduction to the Study of Roman Law*, 3rd edit. (Cambridge 1972), p. 171; R. Wittmann, *Die Körperverletzung an Freien im klassischen römischen Recht* (Munich 1972), pp. 3 ff.; and the authors cited in these works.

5. The translation is that of F. H. Lawson, *Negligence in the Civil Law* (Oxford 1950), p. 103.

6. See now U. von Lübtow, *Untersuchungen zur lex Aquilia de damno iniuria dato* (Berlin 1971), p. 21 and the authors he cites at n. 16; M. Kaser, *Das römische Privatrecht* 1, 2nd edit. (Munich 1971), p. 161, n. 60. Most recently, A. M. Honoré has argued that the words *Ceterarum rerum* are genuine; *Linguistic and Social Content of the Lex Aquilia*, Irish Jurist 7 (1972), pp. 138ff. Though he has shown from Cicero, *pro Quinctio* 3.11, that the genitive is not surprising and that the phrase *ceterarum rerum* could

nal scope of the chapter is much disputed but I accept the view of David Daube that it was concerned with injuries less than death to slaves and animals[7] (perhaps only herd animals, *pecudes*) and not with damage to inanimate things. One of the most powerful arguments for this view is the relationship between *membrum rup<s>it* and *os fregit* of the XII Tables on the one hand, and *fregerit ruperit* of the *lex Aquilia* on the other. Only with a reference back to the XII Tables can one see any reason for the *lex Aquilia* using both verbs, both *fregerit* and *ruperit*. This involves holding that one purpose, perhaps the main purpose, of chapter 3 was to reform the law in the XII Tables on injury to slaves, especially by substituting a different way of calculating damages[8].

If the opinions expressed in the previous paragraph are correct then it should be possible to use chapter 3 of the *lex Aquilia* to aid our understanding of the XII Tables. It seems appropriate to begin with the assertion that *ruperit* in the *lex Aquilia* corresponds to *membrum rup<s>it* in the XII Tables, and that *fregerit* corresponds to *os fregit*. The verbs are likely to be used in both pieces of legislation with the same meaning[9], at least as the verbs were interpreted for the XII Tables when chapter 3 was introduced. There is, it must be admitted, an act of faith here, since there seems no way of proving the assertion. Everything depends upon its plausibility which will seem greater to some scholars than others. Wittmann, for instance, maintains that no help for understanding *membrum ruptum* can be found in the wording of the much later *lex Aquilia*; and he justifies this by pointing out that from the beginning *rumpere* must have had a wide meaning in the context of chapter 3[10]. A wide meaning for *rumpere* will not be denied in this paper.

Nothing in our sources for the XII Tables corresponds to *quod usserit*, "by burning", "because he burned". To this problem we will return[11]. At the

mean "as to other matters" I am not persuaded by his other arguments. To begin with, the aedilician edict *de feris* originally ended, I believe, at '*ita habuisse velit*'; hence little can be deduced (for the *lex Aquilia*) from *ceterarum rerum* in the next sentence of Ulpian's text, D.21.1.42 (*2 ad ed. aed. cur.*); see A. Watson, *Law Making in the Later Roman Republic* (Oxford 1974), pp. 89f. Then, pace Honoré (pp. 142f.), D.9.2.27.6 does not seem to be Ulpian's comment on *ceterarum rerum*. Its main purpose is introductory, to distinguish the scope of chapter 3 from that of chapter 1, and it then opens the discussion of *usserit*. Above all, there is a positive objection to Honoré's reconstruction. On his view *ceterarum rerum* must refer to the contents of chapters 1 and 2, and mean that chapter 3 concerned only matters other than those comprised in the first two chapters. This should then imply that loss inflicted by a breach of an obligation (other than by an *adstipulator* as in chaper 2) would give rise to an *actio legis Aquiliae*. This, we know, was not the case. Indeed, *quod usserit fregerit ruperit* shows that the action under chapter 3 was available only where something was physically damaged. Hence, unless chapter 3 was incredibly badly drafted, *ceterarum rerum* could not have appeared.

7. *On the Third Chapter of the Lex Aquilia*, LQR 52 (1936), pp. 253ff.; cf. e.g. A. Watson, *Law of Obligations in the Later Roman Republic* (Oxford 1965), pp. 235f.; von Lübtow, *Untersuchungen*, pp. 109f. It is not intended to enter upon this controversy here but it is freely admitted that the following discussion depends upon the substantial accuracy of the view taken on the original scope of chapter 3.

8. Cf. e.g. Daube *Third Chapter*, p. 255; von Lübtow, *Untersuchungen*, pp. 22ff., 109ff.

9. Cf. e.g. Daube, loc. cit.; von Lübtow, *Untersuchungen*, pp. 109ff.

10. *Körperverletzung*, p. 4 and n. 12.

11. *Infra*, p. 261.

moment it is enough to suggest that either *quod usserit* relates to a provision of the XII Tables which is now lost[12], or, as I think more likely, it was inserted in the *lex Aquilia* because difficulties had arisen precisely because the burning of humans was not expressly regulated by the old code.

In chapter 3 the phrase *quod usserit ruperit fregerit iniuria* "by wrongfully burning, breaking or breaking off" denotes the ways in which physical injury to the slave cause financial loss – "financial loss" is the meaning of the word *damnum*[13] – to his owner. The phrase must be meant to cover *all* cases where physical injury to the slave involves the owner in financial loss.

But it will be immediately noticed that nothing in chapter 3 corresponds to the clause of the XII Tables, VIII.4, *Si iniuriam faxsit, viginti quinque poenae sunto*. If the assertion made in the preceding paragraph is correct, this can only mean that if the wrong envisaged by the XII Tables' clause was inflicted on a slave[14] this would not cause a financial loss to the master. Thus the clause related to such injuries as would not result in a fall in the market value of the slave – hence not disabling or scarring – or even in medical expenses. So only minor assaults were covered. This harmonises well with the relatively small penalty of 25 *asses*.

When we turn to *fregerit* we find that no case reported on the *lex Aquilia* turns on the meaning of the word. Nor is much thought expended on its interpretation. D.9.2.27.13 relates that the old jurists understood *ruperit* to mean *corruperit*, "spoiled", while §16 informs us that Celsus correctly admits that *fractum* and *ustum* are included in the term *corruptum*[15]. But whereas several other texts discuss *usserit* none refers again to *fregerit*[16]. Yet *os fregit* in the XII Tables seems to admit of only one meaning, namely "broke a bone"[17], and some such meaning should also be attributed to *fregerit* in chapter 3.

This brings us to the crux of the whole problem, the meaning of *membrum rup<s>it*. Above all, the question is whether, in view of the meaning of *os fregit* and the narrow scope attributed to Tab. VIII.4, *membrum rup<s>it* is wide enough to cover all other serious bodily injuries[18]? The evidence from the *lex Aquilia* is that it is.

To begin with, *quod usserit fregerit ruperit* covered *all* types of physical injury to slaves which would result in financial loss to the owner, hence *ruperit* referred to all such injuries other than those caused by burning or breaking a bone.

12. The possibility is raised by Daube, *Third Chapter*, p. 255.

13. See above all, D. Daube, *On the Use of the Term damnum*, Studi in onore di Siro Solazzi (Naples 1948), pp. 93ff.; cf. e.g. Watson, *Obligations*, pp. 236 n. 2; 246 n. 7; von Lübtow, *Untersuchungen*, p. 25.

14. It is possible that the XII Tables' clause concerned only *iniuria* to a free person, but this does not affect the argument here: see *infra*, p. 220.

15. Suggestions of interpolation in the latter text do not affect us: see von Lübtow, *Untersuchungen*, p. 114; H. Hausmaninger, *Zur Gesetzesinterpretation des Celsus*, Studi Grosso 5 (Turin 1972), pp. 265ff.

16. If there had ever been much discussion of *fregerit*, some traces would have survived.

17. The main reason for other interpretations being suggested is, I believe, the desire of scholars to make *membrum ruptum* and *os fractum* cover all types of severe physical injury to humans.

18. Apart from burning?

And the commentary on the *lex Aquilia* itself shows how insignificant *fregerit* was thought to be.

Secondly, the interpretation of *ruperit* in chapter 3 was in fact very wide. In classical law and as early as the law of the late Republic, *ruperit* was treated as being even wider than *membrum rup<s>it* could have been in the XII Tables, but this was due to two particular factors and should not be allowed to obscure the issue. The first of these factors was the extension of chapter 3 to cover damage to inanimate property. The other factor was the *edictum generale*[19] for *iniuria* which was issued probably in the last quarter of the third century B.C., and which removed the last legal relevance for a distinction between *os fractum* and *membrum ruptum*. A very different and slightly later law, a *lex de vere sacro vovendo* of 217 B.C. seems to have used the verb *rumpere* to cover injuries of all sorts to animals[20].

Thirdly, since *quod usserit fregerit ruperit* covered all types of serious physical injuries, there is no room for the suggestion that a further lost provision of the XII Tables – other perhaps than one on burning – dealt with cases of severe injury which did not fall under either *membrum ruptum* or *os fractum*[21]. Such a suggestion would involve holding that the clause had become obsolete and was lost before about 287 B.C., the year when chapter 3 of the *lex Aquilia* was perhaps promulgated[22]. This is inherently improbable especially in view of the slow speed of change in an underdeveloped society such as Rome then was.

19. Further on the *edictum generale* see infra, pp. 260 f.

20. Livy, 22.10.5. As Daube observes, "if the text given by Livy is not the authentic one it still shows how he supposed ancient laws to be"; *Third Chapter*, p. 255 n. 10.

21. Such a view was put forward by K. Binding, *Rechtsvergleichende Vermutungen zu membrum ruptum, os fractum und injuria der Lex XII Tabularum*, ZSS 40 (1919), pp. 106ff.

22. This is the commonly accepted date based on Theophilus, *Paraph.* 4.3.15. The historical credibility of Theophilus is often called in question, but even so scholars tend to prefer such a dating: see e.g. Kaser, *Privatrecht* 1, p. 169; von Lübtow, *Untersuchungen*, pp. 4ff.; T. Mayer-Maly, review of von Lübtow, Göttingische Gelehrte Anzeigen 226 (1974), pp. 128, 131. Recently Honoré, *Linguistic and Social Content*, pp. 145ff., suggests a dating perhaps between 209 and 195 B.C., but his arguments are unconvincing. He argues that the *lex Aquilia* was reforming the measure of damages set by the XII Tables because of the loss of purchasing power of *aes*. But this argument could apply only to *os frangere* not also to *membrum rumpere* and one can think of other motivations for reforming the old measure of damages. The absence of discussion on *fregerit* for the *lex Aquilia* shows how little importance the injuries covered by that word had in the *lex*, in contrast to those covered by *rumpere*. Moreover Honoré seems to think of devaluation only in terms of the reduction of weight of bronze coins, yet an increase in the amount of bronze in circulation between 451 and 287 would result in the fall in the value of a pound of bronze even before the introduction of coinage. Further it is by no means certain that the purchasing power of early Roman bronze coins was tied to the value of the bronze in the coins, and that a reduction in weight would mean a corresponding reduction in purchasing power. The aim of the government was clearly otherwise, though it was not completely successful; see M. H. Crawford, *War and Finance*, JRS 54 (1964), pp. 29ff. at p. 31; *Roman Republican Coinage* (Cambridge, 1975), pp. 626ff. It should also be remembered that contemporaneously and side-by-side and sometimes clearly in association with the massive cast *aes grave* there circulated a separate series —based on Greek measures—of struck coins in gold, silver and bronze. The struck bronze is very light in comparison with the *aes grave* and it simply cannot be maintained that the purchasing power of the bronze in both series was based on weight.

Moreover, it also involves holding in any event that by 287 *rumpere* had extended its meaning to cover the scope of this hypothetical lost clause.

Thus, it would seem that *membrum rup<s>it* covered all physical injuries apart from the most minor or the breaking of a bone. Hence, for instance, a stab wound in the trunk, a flesh wound in the arm, or the putting out of an eye are all, it appears, cases of *membrum ruptum*. This proposition can be maintained only if one can justify this wide scope for *membrum rup<s>it* within the normal early range of meaning of these words. This I believe can be done.

In classical Latin, *membrum* seems to mean "a part of the body"; and was not restricted in sense to "a limb" such as an arm or a leg, but could also apply, for instance, to "an eye"[23]. But the sense may well have undergone changes and it is necessary to look at the word's history. Ernout and Meillet direct our attention[24] to related words in other Indo-european languages: to the Sanscrit *māmsám*, Tokharian *misa*, Albanian *mis*, Armenian *miš*, and the Gothic *mimz*. In all these languages the word has the meaning "flesh" in the sense of "edible meat". The nearest in form to *membrum*, Ernout and Meillet claim, is the Irish *mir*, meaning "piece of meat". Their conclusion is that the initial meaning of *membrum* would therefore be "a piece of the body (of a living being)". The evidence, it seems to me, points to a rather different conclusion, namely that *membrum* initially meant "edible flesh" then "a piece of an edible body" and thereafter "a piece of the body (of a living being)". Later still developed the meaning of classical Latin, namely a part of the body (such as leg, arm or eye). The penultimate stage – which Ernout and Meillet regard as the first – is what I believe concerns us, when *membrum* would include, but not be restricted to, a part such as a leg, arm or eye, and would also be used of the trunk, flesh and so on.

There is no difficulty in ascribing the appropriate meaning to *rumpere* since its basic sense is "to break" or "to burst". No problem is presented, if anything help is provided, by the strange and corrupt text of Festus, "*Rupitīas . . . XII significat damnum dederit*", "*Rupitias* in the XII Tables means "he caused financial loss"". The *excerpta* of Paulus has *Rupitia damnum dederit significat*. Whether one believes that the word *rupitia* did exist but became obsolete leaving no other example[25], or holds that *rupitias* is a corruption for *rupit* or *rupsit* whether in our clause of the XII Tables or another[26], the outcome is the same. Festus' explanation, in leaving out all mention of breaking, cannot be complete, but reveals that for the XII Tables' clause this breaking must be such as causes financial loss.

In early times, therefore, *membrum rumpere* would mean "to burst or break a piece of the body". Thus, *membrum rup<s>it* in the XII Tables could be

23. See A. Ernout and A. Meillet, *Dictionnaire étymologique de la langue latine*, 4th edit. (Paris 1959), p. 395.

24. *Loc. cit.*

25. See e.g. F. Wieacker, *Die XII Tafeln in ihrem Jahrhundert*, Entretiens sur l'Antiquité classique 13 (Fondation Hardt, Vandoeuvres-Genève 1967), pp. 293ff. at p. 301; followed by A. Watson, *Tignum iunctum, the XII Tables and a Lost Word*, RIDA 21 (1974), pp. 337ff., at p. 339.

26. See the *apparatus criticus* in Bruns, *Fontes* p. 30 and *Fontes Iuris Romani Antejustiniani* 1, 2nd edit. by S. Riccobono (Florence 1941), p. 54; also Birks, *Early History*, p. 184.

used of any injury to the body, other than the most minor blows causing no real damage, for which a penalty of 25 *asses* was laid down. The phrase certainly, and the clause of the XII Tables possibly, could also apply to cases where a bone of the victim was broken and there might well be an overlap with the provision, Tab. VIII.3, *Manu fustive si os fregit* ... If this is so[27], this latter provision would not be pointless. It would provide a minimum penalty where a minor bone was broken as a result of a blow from a fist or a stick or club. Where a major bone was broken, or the injury followed upon a more serious assault with warlike weapons, recourse could be had to Tab. VIII.2. This conclusion about the overlap, it will be noticed, provides us with answers to two problems. Tab. VIII.3 – but not Tab. VIII.2 – specifies the way in which the injury was inflicted – "by a fist or stick" – because there was no intention or need for the clause to cover all injuries where a bone was broken; more warlike assaults resulting in an equivalent injury could be dealt with by *Si membrum rup<s>it*. Again, the tariff for injuries under Tab. VIII.3 is not flexible – 300 where the victim is a free man, 150 for a slave – and need not be, since whenever a heavier tariff was appropriate, recourse could be had to Tab. VIII.2.

That retaliation could be inflicted for *membrum ruptum*, only a "pecuniary" fine for *os fractum*, has caused considerable confusion, and has led to the views that Tab. VIII.2 represents an earlier stage of development and that *membrum ruptum* was necessarily a more serious injury than *os fractum*[28]. But a look at other archaic systems shows that talion is not necessarily earlier than a pecuniary fine, and that in some systems the latter may come first[29]. For Rome we cannot tell, but it should be stressed that the XII Tables expressly declare that talion is to be imposed for *membrum ruptum* if the parties do not reach an agreement for composition. Moreover there is just no evidence that talion ever was inflicted. Favorinus in Aulus Gellius, *Noctes Atticae*, 20.1.14ff is even made to say that this law cannot be carried out since the exaction of a just retaliation is impossible. Not too much should be made of this, however, since Favorinus is using a *reductio ad absurdum* in an attempt to show that an apparently cruel law was not so savage[30]. And at *Noctes Atticae*, 20.1.38 we find Sextus Caecilius claiming that if the defendant who had refused compromise did not obey the judge who ordered retaliation, the judge fined him; hence the severity of the law was limited to a fine. This claim is perhaps best taken as referring not to the time of the XII Tables but to a subsequent age[31]. But the Gellius' passages are significant for us in that they reveal there was no memory at Rome of talion ever having been inflicted. Perhaps it never was inflicted, a compromise always being reached[32]; alternatively it must have been very rare. It has been suggested that composition may have been indirectly enforced by the magistrate refusing

27. The lack of interest in *frangere* in chapter 3 of the *lex Aquilia* is in favour of this argument.

28. See now the discussion and the literature cited in Birks, *Early History*, pp. 179ff.; Wittmann, *Körperverletzung*, pp. 4ff.

29. See B. S. Jackson, *The Problem of Exod. xxi. 22-5 (ius talionis)*, Vetus Testamentum 23 (1973), pp. 273ff. at pp. 297ff., and the authors he cites.

30. Birks apparently takes this straight: *Early History*, p. 182.

31. See Simon, *Begriff*, pp. 176f.

32. See A. Watson, *Rome of the XII Tables, Persons and Property* (Princeton N.J. 1975), pp. 123f.

to grant *addictio* to the plaintiff of a wrongdoer who had offered a reasonable compromise[33].

Once one has escaped from the idea that talion (when no composition is agreed on) is necessarily more primitive than fixed compensation, one need not believe that *membrum ruptum* must inevitably be a more serious injury than *os fractum*. Whereas the provision on the latter is laying down a fixed minimum penalty for a particular type of injury, the great merit of the clause on the former is the flexibility of the reparation. All kinds of injuries can be covered[34] and, one hopes, a reasonable composition could be reached on the facts of each case.

Of the three provisions of the XII Tables on *membrum ruptum*, *os fractum* and *iniuria*, only that on *os fractum* expressly provides for the situation where the victim is a slave; and then the penalty is half that which is regarded as appropriate when the victim is a free man. Whether the clauses on *membrum ruptum* and *iniuria* also covered wounding a slave cannot be precisely determined. It has been suggested, for instance, that *membrum ruptum* had an entirely different aspect according to whether the injured person was free or a slave, and that it should not be assumed retaliation would be allowed in the latter case[35]. But much of the force of this argument is removed if we believe that the thrust of Tab. VIII.2 was to ensure that a composition would be achieved. Again, I have suggested elsewhere[36] that the *edictum generale* on *iniuria* (which I believe was primarily concerned with minor assaults[37]) did not at first cover assaults on slaves. If this is so, then since the purpose of that edict was to provide a flexible system of damages without changing the substance of the law in the XII Tables it should follow that Tab. VIII.4 did not cover the situation where the injured person was a slave. The argument is all the stronger because Tab. VIII.4 would not have been replaced by chapter 3 of the *lex Aquilia*. However this might be, if Tab. VIII.2 and 4 related only to injuries to free men, then injuries to slaves, other than *os fractum*, would be covered either by another clause or clauses or, as often, the existing law would be well-known and settled and would not be set out in the XII Tables at all. Nonetheless, whichever of these three possibilities is correct the argument from chapter 3 of the *lex Aquilia* for the meaning of *membrum rup<s>it* and *os fregit* is unaffected. The authors of the *lex Aquilia* chose to use *quod usserit ruperit fregerit* to denote all kinds of injury to slaves which caused financial loss to the owner. *Fregerit* must refer to an injury of the same type as *os fregit*. The choice of *ruperit* must likewise denote the same kind of wounding as *membrum rup<s>it*

33. See Simon, *Begriff*, p. 166; Jolowicz and Nicholas, *Historical Introduction*, p. 171, n. 8.

34. See now, e.g. Jolowicz and Nicholas, *loc cit*.

35. Daube, *Third Chapter*, p. 267.

36. *Obligations*, p. 248.

37. *Obligations*, pp. 248ff. Birks believes *membrum ruptum* and *os fractum* were the root cases of *iniuria; Early History*, pp. 202ff. The important thing, though, is that the *edictum generale* certainly did apply to minor physical assaults as the example in the standard *formula* shows; for the *formula* see above all O. Lenel, *Das Edictum perpetuum*, 3rd edit. (Leipzig 1927), pp. 397ff. A novel, interesting, but in my opinion unconvincing explanation of the decemviral law on *iniuria*, the *edict* and the *formula* under it is in P. Birks, *Lucius Veratius and the Lex Aebutia*, Daube Noster edit. by A. Watson (Edinburgh–London 1974), pp. 39ff.

even if the XII Tables' clause did concern only injuries to free man. Similarly, the absence of any word or phrase in chapter 3 corresponding to *Si iniuriam faxsit*, can only mean that – whoever was envisaged as the victim under that clause of the code – no such injury to a slave was to give rise to an action under chapter 3; hence the injuries in question were such as caused no financial loss to the owner.

Chapter 3 of the *lex Aquilia* covered injuries not just to slaves but also to animals or, at least, to herd animals (*pecudes*). Chapter 1 of the *lex Aquilia* gave an action for the wrongful killing of a slave or herd animal[38]. Yet no trace has survived of any provision of the XII Tables which dealt with the killing of slaves or the killing or wounding of animals. One should not simply conclude from this that the XII Tables contained no such provisions. That is certainly a possibility, but it is at least as likely that the *lex Aquilia* itself, by replacing the clauses, caused them to become obsolete. Our knowledge of the XII Tables descends mainly from Sextus Aelius Paetus Catus' work, the *tripertita*, of around 200 B.C. Some information on most of the clauses which survived until then and were treated in the *tripertita* has, in my view, come down to us. But what was lost by then was, of course, lost for ever, and the lost clauses would primarily be those replaced by a subsequent statute[39].

How then, it may be asked, should one account for the survival of knowledge of the clauses on *membrum ruptum*, *os fractum* and the *iniuria* valued at 25 *asses*? The answer is, of course, that, whether or not they all covered injuries to slaves, they certainly did apply to injuries to free men, and in regard to these injuries the provisions were not replaced by the *lex Aquilia*. The provisions would only fall out of use as a result of the *edictum generale* for *iniuria* which was issued probably in the last quarter of the 3rd century B.C.[40]

The same argument can be applied to the question of whether the XII Tables contained a clause on injuring a free man (and which may also have applied to slaves) by burning[41]. Such a clause relating to burning a free man would not be replaced by the *lex Aquilia* (or by any other statute known to us) hence its chances of survival would be high, especially since it would be so striking. Thus the strong probability is that no such clause appeared in the XII Tables.

A rather more difficult question is whether any help is provided by chapter 3 of the *lex Aquilia* in determining whether the XII Tables' provisions applied only to deliberate assault or also covered negligent or even accidental wounding[42]. Chapter 3 gave an action where the injuring party had acted *iniuria*, that is *non iure*, "without right". Thus, liability under the *lex Aquilia* was by no means restricted to deliberate misconduct by the defendant, but included most cases where the defendant was negligent and some cases where the injury was

38. See, e.g. D.9.2.2*pr*. (Gaius 7 *ad ed. prov.*).
39. See for the argument Watson, *XII Tables*, pp. 6f.
40. See now Watson, *Law Making*, pp. 45ff.
41. In the days before artificial heating and lighting injury to humans by burning, both accidental and deliberate, will have been more common; see, not for comparative law, but for comparable situations, *Exodus*, 21.23ff. In unpremeditated assault a weapon at hand would be used, and this would often be a torch.
42. The Romans of the time were certainly capable of drawing the distinction between deliberate and non-deliberate wounding: see e.g. Tab. VIII. 24a; cf. D. Daube, *Roman Law, Linguistic, Social and Philosophical Aspects* (Edingburgh 1969), pp. 131ff.

even accidental. In course of time *non iure* came to be interpreted as "maliciously or negligently"[43]. It is very tempting and reasonable to hold that a similar standard of liability for acting *non iure* applied to *membrum ruptum, os fractum* and *iniuria* in the XII Tables. But chapter 3 did not deal with injuries to free men, and its main purpose was to provide the master with compensation for his financial loss. Very different principles could apply when a free man was injured; hence if *membrum ruptum* and *iniuria* in the XII Tables did not cover injuries to slaves, the actions might be available only where the injuring party's conduct had been deliberate. Again even for the clause on *os fractum* which certainly did apply to injuries to slaves, if the 150 *asses* is better regarded as a penalty rather than as compensation we cannot be certain that the action would lie for non-malicious damage[44]. The best argument for holding that the actions on the XII Tables' clauses were not restricted to cases of malicious injuring is simply that there is no sign of any such restriction in the wording of the clauses[45].

Finally it would appear that chapter 3 of the *lex Aquilia* did not provide a remedy for damage to inanimate property until probably the second half of the first century B.C.[46] The extension was possible because chapter 3 did not mention slaves and animals expressly[47]. This raises the question of the nature of the previous remedy – there must have been one – for damage to inanimate property. There is no trace of any clause of the XII Tables on the general issue of damage to inanimate property[48], yet such a clause if it had ever existed is almost bound to have survived beyond the time of the *tripertita* if the argument adduced on the survival rate of XII Tables' provisions is correct. Hence it can reasonably be supposed that no such clause ever existed, presumably because when the code was drafted the law was thought to be settled, and caused no difficulties[49].

43. We need not be more precise here but see, e.g. Watson, *Obligations*, pp. 236ff.; von Lübtow, *Untersuchungen*, pp. 82ff.

44. If it be the case—which I do not believe—that this clause covered only deliberate wounding of a slave, this does not entail that no other action was available for non-deliberate wounding.

45. Whether the *edictum generale* originally applied only to deliberate assaults is not certain: for differing opinions see e.g. D. Daube, *Nocere and Noxa* CLJ 7 (1939), pp. 23ff. at p. 46; Birks, *Early History*, p. 203; A. Watson, *Roman Private Law around 200 B.C.* (Edinburgh 1971), p. 156.

46. See e.g. Daube, *Third Chapter*, pp. 260f.; von Lübtow, *Untersuchungen*, pp. 109f.

47. See von Lübtow, *loc. cit.*

48. There are, of course, a few clauses on specific types of injury.

49. I am very grateful to Professor A. M. Honoré, Dr. Alan Rodger and Mr. Sandy McCall Smith all of whom read a draft of this paper.

21

D.7.1.13.2 (Ulpian 18 ad Sab.): The Lex Aquilia and Decretal Actions

In my book, *The Law of Obligations in the Later Roman Republic* [1], I observed that the jurists of the later Republic gave an *actio legis Aquiliae* where the injury was less directly inflicted than was required for the *actio* in classical law. The reason for this, I suggested, was that although decretal remedies were certainly being given by the praetor in the time of Alfenus[2] it is unlikely that they were being given automatically as they seem to have been in classical law. The tendency would be to interpret the *lex* widely so that some remedy would be available to the injured party and only later, with the great development of decretal actions, would it become reasonably possible for the statute to be interpreted in a more restricted way. This view of the development I still think to be correct but the emphasis is not exact. What seems to be rather forced in the jurists' attitude is not the wide interpretation of the *lex* by the Republican jurists, but the narrow interpretation of the *lex* by the classical jurists. There is, to take only one example, a certain absurdity in the distinction drawn by Labeo and accepted by Ulpian [3] in the case where a woman dies from a drug given her by a midwife: if the midwife administered the drug with her own hands, there has been an *occidere* and an *actio legis Aquiliae* will lie; if, however, the midwife handed the drug to the woman for her to take herself, there has only been *mortis causam praestare* and an *actio in factum* will be given [4]. It is difficult to see anything in the wording of Chapter 1 which compelled this narrow understanding of the verb *occidere,* and it should be noted that there is no indication that the word was so restrictively interpreted in other contexts, such as, for instance, the *lex Cornelia de sicariis* of 81 B. C. It looks, in fact, as if the attitude of the jurists of the Empire to the word *occidere* was not really based on any interpretation of the meaning of that word, but on a desire to limit the scope of the action. For one reason or another, probably based on practical considerations, they preferred to give an *actio utilis* or *actio in factum* rather than the *actio legis Aquiliae.* I have no explanation of the juristis' reasons to offer here, but merely want to emphasise that this excessively narrow interpretation of the *lex Aquilia*

(1) (Oxford, 1965), pp. 241 ff.
(2) D. 9. 2. 9. 3 (Ulpian *18 ad ed.*); 19. 5. 23 (Alfenus *3 dig. a Paulo epit.*).
(3) D. 9. 2. 9 pr. (Ulpian *18 ad ed.*).
(4) This, of course, is not to deny that sometimes a reasonable distinction can be drawn between a more direct and a less direct way of doing something: cf. DAUBE, *Collaboration with Tyranny in Rabbinic Law* (London, 1965), pp. 8 f., pp. 72 ff.

— which applies to Chapter 3 as well (5) — only makes sense when the *actio utilis* or *actio in factum* is granted automatically and its treated as being as much part of the ordinary law as the *actio legis Aquiliae* itself. In this connection, it is worth observing the prominence of *actiones in factum* and *actiones utiles* in discussions on the lex *Aquilia.* Nowhere else do decretal actions occupy such an important place.

But how close the connection between the *actio legis Aquiliae* and the decretal action was in the mind of the Roman jurists is best illustrated by D. 7. 1. 13. 2 (Ulpian *18 ad Sab.*).

> *De praeteriis autem damnis fructuarius etiam lege Aquilia tenetur et interdicto quod vi aut clam, ut Iulianus ait: nam fructuarium quoque teneri his actionibus nec non furti certum est, sicut quemlibet alium, qui in aliena re tale quid commiserit. denique consultus, quo bonum fuit actionem polliceri praetorem, cum competat legis Aquiliae actio, respondit, quia sunt casus, quibus cessat Aquiliae actio, ideo iudicem dari, ut eius arbitratu utatur: nam qui agrum non proscindit, qui vites non subserit, item aquarum ductus conrumpi patitur, lege Aquilia non tenetur. eadem et in usuario dicenda sunt.*

Discussions of the text have tended to concentrate either on the nature of the action in respect of usufruct which the praetor promised the owner against the usufructuary (6), or on the evidence which the text provides that the *actio legis Aquilia* did not lie for injuries resulting from omissions (7). But another significant aspect of this text seems to have been neglected. From *denique consultus* to the end of the text, the terms *legis Aquiliae actio, Aquiliae actio* and *lex Aquilia* are used to include the decretal actions which are given in circumstances close to the scope of the *actio legis Aquiliae.* In the first part of the text we are told that Julian said, *inter alia,* that the usufructuary was liable to the *actio legis Aquiliae.* Then we have: *denique consultus, quo bonum fuit actionem polliceri praetorem, cum competat legis Aquiliae actio, respondit, quia*

(5) In respect of the directness of the injury; but not, of course, in so far as *rumpere* was understood as *corrumpere.* But this interpretation of the word *rumpere* occurred in the Republic: D. 9. 2. 27. 13 (Ulpian *18 ad ed.*).

(6) E. g. Lenel, *Das Edictum perpetuum* 3rd edit. (Leipzig, 1927), pp. 368 f.; Grosso, *Usufrutto e figure affini nel diritto romano,* 2nd edit. (Turin, 1958), pp 274 ff.; Wesener, *Synteleia Arangio-Ruiz* I (Naples, 1964) p. 197.

(7) E. g. Ferrini, *Opere* II (Milan, 1929), p. 108; Arangio-Ruiz, *Responsabilità contrattuale in diritto romano* 2nd edit. (Naples, 1935), pp. 230 ff. [The interpolations which he suggests are to be found in the text do not really much concern us]; Lawson, *Negligence in the Civil Law* (Oxford, 1950), p. 160; Albanese, *Annali Palermo* xxi (1950), pp. 21 f.; Beinart, *Studi Arangio-Ruiz* I, p. 301; Cohen, *Studi De Francisci* I, p. 329.

sunt casus, quibus cessat Aquiliae actio. The words *denique consultus* strongly suggest that the question was raised as a result of Julian's statement that the *actio legis Aquiliae* lay against the usufructuary and hence that it was asked by a colleague or a student. Moreover such a question, « What is the point of this remedy when its scope is already covered by another action? » is more typical of a lawyer than of a layman. Yet the question put to Julian is very silly unless the questioner was including under the term *actio legis Aquiliae* the decretal actions surrounding the *lex Aquilia.* There are innumerable situations where a usufructuary could do damage but not directly enough for an *actio legis Aquiliae* to lie though a decretal action would be given. Equally significant is the fact that Julian gives a serious answer. This significance remains even if Julian's reply ended at *cessat Aquiliae actio* ([8]). At the very least, he regarded the question and answer important enough to be given a place in his writings from which, presumably, Ulpian drew his own discussion. But there could be no significance in the point if by *quia sunt casus, quibus cessat Aquiliae actio* Julian was meaning all the situations where a decretal action rather than the *actio legis Aquiliae* would be given. There would be too many of them for the question to merit a serious reply. The text goes on: *nam qui agrum non proscindit, qui vites non subserit, item aquarum ductus conrumpi patitur, lege Aquilia non tenetur.* This is still part of the reason for the existence of the praetorian action on usufruct against the usufructuary. It is in the indicative but, since Ulpian frequently reports reasons given by another but with which he agrees in the indicative ([9]) (as in the preceding *quia s u n t casus, quibus c e s - s a t Aquiliae actio*), it is impossible to tell whether this part of the text also goes back to Julian ([10]) or is Ulpian's own contribution. As has been frequently observed ([11]), the examples here are all cases of omission. They are not instances where there has been a positive act but where the *actio legis Aquiliae* would be refused in favour of a decretal action. This cannot be coincidental and it means that whoever wrote this passage must also have been including such decretal actions within the term *actio legis Aquiliae.* If it does go back to Julian then it is strong confirmation of the attitude already ascribed to that jurist. And we can be confident that Ulpian was thinking along the same lines. The indicatives and *his eadem et in usuario dicenda sunt* show his approval. If, however, *nam* to *tenetur* is Ulpian's own contribution to the discussion then it shows only that Ulpian himself was thinking of the term *actio legis Aquiliae* as in-

---

([8]) Arangio-Ruiz holds *ideo-utatur* interpolated: loc. cit. *Nam - tenetur* may be Ulpian's own addition: cfr. *infra*, p. 169.

([9]) Cf. Magdelain, *Les actions civiles* (Paris, 1954) p. 9.

([10]) As it does as translated by Otto, Schilling and Sintenis; *Das Corpus Iuris Civilis* (Leipzig, 1830), p. 649.

([11]) Cf. *supra*, p. 264, n. 6.

cluding the decretal actions which surrounded it ([12]). To conclude, it seems that in D. 7. 1. 13. 2 an unknown jurist, Julian and Ulpian all include within the term *actio legis Aquiliae* the *ad hoc* praetorian remedies which grew up around it.

It might be suggested, however, that this conclusion does not follow since the instances given of cases where the *actio legis Aquiliae* does not lie are all cases of damage to immoveables, that indirect damage to immoveables resulting from a positive act is relatively difficult to imagine, and that in this context what was being considered was nothing but usufruct of immoveables. It is, of course, true that the instances are all cases of damage to immoveables and that indirect damage to immoveables — especially such as should give the owner a right to an action against the usufructuary — are relatively rare, but I doubt if that is significant for us here. First, it is much more natural in the context of usufruct to think generally of damage by omissions (resulting from idleness rather than malice) to be caused to immoveables. One would, I believe, think automatically rather of the examples in the text than of, say, failure to take action to prevent the spread of disease in a herd. Secondly, usufruct of an estate will virtually always include important moveables, animate and inanimate. So it is hard to believe that what was being thought of here in the abstract was usufruct of an estate which consisted of nothing but immoveables. Thirdly, there is no sign the praetorian action in respect of usufruct given to the owner against the usufructuary was restricted in any way to immoveables.

If this conclusion is correct then a number of deductions can be made. First, the text would prove — what we already know in effect from texts in D. 9. 2. — that the *actiones decretales* which surrounded the *lex Aquilia* had been so developed that in a wide range of circumstances they would be granted automatically and that they could be regarded as a full part of the ordinary law. Secondly, the text would show more clearly than anything else does the great dependence of the jurists on decretal actions for the full sweep of *damnum iniuria datum*. Thirdly, the jurists normally ([13]) treat law from the point of *actiones* but this text would show that even in respect of institutions where this was very much the situation they might on occasion take a broader view. Fourthly, if here the jurists could talk in such a general way of an *actio legis Aquiliae*, they might on occasion have done so elsewhere. That is to say that other texts which talk of an *actio legis Aquiliae* where one might have expected a decretal action might be reproducing the original form of the text and yet not be implying that a direct *actio legis Aquiliae* rather than a decretal action would be given. One possible instance is in the quotation

([12]) There is not the slightest reason to think *nam-tenetur*, interpolated. So far as I am aware this has never even been suggested.

([13]) But not always: see SCHULZ, *Principles of Roman Law* (Oxford, 1936), p. 43.

from Celsus in *Coll.* 12. 7. 10 (Ulpian *18 ad ed.*): *si cum apes meae ad tuas advolassent, tu eas exusseris, quosdam negare legis Aquiliae actionem, inter quos et Proculum quasi apes dominii mei non fuerint.* The form of the action here is not primarily in issue. The real question is whether I have any action at all or whether I have lost ownership of the bees and hence have no action. Celsus himself, as the rest of the text shows, favours the view that I retain ownership of the bees. Hence an action will be available. If Celsus were more concerned with the form of the action, he might have specified a decretal action as Ulpian seems to in similar circumstances in D. 9. 2. 49 pr. (*9 disp.*) ([14]). Fifthly, the illustrations given in D. 7. 1. 13. 2 of situations where no *actio legis Aquiliae* would lie, being all cases of omission, would show that at that time not even a decretal action would normally be given by the praetor where loss was suffered as the result of another's omission.

([14]) Here I wish at all costs to avoid going into the question of the relationship between the *actio utilis* and the *actio in factum.*

22

The Definition of Furtum and the Trichotomy

The following definition of theft is found in D.47.2.1.3. (Paul 39 *ad ed.*)

> Furtum est contrectatio rei fraudulosa lucri faciendi gratia vel ipsius rei vel etiam usus eius possessionisve, quod lege naturali prohibitum est admittere.

It is repeated, but with a variation, in Justinian's Institutes 4.1.1.

> Furtum est contrectatio rei fraudulosa vel ipsius rei vel etiam usus eius possessionisve, quod lege naturali prohibitum est admittere.

The Digest definition appears as above, so far as I am aware, in all editions of the Digest with the exception of those of Haloander, while the one from the Institutes is in that form in the very early editions but not in most of those dating from the end of the first quarter of the 16th to the beginning of the 18th century.

The former definition as we have it, although it does not give a completely accurate picture of the law, makes good sense. It is a much finer definition than those of the classical period which have come down to us outside the *Corpus Iuris Civilis* [1]), and it is regarded as seriously interpolated [2]). Apart from purely formal indications, there are two reasons which make it unlikely that this is to any great extent the work of Paul. First, this would be the only example of an important definition from the pen of Paul. Secondly, we have another definition of *furtum* by Paul and this is much closer to those of Sabinus and Gaius than to that ascribed to him in the Digest.

> P.S. 2.31.1. Fur est qui dolo malo rem alienam contrectat [3]).

If Paul is the author of the *Sententiae*, then there is internal evidence to show that his Commentaries *ad edictum* (from which the Digest definition is taken), are earlier than the *Sententiae* [4]), and it is difficult to understand why Paul, after producing such a good definition, should revert to the traditional, inferior one [5]). If the *Sententiae* are a postclassical compilation from the works of Paul [6]), it is

---

1) Sabinus, reported in Aulus Gellius *Noctes Atticae* XI.18.20., has '*Qui alienam rem adtrectavit, cum id se invito domino facere iudicare deberet, furti tenetur.*' For G.3.195., if indeed a definition is intended, see infra p. 4.

2) Cf. Index Itp.; Jolowicz, *Digest XLVII. 2. De Furtis*, pp. 1—2.; Schulz, *Classical Roman Law*, pp. 580—581.

3) Repeated in Coll. 7.5.2., but with the omission of *dolo malo.*

4) Cf. Ferrini, *Furtum usus possesionisve*, in *Opere* V, p. 107 *et seq*, at p. 109.

5) If, however, Paul intended the *Sententiae* for the education of his son, it is just possible that he would prefer to give the old definition because it is simpler.

6) Cf. Schulz, *Roman Legal Science*, p. 176.

equally difficult to see why the author chose the inferior definition even if it were the earlier. Nor are formal indications of interpolation lacking.

The elements of the definition may be broken down in this way.

Contrectatio rei: In general, *contrectatio* was necessary and sufficient for *furtum*, although there were a few exceptions [7]. Sabinus' definition reported by Aulus Gellius shows that in his time handling, not asportation was the requirement for theft. It is sometimes maintained that *contrectatio* is wider in meaning and can be used to signify 'meddling' whether or not there is actual touching or handling [8]. But those who adopt this point of view produce no evidence for it, and it would appear from the texts — lay and legal — that the word is not so used [9]. On the other hand, *contrectatio* usually has a more restricted sense and means a handling or touching which is improper in some way, whether illicit, immoral, illegal or merely disgusting [10]. *Contrectatio* also requires an objective genitive and this is provided in the present text by *rei*. Here too, one must admit that the definition needs qualification. The *res*, for example, must be *mobilis* [11], and children, wives *in manu*, etc. who are not *res*, may be stolen [12].

fraudulosa: This word is certainly interpolated. It is said that in Latin literature it occurs only in these two texts and, as Schulz has pointed out [13], it cannot have been written by Paul since the jurists avoided uncommon words. Nor, since *contrectatio* means an improper handling, is it necessary.

lucri faciendi gratia: This phrase may or may not be classical. In favour of its classicality are the following points. First and most important, Aulus Gellius reports [14] Sabinus as saying: *Qui alienum iacens lucri faciendi causa sustulit, furti obstringitur* .... Hence, Sabinus seems to have regarded intention to make a gain an essential. Ulpian, too, in the 41st book of his commentary on Sabinus uses almost exactly the same words [15], and in the 1st book of his commentary on the Edict of the Curule Aediles has (D.47.2.66.):

---

7) Cf. *Jolowicz*, *op. cit.*, pp. xx—xxi.
8) E.g. Ferrini, *op. cit.*, p. 113.
9) Cf. *Thesaurus Linguae Latinae*.
10) E.g. Cicero, *De Deor. Nat.* 1.77: *cur non gestiret taurus equae contrectatione, equus vaccae?*; Donatus Terence, *Eun.* 96: *hoc totum nimis blande et cum contrectatione adulescentis dicit meretrix*; Hilarius in Psalm 118 gimel 4: *tamquam per contrectationem mortui quisquam fiat immundus*. Cf. *Thes. Ling. Lat.*; I am grateful to Professor David Daube for bringing this point to my attention. *Contrectare* has similar undertones.
11) E.g. D.47.2.25.pr.; G.2.51.; it must also be a *res in commercio*.
12) E.g. G.3.199; cf. Jolowicz, *op. cit.*, pp. xv—xvii.
13) *Classical Roman Law*, p. 580.
14) *Noctes Atticae* XI.18.21.
15) D.47.2.43.4.

> Qui ea mente alienum quid contrectavit ut lucrifaceret, tametsi mutato consilio id domino postea reddidit fur est: ......

Secondly, without this requirement it would be impossible in many cases to distinguish *damnum iniuria datum* from *furtum*. Thirdly, those who would remove the requirement of gain hold that the presence of *dolus* or an *animus furandi* should be substituted [16]. But if the requirement were simply that there must be *dolus malus*, the difficulty again arises of distinguishing *furtum* and *damnum iniuria datum*. And how other in Roman law would one conceive *animus furandi* than as an intention to make gain? It cannot merely mean 'to deprive the owner' since that could be done by destroying the object, which would give rise not to an *actio furti* but to an *actio legis Aquiliae*. There are, of course, a few exceptions to the requirement [17] but none so serious as to suggest that it should not, in classical law, be part of the definition [18]. Probably it was construed very widely to mean that the thief must intend that someone other than the person from whom the thing was taken, but not necessarily the thief himself, would gain the thing, its use or possession. The arguments in favour of it being an interpolation are also strong. First, there are the exceptional cases just mentioned which can lead, and have led many writers to deny that an *animus lucrandi* was essential [19]. Secondly, the phrase is omitted from the Institutes. The strength of this argument, however, is difficult to estimate. On the one hand, the definition must have a classical basis in book 39 of Paul's commentary on the Edict; yet since the versions in the Digest and the Institutes are certainly not wholly the work of Paul but are identical except for the absence of this phrase from the Institutes the compilers of one must have relied on the definition in the other [20]. And it cannot be doubted that the dependent text is that in the Institutes since Paul's commentary *ad edictum* was not one of the standard sources used for that work, but Theophilus and Dorotheus would be aware of what was in the Digest [21]. But the Digest did contain the words *lucri faciendi gratia*, and therefore, whether their omission in the Institutes be accidental or deliberate, it is not evidence that the phrase was not in Paul. On the other hand, we know very little about the way the Institutes were compiled and it is possible that the compilers, in addition to the Digest, used an independent source — whether an edition of Paul or an anthology of texts of various jurists — which did not have *lucri faciendi gratia*, and this reading they considered preferable. If this

---

16) E.g. Jolowicz, *op. cit.*, pp. lv—lxi; Schulz, *op. cit.*, p. 578.

17) E.g. D.12.4.15; 47.2.48.4; h.t.50.1.

18) Ferrini considered that an *animus lucri faciendi* was a very old requirement, *op. cit.*, p. 107.

19) Cf. Jolowicz, *op. cit.*, pp. lvii, lix—lxi; and the references he gives.

20) This conclusion would not follow if all the interpolations in the definition with the exception of *lucri faciendi gratia* were pre-Justinianic. But this seems most unlikely.

21) Ferrini says (*op. cit.*, p. 111) „Che la definizione delle Istituzioni sia presa dal frammento pauliano, *nemo sanus* vorrà negarlo." Cf. idem, *Opere*, II, p. 399.

were the position, the omission may be good evidence that the words were not in Paul. Lastly, the requirement is not stated in the definition in Paul' Sentences 2.31.1.[22]).

vel ipsius rei vel etiam usus eius possessionisve: These words are undoubtedly an interpolation, whether post-classical or Justinianic [23]). In addition to their appearance which is strange enough, they must depend on either *contrectatio* or *lucri faciendi gratia*. If the former, they are logically absurd since one cannot handle the use or possession of anything. If the latter, they would be ungrammatical. The correct construction, as Schulz points out [24]), would be *lucrum facere ex re* or *lucri facere rem*. For us, however, it is more important to decide whether the compilers regarded them as depending on *contrectatio* or on *lucri faciendi gratia*. The evidence strongly points to the latter. To begin with, and this in itself should be conclusive, *contrectatio usus possessionisve* does not make sense. One just cannot touch or hold the use or possession of anything. Those who maintain that the words do depend on *contrectatio* translate it as 'meddling' or 'usurping' [25]). But for this, as has been said, there is absolutely no justification in any Latin text. Secondly, where, on that view, one might expect to find *contrectatio usus*, one finds instead talk of *contrectatio rei* [26]), e.g. G.3.195—196:

> Furtum autem fit non solum, cum quis intercipiendi causa rem alienam amovet, sed generaliter cum quis rem alienam invito domino contrectat. 196. Itaque, si quis re quae apud eum deposita sit utatur, furtum committit.

Thirdly, there is no doubt that in the Basilica the Byzantine jurists relate the phrase in question to *lucri faciendi gratia*. In his Index at the beginning of B.60.12., Stephanus translates the definition of Paul as 'Theft is the fraudulent handling of a thing for the sake of gain, that is for the sake of gaining the thing itself, or its use or its possession.' This interpretation recurs in B.60.12.1.3. Of course, as Ferrini points out [27]), this cannot be taken as complete proof of the Justinianic interpretation of the passage since the Basilica texts are elaborations made quite some time after the promulgation of the Digest. Nevertheless, it is good supporting evidence. Lastly, *lucri faciendi gratia vel ipsius rei vel etiam usus eius possessionisve* makes perfect sense both logically and legally. The only important factor against this interpretation [28]) is that the words *lucri faciendi gratia* are not in the Institutes. Ferrini who held that *vel ipsius rei* etc were dependent on *contrectatio* said that the

---

22) Nor is it in G.3.195 (or anywhere else although it may underlie his discussion in 3.202.) but this text is probably not a definition. On the other hand, see Gaius D.41.1.5.6.

23) Cf. *Index Itp.*; Schulz, op. cit., p. 580; Jolowicz, *op. cit.*, p. 2.

24) *Loc. cit.*

25) E.g. Ferrini, *Opere*, V, p. 113.

26) This argument is produced by Ferrini (*op. cit.*, p. 112) against himself.

27) Loc. cit.

28) Against this interpretation there is little force in the point that *lucri faciendi gratia* should not be followed by a genitive, since *vel ipsius etc.* is admitted to be an interpolation.

omission in the Institutes shows that at a time when Latin legal language was still well known and properly used it did not grate on anyone's nerves ('non urtava i nervi di nessuno') to talk of *contrectatio usus*. This of course, ignores the possibility of carelessness on the part of the compilers either in accidentally omitting the words or in deliberately cutting them out as unnecessary and failing to notice in their haste the effect that this had on *vel ipsius rei etc*. Further, that very likely *contrectatio usus* and *contrectatio possessionis* would offend the susceptibilities of a jurist of that period is shown by the gloss on the Turin manuscript of the Institutes.

> Contrectatio dicitur a trahere, trahi vero non potest nisi corpus et quod moveri possit, ergo nec contrectari potest nisi corpus et quod mobile, ideoque nec furari. Cum scilicet (non — Sav.) sit contrectatio in incorporalium ergo non est furtum; sed cum res contrectatur fit fraus quandoque ipsius rei, quandoque usus, quandoque possessionis.

Three points emerge from this passage. First, the author bases his argument that incorporeals and immoveables cannot be stolen on the fact that there can be no *contrectatio*, so for him, *contrectatio* cannot mean 'meddling'. Secondly, although he was working from the Institutes, he says '*cum res contrectatur fit fraus quandoque ipsius rei, quandoque usus, quandoque possessionis*' thus refusing the dependence of *usus* and *possessionis* on *contrectatio*. Thirdly, and most significant of all, he says '*nec contrectari potest nisi corpus et quod mobile*'. One would expect not '*corpus*' but '*corporale*'. An adjective would be more natural than a substantive and would balance '*mobile*' The choice of 'a corporeal' (noun) instead of ,corporeal' (adjective) is deliberate and is clearly intended to counteract the inference of the Institutes' text and exclude the possibility that one can handle the use or possession of a moveable. It cannot be doubted that for this very able jurist *contrectatio usus* or *possessionis* was an impossible concept. Admittedly, while the Turin manuscript is of the 6th century A.D. this gloss is dated much later and is thought to be of the 12th century which seriously impairs its evidentiary value [30]). Nevertheless, it does show that at a period when one might have expected purity of legal Latin to be less marked it did grate on a jurist's nerves to talk of *contrectatio usus* or *possessionis*. More powerful evidence that Justinian's compilers did not intend to make *vel ipsius rei etc.* depend on *contrectatio* is found in Theophilus' Paraphrase. If it were their desire — even in the Institutes — to do so, one would expect Theophilus who was one of the three compilers (if one can include Tribonian) to give the same interpretation. But he does not. In the corresponding passage, 4.1.1., he has 'Theft is the wrongful handling of a thing belonging to another, hurting him who suffers the theft, either in respect of the thing itself, its use or possession.' Nor can we account for this extraordinary interpretation by saying that the word ψηλάφησις used to translate *contrectatio* has a rather restricted meaning and cannot be used with χρῆσις or νομή, because firstly, *contrectatio* itself has the same restrictions, and secondly, another word or phrase could and would have been used if Theophilus understood the Institutes' passage as being concerned with 'meddling with the

30) Cf. Alberti, *La „Glossa Torinese"*, Turin 1933.

use or possession'. Therefore, despite the omission of *lucri faciendi gratia* from the Institutes, in the Digest we should take *vel ipsius rei etc.* as depending on these words.

Another possibility which we must not ignore is that *vel ipsius rei* etc are a gloss which was intended originally to explain the first *rei* by a jurist who did not notice that this would make the words ultimately dependent on *contrectatio*. The words were later incorporated into the text by a scribe, perhaps before the insertion of *lucri faciendi gratia* by the compilers. If this is so, then it would account for the acceptance in the Institutes of their dependence on *contrectatio* — the compilers simply accepted the passage without too careful a scrutiny. On this interpretation it becomes even clearer that in the Digest *vel ipsius etc.* depend on *lucri faciendi gratia.* There the compilers noticed the difficulty caused by the gloss, and got round it by deliberately placing *lucri faciendi gratia* after *fraudulosa*, not, as they would otherwise have done (and as some later commentators, e.g. Baldus, did), after *possessionisve*. In other words, they intentionally broke the connection between the first *rei* and *vel ipsius* etc. Therefore, whatever the history of the definition, in so far as they thought about it, it was the compilers' policy to make *vel ipsius etc* depend on *lucri faciendi gratia.*

quod lege etc.: This, so far as we are concerned, may be ignored.

Accordingly, the Digest definition should be translated as follows:

> „Theft is the dishonest handling of a thing with the intention of profiting either from the thing itself or from its use or possession. From such conduct natural law commands us to abstain.

The difficulties in interpreting this definition (and they are not few) are to a certain extent due to a curious recurrent error deriving from an old and now forgotten emendation. Even authors who themselves do not make this error, rely on those who have, and because they have not detected its presence their own commentaries are confused.

Buckland is one who makes the error [31]). He, relying on the Institutes, says that *furtum* was „Defined by Justinian as *contrectatio fraudulosa vel ipsius rei vel etiam usus eius possessionisve*", i.e. he omits the first *rei* which occurs between *contrectatio* and *fraudulosa*. This leads him, incorrectly, to accept the trichotomy with the distinctions *furtum rei, furtum usus* and *furtum possessionis* [32]). Schulz takes his definition from the Digest, but also omits the first *rei* [33]); '*Furtum est contrectatio fraudulosa*

---

31) *Textbook of Roman Law*, 2nd ed., Cambridge 1932, p. 576.

32) *Op. cit.*, p. 577. Altogether, Buckland's position is peculiar. He quotes the Institutes as above in the first edition of his *Textbook* published in 1921 (p. 572), and gives an appropriate translation in the 1st edition of his *Manual of Roman Private Law*, 1925 (p. 317.). Then in his *Main Institutions of Roman Private Law* published in 1931, he gives a translation of the definition in which the first *rei* has not been omitted (p. 327). But in the second edition of the *Textbook* in 1932 (p. 576.) and his *Manual* published in 1939 (p. 318) he has made no corrections.

33) *Op. cit.*, pp. 580—581.

lucri faciendi gratia vel ipsius rei vel etiam usus eius possessionisve'. He rejects most of the definition as unclassical, and he ends his discussion by saying „Students should ignore the trichotomy altogether; it occurs only in this text" [34]). It is possible that there is a common modern source for this error, but if so I have not been able to uncover it, nor have I found other examples in this century. It does not occur in Monro [35]), Jolowicz [36]), Poste [37]) or Lee [38]), or in any of the foreign authors whom I have consulted and who quote either of the definitions, e.g. Huvelin [39]), Kunkel [40]), and Kaser [41]). Nor so far as I can discover, is *rei* omitted from any quotation of the definitions in the late 19th century.

But in the 17th century, the position was very different. Matthaeus whose commentary *De Criminibus* first appeared in 1644, quotes the Digest definition, omitting the first *rei* [42]). He also distinguishes between *furtum rei, furtum usus* and *furtum possessionis* [43]). He seems to be the first jurist to comment on the Digest definition in that form. Similarly, Voet, in his *Commentarius ad Pandectas* 47.2.1. quotes the Institutes' definition omitting *rei.* He, too, distinguishes between the three kinds of *furtum,* and relates the distinction to the definition. At 47.2.5. he says: *Nec tantum proprietatis, sed et usus furtum fieri, ut definitio satis ostendit* . . . .

While Matthaeus' error is almost certainly the result of carelessness (although as we shall see, there was some textual support for his reading) there is another reason for Voet's definition and that is a faulty text of the Institutes. The reading given by Voet is found in all 17th century Dutch editions, e.g. that of Vinnius, but in fact it is much earlier.

The exact date when this error crept into the text could only be discovered with certainty if one examined all the early editions of the Institutes, but in default of that, having examined a number, but by no means all of the early editions, the position seems to me to be as follows.

The manuscripts and printed editions of the Institutes up to the end of the first quarter of the 16th century, and the commentaries on them, give the text which we now have [44]). Then quite suddenly the change occurs, and almost all editions from

---

34) Ferrini points out, *op. cit.*, p. 114, that one has not so much a trichotomy as a dichotomy; on the one hand, there is *vel ipsius rei*, on the other, *vel etiam usus eius possessionisve.*

35) *Digest XLVII. 2. De furtis*, Cambridge 1927, pp. 1—2.

36) *Op. cit.*, pp. 1—2.

37) *Gai Institutiones Iuris Civilis*, 4th ed. ,Oxford 1904, p. 413, He does however, i nsert *lucri faciendi gratia.*

38) *The Elements of Roman Law*, 4th ed., London 1956, p. 385.

39) *Etudes sur le furtum dans le très ancien droit romain*, I, Lyon 1915, p. 783. n. 3.

40) *Römisches Privatrecht*, 3rd ed., Berlin, 1949, p. 252.

41) *Das römische Privatrecht*, Munich 1955, p. 514 n. 10.

42) *Op. cit.*, p. 65.

43) *Op. cit.*, p. 71.

44) E.g. the editions of Baptista de Tortis, Venice 1457; P. Schoeffer, Mainz 1468; J. Chappuis, Paris, 1519; Lyons 1525. Professor R. Feenstra of the University of Leiden also very kindly looked at several editions from 1468—1501, and all had that reading.

the middle of the 16th century omit the first *rei* and insert *lucri faciendi gratia.* One of the last exceptions to this is Wesenbecius' *Commentarius in Institutionum iuris libros quattuor* which appeared at Basle in 1569.

The change is primarily due to Haloander. Even if it happens that some jurist or jurists now obscure emended the text before him, it was certainly due to the popularity of his works that the new text was generally accepted throughout Europe. The first edition of both his Digest and Institutes appeared in 1529, and both contained exactly the same definition viz. '*Furtum est contrectatio fraudulosa lucri faciendi gratia vel ipsius rei vel etiam usus eius possessionisve etc.*' i.e. from both he omits *rei* and in the Institutes, he adds *lucri faciendi gratia.* For neither of these changes had he, it would appear, manuscript support [45]). It is curious to note that although in time his reading of the Institutes prevailed, his emendation of the Digest had not so far as I can discover, a single follower. Haloander retained these emendations in his subsequent editions and they cannot be accidental. He provides no commentary on the texts, and one can only make conjectures as to the reasons for his emendations. It may be that he is making the trichotomy, but there is no evidence for this. More likely, although he inserted *lucri faciendi gratia* in the Institutes, he would make *rei, usus* and *possessionis* dependent on *contrectatio* and so the first *rei* would be superfluous. If this is the case, he was by no means the first to adopt this interpretation in the West. Indeed, his omission of *rei* strongly recalls the text of the work now known as the Brachylogus.

> III.20.1. Furtum autem est contrectatio fraudulosa, quae fit invito domino, alienae rei usus possessionisve.

The origins of this work are disputed, but the more general opinion would seem to be that it was produced in the 12th century in either Lombardy or France. It is unlikely to have influenced Haloander's conjecture since it would not normally be read by jurists in the 16th century, and although we know of at least seven manuscripts then extant (one incomplete) it was not published until 1549, i.e. 20 years after Haloander's first edition. Perhaps more likely to have influenced the conjecture is Baldus' comment on Instit.4.1.1. '*Furtum est contrectatio proprietatis vel usus rei alienae fraudulosa invito domino animo lucrandi*'. Baldus, that is clear,

---

[45]) Cf. Schrader's critical edition of the Institutes published in Berlin in 1832, and Mommsen's two volume edition of the Digest, Berlin, 1870. A glossed edition of the *Corpus Juris Civilis* published at Lyons in 1548 notes on D.47.2.1.3 in the margin *contrectatio fraudulosa lucri etc.* but this is probably a reference to the Haloander reading.

Antonius Augustinus in his *Emendationum et opinionum libri quattuor*, Venice 1543, IV.4, criticized Haloander for omitting the first *rei* since it occurs in the Florentine Pandects and is more consonant with Theopilus' Paraphrase. The glossed edition of the Institutes which appeared at Geneva in 1555, published by G. Symon a Bosco and Gulielmus Gueroult, cites Augustinus with approval and says that the Florentine reading was supported by a Colladonian manuscript (cf. E. Zorzi, *Di una glossa francese alle Istituzioni tratta dall' Ordinario con particolare riguardo al titolo del furto*, in Atti del R. Ist. Veneto di scienze, lettere ed arti, XCII (1932—33), 2nd part, p. 1415 et seq.).

links *vel ipsius etc.* with *contrectatio*. Another, much later, jurist who does the same is de Piro. The edition of his commentary on the Institutes which I used was published at Louvain and is undated, but it is usually regarded as earlier than another edition published in 1482, and it reads: '*Secundo requiritur quod illa res sit mobilis et corporalis quia res immobilis et incorporalis non potest contractari et hoc est quod voluit hic glossa super verbum rei. Potest tamen dici quod usus seu possessio rei potest contractari et sic in usu et in possessione bene fit furtum et de hoc tangitur hic in glossa super verbum usus.*' This text is unlikely to have influenced Haloander, but is nevertheless not without interest. Before *Potest* de Piro is merely recounting the Accursian gloss. From *Potest* to the end of the quotation we can see that he links *vel ipsius rei etc* to *contrectatio*, and that he considers that the gloss did the same. Understood in this way, the text seems to be the work of a jurist who was much under the influence of the authority of the gloss, but who allowed himself a slight criticism of its logic viz. that there can be no *contrectatio* of immoveables or incorporeals, but there can be of the use or possession of something.

Of course, Haloander's emendations were not at once universally accepted. One step in the development is found in the edition of the Institutes by Sylvestro Aldobrandini published in Venice in 1552. He retains *rei*, but adds *lucri faciendi gratia*; that is, the Digest reading. The same reading is adopted by Hotoman, the first edition of whose Institutes appeared in 1560. He comments on *lucri faciendi gratia* in the definition as follows: *Quare necessario adiicienda haec fuerunt. nec manuscriptis quibusdam libris (in his Tigurino) assentio, in quibus haec desunt verba.* The use of *quibusdam* suggests that although he knew that certain manuscripts did not contain the words *lucri faciendi gratia*, he knew or believed that others did. Of these, however, we have no trace. Nevertheless, there was some (fruitless) opposition to the insertion of the words. Reitz in his edition of Theophilus' Paraphrase reports an old controversy. *Movet litem V. C. Cuiacius ad h.§. et ait: otiose in hac definitione adpositum esse illud l u c r i f a c i e n d i g r a t i a: quippe hoc, inquit, nihil aliud quam interpretatio est verbi f r a u d u l o s a. . . . .*' [46]).

Another edition which is important for us is that produced by Ludovicus Russardus and published in Antwerp in 1567 i.e. 38 years after the first edition of Haloander. He gives us the text as amended by Haloander, but notes on it appear in the margin. Note e says: *contrectatio rei. omn & D.*, i.e. Russardus recognises that all the manuscripts of the Institutes, and the Digest have the first *rei*. Note f. refers to *lucri faciendi gratia* and says. *Ita D. abest tamen ab om & Theoph.*, i.e. here too, Russardus admits that he has no direct textual support for the emendation. A somewhat different opinion is found in the edition of L. Pacius (published in 1583) who also adopts the Haloander reading. A marginal note says: *leg. contrectatio rei fraudulosa, ut habent Pand. Flor. etc.* The position seems to be that he believes *contrectatio fraudulosa* to be the correct reading, but that he considers the text should be understood as if *rei* were in, and in support says that *rei* is found in the Digest.

---

[46]) Cuiacius or Cujas lived from 1520 (?) to 1590.

The next step is that the emendations become generally accepted, and no notes are given to show that the editors were aware of the alterations. This is the case with the texts of Mynsingerus (first published in 1569), of Gothofredus (first published in 1583) and the contemporary editions of the *Corpus Juris Civilis cum glossis.* It is worth mentioning that the Accursian gloss which originally referred to the first *rei* in the definition has been transferred in the glossed edition just mentioned to the second (or sole surviving) *rei.* On the authority of these, the reading seems quickly to have become standard. Only a very few jurists in the next century and a half have any other reading. Bachovius, however, whose Commentary was published at Frankfurt in 1628 has *fraudulenta* instead of *fraudulosa*, and Borcholten (Paris? 1652) has the pre-Haloander definition. Now, of course, we have completely returned to the manuscript reading and Haloander's conjectures are forgotten.

As has been said, it is unlikely that Haloander adopted the trichotomy. Nevertheless, there are texts written considerably earlier than the 16th century which could give a good starting point for the division, and at least one jurist, Angelus de Ubaldis (brother of Baldus) could write of *furtum usus* and *furtum possessionis.* In his comment on D.47.2.1.3 he has: *Nota committi furtum ipsius usus, sic inst. eo* §1 *eo. si is qui rem commodasset*; *per hoc sustineo Martinum derelictum ab omnibus in l. falsus C. de furtis.* And on D.47.2.10 which says that the person who has the *actio furti* is he who had an interest in the thing not being stolen, he has: *Nota quod hic dominus facit furtum, subaudi possessionis, et usus. et per hoc sustinui dictum Martini in l. falsus, C. eo., ut ibi dixi in repetitione Paduae.*' The text of Martinus referred to is probably not extant, but to some extent it can be envisaged. As Angelus tells us, it referred to C.6.2.19 which reads:

> Falsus procurator depositum recipiendo vel aes alienum exigendo citra domini voluntatem furtum facit ac praeter rei restitutionem actione dupli furti nec manifesti convenitur.

And the controversy was on the right of action by the person who paid. The glossators first distinguished between the case where the *falsus procurator* had never been so appointed, and where he had but his *mandatum* had been revoked. In the first hypothesis they made another distinction, viz. either the debtor thought he was released and transferred the ownership of the money to the *falsus procurator* because he believed him to be a *procurator in rem suam*, or he handed it over to the *falsus procurator* to take to the *dominus*, but the *procurator* took it intending to keep it for himself. In the latter situation, there was general agreement that the person who paid had an *actio furti* and a *condictio furtiva.* In the former, Accursius held he had not, if he had transferred the ownership of the money to the *falsus procurator*, and he cites D.12.4.14 in support; but, he goes on, Martinus relying on the same text held the opposite. The gloss on the word '*condici*' in D.12.4.14 enlarges on the situation.

> *Condici.* condictio furtiva. Et hic nota quod Martinus dicebat actione furti posse agi contra falsum procuratorem et contra falsum creditorem, si scienter indebitum accipiunt, et eos nummos lucrentur: quamvis in eos sit

> dominium translatum: et *hic*, & *infra de condict. fur. l. quoniam* 2. Sed Ioannes et Azo contra. dicunt enim furtum non fieri ab eo, qui dominus factus est: ut *infra l. proxim. in fine. et patet ex definitione furti*: quia dicitur, furtum est contrectatio rei alienae, etc. ut *Institut. de ob. quae ex delict.* § 1. Nec obstat, quod hic dicit: quia mutat casum. nam supra dixit quando dominium fuerit translatum: et datur tunc condictio ob causam hic quando non, et datur furti: ut *Cod. de fur l. falsus.* Item non obstat *d. l. infra de condict. furt. l. quoniam,* quia et iliam intelligas quando dominium non est translatum in creditorem: ut ibi dices.

The position of Johannes, Azo and Accursius is that in such a case one cannot have theft because there can only be theft of a *res aliena.* Martinus is, of course, still represented as giving the *actio furti,* but no reasons for his view are given. Nevertheless, it is unlikely that his position was that the act amounted to a *furtum usus* or *possessionis* and not to *furtum rei.* First, because if this were his argument one would hardly refute it (as Johannes, Azo and Accursius did) by saying that one could only steal a thing which belonged to another. Secondly, because it is difficult to see how the act of the *falsus procurator* could be conceived in this way — after all, he was not given the money for a limited purpose. It is much more probable that Martinus merely said the payer had the *actio furti* because he had an interest in the safety of the thing. And it is Angelus de Ubaldis alone, who to refute the argument of Johannes and the others, says that the owner can be guilty of theft when he steals the use or possession of something, and therefore he supports Martinus who relied on other arguments.

Another possible starting point for the trichotomy can be found in the Commentary on the Institutes by Angelus Aretinus [47]). On 4.1.1, he has '*Nota quod non tantum fit furtum in proprietate, sed etiam in usu et possessione.* This, however, should not be pressed too far. It is not likely that he intended to say that there were three types of theft, but rather to point out that there could be theft in respect of the gain of the thing, its use or possession. This interpretation is borne out by two quotations from his *Tractatus de Maleficiis*: *Est autem furtum rei alienae contrectatio fraudulenta, invito domino, animo lucrandi facta.*; and *Et advertas quod illud quod dicitur, quod furtum est contrectatio animo lucrandi, intelligas, quod habebat animum lucrandi rem, vel possessionem, vel etiam tantummodo usum rei* [48]).

Similarly, two of the glosses on J.4.1.1 may have influenced the appearance of the trichotomy. The gloss on '*vel ipsius*' reads: *Scilicet rei, id est proprietatis ipsius rei*; and on '*usus*: *ut habes exemplum infra, eod. titul.* § *furtum autem fit.* There is nothing to suggest that Accursius made the threefold division but it is easy to see how these comments could have played a part at a later date in the introduction of the trichotomy by being interpreted in that way. The *casus* on the *lex* may also have been significant: *Quaesivi a legislatore quid esset furtum et quid rapina etc. Et ipse primo ponit definitionem de furto dicens quod furtum est contrectatio rei alienae invito*

---

47) 1422 — after 1451.

48) In the edition published in Coloniae Agrippinae in 1599, these quotations appear on p. 377 and p. 395 respectively.

domino. Et exponit hoc nomen, rei, dicens sive ipsius rei, id est proprietatis, sive possessionis.

None of these texts seem to have produced as an immediate effect the trichotomy, and indeed, there is no sign of it in the Commentaries published in the first thirty years after the appearance of Haloander's emendations. Admittedly in these Commentaries there is also nothing to indicate that their authors rejected the trichotomy, but this is probably the best possible evidence that it was not even thought of. One example at random is Melchior Kling, whose Commentary on the Institutes was published at Frankfurt in 1542. He has: '*Est autem furtum contrectatio fraudulosa rei alienae mobilis, corporalis, vel etiam usus eius possessionisve, quae fit animo lucrifaciendi, invito domino, quod iure naturali est prohibitum committere .... Dico usus, possessionisve, Quia si creditor utitur pignore et depositarius deposito, furtum committunt.*' Thus, he makes *rei, usus* and *possessionis* depend on *contrectatio*, but there is no sign of the trichotomy.

Almost certainly, the man really responsible for the trichotomy is Hotoman the first edition of whose commentary on the Institutes appeared in 1560 and was frequently reprinted. His comment on the text reads: *Furtum non tantum rei, sed etiam usus ac possessionis committitur.* Here quite clearly, he makes the classifications *furtum rei, furtum usus* and *furtum possessionis.* But, as we have seen, in giving the text of the Institutes he retained the first *rei* while adding *lucri faciendi gratia.* Thus it would seem that the trichotomy did not result from the omission of *rei* by Haloander, but that it was rather the fruit of Hotoman's imagination, probably influenced to a greater or less extent by some of the possible starting points just mentioned. Despite the popularity of his works, however, Hotoman's interpretation was not at once widely accepted. For example, the Isagoge to Wesembecius' Commentary on the Institutes published in 1569 which has already been mentioned reads: *quod est contrectatio rei alienae fraudulosa, lucri faciendi gratia vel ipsius rei, vel etiam usus eius possessionisve*; *quod lege naturali prohibitum est admittere.* The punctuation of this, especially the treatment of *lucri* — *rei* as one phrase, makes it absolutely certain that for Wesembecius *rei, usus* and *possessionis* were dependent on *lucri faciendi gratia*, and that he ignored the trichotomy [49]. The Commentary of Duarenus on the Digest which was first published at Lyons in 1583 is similar: *Dicitur Usus possessionisve. Quia furtum facit, non tantum is, qui lucrari vult proprietatem, sed etiam usum eius, aut possessionem* [50]. Indeed, the first whom I have discovered who follows Hotoman (although no doubt there are others who are earlier) is Thadaeus Piso who published a Commentary on the Institutes in Venice in 1600. The relevant part reads: *Non solum rei furtum committitur, sed etiam usus, veluti ..... Item non solum rei et usus, sed etiam possessionis...* But even later than this one finds commentaries where it is doubtful whether or not

---

49) It is interesting to note that in at least some of the later editions e.g. that published at Padua in 1687, the punctuation is altered and a comma is inserted after gratia, thus allowing a different interpretation.

50) Cf. Vulteius, *Comment. in Inst.* Marpurgi 1598.

the author accepts the trichotomy e.g. that of Bachovius (1628) already mentioned. Soon after, however, the trichotomy is generally accepted. For example, Vinnius' edition of the Institutes (first published at Leiden in 1642) has: *Exempla furti usus rei sunt in* § 6, *possessionis* § 10 *inf. eod. l.* 74. *de furt.* And, of course, it is extensively commented on by Matthaeus *De Criminibus*, by Voet and others, and is related to the definition, and so colours all discussions of theft. Perhaps the best example of this is in the Commentary on the Institutes by Borcholten published in 1652. He, as has already been mentioned, gives the correct pre-Haloander reading of the text. Nevertheless, he is so enmeshed in the contemporary concept of theft that he might as well never have been right. He comments as follows:

> *Furtum autem est contrectatio fraudulosa, lucri faciendi gratia, vel ipsius rei, vel etiam usus eius, possessionisve: Quod lege naturali prohibitum est admittere.* Ita Iustinianus furtum hic definit, eamque definitionem sumpsit *ex Paulo* in l.l. finali de furtis [51]) . . . . . *Lucrifaciendi gratia*, addita sunt, pro interpretatione verbi *fraudulosa*. . . . . . Additur in definitione *vel etiam usus eius*. Ut si servi usum habeam, et is servus surripiatur, mihi usus furtum fit, ... Additur in definitione *possessionisve*. Si enim res intervertatur, cuius possessionem dumtaxat habeo, non etiam proprietatem, non usum, non usumfructum, mihi possessionis furtum fit . . . . [52]).

It is almost impossible to understand how, having given the correct definition he could write the first part of this comment. It is worth noting that he takes *lucri faciendi gratia* as being an explanation of *fraudulosa* and nothing more. *Addita sunt* may have no special significance, since *additur* is used in connection with both *vel etiam usus eius* and *possessionis*.

Thus, Haloander's conjectures, especially the omission of *rei*, had an important effect on the later understanding of *furtum*. *Contrectatio* requires to be followed by a noun or nouns in the genitive, and so *vel ipsius rei vel etiam usus eius possessionisve* had to be treated as being directly dependent on *contrectatio*. Admittedly, the conjecture did not cause Hotoman to make the trichotomy, but once made, since the trichotomy was referred by others to the definition in the form given by Haloander, it was an important factor in its retention. Although it cannot be proved, it is also not unlikely that Hotoman's trichotomy would never have become generally accepted had it not been for Haloander's conjecture, because otherwise there is no evidence for it in this text and no indication elsewhere. The close interdependence of Haloander's conjecture and the trichotomy is shown in that of the two jurists of this century who omit *rei*, Buckland accepts the trichotomy [53]), and Schulz who rejects it for classical law says that it should be ignored and that it appears only in this definition [54]). It is perhaps also significant that the approximations to the

---

51) Manilius gives a very similar interpretation in the edition of Costa's Institutes (which gives the correct definition) to which his notes and those of Muratus and Alpinus are added by Van de Water, Leiden 1714.

52) This interpretation of *furtum usus* and *furtum possessionis* is, of course, different from that of modern jurists who retain the trichotomy.

53) *Textbook*, pp. 577—578.

54) *Classical Roman Law*, pp. 580—581.

trichotomy made before the omission of *rei*, especially that of Angelus de Ubaldis, did not win general acceptance. Schirmer, as early as 1884 in a very powerful article [55]), demonstrated the falsity of the trichotomy. But since he did not show that the earlier view which had been almost universally held since the 17th century was closely connected to Haloander's conjecture — which by his time had been rejected — he did not completely kill the earlier theory (witness Buckland), and even those who accept his position are forced to restate it. In other words, to a certain extent modern Romanists are still enmeshed in the consequences of the omission of *rei* [56]).

---

[55]) ZSS 5, p. 207 et seq.

[56]) I am grateful to Professor R. Feenstra of the University of Leiden and Mr. A. M. Honoré, Rhodes Reader in Roman-Dutch Law in the University of Oxford, for very generous advice.

23

Contrectatio as an Essential of Furtum

I HAVE maintained elsewhere [1] that the word *contrectatio* meant " a physical handling which is in some way improper." It is usually argued that there are cases where handling was not needed for *furtum* and Buckland who said that *contrectatio* was necessary [2] took that word in the wider sense of " meddling." Nevertheless, a good case can be put up for saying that physical touching was an essential for theft in classical Roman law and later.

The main texts which are believed to show that touching was not needed are D.47.2.67(66).2 and *h.t.* 37.

> D.47.2.67(66).2. (Paul 7 *ad Plautium*). Eum, qui mulionem dolo malo in ius vocasset, si interea mulae perissent, furti teneri veteres responderunt.

Perhaps the clearest statement of the view that here there is *furtum* without touching is by Huvelin.[3] A mule driver, he says, was passing in the street, driving his mules. Up came a rogue who under some pretext summoned him before the praetor. The mules left alone were killed by chance or strayed or were stolen. The republican jurists gave the *actio furti*. " Notice," he says, " that nothing in the text of the *responsum* indicates that the mules were stolen; the words used (*si mulae perissent*) extend just as naturally to mules which have been killed or have strayed. Likewise nothing suggests that the *in ius vocans* was in league with thieves who took away the mules. Lastly, nothing suggests that he was sued by the *actio furti* as an accomplice. . . . In fact the *in ius vocans* commits a theft even if the mules are lost completely by chance and he is the sole perpetrator of the theft." This interpretation is generally accepted, for instance by Buckland,[4] Jolowicz,[5] Niederländer [6] and Albanese.[7] But despite such distinguished support it is untenable. Since on this view the *in ius vocans* is liable even where the mules wander off or are killed by chance it would mean that there was no need for an

1 " The definition of *furtum* and the trichotomy " (1960) 28 Tijd. p. 197 *et seq.*, at p. 198. ; supra, p. 270.

2 " *Contrectatio* " (1941) 57 L.Q.R. p. 467 *et seq.*

3 *Etudes sur le furtum* (1915) 1 Lyon p. 677 *et seq.*

4 " Digest XLVII. 2 (*De Furtis*) and the Methods of the Compilers " (1930) 10 Tijd. p. 116 *et seq.* at p. 128; " *Contrectatio*," *cit.* pp. 470–471.

5 *Digest XLVII. 2* ; *De Furtis*, Cambridge, 1940, p. 102.

6 " Die Entwicklung des *Furtum* und seine etymologischen Albeitungen " (1950) ZSS, p. 185 *et seq.* at p. 193.

7 " La nozione del *furtum* fino a Nerazio " (1953) 23 *Annali Palermo*, p. 8. This article will be hereafter referred to as Albanese I.

animus furandi, and even Huvelin's supporters do not hold that.[8] Buckland who is aware of this difficulty says [9] "I, *dolo malo*, summon a mule driver to court. The mules, left unguarded, stray and are lost. I am liable for *furtum*. It is not said, but must be assumed, that I acted with a view to this result." But this is very implausible. It is scarcely even foreseeable that if I wrongly summon a mule driver to court his mules will stray: much less am I likely to summon him with the intention that they should wander off.[10]

> D.47.2.37. (Pomponius *19 ad Sab.*). Si pavonem meum mansuetum, cum de domo mea effugisset, persecutus sis, quoad is perit, agere tecum furti ita potero, si aliquis eum habere coeperit.

Huvelin [11] says of this text that the words *si aliquis eum habere coeperit* imply that the person who chased the peacock which was then taken by another is liable to the *actio furti* as accomplice; and his complicity is *ope tantum* since nothing suggests that the first wrongdoer intended that the peacock should come into the other's hands. The use of the indicative, he goes on, in *quoad is perit* would even seem to exclude all idea of delictal intention. The indicative, he says, is unusual and in that clause which is dependent on a statement in the subjunctive one would necessarily expect a subjunctive. This mistake in modal attraction he accounts for by saying that the text has been altered and that originally *quoad is perit* did not depend upon a proposition in the subjunctive. He would reconstruct the text: *Pavonem meum mansuetum, cum de domo mea effugisset, persecutus es quoad is perit; agere tecum furti me posse veteres responderunt.* This cuts out *si aliquis eum habere coeperit* which, Huvelin remarks, has no equivalent in D.47.2.67(66).2.[12] But this reconstruction implies that the compilers gave themselves much more work than they need have done. It is difficult to see why they should want to reframe the text at all,

8 Buckland, *Textbook of Roman Law*, 2nd ed., Cambridge, 1932, p. 577; Jolowicz, *op. cit.* p. lvii, "When Gaius says *furtum sine affectu furandi non committitur*, all that he means is that one cannot commit theft without knowing what one is doing"; Albanese "La nozione *furtum* da Nerazio a Marciano" (1956) 25 *Annali Palermo*, p. 85 *et seq.* at p. 183 n. 168. *Contra*, Albertario "*Animus furandi*," *Studi di diritto romano* III, Milan, 1936, p. 208 *et seq.* But if there was *furtum* when there was *contrectatio* and *dolus malus* (Albertario, *op. cit.* p. 212) most cases of *damnum iniuria datum* and of *iniuria* would give rise to the *actio furti*.

9 "*Contrectatio*," *cit.* p. 470.

10 It is interesting to notice that Buckland who refuses to countenance that assumption of *ope consilio* admits what is, on his interpretation, the much more difficult assumption of *animus furandi*.

11 *Op. cit.* p. 618, n. 6 (p. 619).

12 This reconstruction is followed by Albanese I, p. 52, but rejected by Niederländer (1954) 5 IURA p. 349.

since, if what was wanted was the addition of the qualification, it could have been simply annexed without anything further. Besides, the failure in modal attraction can scarcely be regarded as odd in the second century A.D., and if it is, a more reasonable reconstruction is to substitute *es* for *sis* and ascribe the flaw to scribal negligence. Buckland [13] also holds *si aliquis eum habere coeperit* interpolated, pointing out that the moods of the tenses in the text are somewhat irregular and that this qualification is placed at the end of the text, a normal place for compilers' additions. But, of course, the tense in that phrase is not itself irregular and it is perfectly natural on any understanding for the phrase to appear at the end of the text. I suggest that the phrase is unlikely to be an interpolation and that its significance is illuminated by D.47.2.36.*pr.* (Ulpian *41 ad Sab.*) which also leads us to the true interpretation of *h.t.*67(66).2 and *h.t.*37.

> Qui servo persuasit, ut fugeret, fur non est: nec enim cui alicui malum consilium dedit, furtum facit, non magis quam si ei persuasit, ut se praecipitet aut manus sibi inferret: haec enim furti non admittunt actionem. sed si alius ei fugam persuaserit, ut ab alio subripiatur, furti tenebitur is qui persuasit, quasi ope consilio eius furtum factum sit. plus Pomponius scripsit eum, qui persuasit, quamvis interim furti non teneretur, tunc tamen incipere teneri, cum quis fugitivi fur esse coeperit, quasi videatur ope consilio eius furtum factum.

This text is not usually considered in this connection and does not seem to have been held interpolated [14] though Albanese [15] does suggest that the rule in *plus Pomponius—factum* was not added by Pomponius as his own but is rather a development of the thought of Sabinus which was mentioned by Pomponius. We know that there was a dispute in classical law as to whether a slave who ran away stole himself, and consequently, whether one who induced a slave to do so was guilty of theft *ope consilio*.[16] Ulpian, as we can see, took the view that in general he was not. But, he says, if one induces a slave to run away so that another person can get hold of him then one is guilty of theft, and he adds that Pomponius held that if one persuaded a slave to run away one was not liable to the *actio furti*, but that one became so liable if later another person got hold of the slave *quasi videatur ope consilio eius furtum factum*. Now in this view of Pomponius (or Sabinus) we have another case of *furtum* where it is difficult to see an *animus furandi*. And this *furtum* takes

13 *Op. cit.* p. 471.
14 *Cf. Index Itp.*
15 I. p. 167 n. 166.
16 *Cf.* Buckland, *The Roman Law of Slavery*, Cambridge, 1908, p. 31.

place not when the slave runs off, but when and if he is taken by a third party and we are expressly told that he is liable as if the theft had been carried out by his aid and advice. We have, that is, an exact parallel with the qualification in *h.t.*37.—the man who chased the peacock until it died was liable provided the peacock was taken by someone. And just as this rule in *h.t.*36.*pr.* is attributed to Pomponius, so does *h.t.*37. come from Pomponius *19 ad Sabinum. H.t.*36.*pr.*, therefore, is strong evidence that *si aliquis eum habere coeperit* represents the genuine thought of Pomponius. Moreover, one can now formulate a satisfactory explanation of the decision in *h.t.*37. *H.t.*36.*pr.* shows us that if I deliberately act wrongfully with respect to you and as a result of my wrongful conduct X is enabled to steal from you, I am treated as an accomplice. The *animus furandi* is imputed to me and your *contrectatio* makes me liable. Similarly with *h.t.*67(66).2. There the *in ius vocans* is liable if the mules " disappear." If they are taken by a thief there is no difficulty. If they wander off of their own accord and are not found it can virtually be conclusively presumed that they have been taken by someone who knew that he was not entitled to them and who therefore committed theft. If they are only lost temporarily no doubt there will be no *actio furti* against the *in ius vocans*. Again, therefore, the *in ius vocans* is guilty because by his wrongful act another person was enabled to " contrectate " the mules.[17] So both *h.t.*67(66).2 and 37 are cases where a wrongdoer is held to be an accomplice and it is difficult to maintain that there has been no *contrectatio*.

There is probably further evidence for this interpretation in D.47.2.50.1. (Ulpian *37 ad ed.*).

> Ope consilio furtum factum Celsus ait non solum, si idcirco fuerit factum, ut socii furarentur, sed et si non, ut socii furarentur, inimicitiarum tamen causa fecerit.

This text has attracted very little attention.[18] Two interpretations spring to mind. First, I give you aid and advice to commit a theft but do so, not so that you may gain anything, but in order to injure the person from whom you steal. This interpretation is completely implausible. It seems most unlikely that classical jurists like Celsus and Ulpian would even bother to argue against such a subjective approach. Moreover, if they had so wanted to, they would have

[17] This explanation would not cover the case where the mules were accidentally killed but I doubt if that were envisaged in the text. In the context, it seems most natural to translate *perissent* as " disappeared ": *cf.* Buckland, " *Contrectatio*," *cit.* p. 470 and Jolowicz, *op. cit.* p. 102.

[18] It is held interpolated by Eisele who would emend *furarentur* to *lucrarentur* ((1909) 30 ZSS p. 146) but this does not affect us. Huvelin argues that it is genuine; (1918) 42 NRHD p. 95 and n. 2.

chosen the simpler case where I take your property not because I want to profit from it but in order to injure you. Secondly, where I do not act in order to enable associates to steal but simply to injure you and as a result of my actions thieves take your property. I am liable *ope consilio*. This, I suggest, is the proper interpretation.[19] It is certainly the kind of situation one would expect the classical jurists to concern themselves with. Here too, a man is liable *ope consilio* to the *actio furti* simply because his deliberate wrongful act enabled another to steal.

No problem is caused by the texts where two or more persons are implicated in the theft but only one touches the *res*.[20] All are liable. The definition of *furtum* in D.47.2.1.3 and J.4.1.1 says there must be a wrongful handling but not that all the wrongdoers must handle. It is perhaps misleading to talk of principal and accomplice in this connection [21] since Roman law, like some modern systems such as Scotland and, to a very large extent, France, draw no such distinction. It makes no difference whether the person who does the handling would in our law be called principal or accessory.

Another text which is generally [22] taken as showing that there need be no handling is D.47.2.52.7. (Ulpian *37 ad ed.*).

> Eum creditorem, qui post solutam pecuniam pignus non reddat, teneri furti Mela ait, si celandi animo retineat: quod verum esse arbitror.[23]

Certainly this text does not specifically mention handling but it should be considered in conjunction with some other texts.

> D.41.2.3.18. (Paul *54 ad ed.*). Si rem apud te depositam furti faciendi causa contrectaveris, desino possidere. sed si eam loco non moveris et infitiandi animum habeas, plerique veterum et Sabinus et Cassius recte responderunt possessorem me manere, quia furtum sine contrectatione fieri non potest nec animo furtum admittatur.
>
> D.47.2.1.1. (Paul *39 ad ed.*). Inde sola cogitatio furti faciendi non facit furem. 2. Sic is, qui depositum abnegat, non statim etiam furti tenetur, sed ita, si id intercipiendi causa occultaverit.
>
> D.47.2.68(67).*pr.* (Celsus *12 dig.*). Infitiando depositum nemo facit furtum (nec enim furtum est ipsa infitiatio, licet prope furtum est): sed si possessionem eius apiscatur intervertendi causa, facit furtum. . . .

19 *Cf.* Jolowicz, *op. cit.* p. lxvi.
20 *e.g.*, D.25.2.19; 47.2.50.4.
21 See Buckland, *op. cit.* pp. 469–470.
22 *e.g.*, Huvelin, *Etudes*, *cit.* p. 69; Jolowicz, *op. cit.* p. xxi; Buckland, *op. cit.* pp. 471–472; Albanese I, p. 69.
23 We need not concern ourselves here with the question whether *si celandi animo retineat* is an interpolation: *cf.* Buckland, *op. cit.* p. 471.

In these texts, all concerned with deposit,[24] we are told that there is no theft unless there has been handling. Buckland [25] explains the seeming contrast with D.47.2.52.7. in two ways. Accepting a distinction suggested to him by Professor Daube he says that the cases of *pignus* and *depositum* are not quite the same. In the former, the debt has been paid before the demand is made and the relation of pledgor and pledgee no longer exists. " The holder is merely a man who has my property and refuses to give it to me. If he refuses because he thinks something is still due, there is no theft, but if he does it dishonestly that is a sufficient ' meddling ' to constitute theft. But in the case of deposit, normally, the relation of depositor and depositee still exists; the thing is not yet due for return. It is not surprising if the jurists require some definite act in relation to the thing, determining the relation." Whether this distinction is valid or not,[26] it does not explain why the deposit texts have such wide general statements that there can be no theft without handling. D.41.2.3.18 says *furtum sine contrectatio fieri non potest*,[27] and D.47.2.1.1 has *inde sola cogitatio furti faciendi non facit furem* and it is from this wide statement that the rule as to deposit is directly derived. Again, Buckland suggests there may have been a conflict between Ulpian and Paul and says that such conflicts are common. But if there was such a conflict we could expect an explicit reference to it and no such direct reference exists. An equally plausible, if not more plausible, interpretation of the text is that there has been *contrectatio* by the pledge creditor but this is not mentioned by Mela.[28] It is not necessary always to state explicitly every essential.[29] At the very least, then, the text is not clear evidence that there can be

24 *Cf.* for the similar case of the *procurator*, D.17.1.55 (Papinian). For suggested interpolations, see *Index Itp.*, Serrao *Il procurator* Milan, 1947, p. 130; *contra* Arangio-Ruiz *Il mandato in diritto romano*, Naples, 1949, p. 61.

25 *Loc. cit.*

26 Generally speaking, there would be no time fixed for the return of a deposit. The depositor would be entitled to the return of the object whenever he wished provided he had recompensed the depositee for any expenses or loss. Moreover, if the pledge creditor after payment is merely a man who has my property and refuses to give it to me, it is surprising that the *actio pigneraticia* ever came into existence since it can only be brought when the debt has been paid.

27 Universally held genuine; *cf.* Albanese I, p. 136 and n. 114.

28 It may originally have been clear from the context. *Arbitror* need not indicate any real hesitancy on Ulpian's part. The point may have been by Mela alone and Ulpian is simply confirming it.

29 *Cf.* D.19.5.17.5 where Sabinus holds there is theft although there is no mention of *contrectatio*. It has on occasion been held that Sabinus did not require there to be *contrectatio* and that this text is evidence of that. On that basis, *quia &c* in D.41.2.3.18 must be regarded as a reason given by Paul and not by the jurists whom he cites; *cf.* Albanese I, p. 130 *et seq.* *Potest* is no great argument for this view since the indicative may be used by Paul to show that he agrees with their reasoning—although the indicative would be incorrect in classical Latin, it is not odd in the 2nd century A.D.

furtum without *contrectatio*. Certainly, it cannot have meant for the compilers that there could be *furtum* without *contrectatio*.

> D.47.2.52.22. (Ulpian *37 ad ed.*). Maiora quis pondera tibi commodavit, cum emeres ad pondus: furti eum venditori teneri Mela scribit: te quoque, si scisti: non enim ex voluntate venditoris accipis, cum erret in pondere.

Here, in the first alternative the purchaser is innocent. Nevertheless, the lender of the false weights is guilty of *furtum*. He can be said to have handled fraudulently through the innocent agent. This is not a wide extension of *contrectatio*.[30]

Thus, there are no texts which give a clear decision that there is *furtum* although there has been no handling. Buckland brings forward some hypothetical cases where he feels that common sense would insist on the *actio furti* even where there was no *contrectatio*. The principal one is where I induce your donkey to follow me by holding a carrot before his nose. "Must I pat his neck," asks Buckland, "to make myself a thief?" But that in fact may have been the position.[31] After all, the line must be drawn somewhere even although ridiculous cases may ensue. The history of the English law of larceny is evidence of that. And what better place to draw the line than *contrectatio*? The decision, too, is scarcely more absurd or extreme than that the depositee does not commit *furtum* where he refuses to return the *res*, but the depositor must wait till the depositee touches it. It must not be forgotten that even if the donkey's owner had not the *actio furti* he would have other remedies.

Thus, although it might be rash to hold that there could never be theft unless there were physical touching, it must be said that the evidence for such cases of theft is not nearly so strong as is commonly supposed.

30 Gellius XI.18.14 causes no difficulty since it is adequately explained by the alternative suggestion of Buckland, *op. cit.* p. 469.

31 In practice, of course, it would be impossible for the wrongdoer to retain or sell the donkey without there being a touching.

24

Contrectatio Again

Professor Thomas has recently published an article [1] attacking my proposition [2] that at times persons were held liable *ope consilio* to a theft although they were not acting in concert with the actual *fur*. To this I would like to make a short rejoinder and at the same time correct a howler in my previous article.

1. – Thomas first discusses three texts which I did not deal with – two, indeed, I did not even mention – which he states are flatly contradictory to my thesis. They would, indeed, be so, especially in the case of D. 47, 2, 54 or. and *h. t.* 39 [3], if my thesis had been that all the jurists held that a person could be liable *ope consilio* to a theft when he was not in concert with the *fur*. But my proposition was the much more limited one that certain texts could best be understood on the supposition that in them a person was held liable *ope consilio* although he was not in concert with the thief. Since I had not anticipated that I would be thought to mean anything else I did not deal with those texts which showed that certain jurists took a different view. But D. 47, 2, 54 pr. and *h. t.* 39 are perhaps relevant after all. Thomas says of my view [4] that it is « rather a startling proposition ». Now the sole point of D. 47, 2, 54 pr. (Paul 39 *ad ed.*) is that if one person breaks down a door *iniuriae causa* and others afterwards remove things, he is not liable to the *actio furti*. And in *h. t.* 39 (Ulpian 41 *ad Sab.*) one of the main points is very much to the same effect. But there seems little reason for denying that a person will be held liable in certain circumstances to a particular action unless it c o u l d be held that he is indeed so liable! So my proposition does not seem

1 '*Contrectatio*', *complicity and* '*furtum*', in *Iura*, 13 (1962), 70 ff.

2 Supra, pp. 283 ff.

3 The other text is D. 47, 2, 50, 4.

4 *Op. cit.* 70.

quite so startling. Moreover, jurists usually are much more concerned to refute views which have been produced that to deny possibilities which never have been suggested, so that D. 47, 2, 54 pr. and *h. t.* 39 may be some slight indication not only that it could have been possible for a Roman jurist to hold a man liable at times *ope consilio* to a theft when he was not in concert with the thief but also that some jurists had actually taken that line.

To turn to the texts which I thought best explained by my proposition. First, D. 47, 2, 37 (Pomponius 19 *ad Sab.*) and *h. t.* 36 pr. (Ulpian 41 *ad Sab.*). Thomas accepts my arguments for the genuineness of the former, but gives a different explanation of the factual situation. According to him [5], in both texts Pomponius was thinking of situations where the person who did the taking was in fact in league with the man who is being held liable to the action. But with all respect this is completely contrary to the natural meaning of the Latin. In D. 47, 2, 37 Pomponius says the peacock-chaser is liable to the *actio furti*, '*si aliquis eum habere coeperit*'. Now *aliquis* is very much an indefinite pronoun. It means quite simply 'someone'. If Pomponius was thinking of a case of a colleague then *aliquis* does not express his meaning at all. He ought to have used something like *socius* or possibly *amicus*. The same applies in *h. t.* 36 pr. Ulpian tells us there that Pomponius wrote that a person who persuaded a slave to flee was not then liable to the *actio furti* but became so liable *cum quis fugitivi fur esse coeperit*. Again one has an indefinite pronoun – this time *quis* – where on Thomas' view one would have expected a word showing the relationship between the person who advised the slave to flee and the *fur*. If an indefinite pronoun had been used in just one of these texts is would have caused difficulties enough for Thomas' view, but the use of indefinite pronouns in both of them makes it inconceivable that Pomponius was here restricting liability to the *actio furti* to cases of actual complicity. Nor does anything else in these texts imply a connexion between the first wrongdoer and the actual taker. It does not seem to me that Thomas' argument that in *h. t.* 36 pr. the word *quasi* in the phrase *quasi videatur ope consilio eius furtum factum* means 'as' rather than 'as if' affects my case in the slightest. Assuming for the sake of argument that here *quasi* does mean 'as', the fictional nature of the attribution of complicity is shown by the *videatur*: « as the theft is r e g a r d e d as having been committed by his aid and advice » [6]. Thomas also argues [7]: « Then the remainder of *h. t.* 36 generally continues to be concerned with wrongdoers in direct association one with the other. This surely suggests that *Pomponius scripsit*, etc., in 36 pr. is itself also concerned with persons who were working in association –

[5] *Op. cit.* 82 ff.

[6] This text is also against Thomas' statement (*op. cit.* 71) that none of the texts concerned « mentions that the liability envisaged within them is *ope consilio* ».

[7] *Op. cit.* 84.

and points to a harmonious annotation or clarification by Pomponius of the proposition contained in the previous sentence». But there is no reason in the world why Ulpian in the *principium* discussing a case where there was liability because of complicity should not go on to mention that in similar circumstances Pomponius would give an action where complicity was not in fact present but would be assumed.

To return for a moment to *h. t.* 37. Thomas says [8]: « It comes from Pomponius *ad Sabinum*. Sabinus we know to have been the first to mention even *adtrectare* in relation to *furtum*; it is not by any means beyond possibility that, at that stage of development of *furtum*, the chasing of the peacock *quoad is perit* would have been a sufficient physical relation to the bird to satisfy Sabinus. What does seem pretty clear is that the requirement, *si aliquis ... poterit*, is Pomponius' own qualification of a decision which originally made no such provision. Huvelin's idea of the original substance of the text is correct, though one need not accept his reconstruction literally ». But the statement « What does seem pretty clear is that the requirement, *si aliquis ... poterit*, is Pomponius' own qualification of a decision which originally made no such provision » is arbitrary. The grammar of the text certainly cannot lead one to that conclusion. Firstly, because if the argument is that the text begins in the subjunctive and hence is in indirect speech – Pomponius reporting Sabinus – and then goes on in the indicative and hence is in direct speech, one ought to notice that *agere tecum furti ita potero i. e.*, the main decision, is also in the indicative. Secondly, the construction of the whole of the body of the text is very Pomponian. A conditional sentence with the subjunctive in the protasis (*effugisset, persecutus sis*) followed by the indicative in the apodosis (*potero* [9]) is very typical of Pomponius and has nothing to do with reported speech [10].

Another text which I thought supported the view I was proposing is D. 47, 2, 50, 1 [11]. I dismissed as implausible the interpretation that I give you aid and advice to commit a theft but do so, not so that you may gain anything but in order to injure the person from whom you steal. My reasons for doing so were first that it seemed most unlikely that classical jurists like Celsus and Ulpian would even bother to argue against such a subjective approach and secondly that if they had

---

[8] *Op. cit.* 85 f.

[9] It is impossible to tell whether *coeperit* is future perfect indicative or perfect subjunctive. Either could be appropriate here but it is more likely to be another subjunctive in a *si* clause.

[10] The following examples were taken from his first three books *ad Sabinum*: D. 6, 2, 15; 7, 4, 18; 28, 5, 23 pr.-1-2; 30, 8 pr.-1-2; 32, 44; 37, 1, 9.

For Thomas' point that we know Sabinus to have been the first to use even *adtrectare* in relation to *furtum* see *infra*, p. 301.

[11] *Op. cit.* 529 f.

wanted to, they would have chosen to discuss the simpler case where I take your property not because I want to profit from it but in order to injure you. Thomas, however, thinks that this interpretation is the 'more proper'[12]. He says[13]: « The argument against the ... interpretation would appear considerably to lose force when one notes that 50, 1 to 50, 4 are entirely concerned with liability by complicity so that there is every reason for the jurists not dealing with 'the simpler case' ». But with respect, this seems a circular argument. Thomas appears to be saying in effect: '*H. t.* 50, 1 is a case of complicity. *H. t.* 50, 1 to 50, 4 are all cases of complicity. Hence Ulpian to make the point he is making in 50, 1 could not possibly have illustrated it with a simpler case where there was only one person involved and thus no complicity'. But no! If Celsus and Ulpian had intended to consider the mental state of the wrongdoer they would have been liable to choose the simple case as an illustration but they would have discussed the problem in a different place. That *h. t.* 50, 1 occurs where it does is no argument in favour of Thomas' interpretation. Thomas later goes[14]: « If the text has a particular point of its own, it is this: accepting, for the purpose of the argument, that *contrectatio* by the actual *fur* must be *lucri faciendi gratia*, persons whose liability is only *ope consilio* need not themselves intend to benefit materially, *provided that all are working in concert.* The apparently subjective approach of the text is thus highly relevant – and contrary to W's thesis ». But here we ought to remind ourselves of what the text does say, namely:

> Ope consilio furtum factum Celsus ait non solum si idcirco fuerit factum ut socii furarentur, sed et si non ut socii furarentur, inimicitiarum tamen causa fecerit.

There is absolutely nothing here to suggest that the text is concerned with the *animus lucri faciendi* of any of the parties. If Celsus and Ulpian had wanted to say that a man who gives advice to thieves is liable to the *actio furti* even if he personally does not want to make a gain they could scarcely have been more obscure. To yield such a meaning the text would have to be completely rewritten. Moreover, it is surprising to find Thomas assuming for the benefit of his argument something which he does not accept, namely that *contrectatio* by the actual *fur* must be *lucri faciendi gratia.* If, as in fact Thomas believes, the actual *fur* need not have an intention to make a gain the text could not have been drawing a distinction between the necessity for such an intention in the person who contrectates and the absence of any such necessity in the case of the person liable

[12] *Op cit.* 80.
[13] *Op. cit.* 79.
[14] *Op. cit.* 80.

ope consilio. Further, of course, there is not the slightest indication anywhere that any jurist had even considered that intention to make a gain was relevant to liability *ope consilio.* Of the interpretation of the text which I preferred, namely that I do not act in order to enable associates to steal but simply in order to injure you and as a result of my actions thieves take your property and I am regarded as liable *ope consilio,* Thomas writes that it « would appear to require an explanation of the repetition of *ut socii furarentur* which is not in fact forthcoming ». But the repetition is there to give the right emphasis. Celsus is saying that there is theft *ope consilio* not only if one acts in order that associates might steal, but even if one acts, not so that associates might steal, but simply out of enmity. That is, the theft which does take place is not the work of associates.

To come now to D. 47, 2, 67 (66), 2 (Paul 7 *ad Plaut.*). Thomas here would agree with Buckland's interpretation that the mules simply strayed and that the wrongdoer had acted with the precise intention that they would stray. He, however, sees the case as illustrating a particular stage of development and says – rightly – that Buckland's assumption that Paul approves the decision because he does not expressly dissent is a *non sequitur* [15]. Later he has [16]: « It may be conceded that the original conception of *furtum* in the XII tables was one of asportation of another's movables. But, bearing in mind the cases already considered here as they must have stood in the decisions of the *veteres* and also other cases known to us, a broader picture of *furtum* would appear to have emerged by the beginning of the last century of the republic; and one which would cover all the cases we have referred to, viz., deliberate conduct of A to deprive B of his property – 'deliberate' signifying, of course, design. Hence, for example, the probable correctness of Bulckland's assumption in the case of the muleteer that my conduct was directed to your animals being left to follow their natural tendency and so be lost to you. There is, that is to say, a shift of emphasis from my asportation to your deprivation through my deliberate conduct ». Let us consider these points. First the general development of *furtum.* One would agree that the original conception of furtum was of asportation of movables. It is also clear that in classical law the conception was *contrectatio* [17] (even if there were some exceptional cases). Now Thomas says [18] « it is generally admitted that the republican concept of *furtum* was wider than was admitted in the period after Sabinus ». But whether generally admitted or not, there is not the slightest evidence for this [19] – apart,

---

15 *Op. cit.* 82. Hence, the fact that D. 47, 2, 54 pr. is also a text of Paul is no argument against the interpretation which I have suggested.

16 *Op. cit.* 87.

17 Cf D. 47, 2, 1, 1-2-3; *h. t.* 68 (67) pr.; 41, 2, 3, 18; P. S. 2, 31, 1.

18 *Op. cit.* 86.

19 Nor is any adduced by Thomas. For the texts from the Empire which he refers to see *infra*, p. 298 ff.

that is to say, from the present text whose meaning we are trying to elucidate. Secondly the intention required for theft. Thomas thinks[20] that I am requiring from the *veteres* an *animus lucri faciendi.* This is going a bit far, but on the other hand I would not hold that just any *dolus* would be sufficient for *furtum.* For instance, if A deliberately kills B's slave, B may an *actio legis Aquiliae* but he will not have an *actio furti.* The *dolus* is not the right kind for the *actio furti.* Hence Thomas' formulation that the basis of liability to the *actio furti* was « deliberate conduct of A to deprive B of his property – 'deliberate' signifying, of course, design » is inaccurate. Moreover, it is noticeable that in those texts in which, although he had no intention to make a gain for himself, a person is held liable to the *actio furti* for his own *contrectatio* and not *ope consilio,* the intention of the wrongdoer is nevertheless very specific. Thus,

> D. 47, 2, 48, 4 (Ulpianus 42 *ad Sab.*): Si ego tibi poliendum vestimentum locavero, tu vero inscio aut invito me commodaveris Titio et Titio furtum factum sit: et tibi competit furti actio, quia custodia rei ad te pertinet, et mihi adversus te, quia non debueras rem commodare et id faciendo furtum admiseris: ita erit casus, quo fur furti agere possit.

Here the intention was that someone other than the owner should make a gain out of the use of the *vestimentum* although the gain was not that of the thief himself[21]. There is, I think, only one text in which an *actio furti* is given although it is impossible to see an intention that someone or other will gain:

> D. 12, 4, 15 (Pomponius 22 *ad Sab.*): Cum servus tuus in suspicionem furti Attio venisset, dedisti eum in quaestionem sub ea causa, ut, si id repertum in eo non esset, redderetur tibi: is eum tradidit praefecto vigilum quasi in facinore deprehensum: praefectus vigilum eum summo supplicio adfecit. ages cum Attio dare eum tibi oportere, quia et ante mortem dare tibi eum oportuerit. Labeo ait posse etiam ad exhibendum agi, quoniam fecerit quo minus exhiberet. sed Proculus dari oportere ita ait, si fecisses eius hominem, quo casu ad exhibendum agere te non posse: sed si tuus mansisset, etiam furti te acturum cum eo, quia re aliena ita sit usus, ut sciret se invito domino uti aut dominum si sciret prohibiturum esse[22].

Your slave was suspected of theft from Attius and he was delivered to Attius for torture on the terms that if it were not discovered that he had committed the theft he was to be returned to you. Attius delivered him to the *praefectus vigilum* as a wrongdoer caught in the act and he was accordingly executed. Proculus says that you have an *actio furti* against Attius. There does not seem to be any possibility of profit here for anyone. But the reason for Proculus' decision is important:

---

20 *Op. cit.* 82.

21 Supra, pp. 270.

22 We need not concern ourselves with questions of interpolation of the text.

quia re aliena ita sit usus, ut sciret se invito domino uti aut dominum si sciret prohibiturum esse. That is, there was an improper use of the slave. But it is straining matters very considerably to hold that handing a slave over for execution is using the slave. And Proculus would hardly have given such a far-fetched reason unless it were essential to his view that the *actio furti* ought to be given. This shows that the *dolus* required for the *actio furti* was of a very specific kind. Indeed, it could easily be maintained that it is evidence that there had to be an intention of gain. The appropriation of the use of a thing after all implies the intention to gain. The difficulty of allowing the *actio furti* in the case given in our text is not so much in finding the gain from the use, but in accepting, – as Proculus wants us to accept – that there was any use at all.

This brings us on to the third point, the intention of the wrongdoer in our particular case. Both Buckland and Thomas hold that the muledriver was summoned into court by the wrongdoer with the intention that while he was there his mules would stray. But this is to assume not only that the mules would not be tethered by the muledriver or else would slip their halter, but also that the wrongdoer would foresee that they would not be tethered or that they would escape from the rope. It seems hardly possible to doubt that a Roman of the later Republic who had to leave his mules unattended would normally tether them (unless they were enclosed in a field or some such). And although there is no direct evidence it is inconceivable that a muledriver *in ius vocatus* would not be given time to tether his animals. It is this which makes it so implausible to assert that the wrongdoer acted with the intention that the mules should stray while the muledriver was in court. Thus we are faced with a choice. Either one says that here any evil intention no matter how indeterminate is regarded as making the wrongdoer liable to an *actio furti* in the full extent of the victim's loss even where he had no intention of causing such loss and where there was no *contrectatio*, at all. Or one says that the mules were stolen by a third party[23] and that the person who summoned the muledriver to court was presumed to be an accomplice since it was his deliberate wrogdoing which permitted the theft to occur. Not only would the second alternative seem to be the less extreme but D. 47, 2, 37 and *h. t.* 67 (66), 2 appear to show that the presumption of complicity was an opinion which was held[24].

---

[23] Thus, there would be intention and *contrectatio*. It would, of course, be theft if the mules strayed and were found by a third party who decided to keep them.

[24] It should be noted that D. 47, 2, 67 (66), 1 is, of course, impossible to interpret on its own and must be examined in the light of other texts.

2. – To turn now to a broader topic. Thomas where he says – without producing any evidence – that the Republican concept of *furtum* was wider than was admitted in the period after Sabinus refers en passant to texts of Ulpian citing Mela and to two other texts[25]. Let us see whether in fact these texts do illustrate a wider concept of *furtum*.

First, D. 47, 2, 52, 7 (Ulpian 37 *ad ed.*). Here I wish to add nothing to my previous account of the text[26].

Secondly, D. 47, 2, 52, 22, with which Thomas asks us to compare D. 4, 3, 18, 3. It was when dealing with this text that I made the howler to which I adverted at the beginning of this note. The text reads:

> Maiora quis pondera tibi commodavit, cum emeres ad pondus: furti eum venditori teneri Mela scribit: te quoque si scisti: non enim ex voluntate venditoris accipis, cum erret in pondere.

And I commented[27]: « Here, in the first alternative the purchaser is innocent. Nevertheless, the lender of the false weights is guilty of *furtum*. He can be said to have handled fraudulently through the innocent agent. This is not a wide extension of *contrectatio* ». But this is nonsense. Such an extension would, of course, deprive the concept of *contrectatio* of all its value as a standard for deciding whether or not there was *furtum*. Rather, '*te - pondere*' is an interpolation or gloss: *te* suggests indirect speech but *scisti* is indicative; *accipis* does not harmonise with *erret*[28]. Thus, Mela said nothing at all – so far as we can tell from the text – about the knowledge of the purchaser or of the lender of the weights that the weights were false. Obviously, the knowledge of the lender is assumed (since he is said to be guilty of *furtum*) and in the absence of anything to the contrary, it is reasonable to think that knowledge of the purchaser is also assumed – it is not often that a man would knowingly lend a friend false weights without telling him that they were such. The liability of the lender alone is considered since it is not necessarily clear that he could be guilty of theft even *ope consilio* – he has merely given the thief (purchaser) the necessary implements. Later, concern with the liability of the purchaser, which Mela probably regarded as too obvious to require to be dealt with, led to the addition of *te - pondere* and this by accident made it appear that the lender was always liable to the *actio furti*, whatever the state of knowledge of the purchaser. So this text is no evidence for a wider concept of *furtum*. D. 4, 3, 18, 3 (Paul 11 *ad ed.*) is concerned with a very different case.

---

[25] *Op. cit.* 86 and n. 50.

[26] Supra, pp. 287 ff.

[27] Supra, p. 289.

[28] Of course, this second point, though not the first, is also explicable on the hypothesis that *cum erret in pondere* is a gloss: cf STEIN, *Fault in the Formation of Contract in Roman Law and Scots Law* (Edinburgh, 1958), 95.

It runs:

> De eo qui sciens commodasset pondera, ut venditor emptori merces adpenderet, Trebatius de dolo dabat actionem. atquin si maiora pondera commodavit, id quod amplius mercis datum est repeti condictione potest, si minora, ut reliqua merx detur ex empto agi potest: nisi si ea condicione merx venit, ut illis ponderibus traderetur, cum ille decipiendi causa adfirmasset se aequa pondera habere.

Stein [29] is right to say that the text has been much abbreviated and that apart from the absence of an adjective qualifying *pondera* – Mommsen's suggestion of *iniqua* seems best – it is at first sight difficult to see to whom the loan was made. Stein rightly suggests, however, that the loan was to the seller since he is to weigh out the goods. Nor is it clear to whom the *actio de dolo* is given. For an understanding of the text, the subsidiary nature of the *actio de dolo* must be stressed. Whether it is the buyer or the seller who sues the lender he must have no other action available against the other party. Thus, if the *actio de dolo* is given to the innocent seller, the sale must have been concluded *ut illis ponderibus traderetur*; if to the buyer, the seller must have been innocent and the sale again must have been *ut illis ponderibus traderetur* [30]. This time the loan was made without the borrower being told that the weights were false. One may leave out of account the possibility that the plaintiff is suing by the *actio de dolo* although he has the right of another action against someone else but the right is useless either because this last person is insolvent or cannot be found. Not only is there no indication that Trebatius was thinking of such a narrow case but there is no trace of the appearance of this right before Labeo [31]. Thus, in the second of the above hypotheses, when alone would the text be relevant to us, there could be no question of an *actio furti* against the lender of the weights because the borrower was innocent and there had been no *contrectatio* which, of course, means f r a u d u l e n t handling [32].

Thirdly, D. 47, 2, 52, 23.

> Si quis servo meo persuaserit, ut nomen suum ex instrumento puta emptionis tolleret, et Mela scripsit et ego puto furti agendum.

With this decision one ought to compare the texts which give an *actio legis Aquiliae* where a document is damaged or destroyed: D. 9, 2, 40 (Paul 3 *ad ed.*);

---

[29] *Op. cit.* 96.

[30] Whether *adquin* to the end is an interpolation or represents the substance of what Paul said does not affect us. For the text see the references given by ALBANESE, *Annali Palermo*, 28 (1961), 265 n. 127.

[31] D. 4, 3, 7, 6.

[32] See WATSON, supra, p. 270.

h. t. 41 pr. (Ulpian 41 *ad Sab.*); *h. t.* 42 (Julian 48 *dig.*). Now for an *actio legis Aquiliae* to lie in classical law there had to be physical injury to an object, causing someone financial loss. Here the object is the document and no real difficulty seems to have been experienced in allowing the plaintiff to recover his interesse where this could be measured. The financial value attributed to the document is not that of the materials from which it is made, but of the amount of money due in one way or another of which it either constitutes the obligation or is proof or perhaps more accurately, of the plaintiff's interesse. Similarly with *furtum*. The value of the document is the sum contained in it. If it is interfered with in order that the wrongdoer will not have to pay this sum, there has been *contrectatio* and there is an *animus furandi*. Nor is there any difficulty here in the fact the document was altered by a slave who was persuaded to do so by the debtor. It is a case of complicity. No extension of the conception of *furtum* is involved here [33].

Lastly, Thomas refers to D. 4, 3, 7, 7 (Ulpian 11 *ad ed.*):

> Idem Labeo quaerit, si compeditum servum meum ut fugeret solveris, an de dolo actio danda sit? et ait Quintus apud eum notans: si non misericordia ductus fecisti, furti teneris: si misericordia, in factum actionem dari debere.

The fettered slave is freed and this must involve touching. And if the person who releases the slave does so *non misericordia ductus*, he is liable to an *actio furti* according to Quintus, but if *misericordia ductus* to an *actio in factum*. In the former case, but not the latter there is an *animus furandi* [34]. Not only is no extension of the conception of *furtum* apparent here, but the unknown Quintus is taking a more restricted view of the intention required for theft than « deliberate conduct of A to deprive B of his property » – otherwise he would hold the man who freed the slave *misericordia ductus* liable to an *actio furti* [35]. Incidentally, the Quintus referred to cannot be Quintus Mucius Scaevola but is an otherwise unknown annotator of Labeo. Albanese who holds the contrary argues [36] that the phrase *Cassius apud Urseium scribit* (D. 7, 4, 10, 5) and others similar can mean that Urseius gives the opinion of the earlier Cassius. His instances, however, are not conclusive since in none of them can it be shown that the older jurist died before the working life of the younger began and so the possibility of the older referring to the younger

---

33 *Pace* JOLOWICZ who says (*Digest XLVII. 2. De Furtis* [Cambridge, 1940], 78) « Again Mela is indifferent to *contrectatio* » and ALBANESE (*Annali Palermo*, 23 [1953], 73 f.) who sees here « un'ulteriore testimonianza dell'ampiezza che la nozione di *furtum* ha nel pensiero di Mela ».

34 Though not necessarily an *animus lucrifaciendi* He may may be motivated by a desire to injure the slave's master.

35 Remember that the text says the slave is freed *ut fugeret*.

36 *Op. cit.* 108 ff.

cannot be excluded. In any event, for our text Albanese's suggestion can be dismissed because of the *notans* which must refer to a writer commenting on Labeo and this excludes Q. Mucius Scaevola [37].

None of these texts, therefore, show any signs of a wider conception of *furtum*.

3. - To end on a very different note. It is often stressed that Sabinus is the first so far as we know to mention even *adtrectare* in relation to *furtum* [38]. But this ought not to induce us to put the introduction of wrongful touching as the standard for distinguishing theft too late. It was the standard at least as early as the middle of the 1st century B. C.

> D. 47, 2, 21 pr. (Ulpianus 40 *ad Sab.*): Volgaris est quaestio, an is, qui ex acervo frumenti modium sustulit, totius rei furtum faciat an vero eius tantum quod abstulit. Ofilius totius acervi furem esse putat: nam et qui aurem alicuius tetigit, inquit Trebatius totum eum videri tetigisse: proinde et qui dolium aperuit et inde parvum vini abstulit, non tantum eius quod abstulit, verum totius videtur fur esse. sed verum est in tantum eos furti actione teneri, quantum abstulerunt....

Thus, for Ofilius and, it must be, also Trebatius (since the case of the slave's ear can only be an illustration for such a proposition) removal of a part means theft of the whole. Apart indeed from the use of *tetigisse*, this is explicable only on the argument that the heap of corn is touched as a whole. Had asportation been the test the obvious separability of what was taken from what was left would have restricted the theft to the former [39]. The rest of the part of this *lex* which is quoted and § 8 show what is in effect a later restriction of the theft to what was in fact taken. Not only does the text show that asportation was no longer essential to *furtum* but, much more important, it shows that 'touching' has come to occupy a very special position. If mere meddling with the deliberate intention of depriving the owner of his property had been the standard, again the theft would have been restricted to what the thief took or intended to take. For these Republican jurists *contrectatio* is the touchstone for theft.

---

[37] Further to the text see WATSON, infra, p. 315.

[38] *E. g.*, by THOMAS *op. cit.* 85.

[39] No relevant interpolations seem to have been suggested.

25

D.47.2.52.20: The Jackass, the Mares and Furtum

D. 47.2.52.20 (Ulpian, l. 37 *ad ed.*): *Si quis asinum meum coegisset et in equas suas τῆς γονῆς dumtaxat χάριν admisisset, furti non tenetur, nisi furandi quoque animum habuit. quod et Herennio Modestino studioso meo de Dalmatia consulenti rescripsi circa equos, quibus eiusdem rei gratia subiecisse quis equas suas proponebatur, furti ita demum teneri, si furandi animo id fecisset, si minus, in factum agendum.*

This is a famous, not to say notorius, text and it is normally held to have been interpolated by Justinian's compilers both in respect of the negative decision and of the two clauses which refer to the *animus furandi* (1). In recent years Albanese alone — whose view will be examined shortly — has maintained the classicality of Ulpian's refusal of the *actio furti* but even he thinks the references to the *animus furandi* are additions (2). The general view is based on two main arguments (3). First, the purpose for which the wrongdoer took away the jackass, namely for breeding with his mares, is clearly stated

(1) See Albanese, in *Ann. Palermo*, 25, 1956, 249 f., and the references he gives.

(2) *Loco cit.*

(3) Albertario's attack on the text (in *Studi*, III, Milano, 1936, 225 f.) is based on a desire to show that *animus furandi* is a Byzantine idea. But at the very least, there are enough certainly classical texts which contain the concept or phrase to make it clear that the idea was also familiar to the classical jurists: cf. Jolowicz, *Digest XLVII. 2, De Furtis*, Cambridge, 1940, lvii f.

and it is obviously dishonest. Therefore, it is said, the qualification that he is liable to the *actio furti* only if he had an *animus furandi* is silly. Secondly, this should be a case of *furtum* because there has been a wrongful use of the jackass and in classical law wrongful use of a thing was theft. Albanese, who thinks the decision in the text is classical, does not seem to dispute that there was a wrongful use or that a wrongful use was theft. He argues that the facts of the case do not imply that there was a *contrectatio* — neither *coegisset* nor *admisisset* necessarily involves a *contrectatio* — and so an essential element of *furtum* could be missing: that the text is closely connected with the preceding § 19 which declares *hoc enim iure utimur ut furtum sine contrectatione non fiat* and so no *contrectatio* is in fact envisaged in § 20 (4) (5). But this argumentation is not satisfactory. There seems to be no sign of any connection between § 19 and § 20 and certainly there is not a close enough connection for Ulpian to be justified in omitting all mention of *contrectatio* in § 20 if his decision fundamentally depended on the absence of this element of *furtum*.

The general approach to the text seems very reasonable but there are a few points which cause me to be not entirely happy with it.

First, wrongful use of a thing was just as much theft in Justinian's law as in classical law. It is enough to quote two texts from this title (6):

> D. 47. 2. 40 (Paul, l. 9 *ad Sab.*): *Qui iumenta sibi commodata longius duxerit alienave re invito domino usus sit, furtum facit.*
>
> D. 47. 2. 83 pr. (Paul, l. 2 *sent.*): *Fullo et sarcinator, qui polienda vel sarcienda vestimenta accepit, si forte his utatur,*

(4) « A ben guardare, la fattispecie proposta, con terminologia molto precisa, da Ulpiano non implica che si ipotizzi una *contrectatio* da parte del proprietario delle cavalle nei confronti dell'asino o dei cavalli altrui. Tanto il *coegisset* quanto l'*admisisset* nei loro significati propri non importano necessariamente la *contrectatio*. Se manca, quindi, tale elemento non può configurarsi il *furtum*. Ciò posto, si vede bene anche la coerenza della collocazione di D. 47. 2. 52. 20 nel più ampio squarcio del l. 37 *ad ed.* a noi pervenuto: il frammento segue immediatamente a quel D. 47. 2. 52. 19 nel quale, come s'è visto, è contenuto il rigoroso principio: *hoc enim iure utimur ut furtum sine contrectatione non fiat.* Logica conseguenza di questo principio appare l'esclusione del *furtum* nella fattispecie proposta dal § 20 ».

(5) Hence Albanese holds the references to the *animus furandi* interpolated on the ground that the presence of the *animus* would not remedy the absence of *contrectatio*.

(6) And cf., e.g., D. 47. 2. 55. 1 (Gaius, l. 13 *ad ed. prov.*).

> *ex contrectatione eorum furtum fecisse videtur, quia non in eam causam ab eo videntur accepta.*

And the definition at the begining of the Title, whatever its origins (7) and meaning may be, certainly implies that wrongful use of a thing is theft:

> D. 47.2.1.3 (Paul, l. 39 *ad ed.*): *Furtum est contrectatio rei fraudulosa lucri faciendi gratia vel ipsius rei vel etiam usus eius possessionisve. quod lege naturali prohibitum est admittere* (8).

Hence an original decision by Ulpian that in our text there was an *actio furti* is not likely to have been negatived by the compilers because of a changed attitude to wrongful use as amounting to theft.

Secondly, the offending references to the necessity of an *animus furandi* appear twice in the text, both times after we have been told what the intention of the wrongdoer was. So, on the general view, the person responsible for the introduction of the references to the *animus furandi* must have been doubly careless and doubly silly.

Thirdly, the first reference to the *animus furandi* runs: *nisi furandi quoque animum habuit.* On the general view it seems impossible to account for the *quoque.* In addition to what must there be an *animus furandi*? It is perhaps worth noting that in his translation of the text Jolowicz ignores the *quoque* (9). Moreover, the *quoque* indicates that whoever is responsible — Ulpian or someone later — for *nisi furandi quoque animum habuit* was conscious of the fact that the wrongdoer's intention had already been expressed.

These points make me feel that an attempt to find a new approach might be justified and I should like to suggest another interpretation.

The starting point is this very *quoque.* The text says that if anyone drives off my jackass and puts it among his mares for breeding purposes only, he is not liable to the *actio furti* unless he also had the intention of stealing. The intention of stealing is thus apparently different from the intention of breeding from the jackass. But what could be the object of this intention to steal? Might it be the jackass itself? That is, as frequently happens, the answer to a question envi-

---

(7) Cf., e.g., Watson, supra, 269 ff.

(8) The definition is repeated in I. 4.1.1 though without the *lucri faciendi gratia.*

(9) *Op. cit.*, 76.

sages the possibility of facts which are excluded from the question. Thus, the question: « Someone drove off my jackass and put it among his mares for breeding purposes only. Is he liable to the *actio furti*? ». Answer: « No, unless he also had the intention of keeping the jackass ». I cannot think that this kind of answer to such a question could be regarded as unusual or unnatural. Moreover, although one can understand that the form of the text has caused difficulty to later scholars, it is fair to remember that Ulpian would not be so conscious of the possibility of confusion. He could not foresee that his works might be regarded as interpolated. This approach would, of course, get rid of the objection to the text that twice the *animus furandi* is brought in after we are twice told the wrongdoer's intention. But it does not yet meet the objection that wrongful use is theft and we know from D. 47. 2. 48. 4 (Ulpian, l. 42 *ad Sab.*) that Ulpian accepted that there could be *furtum* even where there was no intention to deprive the owner permanently of the thing. Must one hold, though, that there has been a use? If one gives an animal the opportunity of following its natural instincts and it does, must one say that the animal has been used? It does not seem to me to be the case that one necessarily must hold that there was a use. Certainly, the fact that the intention of the owner of the mares was wrongful and was to make a profit does not, by itself, mean that there was a use. And whereas I would be thought to use your stallion if without your knowledge but acting as your *negotiorum gestor* I harnessed it to a cart and took your produce to market, one would not normally consider though, admittedly, one could — that I used your stallion if, again acting as your *negotiorum gestor*, I introduced it to your mares. The possibility that Ulpian could think there was not a use of the jackass here is heightened when we look at a text concerned with the *lex Aquilia.*

> D. 9. 2. 30. 2 (Paul, l., 22 *ad ed.*): *Si quis alienum vinum vel frumentum consumpserit, non videtur damnum iniuria dare ideoque utilis danda est actio.*

We are concerned now only with the refusal of the *actio legis Aquiliae*. This part of the text does not seem to have been held interpolated and there seems to be agreement as to the reason for the decision, namely that the wine and grain by being consumed served the only kind of purpose for which they were intended and so the requisites for *damnum iniuria datum* have not been satisfied, because there has been no *corruptio* ([10]). Yet, of course, the owner has suffered *damnum*, i.e. financial loss ([11]), and the wine and corn have been effectively destroyed. If Paul could hold here that there was no *corruptio* because the things in question were made to serve the only kind of purpose for which they were intended, then Ulpian in D. 47.2.52.20 could equally hold that a jackass was not used where it was simply enabled to follow its natural instinct and mate with the mares ([12]).

There might, indeed, have been a strong reason for Ulpian wanting to exclude the *actio furti* against the wrongdoer. If not invariably, then at least in almost all cases, the damages awarded to an owner in the *actio furti* were a multiple of the value which the thing stolen had at the time of the theft, not a multiple of his interest ([13]). The Romans did not have a concept of *furtum usus* as opposed to *furtum rei* ([14]) and so, where a thing belonging to another was wrongfully used but the wrongdoer had no intention of permanently depriving the owner, what was stolen was the thing itself. Nowhere — so far as I am aware ([15]) — is the question of the quantum of damages where the thief intends eventually to return the thing discussed and there is no authority for thinking that any difference was made between this case and the one where there was the intention of depriving the owner permanently of the thing. Accordingly, in the present situation, Ulpian might have felt that it was over-severe to punish the wrongdoer in a multiple of the value of the jackass ([16]). The owner of the jackass would be adequately protected by the granting of an *actio in factum*.

([10]) Cf. LAWSON, *Negligence in the Civil Law*, Oxford, 1950, 116 and the authors he cites; ALBANESE, in *Ann. Palermo*, 21, 1950, 176. An article by G. LONGO, in *Ann. Macerata*, 22, 1958, 49-74, where he apparently discusses this text was not available to me.

([11]) Cf. DAUBE, in *Studi Solazzi*, Napoli, 1948, 93 ff.

([12]) The difficult texts, on abduction of another's female slave *libidinis causa*, *Paul sent.* 2.31.12 and 32, D. 47.2.39 pr. (Ulpian, l. 41 *ad Sab.*) and *h.t.*, 8.2 (Paul, l. 2 *sent.*), cannot be approached in the same way. Whatever the attitude of the girls one must say that there is a use since the taker intends to perform the acts himself.

([13]) Cf. now for all, MEDICUS, *Id quod interest*, Köln-Graz, 1962, 232 ff.

([14]) Cf. now WATSON, supra, p. 269 ff.

([15]) But see WATSON, *The Law of Obligations in the Later Roman Republic*, Oxford, 1965, 227 f.

([16]) As Labeo may have done in a different case of wrongful use: Aulus Gellius, *noct. att.*, 7.15.1; see WATSON, *loco cit.*

26

Si Adorat Furto

A well-known fragment of the XII Tables has come down to us from Festus[1]: *"Si adorat furto quod nec manifestum erit"*. He quotes no more since his concern is with a usage of *nec*. The provision is generally taken to refer to an accusation (followed by proof in court) of *furtum nec manifestum* and (reasonably, on this understanding) is completed by *"duplione damnum decidito"*[2]. Against this approach to the provision the arguments of R. Yaron[3] seem to me conclusive. As he says: "the narrative starts at a point which for the XII Tables is untypically early. Their draftsmen are used to express themselves very concisely, apparently believing that it is desirable *inde incipere narrare unde necesse est*. Why bother telling about a charge being brought? The text would necessarily have to continue with a statement concerning proof and conviction, — all this to no evident purpose. In other provisions concerning delict the protasis commences with the deed itself, without any introduction. As a rule, a section will be of the type "*si* (or *qui*)... *faxit*". Then he gives various example to illustrate his point.

Yaron's own solution is to see the clause as concerning false accusation: "If one accuses another falsely of *furtum nec manifestum*...". This seemingly attractive solution is, I find, not convincing, largely because of two difficulties which did not escape Yaron's notice. The first is the use of the future tense in *"quod nec manifestum erit"*. Yaron admits[4] that *erit* is unexpected, and that he has no satisfactory explanation for the future tense. He does, however, call attention to the future *escit*[5] in *"Si intestato moritur, cui suus heres nec escit..."*. But this does not

---

* For Hans-Julius Wolff. [1] *Sv. "nec"*. [2] Cf. e.g. now M. Kaser, *Das röm. Privatrecht* I² (1971) 158 f. [3] *Si adorat furto, T.* 34 (1966) 510 ff., especially at p. 511 f. [4] *Si adorat furto* 513 nt. 13. [5] *Esco* is in fact an old inceptive of *sum* and is used as a future: cf. *Oxford Latin Dictionary* (1971) 621.

seem to be a parallel usage on Yaron's understanding of *"Si adorat etc."*, and in fact the future *escit* does not require any eplanation. The second difficulty is to explain why this provision dealt particularly with *furtum nec manifestum,* and Yaron suggests two possible answers[6]: "First, it may be pointed out that in *furtum nec manifestum* conviction was in the main based on circumstantial evidence. Hence the apprehension of false charges. However, the same problem might arise also in many other situations. The second answer is therefore perhaps more satisfactory: for all we know the Tables may have contained more sections concerning cases of *adorare,* the allegation of delicts not followed by proof. One must remember that 8. 16 owes its survival merely to a grammarian's interest in the particle *nec*". He has himself given the main objection to the first alternative. As to the second answer one must concede it is a possibility. But it is, I submit, a bare possibility. In a separate work I have argued that we have some knowledge of most of the provisions of the XII Tables, and that when we have no record of a clause of that code the reason usually is that no clause ever existed. To a large extent we can even determine which topics were not dealt with in the XII Tables[7]. On Yaron's second alternative there must have been several clauses concerning cases of *adorare,* and it is extremely difficult — for me at least — to believe that all these others have disappeared without trace.

To these two difficulties noted by Yaron one should add a third which is itself high-lighted by the *erit.* The XII Tables are noted for their terse style. Why does this provision have the apparently periphrastic *"Si adorat furto quod nec manifestum erit"*, instead of the seemingly appropriate *"Si adorat furto nec manifesto"?* For reasons which will be given later in this paper one cannot claim as the explanatinon that *furtum nec manifestum* was not yet a technical term or a legal concept.

Any satisfactory explanation of this clause must, I submit, account for the future *erit,* for the fact that the provision specifically concerns *furtum nec manifestum,* and for the apparently periphrastic *"quod nec manifestum erit"*. One reconstruction, and only one reconstruction, fits, namely *"Si adorat furto quod nec manifestum erit... manifestum esto"*. In certain circumstances what is *furtum nec manifestum* is to be *furtum manifestum.* The future with *erit* is appropriate, and the text on this understanding is quite a close parallel in structure to *"Si intestato moritur, cui suus heres nec escit, agnatus proximus familiam habeto"*. In

---

[6] *Si adorat furto* 516 f. [7] See my forthcoming book, *Rome of the XII Tables:*

both the relative clause is almost conditional. The provision in question refers to *furtum nec manifestum* because it deals with a rule which applied only to *furtum nec manifestum*. It is *furtum nec manifestum* — and not *iniuria* or some other delict — which is to be something else. But the lynch-pin of the reconstruction is that the periphrasis is now explicable. The provision with "*quod nec manifestum erit*" is much neater than "*Si adorat furto nec manifesto... furtum manifestum esto*". But this could not be said if the clause ended in any other way; see for instance, "*Si adorat furto nec manifesto... duplione damnum decidito*".

If this approach to the provision is correct there can be little doubt about the original content of the clause: it concerned the search *lance licioque*. Gaius tells us that if anything is found in such a search 'iubet id lex [i.e. the XII Tables] furtum manifestum esse'[8]. This leads him to the famous:

Gai 3.194. *Propter hoc tamen quod lex ex ea causa manifestum furtum esse iubet, sunt qui scribunt furtum manifestum aut lege intellegi aut natura: lege id ipsum de quo loquimur, natura illud de quo superius exposuimus. sed verius est natura tantum manifestum furtum intellegi; neque enim lex facere potest ut, qui manifestus fur non* sit, *manifestus sit, non magis quam qui omnino fur non sit, fur sit, et qui adulter aut homicida non sit, adulter vel homicida sit. at illud sane lex facere potest, ut proinde aliquis poena teneatur atque si furtum vel adulterium vel homicidium admisisset, quamvis nihil eorum admiserit.*

For us the main importance of Gaius' testimony is that it shows that following a successful *quaestio lance licioque* what was not *furtum manifestum* before is expressly declared by the XII Tables to be *furtum manifestum*[9]. Gaius thus, incidentally and conclusively, also reveals that the terminology and concept of *furtum manifestum* existed at the time of the XII Tables. This necessarily entails the existence of *furtum nec manifestum*. Hence since *furtum manifestum* was a technical term, so will *furtum nec manifestum* have been. Accordingly, the form of "*Si adorat furto quod nec manifestum erit*" cannot be explained on the basis that there was as yet no term, "*furtum nec manifestum*". Moreover, if the term "*furtum nec manifestum*" had not existed, one would rather have expected the clause to read "*Si adorat furto quod manifestum non erit*".

We cannot tell whether our clause originally contained a mention

---

Persons and Property. [8] Gai 3.192. [9] Cf. e.g. Daube, *Greek and Roman Reflections on Impossible Laws, Natural Law Forum* 12 (1967) 1 ff. at p. 25 ff.

of the *quaestio lance licio* or whether its relationship with that search was simply clear from the context. Our clause may, indeed, have stated only "*Si adorat furto quod nec manifestum erit manifestum esto*". What does seem fairly certain is that the *quaestio* itself was not fully described in the XII Tabes [10], hence cannot itself have been a complete innovation though the code may have been confirming an existing practice [11].

No argument against this understanding of the provision can be drawn from the use of the verb *adorare.* Probably it means here something like "to charge, accuse", which is the sense normally attributed to it in this context [12].

Finally, it is cheerfully conceded that the understanding of the clause "*Si adorat furto etc.*" which is proposed here cannot be regarded as proven. All that is hoped is that the solution suggested is inherently plausible and free from substantial objection.

---

[10] Cf. J.G. Wolf, *Lanx und licium, Sympotica Wieacker* (1970) 59 ff. The convincing argument is that if the search had been described in the code there could not have been such doubt in classical times as to what was involved in the *quaestio.* [11] Cf. Wolf, *Lanx und licium* 76. [12] But it should be admitted that the early usage and meaning of *adorare,* outside the religious sphere, is not entirely clear, even though Festus, *s.v. adorare* has "*Adorare apud antiquos significabat agere; unde et legati oratores dicuntur, quia mandata populi agunt*". M. Lemosse translates *adorare* as 'to confess', with the subject being the thief; 'Les actions pénales de vol', *Droits de l'Antiquité et Sociologie juridique, Mélanges H. Lévy-Bruhl* (Paris, 1959), pp. 179 ff at p. 184. This, however, just does not square with what we know otherwise about the word. Interestingly, P. Huvelin, who has a very different interpretation of the clause we are discussing, writes: "Il faut sans doute traduire: *Si adorat furto...* par: Si une personne en accuse une autre de vol..., et se garder de vouloir entendre étroitement ces mots, comme on le fait ordinairement, du fait d'intenter une action en justice. *Si adorat furto...* peut s'appliquer aussi bien à une réclamation extrajudiciaire. Dans la procédure extrajudiciaire de la *quaestio lance licioque,* il existait aussi, semble-t-il, une sorte de sommation du volé au maître de maison (*ad dominum appellare*). La disposition sur le *furtum lance licioque conceptum* pouvait commencer aussi par les mots *si adorat furto*"; *Études sur le Furtum dans le très ancien Droit romain* 1 (reprinted Rome, 1968) 72.

27

Actio de dolo and actiones in factum

The relationship of the *actio de dolo* and of *actiones in factum* has received little attention and the problems seem to have passed largely unnoticed. The fundamental issue is whether, since we are told that the *actio de dolo* is available only where there is no other action, it is subsidiary also to an *actio in factum*. The question would seem to be raised especially in situations akin to those covered by the *lex Aquilia*. The few scholars who have touched on the point seem in the main agreed that in classical law the *actio de dolo* was subsidiary to *actiones in factum,*[1], but it is doubtful whether this was really the case.

The problem is perhaps best approached by tracing the historical development of the *actio de dolo*.

The *actio de dolo* was probably introduced by Aquilius Gallus when he was peregrine praetor in 66 B.C. The scope of the action was originally narrow and was limited to cases where there was actual deception: where one thing was pretended but another done.

> Cicero De nat. deor. 3.30.74. Inde everriculum malitiarum omnium, iudicium de dolo malo, quod C. Aquillius, familiaris noster protulit; quem dolum idem Aquillius tum teneri putat, cum aliud sit simulatum, aliud actum

The use of *everriculum* (dragnet) might give the impression that the *actio de dolo* was very wide indeed, but equally it might mean nothing more than that unlike the other actions which Cicero has just named, it was not restricted to a particular type of situation. And that this latter interpretation is the correct one is shown by the last part of the text where Cicero tells us that Aquilius held that that *dolus* was punishable when *aliud*

[1] Eisele SZ 18 (1897) pp. 22-23 holds that in D.19.5.14 pr. *si dolo, dolo tenetur* is interpolated since the *actio de dolo* is subsidiary and yet in the same text an *actio in factum* on the *lex Aquilia* is given when the deed is done *sine causa*. He is followed by Pringsheim SZ 41 (1920) p. 255, n. 4, and Krüger, Stereotype Digest ad h. 1, But De Francisci accepts that part of the text as genuine without, however, any discussion or citation: Συνάλλαγμα, Pavia 1913 p. 335. The contrary view is expressed by Heldrich in discussing D.4.3.1.4: Das Verschulden beim Vertragsbschluß, Leipzig 1924 p. 2.

sit simulatum, aliud actum. Further evidence to the same effect is found in D.4.3.1.2 (Ulpian 11 ad ed.):

> Dolum malum Servius quidem ita definiit machinationem quandam alterius decipiendi causa, cum aliud simulatur et aliud agitur. Labeo autem posse et sine simulatione id agi, ut quis circumveniatur: posse et sine dolo malo aliud agi, aliud simulari, sicuti faciunt, qui per eiusmodi dissimulationem deserviant et tuentur vel sua vel aliena: itaque ipse sic definit dolum malum esse omnem calliditatem fallaciam machinationem ad circumveniendum fallendum decipiendum alterum adhibitam. Labeonis definitio vera est.

The Republican Servius, we are told, defined fraud as a machination to deceive another when one thing is pretended and another done. This is in complete harmony with the text of Cicero. On the other hand, the jurist of the early Empire, Labeo, has widened the definition to 'any stratagem, trick or machination used to circumvent dupe or ensnare another'. How far Labeo was prepared to go in this is shown by another text, D.4.3.7.6 (Ulpian 11 ad ed.):

> Si quadrupes tua dolo alterius damnum mihi dederit, quaeritur, an de dolo habeam adversus eum actionem. et placuit mihi, quod Labeo scribit, si dominus quadrupedis non sit solvendo, dari debere de dolo, quamvis, si noxae deditio sit secuta, non puto dandam nec in id quod excedit.

Labeo, therefore, would give an *actio de dolo* against a person who brings it about that another's animal does damage where the *actio de pauperie* against the owner would be valueless. Thus Labeo stretched the *actio de dolo* in two directions:[2] first to include cases where there were negotiations between the parties, but false representations were not made; secondly, to situations where there was no direct relationship between the parties.[3] It would, however, be dangerous to assert that the second extension was accepted immediately by all of his contemporaries. That it was accepted by Ulpian, as was Labeo's definition, is clear from the text *et placuit mihi, quod Labeo scribit.*[4] But Ulpian's very emphasis on his agreement suggests that the matter had been and perhaps still was disputed.

[2] He also widened its scope to the extent that he declared it should be given, not only where there was no other action, but also where it was doubtful whether there was another action: D.4.3.7.3.

[3] Probably Labeo personally should not be given too much credit for the extension. His elder contemporary, Trebatius, (cf. Kunkel, Herkunft und soziale Stellung der römischen Juristen, Weimar 1952, pp. 28 and 114) also gave the *actio de dolo* when there were no negotiations between the parties: D.4.3.18.3. Perhaps Labeo's biggest individual contribution was to widen the definition to cover the new and not universally accepted extensions.

[4] Whether *quamvis – excedit* is genuine or interpolated as suggested by Pernice, Labeo,

Other evidence is not lacking that the second extension was not completely accepted.

> D.4.3.7.7 (Ulpian 11 ad ed.) Idem Labeo quaerit, si compeditum servum meum ut fugeret solveris, an de dolo actio danda sit? et ait Quintus apud eum notans: si non misericordia ductus fecisti, furti teneris: si misericordia, in factum actionem dari debere.

That Quintus made a note on Labeo at all, and that Ulpian should cite it prove that Labeo's decision must have been different. And that decision probably was that you were liable *simpliciter* to the *actio de dolo*. The *actio furti* would be excluded because you released the slave *ut fugeret*. Legally it is irrelevant that your intention is morally good. If you cheat a wealthy profiteer to give to charity, you are nonetheless guilty of fraud. It is unlikely that it was on the ground of morality that Quintus excluded the *actio de dolo*:[5] *misericordia* is only introduced to exclude the intention of profiting from the release. Further, I hope to show later that it was not because a decretal *actio in factum* ousted the *actio de dolo*. This leaves as an explanation Quintus' refusal to accept that an *actio de dolo* could lie where a man wilfully caused another financial loss but there was no actual deception in the course of negotiations.[6]

> D.4.3.18. 5 (Paul 11 ad ed.) Si servum, quem tu mihi promiseras, alius occiderit, de dolo malo actionem in eum dandam plerique recte putant, quia tu a me liberatus sis: ideoque legis Aquiliae actio tibi denegabitur.[7]

Plerique recte putant suggests that even in the time of Paul, there was doubt as to whether the *actio de dolo* was available when there was no question of negotiations between the injured party and the wrongdoer.[8]

Turning to the relationship of the *actio de dolo* and *actiones in factum*, there can be little doubt that the existence of an edictal *actio in factum* ousted the

2.i., Halle 1895, p. 210, n. 1, need not concern us here.

[5] This reason may, however, have influenced Ulpian's seeming acceptance of Quintus' position. More than other classical jurists, Ulpian was influenced by non-legal considerations. Cf. D.9.2.23.1 where Julian's view is correct on principle but for equitable reasons is not accepted by Ulpian.

[6] There is also the possibility that Quintus would have allowed an *actio de dolo* but considered an *actio in factum* more appropriate; cf. infrà p. 397, but given the tenor of the text that seems rather unlikely.

[7] *Ideoque – denegabitur* may be interpolated; cf. Index Itp. That, however, does not affect the present point.

[8] In P.S.1.8.1, we find the old narrow definition: *Dolus est, cum aliud agitur, aliud simulatur*. Our present text, however, could also be explained on the ground that the doubt whether an action lay existed because the plaintiff had only a contractual right to the slave. Cf. in general for the historical development of the *actio de dolo*, Arangio-Ruiz, Istituzioni di diritto romano, 14th ed., Naples 1960, pp. 103-104; Kaser, Das römische Privatrecht 1, Munich 1955, p. 524.

possibility of suing by the *actio de dolo*. There is no text which gives the *actio de dolo* where an edictal *actio in factum* is appropriate. Moreover, there are a number of such *actions in factum* which lay for fraud only. The majority of these, however, were given in situations which were not originally covered by the *actio de dolo* since there were not (or need not be) dealings between the parties in which actual deception was practised, e.g. *De eo per quem factum erit quominus quis in iudicio sistat*;[9] *de alienatione iudicii mutandi causa facta*;[10] *de servo corrupto*;[11] *de sepulchro violato*.[12] But this does not apply to all. At least one, *Si mensor falsum modum dixerit*,[13] could only be brought where there were such dealings.[14] Whether this praetorian action was introduced before or after the *actio de dolo* cannot now be discovered, but it was probably earlier. There is also some slight positive textual evidence that an edictal action ousted the *actio de dolo*. In D.4.3.1.4., we are told that an *actio de dolo* cannot be brought if another action is available, *si sit civilis vel honoraria*. This may well be interpolated,[15] and as regards praetorian actions, is, as we shall see, too wide for classical and Justinianic law. But if it means anything at all, it must be that no *actio de dolo* could be brought where an edictal action could.

But the position was not the same where the choice was between an *actio de dolo* and a decretal *actio in factum*. There the *actio de dolo* was not excluded. This is simply demonstrated.

First, if this were the position, the *actio de dolo* would never have been introduced, not only because it would have been superfluous, but also because it could never have been used. It would seem reasonable to believe that every time the praetor would grant an *actio de dolo* he would also have been willing to grant an *actio in factum*. This, however, would not prevent the *actio de dolo* from being introduced or being celebrated as a momentous innovation. It is one thing to have to go to the praetor to ask for an *ad hoc* remedy which would always, especially to laymen, seem very uncertain even when it was not, quite another to know that there is a general action covering fraud as defined by the praetor. And if it be argued that the praetor's powers of granting decretal actions were more restricted in the Republic than they were later, then at least the *actio de dolo* would have become obsolete in the classical period.

Secondly, we have a number of texts where, for one reason or another, an *actio de dolo* is not available, and we are told that an *actio in factum* must

9 D.2.10.1 pr; h.t. 3 pr. It seems easiest to refer to these actions by the Title of the Digest in which they are discussed.

10 D.4.7.1 pr.

11 D.11.3.1 pr.

12 D.47.12.3 pr.

13 D.11.6.1 pr.

14 Thus the action is refused even if the *mensor* deliberately delays to hand in his report: D.11.6.5 pr. The end of the text is interpolated; cf. Index Itp.

15 Beseler SZ 45 (1925) p. 434; Heldrich loc. cit.

be given. Logically, if in the less straightforward case an *actio in factum* is given, it must also have been available in the more usual case unless another action, namely the *actio de dolo* were preferred. One example will suffice.

D.4.3.11.1 (Ulpian 11 ad ed.) Et quibusdam personis non dabitur (*scil. actio de dolo*), ut puta liberis vel libertis adversus parentes patronosve, cum sit famosa. sed nec humili adversus eum qui dignitate excellet debet dari: puta plebeio adversus consularem receptae auctoritatis, vel luxurioso atque prodigo vel alias vili adversus hominem vitae emendatioris. et ita Labeo. quid ergo est? in horum persona dicendum est in factum verbis temperandam actionem dandam, ut bonae fidei mentio fiat.[16]

Thus certain classes are refused an *actio de dolo* against certain others and an *actio in factum* is given. It is irrelevant that the *actio in factum* may be based on the *actio de dolo*, and the significant fact is simply that if an *actio in factum* is given there, it would also have been granted by the praetor in cases involving persons who were of similar digity if the *actio de dolo* had not been preferred to it.[17] Therefore, the fact that a decretal *actio in factum* could be given does not mean that the *actio de dolo* is excluded.

Thirdly, there are situations for which the texts sometimes give an *actio in factum*, sometimes an *actio de dolo*.

D.9.2.27.21 (Ulpian 18 ad ed.) Si quis de manu mihi nummos excusserit, Sabinus existimat damni iniuriae esse actionem, si ita perierint, ne ad aliquem pervenirent, puta si in flumen vel in mare vel in cloacam ceciderunt: quod si ad aliquem pervenerunt, ope consilio furtum factum agendum, quod et antiquis placuit. idem etiam in factum dari posse actionem ait.

Although it is probable that Sabinus gave the direct action in such a situation and that the attribution to him of the *actio in factum* is an interpolation,[18] it would seem to be generally agreed among scholars that other classical jurists gave an *actio in factum*.[19]

D.19.5.14 pr. (Ulpian 41 ad Sab.) Qui servandarum mercium suarum causa alienas merces in mare proiecit, nulla tenetur actione: sed si sine causa id fecisset, in factum, si dolo, de dolo tenetur.

[16] The text is probably interpolated but it is nevertheless agreed that the *actio in factum* would be given in classical law, although perhaps not in respect of all the classes here mentioned. Cf. De Francisci, op. cit. 2, pp. 910-911; and the other works cited in the Index Itp.

[17] Cf. C.5.21.2 where we are told that penal actions (which include the *actio de dolo*) do not lie between spouses and the *actio in factum* is given.

[18] Cf. Index Itp. The name of some other jurist should be substituted for "*Idem*".

[19] Cf. Rotondi, Scritti Giuridici 2, p. 454) Lawson, Negligence in the Civil Law, 2nd ed., Oxford 1955, p. 108. See also Gai. 3.202; D.19.5.14.2.23; 41.1.55; 47.2.50.4.

The only suggested interpolation with which we need be concerned is that proposed by Eisele who is followed by Krüger and Pringsheim.[20] They would excise *si dolo, de dolo*. Two reasons are given for this. First, *de dolo teneri*, it is said, is unusual. But this does not seem correct. Papinian also uses the expression[21] which is found in four other texts of Ulpian.[22] Secondly, Ulpian gives an *actio in factum legis Aquiliae* where the act was done *sine causa*, and since the *actio de dolo* is subsidiary it should likewise be excluded even where the act is dolose. But enough has already been said to show that the *actio de dolo* is not ousted by the availability of a decretal *actio in factum*. There is also a reasonable contrast between *sine causa* and *si dolo*. The former amounts to *culpa* since the goods are thrown overboard without good reason.

D.4.4.9.6 (Ulpian 11 ad ed.) Adversus libertatem quoque minori a praetore subveniri impossible est,

D.4.4.11 pr. (Idem) Verum vel de dolo vel utilis actio erit in id quod minoris interfuit non manumitti: . . .

A minor was fraudulently persuaded to manumit his slave. The *libertus* cannot be reenslaved but Ulpian will allow the minor a choice of the *actio de dolo* or an *actio utilis* modelled on the edict *De minoribus viginti quinque annis*.[23] There have been no suspicions of interpolation.

Another slightly more dubious example is in D.9.2.41 pr. (Ulpian 41 ad Sab.) and D.4.3.35 (Ulpian 30 ad ed.). At the beginning of the former, the question is raised whether a testator whose will is destroyed by another has an *actio damni iniuriae*. The question is answered in the negative since his interest cannot be measured, but we are told the position is different in the case of his heir or legatee. In the latter text the person with whom a will is deposited destroys it after the testator's death and the heir and legatees are given an *actio de dolo*. Given the decision in this second case and the fact that in D.9.2.41 pr. only an *actio damni iniuriae* was being considered, it becomes clear that in that text the heir and legatee were given only an *actio in factum* based on the *lex Aquiliae*. Neither text in so far as we are interested in them has been held interpolated. It is unlikely that the difference in time of the destruction (in the former text the will is destroyed before the testator's death, in the latter, after) would cause the decisions to be distinguished.[24]

[20] Supra p. 313, n. 1.

[21] D.23.3.69.7.

[22] D.4.2.14.3; 4.3.9.4; 7.4.5.3; 17.1.10.7. Cf. *ex dolo teneri* which is a favourite expression of Ulpian's (it occurs ten times in texts of his) but is found in no other jurist.

[23] It is just possible that two situations are envisaged and, say, the *actio de dolo* is given against the former slave, the *actio in factum* against a third party. But there is not the slightest evidence for this in the text and it is difficult to see any reason for making the distinction.

[24] Cf. D.9.2.23.8; h.t.13.2; h.t.43.

But if the above shows that a decretal *actio in factum* did not oust the *actio de dolo*, it is equally clear that such an *actio in factum* could be given even when there was *dolus*. Numerous examples are found in connection with the *lex Aquilia*.

> D.9.2.9.3 (Ulpian 18 ad ed.) Si srvum meum equitantem concitato equo effeceris in flumen praecipitari atque ideo homo perierit, in factum esse dandam actionem Ofilius scribit: quemadmodum si servus meus ab alio in insidias deductus ab alio esset occisus.

This text has never been held interpolated. In the second hyothesis envisaged it is obvious that the wrongdoer was guilty of *dolus*, not merely of *culpa*. This decision, like the first in the text, is referable to the Republican jurist Ofilius as is shown by the subjunctive *esset occisus*.

> D.9.2.11.1 (Idem) Si alius tenuit, alius interemit, is qui tenuit, quasi causam mortis praebuit, in factum actione tenetur.

This text, too, is universally regarded as genuine[25] and again there cannot be any question of *culpa*. There are also other texts on the *lex Aquilia* where an *actio in factum* is given although *dolus* as well as *culpa* is certainly envisaged, e.g.

> D.9.2.11.5 (Idem) Item cum eo, qui canem irritaverat et effecerat, ut aliquem morderet, quamvis eum non tenuit, Proculus respondit Aquiliae actionem esse: sed Iulianus eum demum Aquilia teneri ait, qui tenuit et effecit ut aliquem morderet: ceterum si non tenuit, in factum agendum.[26]

Two reasons can be given for preferring in these circumstances an *actio in factum* to an *actio de dolo*. First, an *actio in factum* modelled on the *lex Aquilia* was given for damage done *corpori sed non corpore* before it were ever possible to bring an *actio de dolo* in the same situation. We saw from D.9.2.9.3 that Ofilius, a jurist of the Republic, gave such an *actio in factum*, but it would appear that not until the early Empire was it conceived that an *actio de dolo* could be given where there were no negotiations between the parties. Moreover, even then the general extension was probably not pacifically accepted. Once it was established that in a particular type of situation an *actio in factum* would lie, legal conservatism would make it difficult for the *actio de dolo* to insinuate itself. And, indeed, there is no evidence for its existence in this sphere before Ulpian. Secondly, it is usually difficult to prove a state of mind. If an *actio in factum* would be given on account of a wrongful act whether done negligently or wilfully, such as is the case with

[25] The Index Itp. says that it was held interpolated by Albertario in 21.1. Rivista del diritto commerciale (1923) p. 506, n. 4, but this seems to be an error.
[26] Cf. D.9.2.7.6; h.t.9.2.

an action based on the *lex Aquilia*, it is obviously more satisfactory to proceed on that rather than risk suing on an *actio de dolo* where fraud has to be proved. A third reason can also be given in respect of D.9.2.11.1. There we have two wrongdoers, one of whom clearly is liable under the *lex Aquilia*, the other not so liable. But in the circumstances it is reasonable that an action should be given against both. However, unless the former could not be found or was bankrupt, an *actio de dolo* could not be given against the latter since the plaintiff had someone else he could sue for his loss.[27] Thus, often an *actio in factum* would be the only appropriate remedy.

Needless to say, these reasons for preferring an *actio in factum* to the *actio de dolo* apply also in circumstances apart from the *lex Aquilia*. Indeed, the second reason could be stated more generally and one might say that whenever a situation exists where an *actio in factum* would be given whether or not there is *dolus*, an *actio in factum* tends to be preferred to the *actio de dolo*. A good example is in D.19.4.1.1 (Paul 33 ad ed.):[28]

> Unde si ea res, quam acceperim vel dederim, postea evincatur, in factum dandam actionem respondetur.

Paul is discussing the transfer of goods for goods which he shows is not the same as sale. Accordingly the actions on sale are excluded and where one party is evicted from the goods transferred to him he is given an *actio in factum*. Paul does not trouble to distinguish the cases where there was *dolus* on the part of the transferor and where there was not.[29]

Again, the *actio de dolo* is, in practice, usually ousted where the praetorian decretal action available is an *actio* with the *formula in ius concepta* plus a fiction, or even an edictal *actio in factum* plus a fiction.

> Gai.4.37. Item civitas Romana peregrino fingitur, si eo nomine agat aut cum eo agatur, quo nomine nostris legibus actio constituta est, si modo iustum sit eam actionem etiam ad peregrinum extendi, veluti si furt*i* agat peregrinus aut cum eo agit*ur*, *nam si cum peregrino agatur*, formula ita concipitur: IUDEX ESTO, SI PARET *LUCIO TITIO A DIONE HERMAEI FILIO OPEVE* CONSILIO DIONIS *H*ERMAEI FILI*I* FURTUM FACTUM ESSE PATERAE AUREAE, QUAM OB REM EUM, SI CIVIS ROMANUS ESSET, PR*O* FURE DAMNUM DECIDERE OPORTERET, et reliqua, item si peregrinus furti agat, civitas ei Romana fingitur, similiter, si ex lege Aquilia peregrinus damni iniurae agat aut cum eo aga*tur*, ficta civitate Romana indic*i*um datur. 38. Praeterea aliquando fingimus ad*ver*sarium nostrum capite deminutum non esse. nam si ex contractu nobis obligatus obligatave sit, et capite deminutus deminutave fueri*t*, velut mulier per coemptionem, masculus per adrogationem, desinit iure civili debere nobis, nec

[27] Cf. D.43.1.8; h.t.2; h.t.3; h.t.4; h.t.5; h.t.6.
[28] So Krüger, but the mss. have 32.
[29] Cf. D.19.5.27; D.19.4.1.1 is widely held interpolated, but the *actio in factum* is

directo intendi prodest sibi dare eum eamve oportere, sed ne in potestate eius est ius nostrum corrumpere, introducta est contra eum eamve actio utilis rescissa capitis deminutione, id est in qua fingitur capite deminutus deminutave non esse.

The fiction, *si civis Romanus esset*, is perhaps the oldest and commonest in Roman law, and Gaius tells us in 4. 37 that where theft has been committed and one of the parties to the action is a peregrine the action given will be the *formula* of the *actio furti* plus such a fiction. And in the case of *furtum* the wrongful conduct must have been deliberate. It might, however, be objected that this text is not good evidence in that it merely shows again that where the *actio de dolo* would originally have been excluded because there were no negotiations between the parties and the praetor granted an *ad hoc* remedy the latter action continued to be preferred even when the *actio de dolo* become possible. But Gai.4.38 is rather different. There we are dealing with contractual obligations which are extinguished *iure civili* by *capitis deminutio*, and Gaius gives the civil law formula with the fiction that the defendant has not undergone *capitis deminutio*. In the case of bilateral contracts the plaintiff must have performed, or be willing to perform his part before he is granted an action and usually it would be very dishonest for the defendant to try to escape from his obligation on the ground of his change of status. This dishonesty is emphasised by Gaius: *sed ne in potestate eius sit ius nostrum corrumpere*.

Another good example is in D.28.5.47 (Africanus 2 quaest.) This text tells us that where one of the parties to a mandate is a *filiusfamilias* and the mandate is performed after he becomes *sui iuris*, Juian would give, not a direct *actio mandati*, but an *actio utilis*. Here the fiction would be *ac si paterfamilias esset*.[30] And again the defendant's conduct seems dolose.

An example of an action with the edictal *formula in factum* plus a fiction is in D.15.3.20 pr. (Scaevola 1 respons.):[31]

Pater pro filia dotem promisit et convenit, ut ipse filiam aleret: non praestante

generally regarded as genuine.

[30] Cf. Desserteaux, Capitis deminutio 2, Paris 1919, pp. 243-246 especially at p. 246, n.6. The text has been much discussed and a number of interpolations have been postulated. Only those, however, suggested by Costa (Papiniano 4, Bologna 1899, p. 34, n. 15) and Bortolucci (Actio Utilis 1, Modena 1909, p. 50, n. 1) and opposed by Lenel (Edictum Perpetuum, 3rd ed., Leipzig 1927, p. 296, n. 5) would oust completely the reference to the *actio utilis*. Considering that *formulae* were abolished in 342 A.D., the compilers would have no reason to change *actio mandati* to an *actio utilis*. If the text is interpolated the alteration must be early.

[31] Cf. D.15.3.21. So far as we are concerned both texts are held interpolated by Albertario alone (Scritti 4, pp. 196-200) and his arguments are adequately dealt with by Solazzi (Scritti 2, pp. 558-560) and Berger (Kritische Vierteljahresschrift für Gesetzgebung und Rechtswissenschaft 50, 1912 p. 441). Cf. Garrido, Ius Uxorium, Rome-Madrid 1958, p. 24 and n. 55.

patre filia a viro mutuam pecuniam accepit et mortua est in matrimonio. respondi, si ad ea id quod creditum est erogatum esset, sine quibus aut se tueri aut servos paternos exhibere non posset, dandam de in rem verso utilem actionem.

Here too, the behaviour of the *pater* smacks of *dolus*, but an *actio utilis de in rem verso* is preferred.[32]

Thus, in practice, a decretal praetorian action was often preferred to an *actio de dolo*. It is indeed, only too easy to overestimate the frequency with which the latter occurred. It is perhaps worth noting that the *actio de dolo* does not occur at all in Gaius' Institutes and it is given in only about 41 texts in the whole of the Digest. And of these texts, only 11 are outside of the title '*De dolo malo*'.[33] Moreover, in some of these texts the reference to the *actio de dolo* is generally admitted to be interpolated,[34] while other texts are concerned not with concrete situations but merely state that an *actio de dolo* will lie against a defined class of persons.[35] Very generally, one can say that the *actio de dolo* is given only in situations where there is no established action on which a decretal remedy can be modelled, and where liability will be considered appropriate only if there were *dolus* so that there would be no advantage in setting up an *actio in factum*.

One can build up a picture of the situations in which the *actio de dolo* is usually preferred.

Firstly, the *actio de dolo* is given where the wrongdoer is sued and fraudulently has himself acquitted. The original obligation is, of course, extinguished. Moreover, there is no *actio* on which an *actio in factum* could easily be modelled and liability would not be appropriate if the acquittal were the result of mere carelessness on the part of anyone.

D.4.3.20.1 (Paul 11 ad ed.) Si persuaseris mihi nullam societatem tibi fuisse cum eo cui heres sum, et ob id iudicio absolvi te passus sim: dandam mihi de dolo actionem Iulianus scribit.[36]

Secondly, we find the *actio de dolo* given where one person fraudulently persuades another that something is the case when it is not and the latter acts to his disadvantage.

[32] Cf. D.4.4.11. pr. where the situation is one where typically the *actio de dolo* is given, but since the plaintiff is a minor an action with a fiction can easily be prepared and Ulpian gives a choice of the *actio de dolo* or an *actio utilis*. Suprà p. 396.

[33] The *actio de dolo* is much less common than the *exceptio doli*. Dolus originally had a wider meaning in the latter than in the former.

[34] E.g. D.11.6.5 pr; 21.2.21 pr; 46.3.95.1; 4.3.7.3.

[35] E.g. D.4.3.13 pr., 1.

[36] Biondi's assertion that a reference to *restitutio in integrum* has been excised, does not affect the argument (Studi sulle Actiones Arbitrariae, Palermo 1913 p. 102, n. 2). Cf. for absolution followed by the *actio de dolo*, D.4.3.9.4; h.t.21; h.t.39.

D.4.3.8 (Gaius 4 ad ed. prov.) Quod si cum scires eum facultatibus labi, tui lucri gratia adfirmasti mihi idoneum esse, merito adversus te, cum mei decipiendi gratia alium falsum laudasti, de dolo iudicium dandum est.[37]

Thirdly, the *actio de dolo*, rather than an *actio in factum* is found in situations involving a stipulation.[38]

D.4.3.1.4 (Ulpian 11 ad ed.) Ait praetor: 'si de his rebus alia actio non erit' merito praetor ita demum hanc actionem pollicetur, si alia non sit, quoniam famosa actio non temere debuit a praetore decerni, si sit civilis vel honoraria, qua possit experiri: usque adeo, ut et Pedius libro octavo scribit, etiamsi interdictum sit quo quis experiri, vel exceptio qua se tueri possit, cessare hoc edictum. idem et Pomponius libro vicensimo octavo, et adicit: et si stipulatione tutus sit quis, eum actionem de dolo habere non posse, ut puta si de dolo stipulatum sit.

Beseler[39] although he agrees with the proposition, holds the reference to the stipulation interpolated. He argues that it does not follow well on Pedius' discussion. Pomponius' decision he says, comes straight from the Edict, not by analogy as does Pedius'. This looks sound and may well be so, but it does not explain why the compilers (or a glossator) thought it worthwhile to emphasise that even if (*et si*) there were an action on the stipulation, the *actio de dolo* would be excluded. Another interpretation, I suggest, is possible. We have already seen that originally the *actio de dolo* had a very narrow scope.[40] There had to be actual cheating on the part of the wrong-doer and so there had to be negotiations between the parties. I submit that the main purpose in introducing the *actio de dolo* was to give some measure of protection to the parties of a verbal obligation just as the parties to as *bonae fidei* contract were protected by the inherent nature of their agreement. The narrower one delimits the original scope of the *actio de dolo* in this way, the easier it is to understand why it was infaming.[41] The position is inverted at the beginning of this text. The action is not subsidiary because it is infaming, but it is infaming because it was conceived of as protecting parties who were, one might say, in a fiduciary relationship but were not in the particular circumstances of the case protected by the *ius civile*. Accordingly since the *actio* was meant primarily

[37] Beseler would excise *merito: cum-laudasti*, but this does not alter the sense of the text: Beiträge 3, p. 62. Cf. D.47.2.43.3; 4.3.9.1; h.t.23; h.t.38; h.t.40.

[38] D.4.8.31; 4.3.14; h.t.5; h.t.7.3; h.t.19.

[39] SZ 45 (1925) pp. 434-435.

[40] Supra pp. 313-315.

[41] It would be absurd to hold that it was intended at the outset to make a man infamous because his *dolus* did not fall into any of the recognised catgegories which were covered by other actions, e.g. the *actio empti*, which were not infaming. The position in this respect is ridiculous in classical law and this is best explained as a by-product of juristic development.

to protect parties to a stipulation the jurists felt constrained to stress the fact that if an action were available on the stipulation the *actio de dolo* was ousted.[42]

Lastly, there are a number of other individual situations where for similar reasons an *actio de dolo* is given in preference to an *actio in factum*. For example if a slave fraudulently obtains his freedom he cannot be reenslaved and his former owner is given an *actio de dolo* against him.[43] Or where the defendant with fraudulent intention makes the plaintiff a gift and he suffers loss as a result.[44]

Conclusions

a) An edictal *actio in factum* excluded the *actio de dolo*.

b) A decretal *actio in factum* did not exclude the *actio de dolo*, nor vice versa. There was no legal principle regulating the choice between them, but certain rules operated in practice.

1) For historical reasons an *actio in factum* was preferred in cases not involving negotiations between the parties. Indeed, the *actio in factum* was usually given where the conduct was dolose but did not involve actual cheating.

2) An *actio in factum* was also preferred where it was reasonable to give an action for *culpa* as well as for *dolus*, or even where a remedy was called for on the facts.

3) Again, a decretal action was given where it could be based on a *formula in ius* or an edictal *formula in factum* plus a fiction.

4) The *actio de dolo* was preferred in the converse of these, i.e. where there was actual cheating in negotiations; where it was difficult to model the remedy on an existing action; and where it was reasonable that liability should lie for fraud only.[45]

[42] Cf. D.4.3.7.3 and Beseler's reconstruction thereof: op. cit. p. 435.

[43] D.4.3.7. pr; h.t.7.8; cf. D.4.3.24; h.t.32. Where the former owner were a minor, Ulpian would give a choice of the *actio de dolo* and an *actio utilis* modelled on the edict *De minoribus viginti quinque annis*: D.4.4.11. pr; cf. supra pp. 318, 322, n. 32.

[44] D.4.3.34; 39.5.18.3.

[45] An interesting text is D.19.5.5.2 *in fine* where Paul tells us that if I give you a slave on the condition that you manumit one of your slaves and you do so, and you are evicted from the one I gave you, then if I gave you my slave *sciens* Julian would give the *actio de dolo* against me, if *ignorans* an *actio in factum*. This seems contrary to the rule expounded but is easily explained. Other jurists starting from Aristo would give an *actio civilis incerti* in the *do ut facias* situation but Julian was much more reactionary and would allow only a praetorian remedy. (Cf. Monier, Manuel Elémentaire de droit romain 2, 2nd ed., Paris 1940, pp. 242-243 and the works he cites.) Julian, being in conflict with others, wants to stress his opinion that the remedy is exceptional and so he distinguishes between cases which involve fraud and those which do not.

c) The *actio de dolo* was ousted and a decretal *actio in factum* would be given where it was reasonable to make a wrongdoer liable, but an action was also available against another party.
d) And, of course, an *actio in factum* was given where it was felt to be improper that the plaintiff should be able to make the particular defendant *infamous*.
e) The *actio de dolo* was relatively uncommon.[46]

[46] I am indebted to Professors Kunkel and Daube for very valuable criticism.

28

Liability in the Actio de Positis ac Suspensis

It is perfectly clear that the *actio de positis ac suspensis* lay against the *habitator* not the person who placed or suspended the dangerous object on or from an eave or projecting roof, but the basis of liability of the *habitator* is not so certain. So far as I am aware, it is always assumed, without any real discussion [1], that liability was the same as in the *actio de effusis vel deiectis* and followed simply from the fact that the dangerous act occurred in the premises occupied by the defendant. But this is nowhere stated in the texts and a rather different position, namely that the *habitator* had to be aware that the object hâd been placed on the eave or projecting roof and had allowed it to remain there, is much more in accordance with the evidence. Moreover, since the purpose of the two actions is very different—the *actio de effusis vel deiectis* being remedial, the *actio de positis ac suspensis* preventive—it ought not to be too lightly assumed that liability is the same in both cases.

D. 9, 3, 5, 10 (Ulp., 23 *ad ed.*):

> Positum habere etiam is recte videtur, qui ipse quidem non posuit, verum ab alio positum patitur: quare si servus posuerit, dominus autem positum patiatur, non noxali iudicio dominus, sed suo nomine tenebitur.

This text never seems to have been held interpolated [2]. We are told that a person is also regarded *positum habere* if he did not place the object himself but allows it to have been placed by another. Since this is meant as a commentary on the meaning of the wording of this part of the edict we must pay particular attention to what is, in fact, said. We are not told that a person is regarded *positum habere* if he is the principal

---

[1] For instance, among modern scholars Stojčević, *Sur le caractère des quasi-délits en droit romain, IVRA* 8, 1957, pp. 57 ff. at p. 66; also, by implication, Stein, *The Nature of quasi-delictal Obligations, Rev. int. dr. antiq.*, 1958, pp. 563 ff. The same is also true for jurists of earlier centuries.

[2] *Cf. Ind. Itp.*

occupier of the premises, but if he allows the object to have been placed. This must imply not only knowledge on the part of the defendant but the authority and the ability, if he had so wished, to remove the object [3]. This control will reside in the *habitator*. The conclusion is strengthened by the link between the first part of the text and *quare si servus* to the end. The use of *quare* shows that there is thought to be a logical connexion between the two parts of the text and it can only be this: since the *habitator* is liable only if he allows the object to remain in its dangerous place, therefore he is liable on his own account if he suffers an object placed by his slave to remain, whereas if he does not know of the slave's act there can be only the noxal action [4]. The distinction in the second part of the text between sufferance and absence of knowledge must be a reflection, however imperfect, of some similar distinction in the first part.

Moreover, the form of the edict *Ne quis in suggrunda* [5] should be contrasted with that of *De his qui deiecerint vel effuderint* [6]. The former has *ne quis . . . positum habeat*: that is, a direct warning against a certain type of conduct. The latter, on the other hand, is much more abstract: if certain conduct occurs with resultant injury, an action will be given. In the former the person liable is he to whom the warning is given, in the latter it is *is, qui ibi habitaverit*. This difference of form suggests strongly that the basis of liability was not looked upon as being the same in the two cases [7]. The connexion of the defendant with the wrongful conduct is much closer in *Ne quis in suggrunda*.

Nor is D. 44, 7, 5, 5 (Gaius, 3 *aur.*), which is repeated in J. 4, 5, 1, good authority for the view that the *habitator* was automatically liable.

> Is quoque, ex cuius cenaculo (vel proprio ipsius vel conducto vel in quo gratis habitabat) deiectum effusumve aliquid est ita, ut alicui noceret, quasi ex maleficio teneri videtur: ideo autem non proprie ex maleficio obligatus intellegitur, quia plerumque ob alterius culpam tenetur aut servi aut liberi. cui similis est is, qui ea parte, qua volgo iter fieri solet, id positum aut suspensum habet, quod potest, si ceciderit, alicui nocere . . .

To take the text as it stands. *Cui similis est* which links the two cases ought not to be understood as saying that the basis of liability is the same. It means nothing more than that in our case the *habitator* also *non proprie ex maleficio tenetur* and this is because the defendant may be liable because of the positive act of a slave or free man: he himself need

[3] *Cf.* D. 50, 17, 50; 50, 17, 109; 47, 6, 1, 1; 9, 4, 3.

[4] Specially provided by the edict, *insciente domino*: D. 9, 3, 5, 6; *cf.* Lenel, *Edictum Perpetuum*, 3rd edit., Leipzig, 1927, p. 174.

[5] Lenel, *loc. cit.*

[6] Lenel, *op. cit.*, pp. 173 f.

[7] Especially if we take seriously Ulpian's statement in D. 9, 3, 5, 7 that the former is a part of the latter edict.

not have done anything positive and mere inaction is not a *maleficium*. If, on the other hand, we say with Stein [8] that *quia plerumque ob alterius culpam* is an addition to the original statement that the *habitator non proprie ex maleficio obligatus intellegitur*, then *cui similis est* implies only that the *habitator* in the *actio de positis ac suspensis* was not really liable *ex maleficio*—since no harm has occurred, to allow the object to remain is hardly a *maleficium*. Stein, however, is not convincing since the *ideo autem* demands that a reason be given. It is perhaps just possible (though there is no reason to assume this) that the whole of *ideo—liberi* is an addition. If so, *cui similis est* would be saying nothing more than that the *habitator* in our case was also liable *non proprie ex maleficio* and no further similarity between the two cases need be assumed.

Moreover, in this text too, we should point to the difference in language used to describe the liability in the two cases. The defendant is described in the first as *is ex cuius cenaculo deiectum effusumve aliquid est*, in the second *is qui positum aut suspensum habet*. Again the connexion of the defendant with the act in question is marked for the edict *Ne quis in suggrunda*, and the absolute nature of his liability for the edict *De his qui deiecerint vel effuderint* is stressed.

Nothing can be deduced from the first part of D. 9, 3, 5, 12.

> Si id quod positum erat deciderit et nocuerit, in eum competit actio qui posuit, non in eum qui habitaverit, quasi haec actio non sufficiat, quia positum habuisse non utique videtur qui posuit, nisi vel dominus fuit aedium vel inhabitator. . . .

The text is quite clearly very corrupt as a result of a careless scribe [9] and any attempt to reconstruct it must rely heavily on *a priori* reasoning. In any event, in so far as it may be maintained that the text talks of giving an action under this edict against the *dominus aedium* or *inhabitator* there is no indication that the *dominus aedium* or *inhabitator* is liable even when unaware of the placing. Everything depends on the interpretation of *positum habuisse*.

Thus, it would appear that the *habitator* had to be at fault for the action under the edict *Ne quis in suggrunda* to lie against him. If this is correct then it is a further argument against the view of Buckland that vicarious liability was the common quality of the quasi-delicts [10] and against the view of Stein that the common quality was strict liability. The *actio de positis ac suspensis* could not be classed as a delict simply because no injury had occurred [11].

---

[8] *Op. cit.*, p. 564.
[9] *Cf.* MOMMSEN, *Digesta Iustiniani Augusti* I, Berlin, 1870, *ad h. l.*
[10] *A Textbook of Roman Law*, 2nd edit., Cambridge, 1932, p. 599.
[11] *Cf.* STOJČEVIĆ, *op. cit.*, p. 67.

A useful, though not absolutely exact, parallel may perhaps be drawn from the English law of nuisance. In that part of the law of torts, the occupier of premises is liable if he causes a nuisance or if he "continues" a nuisance. To "continue" a nuisance means to permit to remain a danger of which one had, or ought to have had, knowledge. A clear understanding of the position may be gained from Fletcher Moulton L.J.'s judgment in *Barker v. Herbert* [1911] 2 K. B. 633 at p. 641 ff: ". . . In a case where the nuisance is created by the act of a trespasser, it is done without the permission of the owner and against his will, and he cannot in any sense be said to have caused the nuisance; but the law recognizes that there may be a continuance by him of the nuisance. In that case the gravamen is the continuance of the nuisance, and not the original causing of it. An owner of premises may have a duty to prevent the continuance of the nuisance, but it is obvious that, just as, where the allegation is that he has caused the nuisance, it must be proved that it was there by his act or that of someone for whose action he is responsible, so, where it is alleged that he is responsible for the continuance of the nuisance, it must be proved that it was continued by his permission. He cannot be said to have permitted the continuance of that which was not caused by him, and of which he had no knowledge; and when I say of which he had no knowledge, of course I include the knowledge of the servants and agents for whom he is responsible. If they have knowledge of the nuisance, their knowledge must be attributed to him. I also realize that cases may arise in which his or their want of knowledge may be due to neglect of duty."

VI

Forms

29

The Imperatives of the Aedilician Edict

A well-known peculiarity of form of the aedilician edicts is their use of the future imperative in laying down rules. Thus, Aulus Gellius, 4.2.1, tells us of a clause which was obsolete in his day.

> In edicto aedilium curulium, qua parte de mancipiis vendundis cautum est, scriptum sic fuit: 'Titulus servorum singulorum scriptus sit curato ita, ut intellegi recte possit, quid morbi vitiive cuique sit, quis fugitivus errove sit noxave solutus non sit'.

And in Julian's redaction of the edict *De mancipiis vendundis* there appears *palam recte pronuntianto* and *ea omnia in venditione pronuntianto*[1]). And *De iumentis vendundis* has *palam recte dicunto* and *de cetero quoque pecore omni venditores faciunto*[2]). The problem is that the imperative does not appear in the praetorian Edict nor, with two significant exceptions[3]), in *senatusconsulta*, but the future imperative is common in *leges* proper. How to explain its presence in the aedilician Edict? Daube, who has recently studied the problem in depth[4]), rightly excludes the possibility that the imperative here derives from that of true legislation. He also shows the weakness of the general argument[5]) that the imperatives reflect the nature of the aedilician provision as police-measures: statutes which are not police-measures use imperatives, praetorian edicts which are in the nature of police-

---

1) D. 21, 1, 1, 1 (Ulpian 1 *ad ed. aed. cur.*).

2) D. 21, 1, 38*pr.*, 5 (Ulpian 2 *ad ed. aed. cur.*).

3) Which, however, do not here really concern us: see Daube, *Forms of Roman Legislation* (Oxford 1956) pp. 87ff.

4) *Forms*, pp. 91ff.

5) Cf. e. g. Karlowa, *Römische Rechtsgeschichte* I (Leipzig 1885), p. 462.

measures do not. Also, he observes that from the general philological point of view there is nothing in the future imperative making it particularly suitable for police-measures[6]).

He himself develops the following thesis: There is also a non-legal branch of ancient Roman literature where the future imperative is frequent, namely, the writings on husbandry. Thus, Cato's *De agri cultura* contains some 200 such imperatives. 'The conclusion is plain. The imperatives in the aedilician Edict derive from the treatises on husbandry. Their original setting in life is not in the court of the aediles nor, indeed, in any statutes – how could it have been there? – but in a circle of technical experts, whose suggestions deserved to be made part of the law. The teachers of husbandry, that is, recommended certain ways of negotiating an agreement, and the aediles announced that they would give actions if these were disregarded'. The didactic *titulus scriptus sit curato ita* no longer, he claims, creates any difficulty: it is exactly what one would expect in a guide. Cato has: *boves aquam bonam bibant curato*[7]); *vilicae quae sunt officia curato faciat*[8]).

So far, Daube feels, he is on safe ground, but he also hazards the conjecture that it was Cato himself who, when aedile in 199, prompted the publication of the earliest edict on the sale of slaves. (Since Cato was a plebeian aedile, not a curule one, he did not himself have the right to issue edicts). In support of this he urges the fact that after Cato the future imperative fades out of agricultural treatises: it does not occur in Varro at all, and is very rare in Columella and Pliny. Daube then shows that the evidence for the traditional dating of the *De agri cultura* around 160 B.C. is not strong and suggests that that book is an early production of Cato whose style was already formed by 199 B.C.

This thesis of Daube seems to me implausible and I should like to argue its fragility.

First of all, to look at a point which is of little importance to

---

[6]) *Forms*, pp. 91f.

[7]) 73.

[8]) 143.1.

the main argument, namely the supposedly didactic *titulus scriptus sit curato ita.* Its true significance, I submit, is revealed by the texts of Cato which were quoted: — in both of them the person addressed has to see to it that another person (or other animals) do something[9]. *Curato* with this force is also common in legislation[10]. Thus, the edict is making the addressee responsible for the proper writing of the labels, but is not demanding that he write them himself[11].

Secondly, it is not really exact to say that the future imperative is frequent in writings on husbandry. It is common in Cato, but — as Daube himself says — does not occur in Varro and is very rare in Columella and Pliny. This may, prima facie at least, appear to render it more plausible that Cato was responsible for the edict, but it makes very doubtful the claim that the setting in life of the edict was agricultural treatises. Cato, however, is not alone among Roman writers to favour the use of future imperatives. Such imperatives are also frequent in Plautus[12]. One might think, with Kühner-Stegmann[13], that the future imperative was common in the 'Volkssprache' and hence found in abundance in Plautus. Or, since the future imperative is frequent in both Cato and Plautus, one might prefer the view that this is an old usage which became obsolescent in the later Republic. In favour of this latter opinion is the fact that any original distinction in usage

---

9) This is also true of another Cato text with *curare*, 2.5, and perhaps also of 67.1.

10) Cf. e.g. *lex Mamilia Roscia Alliena Fabia* (59 B. C.) cap. 3,5; *lex Iulia municipalis* (45 B. C.) at e.g. lines 149, 156.

11) Though the point will not be insisted upon here, it should be noticed that this edict may not have given the buyer any remedy on the sale, but have established only a quasi-criminal action under the control of the aediles. In favour of this possibility it should be observed that what concerns the buyer is whether or not he is informed of defects, not specifically that the defects be written on the label.

12) Some instances: *As.* 228; 239; 801; *Ba.* 729; 741; 1175; *Capt.* 11; 452; 721; *Cas.* 210; *Merc.* 770; *Mil.* 525; 566; *Poen.* 1281; *Pseud.* 647; *Rud.* 578; 858; *St.* 148; *Tri.* 295.

13) *Ausführliche Grammatik der lateinischen Sprache*, II. I, 4th edition (reprinted Munich 1962), p. 196.

between present and future imperatives[14]) was becoming blurred as early as Plautus: the present occurs where one might expect the future[15]), and the future where one might expect the present[16]). In either event, one must doubt any particular association of Cato — as well as of agricultural treatises in general — with the future imperative of the aedilician edict.

Thirdly, although Daube correctly points out that the two texts which are relied upon for the view that Cato did not begin writing until he was an old man[17]) omit any mention of practical manuals, he does not produce any further evidence that the *De agri cultura* is an early work. And the two texts referred to do at least show that the main period of Cato's writing was his old age. The balance of probability is, I feel, still in favour of the *De agri cultura* being a late work and, if this is so, its use of future imperatives is no evidence that the form of the aedilician edict has any connection with Cato's aedileship in 199.

Daube also produced what is for him — if I read him correctly — a very subsidiary argument for linking Cato and the form of the aedilician edict. He observes that in the two Cato passages on which he relies, 73 and 143.1. '*curato* is construed with the simple subjunctive — i.e. without *ut* — just as in the edict under discussion, and that the arrangement of the words also is similar'[18]). In this observation he is, of course, correct, but I doubt whether much weight should be given to it. First in final clauses it is extremely common, especially in pre-classical Latin to omit *ut*[19]). Indeed the omission of *ut* is not unusual in a subjunctive clause dependent upon *curare*[20]). Secondly, in talking of the

---

[14]) Cf. e.g. Leumann-Hofmann-Szantyr, *Lateinische Grammatik* II (Munich 1965), p. 340.

[15]) E.g. *As.* 97; 367; *Cas.* 146; *Merc.* 115f; *Mil.* 864; *Tri.* 1108; cf. Kühner-Stegmann, *Grammatik* II. I, pp. 197f.

[16]) E.g. *Ba.* 741; *Capt.* 11; 452; *Rud.* 578; cf. Kühner-Stegmann, *Grammatik* II. I, p. 198.

[17]) Nepos, *Cato*, 3.2; Cicero, *Cato maior*, 11.38.

[18]) Forms, p. 95.

[19]) Kühner-Stegmann, *Grammatik* II. II, pp. 227ff.

[20]) Cf. texts listed in *Thesaurus Linguae Latinae* IV (Leipzig 1906-1909), 1499.

arrangement of the words as being similar Daube presumably means primarily that the imperative comes after the main part of the command. But this, too, is a frequent usage[21]).

Thus, we should look for a different setting in life of the future imperatives in the Aedilician Edict. An important clue, I suggest, is to be found in a comparison of two parodies of edicts in Plautus. The first is from line 16 of the prologue to the *Poenulus*:

> 'bonum factum † esse †, edicta ut seruetis mea.'
> scortum exoletum ne quis in proscaenio
> sedeat, neu lictor uerbum aut uirgae muttiant,
> neu dissignator praeter os obambulet
> neu sessum ducat, dum histrio in scaena siet.
> diu qui domi otiosi dormierunt, decet
> animo aequo nunc stent uel dormire temperent.
> serui ne opsideant, liberis ut sit locus,
> uel aes pro capite dent; si id facere non queunt,
> domum abeant, uitent ancipiti infortunio,
> ne et hic uarientur uirgis et loris domi,
> si minu' curassint, quóm eri reueniant domum.
> nutrices pueros infantis minutulos
> domi ut procurent neu quae spectatum adferat,
> ne et ipsae sitiant et pueri pereant fame
> neue essurientes hic quasi haedi obuagiant.
> matronae tacitae spectent, tacitae rideant,
> canora hic uoce sua tinnire temperent,
> domum sermones fabulandi conferant,
> ne et hic uiris sint et domi molestiae.
> quodque ad ludorum curatores attinet,
> ne palma detur quoiquam artifici iniuria
> niue ambitionis caussa extrudantur foras,
> quo deteriores anteponantur bonis.
> et hoc quoque etiam quod paene oblitus fui:
> dum ludi fiunt, in popinam, pedisequi,
> inruptionem facite; nunc dum occasio est,
> nunc dum scribilitae aestuant, occurrite,
> haec imperata quae sunt pro imperio histrico,
> bonum hercle factum pro se quisque ut meminerit.

---

[21]) Many instances are to be found in the texts illustrating the imperative in Kühner-Stegmann, *Grammatik* II. I, pp. 196ff.

The other from line 803 of the *Captivi*:

ERGASLIVS prius edico, ne quis propter culpam capiatur suam:
continete uos domi, prohibete a uobis uim meam.
HEGIO mira edepol sunt ni hic in uentrem sumpsit confidentiam.
uae misero illi, quoius cibo iste factust imperiosior!
ER. tum pistores scrofipasci, qui alunt furfuribus sues,
quarum odore praeterire nemo pistrinum potest:
eorum si quoiiusquam scrofam in publico conspexero,
ex ipsis dominis meis pugnis exculcabo furfures.
HE. basilicas edictiones atque imperiosas habet:
satur homost, habet profecto in uentre confidentiam.
ER. tum piscatores, qui praebent populo piscis foetidos,
qui aduehuntur quadrupedanti, crucianti cantherio,
quorum odos subbasilicanos omnis abigit in forum,
eis ego ora uerberabo surpiculis piscariis,
ut sciant alieno naso quam exhibeánt molestiam.
tum lanii autem, qui concinnant liberis orbas ouis,
qui locant caedundos agnos et dupla agninam danunt,
qui Petroni nomen indunt uerueci sectario,
eum ego si in uia Petronem publica conspexero,
et Petronem et dominum reddam mortalis miserrumos.
HE. eugepaé! edictiones aedilicias hicquidem habet,
mirumque adeost ni hunc fecere sibi Aetoli agoranomum.

The first of these, that from the *Poenulus*, is a parody of a praetorian edict. This emerges from the reference to lictor in line 18 since the praetors — as magistrates with *imperium* — were accompanied by lictors, but the aediles were not. The other parody, from the *Captivi*, is of course of an aedilician edict. It should be observed, en passant, that neither edict relates to private law. The provisions of the former are concerned with the smooth running of the theatrical performance, of the latter with the standard of hygiene in the streets. Both, one might say, are police-measures. But of more interest to us now are the forms.

The edict in the *Poenulus* so far as line 39 properly mirrors the forms of the praetorian Edict. There are here no imperatives, but the habitual *ne quis . . . sedeat*, *neu . . . muttiant*, *aes pro capite dent*, *domum abeant* and so on. And the commands are correctly in the third, not the second, person[22]. The edict of the *Captivi* has imperatives, *continete*, *prohibete;* as well as the form *ne quis . . . capiatur* which is not surprising in an aedilician edict[23].

But now, the imperatives of Plautus' aedilician edict differ markedly from any surviving in a true edict in that they are present imperatives, not future. The question must be put. Was Plautus sensitive enough to legal form not to have imperatives in the main part of the praetorian parody to line 39 and yet to have them in the aedilician, but not sensitive enought to give the proper tense of the imperatives? Or was he fully sensitive to legal form and did give a standard formulation for an aedilician edict[24]? No answer can be given with certainty, but it would be surprising if a skilled dramatist could give such evidence of sensitivity to form in parody and at the same time make such a blatant error in the tense. The Plautine passage is some indication that present imperatives were appropriate to an aedilician edict.

Even if this tentative conclusion is not fully accepted, the parody in the *Captivi* brings out another point. A future imperative in the singular, judged solely by its appearance, could be second person, third person or impersonal. Daube has already suggested that in the edict preserved in Aulus Gellius *curato* is likely to be in the second person[25]. The present imperatives in the *Captivi* – inevitably second person – make it virtually certain that this is correct.

The imperatives, then, of the early aedilician edicts are very different from those of true legislation. For the imperatives of *leges* proper are all either third person or impersonal. (Perhaps it would be more precise to say that there are in *leges* no present imperatives, and no future imperatives which appear to be second person; but many future imperatives in statutes from the earliest

---

22) For the significance of lines 40ff see *infra*, p. 341.

23) Thus, *De mancipiis vendundis* of Julian's redaction has *Qui mancipia vendunt, certiores faciant emptores*: D. 21, 1, 1, 1.

24) It must be remembered that most aedilician edicts would concern minor regulations of the street and market and have not survived.

25) *Forms*, p. 92.

times are clearly third person or impersonal, and it is very likely that they all are). Interestingly, it is a fact well-known to philologists that in ordinary speech (in early times) the second person future imperative is common, but the third person future imperative is virtually confined to the language of *leges*[26]). We are confirmed in the assumption already made that the setting in life of the imperative in the aedilician edict does not come from *leges*, and is something entirely different.

Thus, commands and so on in *leges* are in the third person or are impersonal and may have the form of an imperative or iussive subjunctive; in praetorian *edicta* they are in the third person and have the form of a iussive subjunctive; in aedilician *edicta* they may be either in the second person or third person and may have the form either of an imperative or iussive subjunctive[27 28]).

Imperatives are more imperious, more blatantly commanding, than iussive subjunctives; hence they are very appropriate to *leges*, orders of political superiors to political inferiors. The use of the third person is more impersonal, less direct and less intimate than the use of the second person; hence it is right for orders to the population at large. But the aediles had a limited jurisdiction, above all control over the streets and markets, and the persons to whom their edicts were primarily addressed formed a determinate group, neither rich nor reputable, small stallholders or slave-dealers. The addressees were clearly both the social and political inferiors of the aediles. Hence, second person imperatives — blatantly commanding, direct and rather personal — are exactly right for aedilician edicts. The setting in life of these second person imperatives, that is, is to be found in the (limited) scope of the aedilician edicts themselves[29]), and the

---

[26]) Cf. Leumann-Hofmann-Szantyr, *loc. cit.*

[27]) So far as our surviving sources go, the second person is used only with the imperative.

[28]) The second person in praetorian *interdicta* is a very different usage.

[29]) There is nothing about imperatives which would make them appropriate only for *leges*. Indeed, if there was, there could never be an explanation — of any kind — of the imperatives in aedilician edicts.

class of persons (and their relationship to the aediles)[30]) to whom they are addressed[31]).

But the edicts *de mancipiis vendundis* and *de iumentis vendundis* as recorded for us in Julian's Edict have the future imperatives in the third person. This change should not, I think, be regarded as particularly significant. In the first place it is absolutely natural for aedilician edicts to be cast in the third person. Even that of the *Captivi* is much more in the third than in the second person. Secondly, since there is no distinction in form between the future imperative second and third persons it would be relatively easy for an edict like that recorded in Aulus Gellius in the second person to be remodelled in the third person even without any conscious desire to make a change of this kind.

To turn now to the parody of the praetorian edict from line 40 of the prologue of the *Poenulus*. It will have been noticed that present imperatives — and in the second person at that — occur in lines 41 and 42: *facite*, *occurrite*. And these, of course, are not appropriate in form for a praetorian edict. But far from casting doubt either on the correctness of the arguments produced above or on Plautus' sensitivity to form, these lines are additional evidence for both. Plautus distinctly breaks with the formality of the Edict at line 40: *et hoc quoque etiam quod paene oblitus fui*. There is a marked change of tone. He is now reaching a climax and wants immediacy and urgency: hence what is needed — as we have seen — are imperatives in the second person: *facite*, *occurrite*[32]). At this point any contact of form with that of the aedilician Edict is an irrelevancy for the dramatist.

---

[30]) The very nature of the aediles' function as 'clerks of the market' would on occasion require them or their attendants to take direct action: cf. e.g. some of the jokes in Plautus, *Captivi*, 803ff; the conduct of the aediles of Hypata in Apuleius, *Metam.* 1.24f.

[31]) It is doubtful how much support can be gained for this conclusion from Hegio's *basilicas edictiones atque imperiosas habet* (*Captivi* 811) followed by his *edictiones aedilicias hicquidem habet* (823). *Basilicae* and *imperiosae* are used primarily of the substance, not the form.

[32]) The significance of this change of third person to second person at the

It is not intended here to enter into any wider discussion of the early history of the aedilician edict, but a few points may be noted. Though the date of the *Captivi* is uncertain a date not later than 189 would be generally accepted[33]). Hence, the curule aediles were issuing edicts by this time at the latest. But since the Plautine edict is concerned with police-measures it is in itself no indication either for the existence of an edict on the sale of slaves or that aedilician edicts were in any way modifying private law[34]). Nor is there any other evidence from Plautus: *Mercator* 418f[35]) concerns a *pactum displicentiae*, and, *pace* Daube[36]), there is no reason to link the lines with the aedilician edict. Neither, *pace* Impallomeni[37]), can any argument be drawn for the existence of *De mancipiis vendundis* in 169 B.C. from Aulus Gellius, *Noctes Atticae* 17.6. Cato when recommending the *lex Voconia* of that year had spoken of *servus recepticius*[38]) and Gellius rightly takes this as meaning a slave whom the woman kept back for herself when constituting a dowry for her husband[39]). But the Augustan Verrius Flaccus thought this meant a slave who was sold and

---

climax of the speech can be well-illustrated by the (otherwise very different) Sermon on the Mount: *Matth.* 5.2-11. After eight 'Blessed are —', Μακάριοι οἱ in the third person, Jesus proclaims 'Blessed are ye, — 'Μακάριοι ἐστε, second person. We need not here enter more closely into the setting-in-life of the Sermon on the Mount, but see Daube *Forms* p. 3; Davies, *The Setting of the Sermon on the Mount* (Cambridge 1964).

33) Lindsay, *The Captivi of Plautus* (London 1900), pp. 106, 144, 320 gives arguments for 193; Sedgwick *Plautine Chronology*, American Journal of Philology 70 (1949), pp. 376ff at p. 379 thinks of 189; cf. Duckworth, *The Nature of Roman Comedy* (Princeton 1952), p. 55.

34) Elsewhere I have argued that it was not until about 100 B.C. that the praetor's Edict was so developed that individual edicts could be issued giving totally new actions on substantive law: *The Development of the Praetor's Edict* to appear in *JRS* 69 (1970).

35) CHARINUS: quid si igitur reddatur illi unde empta est? DEMIPHO: de minime gentium. CH: dixit se redhibere si non placeat.

36) *Forms*, p. 97.

37) *L'editto degli edili curuli* (Padua 1955), pp. 92f.

38) 17.6.1.

39) 17.6.6.

returned because of a fault[40]). This view of Verrius Flaccus certainly demands the existence of the aedilician edict *De mancipiis vendundis* permitting redhibition but there seems little justification for holding that the idea would not have occurred to Flaccus if the edict had not existed in 169, or that Gellius would have urged the non-existence of the edict as another argument against Flaccus. Neither Flaccus nor Gellius need have had any precise knowledge of the date of introduction of *De mancipiis vendundis*. Certain it is, though, that an aedilician edict on the sale of slaves existed by the middle of the second century B.C., for we have an opinion of Cato — either Cato Censorinus who died in 149 or his son Cato Licinianus who died in 152 — that a slave who had lost a finger or a toe was *morbosus*[41]). We cannot tell, however, whether Cato was commenting on an edict like that recorded in Aulus Gellius or like that of Julian's redaction[42].

---

40) 17.6.2.

41) D. 21, 1, 10, 1 (Ulpian 1 *ad ed. aed. cur.*).

42) Which it was might be of considerable moment if the idea brought forward, *supra*, n. 11, has any substance.

30

Two Studies in Textual History

1. The texts of Ulpian 18 ad edictum in the Collatio

This study is an attempt to show that Ulpian's *liber 18 ad edictum* was not subjected in postclassical times to a re-editing in the sense of a thorough going over with the purpose of making a modernised version of the book [1] and that pre-Justinianic corruptions are not so extensive as has sometimes been suggested.

(I). — *Coll.* 12.7.8 (Ulpianus *18 ad ed.*):

> Item libro VI ex Vibiano relatum est: si furnum secundum parietem communem haberes, an damni iniuria teneris? et ait <*Proculus*> agi non posse Aquilia lege, quia nec cum eo qui focum haberet: et ideo aequius putat in factum actionem dandam. Sed non proponit exustum parietem. Sane enim quaeri potest, <*si*> nondum mihi damnum dederis et ita ignem habeas, ut metuam ne mihi des, an aequum sit me actionem, id est in factum impetrare? Fortassis enim de hoc senserit Proculus. Nisi quis dixerit damni non facti sufficere cautionem.

Of this text Schulz says [1bis] "Whoever still denies the fact of a pre-Justinian revision of the texts in the Collatio must prove

---

[1] This seems the sense of 'edition' in H. J. Wolff, *Ulpian XVIII ad edictum in Collatio*, Studi Ferrini IV (Milan, 1949) pp. 64ff, perhaps most clearly at p. 82 n. 1; and in Schulz, *Roman Legal Science* (Oxford 1946) p. 200. It is not the meaning given by Wieacker to 'Ausgabe' For Wieacker an 'edition' appears to be the renewal of a work through planned multiple copying after a thorough correcting of the text and comparison of manuscripts, but he does not maintain that the 'editor' took this as an opportunity to modify the work. Thus, for him, corruptions, glosses and paraphrases are not evidence of planned alteration by the 'editor': *Textstufen klassischer Juristen* (Göttingen 1960) pp. 72ff. So in what follows the main disagreement with Wieacker is as to the extent of corruptions in the texts, not as to whether they had undergone 'editions' in his sense of the word.

[1bis] *Loc. cit.*

the authenticity of the words in Coll. 12.7.8: *sed non . . . cautionem*, which is simply impossible". And Wieacker, who in discussing the modifications to the text of Ulpian's Commentary on the Edict especially as shown by the Collatio quotes Schulz with approval, writes "That the common text cannot have been written by Ulpian is shown clearer here than anywhere else" [2]). Here I wish to try the impossible. The Collatio text, I will maintain, is genuine and the contrary view is due to a failure to grasp Ulpian's bewilderment at Proculus' decision.

The verb *proponere* in this context if it were not qualified by a negative would mean something like 'to state that . . .' or 'to put the case that . . .' and would be unambiguous. But when it is negatived as in *Sed non proponit exustum parietem* it becomes ambiguous. Linguistically, it could mean "But he does not put the case of the wall being burnt down" *i.e.*, he was expressly concerned with the case where the wall was not burnt down. This seems to be the accepted translation of the sentence [3]). But equally it can mean linguistically "But he does not state that the wall was burnt down" i.e., he said nothing one way or another which tells us whether the wall was or was not burnt down. And in the context this second, and usually ignored, interpretation is the correct one. First, the text goes on to say "For indeed it may be asked whether, if you have not yet done me any damage but you keep your fire in such a way that I fear you will do me damage, it is right that I should obtain in the interim an action, that is, *in factum*. Perhaps that was what Proculus was thinking of". Now, if Proculus had expressly stated that the wall was not burnt down, this must have been what he was thinking of. There is no other real possibility. So

---

[2]) „Deutlicher als irgendwo anders zeigt sich hier, daß der gemeinsame Text von Ulpian nicht geschrieben sein kann". (*Op. cit.*, p. 244). See also the authorities cited by Schulz and Wieacker.

[3]) *Cf.* for instance, Lawson, *Negligence in the Civil Law* (Oxford 1950), p. 149. H. J. Wolff's treatment of the text is interesting: he declares that the fact that there was a fire is self-evident, but that *sed non proponit exustum parietem* is not classical but is an addition written by someone who misunderstood the first two sentences of the text: *op. cit.*, pp. 73—4.

that there could be no place for the *fortassis*. Secondly, even logically, if Proculus had expressly been concerned with the case of a wall which had not been burnt down, *sed non proponit exustum parietem* is odd. Why should we be told that Proculus did not put the case of the wall being burnt down? Why, after all, if he were discussing one case, should he have discussed the other? Moreover if the writer had wanted to tell us that Proculus was concerned with the case where the wall was not burnt down he should have written *sed proponit non exustum parietem.* The pattern which begins to emerge is that the writer of the text as it stands (whether Ulpian or not) is puzzled by Proculus' decision so he tries to explain it by suggesting that Proculus was concerned with a case of threatened damage though later in the text he rejects the giving of an *actio in factum* for that.

That Proculus was considering a case where the wall was burnt down can hardly now be doubted [4]). He was concerned with the *lex Aquilia* since the root of the question is *an damni iniuria teneris?* and for such an action there had to be financial loss [5]) caused *quod usserit fregerit ruperit iniuria*. It is impossible that at the beginning of the classical period the jurists could even raise the question whether an *actio legis Aquiliae* would lie where there was as yet no financial loss and no burning, breaking or destroying. Nonetheless, Proculus refused to give a direct *actio legis Aquiliae* where a common wall was burnt down as a result of a stove, probably moveable, being placed against it. Any explanation of the decision must take into account Proculus' reason *quia nec cum eo qui focum haberet*. Two reasons for the refusal of a direct action can be suggested. First, the damage was not done directly enough, *i.e.*, it was *corpori sed non corpore*. This is generally accepted [6]) but is perhaps not completely satisfactory. Especially where there was a fireplace, which would really be part of the wall, it would be difficult to

---

[4]) *E.g.* Wolff, *loc. cit.;* Wieacker, *op. cit.*, pp. 244—5; *contra*, Lawson, *op. cit.*, p. 104, note on D. 9.2.27.10.

[5]) *Cf.* Daube, *On the use of the term 'Damnum'*, Studi Solazzi, pp. 93ff.

[6]) *Cf.* the references given by Wieacker, *op. cit.*, p. 245 n. 119; Lawson, *loc. cit.*,

argue that the damage was indirect. Ulpian tells us in the same fragment at § 3 that Labeo held that if someone intended to burn down a tenement and the fire spreads to that of a neighbour, he will be liable under the *lex Aquilia* to the neighbour also; and no less to the tenants on account of any goods of theirs which have been burnt. The damage here must have been less direct than in our text [7]). Admittedly, Ulpian also tells us in § 5 that Celsus would give only an *actio in factum* where a person set fire to stubble and the fire spread, *quia non principaliter hic exussit, sed dum aliud egit, sic ignis processit* [8]). Alternatively, and this seems to me more likely, the decision is a survival from the time when *iniuria* in *damnum iniuria damnum* meant *non iure* and not *culpa aut dolo*. Beinart has shown that even in classical law cases survived where liability was not for negligence but for acting without right [9]). Here the argument was, I suggest, that one had a right to light a fire in one's fireplace even if the fireplace were built into a common wall and so one was not liable under the *lex Aquilia* if the wall were burnt down as a result. Therefore, one equally had the right to have a moveable stove and to place it against a common wall and again there was no Aquilian liability [9bis]). But Proculus thought it was only proper that the owner of the stove should be made to suffer since he had caused the damage, so he allowed an *actio in factum* against him.

The same explanation may account for the difference in the decisions in § 3 and § 5. In § 3 the burning of even one's own tenement is not only malicious but clearly also without right especially since it was let [10]). But the burning of stubble in § 5

---

7) *Cf.* Lawson, *loc. cit.*

8) For this text *cf. infra* p. 249.

9) *The relationship of 'iniuria' and 'culpa' in the 'lex Aquilia'*, Studi Arangio-Ruiz, I, pp. 379ff. Not all of his examples are convincing, but this seems the best explanation of the text on the liability of the javelin throwers, D. 9. 2.9.4 and J. 4.3.4.

9bis) *Cf.* D.8.2.13 pr.; 8.2.19 pr.

10) That is to take the most extreme interpretation possible of Coll. 12.7.3. Much more likely, *meam* which appears in D.9.2.27.8 has been omitted and this is a case of arson by a third party.

was a normal and rightful agricultural occupation [11]). The text is with § 4 perhaps worth quoting:

> 4. Sed si stipulam in agro tuo incenderis ignisque evagatus ad praedium vicini pervenerit et illud exusserit, Aquilia lex locum habeat an in factum actio sit, fuit quaestio. 5. Sed plerisque Aquilia lex locum habere non videtur, et ita Celsus libro XXXVII digestorum scribit. Ait enim 'si stipulam incendentis ignis effugit, Aquilia lege eum non teneri, sed in factum agendum, quia non principaliter hic exussit, sed dum aliud egit, sic ignis processit'.

This is the punctuation adopted by the editors but something is clearly wrong [12]) since if *si stipulam* — *processit* is in direct speech we should not have the accusative and infinitive construction in *eum non teneri* and probably also in *sed in factum agendum*. Rather, the text should be punctuated

> . . . Ait enim si stipulam incendentis ignis effugit, Aquilia lege eum non teneri, sed in factum agendum: quia non principaliter hic exussit, sed dum aliud egit, sic ignis processit.

That is to say, that as far as *agendum* we have the thought of Celsus in indirect speech, while the reason given for the decision, which is in the indicative, is Ulpian's own. The only thing wrong grammatically with this reconstruction is the indicative *effugit* instead of the subjunctive *effugiat* but scribal slips are extremely common in the Collatio [13]). It is easier to account for *effugit* than for *eum non teneri*. Accordingly, it might be dangerous to affirm that Celsus refused the action on the ground that the damage was not done *corpori corpore*.

To return to § 8. Whichever of these explanations is the more correct, Proculus gave only an *actio in factum* and this decision so puzzled Ulpian that he suggested that perhaps Proculus was thinking of the situation where the wall was not burnt down. Ulpian was bewildered, I suggest, because for him liability under the lex depended on *culpa* or *dolus* not on whether one was

---

11) *Cf.* Virgil, G. 1. 84ff.

12) Kunkel suggests that *quia* — *processit* may be a gloss; '*Diligentia*' *ZSS*, XLV (1925), p. 266ff. at p. 330 n.1.

13) *Cf.* the numerous texts which are repeated in other sources.

acting *iure* or *non iure*, and because the damage seemed to have been caused too directly for the *actio legis Aquiliae* to be excluded.

However, Ulpian's tentative solution did not satisfy even him and he hesitatingly rejected it, saying, "Unless it be said the *cautio de damno infecto* will suffice".

Thus, the text as it stands makes perfect sense and is not objectionable grammatically. Indeed, the only flaw in the text is the omission of *Proculus*. The text shows Ulpian relating a previous case which, because of the changing law, he is unable to understand. He suggests a possible explanation of the decision but rejects it as bad law.

The text might be translated:

> If you had a stove against a common wall, are you liable for wrongful damage? And <Proculus> says there can be no action on the *lex Aquilia* since there would be none against a person who had a fireplace; and so he thinks it fairer that an *actio in factum* be given. But he does not state that the wall was burnt down. For indeed, it may be asked whether, if you have not yet done me any damage but you keep your fire in such a way that I fear you will do me damage, it is right that I should obtain in the interim an action, that is *in factum*. Perhaps that was what Proculus was thinking of. Unless it be said that the *cautio de damno infecto* will suffice.

As Wieacker has shown [14]), the corresponding text in the Digest, D. 9.2.27.10, derives from a text in the same state as that in the Collatio. He himself says "It is perhaps the most astonishing finding of the whole investigation of textual layers that no better text than the formally and substantively very corrupt Collatio text can have been available to the Compilers, and that they (other than as to their correct emendation *Proculus*) were not in a position to fill the large gaps of the first sentence after *nec cum eo qui focum haberet* <....> from sources which had been better transmitted" [15]). It would indeed

---

[14]) *Op. cit.*, p. 243.

[15]) „Es ist vielleicht der auffallendste Befund der ganzen Textstufenforschung, daß den Kompilatoren kein besserer Text als der mechanisch und inhaltlich tief zerrüttete der Collatio vorgelegen haben kann, und daß sie (anders als bei ihrer richtigen Emendation *Proculus*) außerstande waren, die große Lücke des ersten Satzes hinter *quia nec cum eo* <....> aus besserer Überlieferung zu schließen".

be so incredible that the text, if it were in fact badly corrupted, had survived only in that state, that this is one of the strongest possible arguments for holding that the text is authentic and that up till now we have merely misunderstood it.

Before we look at other texts in the Collatio from Ulpian *18 ad edictum* let me say that, in general, it is impossible to prove that any text is genuine. I merely wish to maintain that if Coll. 12.7.8 is accepted as genuine the evidence from other texts for a pre-Justinianic revision of Ulpian's commentary on the Edict is very slight — indeed, it is perhaps for that reason that so much stress is placed on that text by modern writers. All the other flaws in the Collatio are explicable as scribal errors or, in a few cases, as marginal glosses which have been incorporated. Moreover, such a revision is *a priori* unlikely. In a period so close to the classical age it is difficult to understand why the re-editing of such a work as Ulpian on the Edict should be considered necessary. Further, if re-editing were the custom it is amazing that Gaius' Institutes should have survived in so pure a form, and even more surprising that those parts of Gaius' Institutes excerpted for the Collatio [16]) should be free from deliberate alteration but not those excerpted from Ulpian on the Edict.

(II). — For the text of Coll. 12.7.7 let me give the reading of the Berlin (B) manuscript [17]).

Si forte servus, quae idem [*eidem* - W] conductores [*qui idem conductor est* - M] coloni [*colonia* - W] obdormissent [*obdormisset* - M] et villa fuerit exusta, muneris [*munerari* - V, W; *Neratius* - M] scribit ex [*et* - V] loca [*locata* - V, W; *locato* - M] conventu [*conventum* - W, M] praestare debere, si neglegens in legendis [*in eligendis* - W; *neglegendis* - V, *in elegendis* - M] ministeriis fuit tenetur. [omit *tenetur* - V, W, M]. ceterorum [*ceterum* - M] si alius ignem subierit [*subiecerit* - V, W, M] fornaci, alius neglegenter custodierit, [*an* insert M] tenetur? namque qui non custodit, si nihil hic [*nihil* - W, M; *si nihil* - V] fecit; qu(a)e [*qui* - V, M] recte ignem subiecit, non peccavit: quemadmodum si hominem [*si hominem* - omit W] medicus

---

16) Coll. 16.2: *cf* G. 3.1-10.

17) In the text, V = the Vercelli ms; W = the Vienna ms; and M = Mommsen's edition in *Collectio librorum iuris anteiustiniani* III (Berlin 1890) p. 178f.

> recte secuerit, sed neglegenter vel ipse vel alius curaverit, Aquilia cessat. quid ergo est? et hic puto ad exemplum [*exemplo* - W] Aquiliae dandam actionem tamen [*tam in* - M] eum, qui [*ad* - insert V, M] fornacem obordimivit [*obdormit* - V, W; *obdormivit* - M] vel neglegenter [*custodit quam et in medicum qui neglegenter* - V, W, M (the last, however, omits *et*] curavit, sive homo periit, sive debilitatus est. ne [*nec* - W, M] quisquam dixerit in eo [*eum* - V] qui obdormivit [*obdormiit* - V, W] rem eum humana [*humanam* - V, M; *humaria* - W] et naturalem passum, cum deberet vel ignem extinguere vel ita [*velut* - V] munire ut non evacaret [evaderet - W; evageretur - M].

Mommsen's emendations are taken mainly from the Digest. This is a fairly typical Collatio text and shows that the manuscripts which we have are full of scribal errors and that, in general, as a more detailed comparison would prove, the compilers of the Digest used a much better manuscript of Ulpian.

I would suggest that the text as written by Ulpian could very well be that given in the Mommsen edition with the deletion of *qui idem conductor est* and the substitution of *tenentur* for *tenetur*.

Forte may have been *fornacarius* in the original since the Digest has *fornicarius* (a Freudian slip?) but that has no significance here.

Quae idem conductores or *qui idem conductor est* is best understood — indeed, can only be understood — as an explanatory gloss on *coloni* [18]). That it is an intrusion is shown by its senseless position after *servus* rather than after *coloni*. It certainly is no evidence for re-editing. Moreover, the effect of its intrusion in the Collatio mss was the plural *obdormissent*. There is no sign of this plural or of the offending phrase in the Digest so that it is possible that the gloss is later than the compilation of the Collatio.

Tenentur for *tenetur* [19]) is more far-reaching. There is no *a priori* difficulty in suggesting such a scribal error especially since *tenetur* does not make obvious nonsense. But if we accept

---

18) *Cf* Beseler, *Beiträge zur Kritik der römischen Rechtsquellen*, IV (Tübingen 1920), p. 232; Wolff, *op. cit.*, p. 72.

19) Alternatively, something like *uter* or *alteruter* may have dropped out after *tenetur:* cf Lawson *op. cit.*, p. 148.

tenentur as the original reading the main difficulties of the text disappear. One of the outstanding problems is the sudden switch from the *actio ex locato* to the *actio legis Aquiliae* and this has led to the suspicion of a lacuna in the text [20]). This, however, is not necessary. Wolff has already pointed out [21]) that Ulpian was primarily concerned with the *lex Aquilia* and the question of the *actio ex locato* is brought in as an introduction to the consideration of the *lex Aquilia.* But he goes on to assume that Ulpian must have considered the same case as Neratius but from a different standpoint. This need not be so. Neratius' case is brought in as something positive from which the discussion can proceed. If Neratius would give an *actio ex locato* in these circumstances, no one in Ulpian's time could doubt that similarly an *actio legis Aquiliae* would lie. It is an obvious case. Hence, Ulpian could proceed immediately to the situation which does interest him, namely, where two persons are involved one of whom lights the fire and the other, who is supposed to watch it, falls asleep. At the same time he quite naturally moves from the more specific case where the negligent person was a slave to a more general one where the status of the parties is irrelevant and is not really considered, though the assumption must be, as the latter part of the text shows, that they are freemen.

At this stage an opponent might argue that such a switch to *tenentur* cannot be justified in view of the Digest's *tenebitur* which means that the singular must date back not only to before the Collatio mss but also to before the compilation of that work. But the Digest text adds, if anything, further evidence that there was such a scribal error. It reads *an tenebitur qui subiecerit?* Now, the discussion which follows is completely general and Ulpian is considering not only the person who lit the fire, but also the person who watched. Accordingly, *qui subiecerit* is nonsense and is a stupid addition. It shows that a reader in the time of Justinian or before was puzzled by this part of the text. One has, therefore, to say either that before the compilation of

---

20) Kunkel, *op. cit.*, p. 329f.; Wolff, *op. cit.*, p. 70.

21) *Loc. cit.; cf.* Lenel, *Palingenesia,* II, 522ff.

the Collatio the text was re-edited and failed to make sense, or that there was a minor scribal error which led to bewilderment. The latter seems, at the very least, just as likely.

(III). — Coll. 7.3.2,3:

> Sed et quemcumque alium ferro se petentem qui occiderit, non videbitur iniuria occidisse. Proinde si furem nocturnum, quem lex duodecim tabularum omnimodo permittit occidere, aut diurnum, quem aeque lex permittit, sed ita demum, si se telo defendat, videamus, an lege Aquilia teneatur. Et Pomponius dubitat, num haec lex non sit in usu. 3. Et si quis noctu furem occiderit, non dubitamus, quin lege Aquilia <*non*> teneatur: sin autem, cum posset adprehendere, maluit occidere, magis est, ut iniuria fecisse videatur: ergo etiam lege Cornelia tenebitur.

This is repeated in a shortened version in D. 9.2.5*pr.*:

> Sed et si quemcumque alium ferro se petentem quis occiderit, non videbitur iniuria occidisse: et si metu quis mortis furem occiderit, non dubitabitur quin lege Aquilia non teneatur. sin autem cum posset adprehendere, maluit occidere, magis est ut iniuria fecisse videatur: ergo et Cornelia tenebitur.

There is a two-fold difficulty in holding that this text has not been re-edited. First, there is the sentence *et Pomponius dubitat, num haec lex non sit in usu* which grammatically must refer to the *lex Aquilia* but which, it is often argued [22]), must in fact mean the XII Tables. Secondly, there is lack of agreement between the categorical statement at the beginning of § 3 and the rest of the fragment from *sin autem;* and not only the killing of a slave at night but also killing by day should be discussed after the distinction mentioned in § 2.

To take the second difficulty first. *Et si quis noctu furem occiderit* becomes in the Digest *et si metu quis mortis furem occiderit.* The Digest reading, I suggest, is the original and *noctu* is nothing but a scribal error [23]). First, it is easy to see how one reading could become the other. *Noctu* and *metu* look much alike, and

---

22) *E.g.* Wolff, *op. cit.*, p. 67 and the references he gives n. 1; Wieacker, *op. cit.*, p. 236.

23) *Cf* Lawson, *op. cit.*, p. 82, on D. 9.2.5 *pr.*

if *metu* were changed to *noctu*, *mortis* would soon drop out in subsequent transmission as an absurdity. Secondly, *mortis* is less likely to have been inserted if the original reading had been *noctu*, than it is to have been omitted if the text had run *metu quis mortis*. Thirdly, deliberate interpolations apart, the Digest reading is in general much closer to the Ulpianic text than the Collatio mss are. Thus, if we consider for the moment only the possibility of scribal errors, it is much more likely that the Digest reading here is the original. Fourthly, there is no real possibility of deliberate interpolation in the Digest. The immediately preceding Digest text, 9.2.4.1 from Gaius *7 ad ed. prov.*, runs:

> Lex duodecim tabularum furem noctu deprehensum occidere permittit, ut tamen id ipsum cum clamore testificetur: interdiu autem deprehensum ita permittit occidere, si is se telo defendat, ut tamen aeque cum clamore testificetur.

This text draws the distinction which is made in the Collatio between killing a thief at night and a thief by day [24]), and that distinction of the XII Tables is presented as if it were good law. Then comes our text, in which because of *metu quid mortis* and *sin autem cum posset adprehendere &c* the law is presented as totally different. Both of these texts come from the same Mass. It is most unlikely, especially in view of their close proximity, that the compilers could have been paying so much attention to interpolating the substance of one and yet fail to notice that the substance of the other was precisely what they did not want. More plausibly, the compilers were not specially interested in this point and failed to notice that the texts, as they stood, contradicted one another. Moreover, the reading in D. 9.2.5*pr.* corresponds to the view of Ulpian expressed in D. 48.8.9 (*33 ad ed.*) while Coll. 7.3.2,3 does not [25]).

> Furem nocturnum si quis occiderit, ita demum impune feret, si parcere ei sine periculo non potuit.

---

[24]) Whether either or both of the references to *clamor* are genuine, glossed or interpolated is here unimportant.

[25]) Nevertheless, *metu quis mortis* is widely held interpolated. Add to the references in the *Index Itp.* and *Supplementum*, Wieacker, *op. cit.*, p. 235.

But if *metu quid mortis* is what Ulpian wrote and *noctu* is a scribal error (the scribe may also have been confused by *nocturnum* above) the lack of agreement between the various parts of the Coll. 7.3.2 and 3 disappears. The question is raised whether a thief at night or by day is allowed to be killed in the circumstances permitted by the XII Tables, and the answer given by Ulpian is quite simply that if a man kills a thief when he is afraid for his own life he is not liable, but if he prefers to kill when he could have arrested him (as, of course, it was his duty to do) he is liable. No distinction need be drawn between killing by night and by day although, no doubt, in practice there would be greater indulgence for one who killed a thief at night.

As for the other difficulty, *et Pomponius dubitat, num haec lex non sit in usu*, three separate possibilities seem to me just as likely as the view of Wolff and Wieacker that it must be the shortening of some reference to Pomponius by Ulpian, and, accordingly, proof of re-editing.

To begin with, it may simply be a gloss which has been intruded. Cross references of this sort are extremely useful and common — a glance at the *glossa magna* or at books used by students is sufficient proof of that.

Secondly, the state of this part of the text (if it is unsatisfactory) may be the result of scribal error. All three Collatio mss have the same reading, namely, *et Pomponius dubitat. Kp dcliii. NUNC hec lex non sit in usu* [26]). *Kp dcliii* and *NUNC* mean that *Pomponius dubitat* was regarded as ending a section. Of course, the editors' practice of running on *dubitat* with what follows is entirely justified but it cannot be doubted that there was great confusion as the result of some scribal error. In the circumstances, if the simple reconstruction is not entirely satisfactory, it would be rash to blame the state of the text on careless re-editing.

Thirdly, it could be maintained that the text as it stands makes perfectly good sense. *Haec lex*, as Wolff and Wieacker say, does

---

[26]) *Cf* the facsimile of the Berlin ms in Hyamson, *Mosaicarum et Romanarum Legum Collatio* (Oxford 1913), p. 25.

refer grammatically to the *lex Aquilia* and it might really be that statute which Pomponius meant. Berger maintained against the current view that this was so [27]) and his arguments never seem to have been refuted, though Wolff and Wieacker disagree with him. He claims that Pomponius and Ulpian are merely concerned with the availability of the *actio legis Aquiliae* for the case under consideration, and that those who maintain the opposite were perhaps misled by *in usu esse*. If that phrase, he says, is taken to mean 'no longer in force' ('nicht mehr in Geltung') it is just as wrong for the XII Tables as for the *lex Aquilia* [28]).

Thus, the state of Coll. 7.3.2,3 is also no evidence for a post-classical re-editing of Ulpian *18 ad edictum*.

(IV). — Coll. 7.3.1:

> Iniuria occisum esse merito adicitur: non enim sufficit occisum, sed oportet iniuria id esse factum. Proinde si quis servum latronem occiderit, lege Aquilia non tenetur, quia <*iniuria*> non occidit.

This is repeated word for word in D. 9.2.3. Wieacker says [29]) that in the first sentence *non enim sufficit occisum, sed oportet iniuria id esse factum* is so platitudinous ('so seicht') that one is permitted to decide without any further evidence that the text cannot have been so written by Ulpian. But no scientific work can ever be free from platitudes. And, as its position in the Collatio and Digest shows, this text was Ulpian's introduction to a discussion of the meaning of *iniuria* in the *lex Aquilia*. Accordingly, it is natural in this place to stress the importance of the word. No one else has suspected this as interpolated.

---

[27]) Studi Albertoni, I (Padua 1935), p. 391 n. 29: with full bibliography.

[28]) It might perhaps be argued that *haec lex* equals 'that provision of the XII Tables' and that it could be doubted whether that provision was in force. But *lex* used to mean a provision of the XII Tables would be especially inappropriate here where the whole enactment had just been called *lex duodecim tabularum*. Besides, it is not clear that *lex* was ever used to describe a clause of the *lex duodecim tabularum*.

[29]) *Op. cit.*, p. 234.

(V). — Coll. 7.3.4.

> Iniuriam autem accipere hic nos oportere non, quemadmodum et circa iniuriarum actionem, contumeliam quandam, sed quod non iure factum est, hoc est contra ius, id est si culpa quis occiderit. Et reliqua.

This is much the same as D. 9.2.5.1. Here, *sed quod non iure factum est, hoc est contra ius, id est si culpa quis occiderit* is regarded as proof of re-editing. There is, as Niedermayer says [30], "a conglomeration of rational impossibilities" ('eine Häufung von gedanklichen Unmöglichkeiten') [31]. But precisely this conglomeration of impossibilities should put us on our guard against the supposition of a re-editing of the text. Editors are always far less likely to write rubbish of this kind than they are to accept it when it is laid before them. Rather, such nonsense should be blamed on a scribe introducing a marginal gloss. I would agree with Wolff [32] that *hoc est contra ius* is a gloss and the rest of the text, which is quite sensible, is what Ulpian wrote. Beinart [33] asserts the genuineness of the whole text and says "that Ulpian after having in the preceding paragraphs said something of the term *iniuria* in the *lex* with illustrations from the older defences, and without having expressed the meaning of *iniuria* up to that stage, thought it high time to expound the meaning. He thus states it does not mean *contumelia* here but *non iure* (its original meaning), presumably to explain the preceding passages D. 9.2.3 and 5*pr.*, but immediately hastens to assert its sense of *culpa*, for it was too important to leave that out". Anyone who urges that the whole passage is the work of Ulpian fails to take into account the ugliness of *hoc est*, *id est*, which is too great even for one who like Ulpian had little sense of style. But, if we accept *hoc est contra ius* as a gloss, Beinart's position is very attractive.

---

30) *Voriustinianische Glossen und Interpolationen und Textüberlieferung* Atti del congresso internazionale di diritto romano, I (Rome 1934), p. 351ff.

31) *Cf* Wieacker, *op. cit.*, p. 237; Beseler, *op. cit.*, III (Tübingen 1913), p. 59.

32) *Op. cit.*, p. 78.

33) *Op. cit.*, p. 298f.

Kunkel argues [34]) that there is no real distinction between *contumelia* and *sed quod non iure factum est* since *iniuria* likewise in the *actio iniuriarum* meant *quod non iure factum est*. But there is a valid distinction. *Contumelia* implies an act which is, in itself, wrongful; *quod non iure factum est* refers to an act for which one has no positive legal right, but which is not necessarily contrary to law, although it may give rise to an action if loss is caused.

(VI.) — Coll. 12.7.1.

> Item si insulam meam adusseris vel incenderis, Aquiliae actionem habebo, idemque est, et si arbustum meum vel villam meam.

This reappears in D. 9.2.27.7 as:

> Item si arbustum meum vel villam meam incenderis, Aquiliae actionem habebo.

In the Collatio, *idemque est, et si arbustum meum vel villam meam* is certainly odd. As Wieacker says [36]), it is very elliptical. Moreover, it is difficult to see why Ulpian (or, to be honest, anyone) thought that it added anything. One must agree with Wieacker that this part of the text is better explained as a marginal gloss than as the result of a mechanical omission. But that, of course, is no evidence of re-editing.

The Digest text suggests that Justinian's compilers had before them a text much as that of the Collatio, which they neatly altered [37]).

(VII). — Coll. 12.7.3:

> Item si quis insulam voluerit exurere et ignis etiam ad vicini insulam pervenerit, Aquilia tenebitur lege vicino etiam, non minus inquilinis ob res eorum exustas, et ita Labeo libro XV responsorum refert.

---

34) *Exegetische Studien zur aquilischen Haftung*, *ZSS* XLIX (1929), p. 158ff at p. 168.

35) Even if the distinction were not happy, what is meant is clear. Compare the distinction drawn for the *lex Aquilia* between *occidere* and *mortis causam praestare: occidere* certainly is *mortis causam praestare*. Cf. Schulz, *op. cit.*, p. 131.

36) *Op. cit.*, p. 238.

37) *Cf* Wieacker, *loc. cit.*

D. 9.2.27.8:

> Si quis insulam voluerit meam exurere et ignis etiam ad vicini insulam pervenerit, Aquilia tenebitur etiam vicino: non minus etiam inquilinis tenebitur ob res eorum exustas.

The sole flaw in this Collatio text [38]) is the absence of *meam* which, almost certainly wrongly, gives the impression that the tenement was set on fire by the owner [39]). This lack, which is not reproduced in the Digest should be attributed to a scribal slip.

(VIII). — Coll. 2.4.1:

> Rupisse eum utique accipiemus, qui vulneraverit, vel virgis vel loris vel pugnis caedit, vel telo quove alio vis genere sciderit hominis corpus vel tumorem fecerit: sed ita demum, si damnum datum est. Ceterum si in nullo servum pretio viliorem deterioremve fecerit, Aquilia cessat iniuriarumque erit agendum. Ergo et si pretio quidem non sit deterior factus servus, verum sumptus in salutem eius et sanitatem facti sunt, in haec nec mihi videri damni Aquilia lege <*agi*> posse.

D. 9.2.27.17:

> Rupisse eum utique accipiemus qui vulneraverit vel virgis vel loris vel pugnis cecidit vel telo vel quo alio, ut scinderet alicui corpus vel tumorem fecerit, sed ita demum si damnum iniuria datum est: ceterum si nullo servum pretio viliorem deterioremve fecerit, Aquilia cessat iniuriarumque erit agendum dumtaxat: Aquilia enim eas ruptiones quae damna dant persequitur. ergo etsi pretio quidem non sit deterior servus factus, verum sumptus in salutem eius et sanitatem facti sunt, in haec mihi videri damnum datum: atque ideoque lege Aquilia agi posse.

Wolff thinks no more than a few inconsequential glosses are to be found here: nevertheless, his deletions account for more than one half of the text [40]). Wieacker thinks that the text has

---

[38]) *Cf* Wolff, *op. cit.*, p. 81; Wieacker, *op. cit.*, p. 239.

[39]) *Cf supra* p. 348 and note 10.

[40]) *Op. cit.*, p. 78f: [*vel virgis - caedit vel*] [*sed ita - datum est*] [*pretio viliorem*] [- *ve*] [*ergo et - posse*].

been much altered but that the decision that medical expenses are not recoverable is classical, and that the opposite decision in the Digest is Justinianic [41]). His main criticism is of *sed ita demum si damnum datum est* which, he says, is not only simple-minded but mad: in the case of *vulnerare*, *scindere*, *tumorem facere*, a *damnum corpore corpori datum* was (unlike other cases of injury) beyond doubt [42]). But Daube has already proved [43]) that in classical law and even in the time of Justinian *damnum* meant always financial loss, never physical injury, and that the phrase *damnum corpore corpori datum* is mediaeval and misleading. Thus, the text is making a perfectly valid and sensible point: it is not enough that a slave be wounded, cut or bruised, but his master must also suffer financial loss as the result. This also makes it likely that the decision in the Collatio that medical expenses cannot be recovered is corrupt and that the Digest shows the original [44]). If this is accepted, it is further evidence against re-editing. Any such re-editing is always regarded as having taken place before the compilation of the Collatio [45]). One would have to argue, therefore, that while the Collatio retained the re-edited decision, Justinian altered it back to the classical law. Such a to-and-fro movement is not very likely and a scribal error in the Collatio is much more plausible. I would suggest that the Collatio text is genuine Ulpian apart only from a few scribal errors. The *caedit* of the editions should be *ceciderit:* B has *cedit*, V and W *occidit*. The last sentence should be as in the Digest.

To sum up. First, Coll. 12.7.8 which is used as the main support for the view that Ulpian's 18th book on the Edict was

---

41) *Op. cit.*, p. 233f.

42) „Nicht nur einfältig, sondern unsinnig: bei *vulnerare*, *scindere*, *tumorem facere* war (im Gegensatz zu anderen Schädigungshandlungen) ein *damnum corpore datum* außer jedem Zweifel".

43) *Loc. cit.*

44) Daube leaves the question of Ulpian's decision open: *op. cit.*, p. 134 n. 201.

45) Schulz, *op. cit.*, pp. 200 and 312; Wolff, *op. cit.*, p. 82ff; Wieacker, *op. cit.*, p. 246ff.

re-edited in postclassical times makes perfect sense and there is no reason to suppose it is not as it was written by Ulpian. Secondly, there are far fewer flaws in the texts than are ordinarily supposed — even by Wolff with whom I am here in a large measure of agreement. Thirdly, such flaws as exist can be plausibly attributed to marginal glosses or scribal errors. It is no objection that some of the scribal errors suggested appear in all three of the Collatio mss. Even in the texts we have examined there are common errors which no one would deny, *e.g.*, in 12.7.7 *muneris* in B and *munerari* in V and W instead of *Neratius*, in 7.3.1 *et Pomponius dubitat Kp dcliii NUNC hec lex*. Moreover, Schulz has shown that all three mss date back to an archetype which was itself extremely corrupt [46]). It is suggestive that most of the scribal errors which have had to be postulated are not found in the Digest whose compilers must have used a far better ms of Ulpian. Finally, there is no real evidence for a postclassical re-editing of Ulpian *18 ad edictum*, and such a re-editing is, on *a priori* grounds, rather unlikely [47]).

2. Tricks of advocacy in the Libri disputationum.

The problematical literature of the Roman jurists has a variety of names and three of these — *libri responsorum*, *quaestionum* and *disputationum* — are suggestive of different types of problem. *Responsa* were written replies in specific cases addressed to *iudices* or magistrates or the parties involved in litigation. *Quaestiones* may be said to be written replies to queries raised mainly by other jurists and usually in hypothetical cases. *Disputationes*

---

46) *The manuscripts of the 'Collatio Legum Mosaicarum et Romanarum'*, BIDR 55—56 (1951), p. 50ff, especially at p. 56: 'The existence of the archetype is proved by the already well known fact that the text in BVW is narred by a considerable number of blunders, common to all three, which cannot be ascribed merely to chance and coincidence".

47) A number of friends have kindly read and criticised this study to my profit, but thanks are above all due to Mr. A. M. Honoré and Professor F. Wieacker, perhaps especially to the latter whose own view of the state of the texts is so different.

were the oral arguments of the jurists whether in teaching or in a *consilium*. Although the matter does not seem to have been much considered in modern times there would seem to be agreement that even the leading jurists took part in such disputations [1]). The use of the word *dixi* is said to be proof enough of this [2]). What I wish to show here is that the form of a number of texts from the *libri disputationum*, of Ulpian especially, but also of Tryphoninus, is directly due to their origin in verbal legal argument. The form of a legal text, no less than that of a building, depends upon its function [3]).

Responsa, on the whole, merely state what the jurist regards the law to be. Their authority rests upon the reputation of the jurist and not on the value of any arguments. *Quaestiones* are less pure. Now the jurist generally is seeking to convince his fellows that what he thinks is the right view. Logical legal arguments are needed. But, since *Quaestiones* are written and are meant to be objective and are intended for other jurists, rhetoric has no place. *Disputationes* one would expect to be much more extreme. The jurist is presenting orally an argument for one particular side, not even inevitably the better side. They should be a mixture of law and rhetoric.

Thus, if the oratorical flourishes in a text are marked enough, one may be able to say that the text originated as part of a disputation. And if a text could have arisen in this way it should not be automatically condemned as interpolated because it is rhetorical. Ulpian's *libri disputationum*, I suggest, provide examples.

D. 41.2.34*pr*. (*7 disput.*):

> Si me in vacuam possessionem fundi Corneliani miseris, ego putarem me in fundum Sempronianum missum et in Cornelianum iero, non adquiram

---

[1]) *Cf.* Krüger, *Geschichte der Quellen und Litteratur des römischen Rechts*, 2nd edit. Munich, 1912, p. 151; Schulz, *Roman Legal Science*, Oxford 1946, p. 225, 'though doubtless only occasionally and before select audiences."; Berger, *Encyclopedic Dictionary of Roman Law*, Philadelphia 1953, *s.v. Disputationes, Responsa* and *Quaestiones*.

[2]) Schulz, *loc. cit.*

[3]) *Cf.* Daube, *Slightly different*, IURA 12 (1961), pp. 81ff.

> possessionem, [nisi forte in nomine tantum erraverimus, in corpore consenserimus].[4]) quoniam autem in corpore consenserimus, an a te tamen recedet possessio, quia animo deponere et mutare nos possessionem posse et Celsus et Marcellus scribunt, dubitari potest: et si animo adquiri possessio potest, numquid etiam adquisita est? sed non puto errantem adquirere: ergo nec amittet possessionem, qui quodammodo sub condicione recessit de possessione.

There are two rhetorical devices in this text.

The first is the stress on an argument which seems to be against interest but is, in fact, unimportant or even irrelevant. One notices at once the prominence given to the point that one can lose possession by intention. Ulpian tells us that he accepts this and that it was also the view of Celsus and Marcellus. Now, to begin with, the citations are not necessary since the law was clear [5]). Indeed, even if the point had not generally been accepted, there was no need to give it such importance since Ulpian is going on to say that it does not apply here. That does not mean, however, that Ulpian is behaving irresponsibly. He has gained a lot by this treatment of the point. He gives the impression of being fair-minded in bringing forward an argument which could have been adduced against him and, at the same time, states it in the form best suited to his own case. Most important of all, attention is directed to this and so is distracted from the essential weakness of Ulpian's case. After all, it is much easier to hold that one has conditionally formed an intention to possess than that one has conditionally lost such an intention [6]).

The second device is that of the false rhetorical question; that is, one to which an answer can be given which is different from the one which the questioner seems to regard as inevitable. This can be used in three ways. The orator in full flood may insert such a question hoping that the possibility of a contradictory answer will not be noticed in the excitement. Or he can put the question into the mouth of his adversary and then himself give

---

4) Interpolated: *cf. Index Itp.*

5) *E.g.* D. 41.2.3.6.

6) Cf. D. 41.2.18.1. (Celsus 23 *dig.*).

the counter argument. Or again, he may simply put the question as one that anybody might ask and then give the counter answer. This last is the subtlest — it avoids the danger of appearing to try to make one's adversary seem a fool and gives the adversary less chance of a rejoinder. That is the one found here. Ulpian asks "And if one can acquire possession by intention, surely it is also acquired here?" Then he replies "But I do not think that a person who is under an error does acquire" [7]).

Precisely the same use of a false rhetorical question is found in a text from Ulpian's *liber quartus disputationum*, D. 37.5.16. The following case on *bonorum possessio contra tabulas* is put: if there are two sons, one of whom was in his father's *potestas* and was passed over in the father's will, and the other, who had been emancipated, was instituted heir, the edict is breached in respect of him who was in *potestas.* If both should ask for *bonorum possessio contra tabulas*, then he who was in *potestas*, since he will take *ab intestato*, will not pay the legacies to *liberi* and *parentes.* Ulpian then says "Surely the *emancipatus* himself would not have to pay the legacies since the property was being taken from him by one who would not have to pay if he were sole heir? But the better view is that he must pay the legacies to *liberi* and *parentes*", *i.e. Emancipatus vero numquid nec ipse praestat, quia ei rem auferret, qui praestaturus non erat, si solus esset? sed verius est vel hunc saltem debere liberis et parentibus praestare legata.* Biondi [8]) held *sed verius &c.* interpolated on the ground that *sed verius est* was one of the habitual phrases of the Byzantines to cut out neatly doubts and discussions. This is

---

7) Interpolations have often been signalled in the text but the reasons given are unconvincing: *cf. Index Itp.*, especially Beseler, *Beiträge zur Kritik der römischen Rechtsquellen*, 4, Tübingen 1920, pp. 163—4 (not p. 153). It is, of course, not a case of acquisition of possession *animo solo* but the *animus* in the circumstances is naturally very much emphasised. The heaping up of *deponere* and *mutare* to which Beseler objects is rhetorical.

8) BIDR 29 (1918), pp. 227—8; *sed verius &c* is also held interpolated by La Pira *La successione ereditaria intestata e contro il testamento in diritto romano*, Florence 1930, pp. 96, 102 n. 1, 109, 357 and 364, which I have not been able to see.

too simple. Many genuine texts have *sed verius est*. But even on Biondi's view *emancipatus vero* would be introducing a false rhetorical question [9]).

A third everday advocate's trick is to administer a *coup de grâce*. That is, when he appears to have finished his case, he leads another point — the strongest of all — and immediately sits down. A clear example of this is given by Ulpian in D. 50.2.2.2 (*1 disput.*).

> In filiis decurionum quaestio est, utrum is solus decurionis filius esse videatur, qui conceptus et natus est ex decurione, an vero et is, qui ante natus est, quam pater decurio fieret. et quidem quantum pertinet, ne fustibus castigetur et ne in metallum detur, non nocet plebeio patre esse natum, si postea honor decurionis patri eorum accesserit. in avo quoque Papinianus idem respondit, ne patris nota filius macularetur.

There is general agreement that *ne patris nota filius macularetur* should not be there, Mommsen [10]), for instance, would delete it altogether, while Lenel [11]) would place it at the end of § 3 or § 7. In this text the question is asked whether, in respect of certain privileges, he alone is regarded as the son of a *decurio* who was conceived and born while his father held that office or whether a son who is born earlier is also *filius decurionis*. Ulpian replies that the position of a son is not adversely affected if he is born while his father is a plebeian if later the father obtains *honor decurionis*. Then, after he has given his opinion, he adds almost as if it were an afterthought, that Papinian replied the same [12]) in the case of a grandfather. No room for argument appears now to be left and in a straight account one would have expected this authority to be given in the course of the discussion [13]). Here we have an easy case supported by the authority of a much more

---

9) The text seems to be held genuine by Voci, *Diritto ereditario romano*, 2. i., Milan 1956, p. 360.

10) *Digesta Iustiniani Augusti*, 2, Berlin 1870, *ad h. l.*

11) *Palingenesia*, 2, 388 n. 1.

12) *Papinianus idem respondit:* Does this imply in a *responsum?*

13) The case is far different from that in which a jurist, having given his decision, adds that it is also the view of certain others.

difficult one. This is a common enough situation in practice but not at all what one would expect in objective writings of a jurist.

A text which even at first sight seems odd is D. 24.3.21 (Ulpian *3 disput.*).

> Sed et si ideo maritus ex dote expendit, ut a latronibus redimeret necessarias mulieri personas vel ut mulier vinculis vindicet de necessariis suis aliquem, reputatur ei id quod expensum est, sive pars dotis sit, pro ea parte, sive tota dos sit, actio dotis evanescit. et multo magis idem dicendum est, si socer agat de dote, debere rationem haberi eius quod in ipsum impensum est, sive ipse maritus hoc fecit sive filiae ut faciat dedit: sed et si non pater experiretur, sed post mortem eius filia sola de dote ageret, idem erit dicendum: cum enim doli exceptio insit de dote actioni ut in ceteris bonae fidei iudiciis, potest dici, ut et Celso videtur, inesse hunc sumptum actioni de dote, maxime si ex voluntate filiae factus sit.

This tells us that if the husband uses the dowry to buy back relatives of his wife from robbers or to release one of them from chains the amount so spent cannot be recovered from him in the *actio dotis*, or *actio rei uxoriae* as it was in classical law. Much more must this be said, we are told, if his wife's father brings the action where the father himself was the cause of the expenditure but the same must be said even if the action is by the wife after her father's death. If the general principle is exact, then the *multo magis idem* [14]) *dicendum est si pater agat &c* is odd. But for us the important thing is the *sed et si non pater experiretur, sed post mortem eius filia sola de dote ageret* which appears to introduce a more difficult case. But legally there can bc no difference on this point between an action by the father-in-law and an action by the wife. If the husband was right in making the expenditure he was right whether the action was brought by one or the other. The absurdity of any other decision is plain when one reflects that otherwise it could mean that if the husband without good reason divorced his wife during her father's lifetime he would have to pay back less than if he had waited until his father-in-law died. From the strictly legal point of view there was no reason for Ulpian to say *sed et si &c* — indeed, he

---

14) Delete *idem* - Mommsen.

implies what is incorrect. But the treatment, on that account, must not be thought worthless. The facts of the disputation would seem to be that the wife brings an *actio rei uxoriae* claiming even what her husband had expended on behalf of her father. Ulpian starts with the general principle that dowry spent on freeing relatives of the wife cannot be recovered, then takes the case of the wife's father suing for what had been spent on him and finally comes to the point in issue. Quintilian tells us [15] that one of the prime cares of orators must be to avoid seeming *contumeliosi, maligni, superbi, maledici in quemquam hominem ordinemve*. One of the best ways to appear to have the qualities contrary to these is to express sympathy with the other party — sympathy, if possible, which is irrelevant. Ulpian wants to say, in effect, that we can understand why a woman unjustly divorced would want to bring an action, however unfounded, against her husband. But this would be dangerous, exposing his client's wrong and obtaining perhaps too much sympathy for the woman. So he compares an action by the father-in-law to one by the wife, saying that it is clearer that an action would be denied to the former though the latter must also fail. This seems to show Ulpian being more than scrupulously fair. Indirectly he seems to be sympathising with the woman without, at the same time, suggesting that the husband's conduct was wrongful. The audience, however, would quickly spot and fasten on the fact that there could be no difference between an action by the *socer* and one by the *uxor*. And, of course, the example chosen shows the plaintiff, not the defendant, in a very bad light [16]).

D. 17.1.29*pr*. (Ulpian 7 *disput*.).

> Si fideiussor conventus, cum ignoraret non fuisse debitori numeratam pecuniam, solverit ex causa fideiussionis, an mandati iudicio persequi possit id quod solverit, quaeritur. et si quidem sciens praetermiserit exceptionem vel doli vel non numeratae pecuniae, videtur doli versari (dissoluta

---

15) In discussing the value and purpose of the *exordium*, *Inst. Orat*. 4.1.10.

16) For irrelevant sympathy compare the speech of P. Vinicius in Seneca the Elder's *Controversiae*, 1.2: "Fortuna, inquit, haec me coegit pati; misereri debent omnes mei'. et ego misereor tui, puella; sed non facimus miserandas sacerdotes. non est apud nos maximus honor ultimorum malorum solatium".

enim neglegentia prope dolum est): ubi vero ignoravit, nihil est quod ei imputetur. pari ratione et si aliqua exceptio debitori competebat, pacti forte conventi vel cuius alterius rei, et ignarus hanc exceptionem non exercebit, dici oportet mandati ei actionem competere: potuit enim atque debuit reus promittendi certiorare fideiussorem suum, ne forte ignarus solvat indebitum.

A guarantor pays the creditor unaware that the latter never gave the money to the principal debtor. Can the guarantor recover from the debtor by the *actio mandati?* Such is the problem in the text. But instead of a straight answer we are told that if the guarantor had knowingly omitted an *exceptio doli* or *non numeratae pecuniae* he was guilty of *dolus* or *culpa lata*, but not if he had acted unawares. From this presentation, it emerges that the guarantor was blameless — which we knew from the start. That is to say, the statement of facts excluded the possibility of fraud or gross negligence on the part of the guarantor, yet it is precisely the situation where the guarantor acts wrongfully which is stressed. Why? Interpolations have often been suggested [17]) but none of the reconstructions really helps. The problem would then be to explain how the compilers or a glossator came to discuss this other situation in this way: *et si quidem* shows that the discussion was meant to help with the main problem — it is not just another case. Any signs of tampering are much more likely to be due to the text's being shortened [18]). Perhaps, however, we should first decide why the principal question was ever raised since at first sight there is only one possible answer. The only explanation I can think of is that guarantor might have been expected to sue the creditor first and only bring the *actio mandati* for what he failed to recover. This is, at any rate, the position of Celsus in D. 12.6.47 where the guarantor paid *suo nomine*. It would also account for Ulpian's *puto* in D. 17.1.29.2 [19]). If that is the point of the principal question the introduction of the fraudulent guarantor is a good red herring. The fraudulent

17) *Cf. Index Itp.*

18) *Cf.* Watson, *The Contract of Mandate in Roman Law*, Oxford 1961, p. 177.

19) *Cf.* Watson, *loc. cit.*

surety has no action because of his wickedness, but the innocent guarantor cannot be classed with him. Therefore, the argument goes, he must be allowed to sue the principal debtor. Alternatively, it might simply be a false statement against interest. Ulpian would be admitting, that is, that his client would have no case if he had acted fraudulently or with gross negligence, but in fact he is free from fault. Or it may simply be an attempt at a more dramatic presentation. In the present (truncated) state of the text it is difficult to be more precise. But one can say that the form of the text is not suited to objective presentation of the law whereas it is a common rhetorical device, for a variety of reasons, to discuss a situation which is not directly involved. A fine example is given by Quintilian, *Declamationes*, CCXLIX [20]). A husband, it is laid down, cannot bring an action against his adulterous wife unless he first sues the adulterer. In the situation for dispute, the husband begins an action against the adulterer, war breaks out, the adulterer fights bravely and, as a reward, is released from the lawsuit. The husband wants to bring an action against his wife. In the speech for the husband it is at first argued as if no action had been begun against the adulterer, showing that exceptions should be made in certain cases. Then Quintilian goes on, *Haec dicerem, si non incohassem, si nihil fecissem*, and turns to the actual facts of the case. No doubt the main intention here is to present the case more vividly by imagining the situation of the plaintiff to be more difficult even than it is.

Another paragraph of the same text provides a further oratorical example, D. 17.1.29.4:

> Quaedam tamen etsi sciens omittat fideiussor, caret fraude, ut puta si exceptionem procuratoriam omisit sive sciens sive ignarus: de bona fide enim agitur, cui non congruit de apicibus iuris disputare, sed de hoc tantum, debitor fuerit nec ne.

We are told that sometimes even if a guarantor knowingly fails

---

20) The better modern opinion is that the *Declamationes* are not the work of Quintilian himself, but that the collection was made at least before the end of the 2nd century A.D.

to use an *exceptio*, for instance an *exceptio procuratoria*, he is free from fraud. For the action is *bonae fidei* in which it is not proper to insist upon the needle points of the law.

The text has often been held interpolated [21]), but most of the criticisms stem from Beseler [22]) who alone seems to give reasons. He holds the whole text a fabrication of the compilers. His arguments are these. First, it lies between two texts which, he says, are entirely emblematic. This is not a strong argument. Secondly, a person who *ignarus* acts wrongly is only too clearly not dolose. This is certainly true, and *sive sciens sive ignarus* must be interpolated; but that proves nothing for the rest. Thirdly, the omission of another dilatory *exceptio* may, he says, be harmless but the failure to use the *exceptio procuratoria* is a grave offence of the guarantor since it entails payment to the wrong person. The example, too, may be interpolated, that is, the whole of *ut puta* — *ignarus* may be an addition but that is not a necessary conclusion. The whole point of the example is that the omission of the *exceptio* does harm the principal debtor. But usually, although payment would be made to the wrong person—because the procurator was a person who should not have been so appointed or the creditor could not appoint a procurator — the creditor would get the money and the principal debtor would not have to pay again, and an equitable result would be reached [23]). Fourthly, and almost as a *coup de grâce*, Beseler says „Der wunderliche Floskel *bonae fidei non congruit de apicibus iuris disputare*". But it is precisely the marvellous rhetorical flourish which in a *liber disputationum* should incline us to hold the text genuine [24]).

After Beseler's attack one need not dwell on the rhetorical nature of *non congruit de apicibus iuris disputare*. But it may be

---

21) *Cf. Index Itp.*

22) *Beiträge cit.*, 1, Tübingen 1910, p. 49.

23) The text, of course, should not be taken as meaning that the guarantor will always be free from fraud if he knowingly fails to use the *exceptio procuratoria*.

24) A further argument that Longo says that *apex* is used by Justinian 8 times although it occurs only once in the Digest appears to be given little weight even by Beseler.

noticed that precisely because the *actio mandati* is *bonae fidei* and there should be no distinction between law and equity the phrase is more rhetorical than if it had been used in a situation depending on strict law.

Most interesting of all for us is D. 15.1.32*pr*. from Ulpian's *liber secundus disputationum*.

> Si ex duobus vel pluribus heredibus eius, qui manumisso servo vel libero esse iusso vel alienato vel mortuo intra annum conveniri poterat, unus fuerit conventus, omnes heredes liberabuntur, quamvis non in maiorem quantitatem eius peculii, quod penes se habet qui convenitur, condemnetur, idque ita Iulianus scripsit. idemque est et si in alterius rem fuerit versum. sed et si plures sint fructuarii vel bonae fidei possessores, unus conventus ceteros liberat, quamvis non maioris peculii, quam penes se est, condemnari debeat. sed licet hoc iure contingat, tamen aequitas dictat iudicium in eos dari, qui occasione iuris liberantur, ut magis eos perceptio quam intentio liberet: nam qui cum servo contrahit, universum peculium eius quod ubicumque est veluti patrimonium intuetur.

The sense of this and the opposition of *ius* and *aequitas* is confirmed by a fragment of a fifth century codex found in Egypt. It covers the second situation in our text and it seems, although this is a reconstruction, that here, too, Ulpian cited Julian [25]).

The text tells us that, if a slave has been freed and his master had appointed two or more persons as his heirs, an action brought against one of the co-heirs in respect of the *peculium* will release the others although the defendant will not be bound to pay a greater amount than that part of the *peculium* which he holds. Then we are told that this was also the opinion of Julian. Further, even if there are several *fructuarii* or *bonae fidei possessores* an action against one will free the others, although the defendant pays only the amount of *peculium* he holds. (On the standard reconstruction of the *codex* fragment, this decision is also referred to Julian). But, it goes on, that results from law, and equity demands the contrary. An action should be given against those who are freed by an accident of the law. Thus, the form of the text is this. There is a categorical statement of what the law is.

---

25) The fragment is reproduced in F.I.R.A., 2, 2nd edit., p. 308.

Authority is then produced to support it. That is much more forceful than having "Julian says the law is . . .". Next, a more extreme case is advanced with the same decision. Then the contrary solution is pressed on the ground of equity. The opposition of law and equity to gain a victory over the former is a standard rhetorical device. Two illustrations may be taken from Quintilian's *Declamationes.* In *Declamatio* CCLXXX the orator gives a clear statement of the law and then proceeds: *Haec ex lege manifesta sunt, illa ex aequitate.* A good parallel to our text is in *Declamatio* CCCXX where the orator says "Perhaps it may seem inane to praise the law. For it is clear that our very able ancestors and founders of this State wisely proposed it and, since the State has used this provision so long, it has been approved. But the case demands that we look also to the equity of the law".

In the *Institutio Oratoria* [26]), Quintilian says it would be stupid to warn orators not to say anything against the judge, except that they do so. Similarly, where the law is clear it should not be openly attacked but even, or especially, where it is contrary to one's case it should be praised or presented as strongly as possible. One should demand, however, that for reasons of equity the present case should be treated differently. It is another way of appearing not only reasonable and fair-minded but also confident of the rightness of one's position. It also involves flattery of the judge's good sense. The rhetorical nature of our text appears even more distinctly when onc remembers that a jurist of the standing of Ulpian could have (and would have in an objective treatise) made his case rest on his authority in opposition to that of Julian.

The text, of course, has been suspected of interpolation [27]). Schulz says of it [28]) "The passage cannot be genuine: apart from the sentimental *aequitas dictat* the whole antithesis of *ius* and *aequitas* belongs to Aristotelian rhetoric, not to Roman juris-

---

26) 4.1.11.

27) *Cf. Index Itp.*

28) *Roman Legal Science cit.*, pp. 240—1.

prudence". Most recently, Wieacker [29]) has admitted the classicality of the antithesis between *aequitas* and *ius* from at least the time of Constantine (he refers to C. 3.1.8 of 314 A.D. and C. 1.14.1 of 316 A.D.). But he maintains that the antithesis in our text is an interpolation of late rhetorical style although, since it can have no place in the magistrates' courts *extra ordinem*, it must have been inserted before the end of the fourth century A. D. But in accordance with the material for comparison (see, he says, C. 4.6.8) he would not date it before 294 A. D. But I hope that by this time enough has been said of the *libri disputationum* to show that the material for comparison must include rhetorical works, and they show that in the courts this antithesis was, even before the time of Ulpian, a commonplace. Whatever impression of the law juristic texts may give us, other writings show that in the daily working of the courts there was plenty of scope for rhetoric. The close similarity of the form of our text to that of, for example, *Declamatio* CCCXX is strong evidence of the former's classicality.

The form of D. 28.5.35 and of D. 29.1.19, both from Ulpian's *liber quartus disputationum*, is also due to their being disputations, but one cannot properly speak here of tricks of advocacy. In the former, Ulpian proceeds to the solution of the problem by way of discussing at some length a clearer case, in the latter by producing related situations where the law was more settled and showing how far they were similar to and how far different from the main question.

Although we have far fewer texts from Tryphoninus' *libri disputationum* they too show traces of rhetorical influence.

D. 23.2.67.1 (Tryphoninus 9 *disp.*):

> De uno dubitari potest, si avus tutelam gessit neptis ex filio emancipato natae, an nepoti ex altero filio eam collocare possit sive emancipato sive manenti in potestate, quia par affectionis causa suspicionem fraudis amovet. sed etsi senatus consultum stricto iure contra omnes tutores nititur, attamen summae affectionis avitae intuitu huiusmodi nuptiae concedendae sunt.

---

29) *Textstufen klassischer Juristen*, Göttingen 1960, pp. 385—8.

After saying in the *principium* that a son of the tutor could not marry his father's ward while the father was liable to an accounting action, Tryphoninus goes on to say that doubt can arise in one case. If a grandfather is tutor to his emancipated son's daughter, can he give her in marriage to another grandson, whether born of a son in potestas or not, since reasons of affection remove the suspicion of fraud? But, the text continues, even if at strict law the *senatus consultum* operates against all tutors, nonetheless marriages of this sort must be allowed because of the great affection of grandparents. Not only is there here an implied antithesis between law and equity but the language is very emphatic — more like that of a legislator than of a jurist writing a textbook. Indeed, for that very reason the text has often been held interpolated [30]). But to speak with authority is also the mark of the orator. To convince others, he must appear convinced himself. The language is also rather formal but that is appropriate to the text and is not surprising in Tryphoninus. Other evidence will have to be produced before the interpolation of the text can be accepted. The very fact that the question was ever raised at all is proof of the existence of that concept of *aequitas* on which the decision is based.

Lastly, we may consider the subject of D. 16.3.31, also from Tryphoninus *liber nonus disputationum*. We are told that the *bona fides* demanded in contracts requires *summa aequitas*. If someone makes a deposit with you and then, found guilty on a capital charge, he is deported, should you return the deposit to him or deliver it to the State? If, we are told, we look to the *ius naturale* and the *ius gentium* we would return it to the criminal, if to the *ius civile* then to the State. Again, if a robber deposits with Seius something stolen from me, should he return it to the robber or to me? These problems smack of the schoolroom, and an almost precisely parallel case is given in Quintilian, *Declamationes* CCXLV. The law, it is said, punishes a depositee who denies the deposit with fourfold damages. A man who had a spendthrift son deposited money with a friend and told him to

---

30) *Cf. Index Itp.*

return it to his son when he had improved. The son, still a spendthrift, demanded the money and the friend denied the deposit and was successful in an *actio* (*depositi*) brought by the son. Later, the son reformed and the friend gave him part of the money. The son now brings the action for the fourfold penalty.

The following conclusions, I suggest, should be drawn from the foregoing investigation.

First, the form of many of the texts in the *libri disputationum* should be ascribed to an original rhetorical function rather than to the effect of subsequent interpolation. Although they lack the 'couleurs de rhetorique Ciceromane' they show most of the standard tricks of advocacy.

Secondly, they originated as schoolroom exercises. Rhetorical texts have three possible origins. They may derive (a) from debates in the *consilium* of a magistrate, (b) from speeches in open court (whether delivered by the writer or someone for whom he was acting) or (c) from teaching. Quintilian tells us that the good orator modulates his speech to the type of audience he has [31]). The more educated, intelligent and experienced his hearers, the less scope for rhetoric — or, at least, for undisguised rhetorical devices. For instance, it is accepted as a commonplace among English barristers that there is more scope for oratorical powers before a jury than before a judge, and more before a County Court judge than a judge of the High Court, while flights of rhetoric are virtually unknown before the House of Lords. Remarkable oratorical powers are the distinguishing feature of all the great demagogues. Of course, also, the smaller the audience the less room for advocacy. The rhetoric in the *libri disputationum*, although skilful, is too obviously employed, I think, for the speeches to have been made in a *consilium* before other leading jurists. So that (a) can be ruled out. Again, the cases do not give the impression of being particularly important in themselves, so it is unlikely that they are the result of speeches written for court by one of the leading jurists. So (b) can also be excluded. That

---

31) *Inst. Orat.* 3.8.

leaves (c). Comparison with Seneca the Elder and Quintilian suggests that the rhetoric here is of the standard which would be greatly appreciated by students. But the standard is not high enough for the speeches to have been delivered before select audiences only as Schulz suggests [32]). It would, however, be rash to allege that leading jurists spent a great deal of their time teaching the young. There may have been a situation similar to that which prevails in this country today. Most judges of the High Court and of the House of Lords are asked from time to time by students to judge their moots and a fair proportion are not unwilling to do so. Scarcely a term goes by in this University without several judges appearing for such procedures. The judge listens to the arguments for both sides and gives his verdict — usually in favour of the side which has argued better even although its legal case may have been the weaker. The Roman jurist, having the same interest in legal education, may have done likewise, perhaps even adding a model argument which is what is recorded in the *libri disputationum*. It is not in itself an argument against the siting of the *disputationes* in a classroom that some of the same rhetorical devices are found in other books of the problematic type. It is clear from the use of *dixi* in some of the texts from these works that these too are at times concerned with *disputationes* [33]). Likewise, it would be dangerous to affirm that all of the texts in the *libri disputationum* do come from actual disputations.

Thirdly, the persons taking part in such disputations were Ulpian and Tryphoninus themselves. One can understand why a jurist even of Ulpian's reputation would, for idealistic motives, take a share in teaching the young, but not why he would collect the disputations of someone of meaner fame. The only fact which may be brought against this conclusion is that in D. 39.5.13 (*7 disput.*) Ulpian uses exactly the same arguments found in a

---

32) *Op. cit.*, p. 225.

33) *E.g.* D. 13.5.25; 21.2.64.2; and 47.12.10; all from Papinian's *libri quaestionum.*

text of Julian, D. 41.1.37.6 (*44 dig.*) [34]). But the best explanation is that this is a direct borrowing by Ulpian for his own rhetorical purposes, not that he is merely collecting texts from Julian or from Julian's source.

---

[34]) The text of Ulpian, as is well known, is interpolated. The decision given in the two cases of the slave and of the procurator must be the same. The use of *nam et si* must be distinguished from that of *sed et si*. *Sed et si* is found in objective accounts where the jurist, having given his decision, proceeds to maintain that the same applies in a more difficult case. *Nam et si* occurs in rhetorical texts where a decision is given and it is supported by the argument that the same decision is given in a more extreme case. D. 41.1.37.6 is, therefore, in itself some evidence that Julian, too, took part in such disputations.

31

Change to Third Person in Javolenus Libri Epistularum

A change of person in a text — normally from the first to the third person — is frequently regarded as a sign of interpolation. This is also the case with the form which we are interested in here [1]. A question is asked in the first or second person; the answer is separated from the question by « *respondi* » or « *respondit* »; and the answer is given in direct speech in the third person. This form occurs regularly only in the *libri epistularum* of Javolenus. The object of the present note is to examine this particular form in Javolenus' *libri epistularum* and to decide whether it is a sign of interpolation [2].

It should be said at the outset that the form does not necessarily look suspicious. The answer is distinctly separated from the question, and an answer in a more abstract way (and the third person is more abstract than the first or second) need not seem out of place. However, this is a purely *a priori* argument and should not be stressed. On the other hand, we should not immediately look for help to other aspects of the form of the answer — the interpolation, or at least the suggestion of interpolation, might extend to these as well. But it would be a different matter if the switch from the first or second to third person corresponded to a peculiarity in the form of the question [3]. And there is a pattern in the relevant texts which is not repeated with the same regularity in the texts of Javolenus' *libri epistularum* where, despite a separation of the question and answer by « *respondit* », there is no switch to the third person.

---

[1] In connexion with D. 19.2.21 (Jav. 11 *ep.*) Daube (*CLJ.* 10 [1948-50] 82) very carefully assesses the value of a change of person as an indication of interpolation: « In the first part of the fragment it is 'I' who am selling: '*cum venderem fundum*'. In the portion here suspected of being an addition it is 'the vendor': '*sed non amplius praestat is venditori*'. Overmuch attention need not be paid to formal inconsistencies of this kind: they are known to occur in the works of the most brilliant interpolationists. They do gain in significance, however, where, as in this case, corruption is suggested by the substance of a text ». But even Daube draws no distinction between the present form and other cases of a switch of person: cf. THOMAS, *Iura* 10 (1959) 106. [2] There will be no attempt to decide how far there are interpolations in the texts. [3] Nothing will be said about a switch from first to second person (or vice

There are seven texts — D. 8.4.5 (book 2 — first situation only); D. 7.1.54 (book 3); D. 47.2.75 (book 4); D. 41.3.21 (book 6); D. 31.41.1 (book 7); D. 19.2.21 (book 11); and D. 19.2.51 pr. (book 11) — where there is a switch from 'I' to 'he' and one — D. 35.2.61 (book 4) — where there is a switch from 'you' to 'he'. In all the questions, the main fact situation is stated in a positive, not a hypothetical, way — 'I did this', not 'If I did this' — and in all except D. 8.4.5 it is stated in the past.

No such regular pattern occurs where there is no switch to the third person. Leaving aside the particular switch of 'I' to 'you' (which may be a special case) the questions present the following aspects. In D. 12.1.36 (book 1), the facts behind the question are stated in a positive form and the verbs are in past time. In the second situation in D. 8.4.5 (book 2) the facts are stated in a hypothetical form and in the present tense. In D. 18.1.64 (book 2) the facts are stated positively and in past time. In D. 29.2.76 pr. (book 4) the facts are stated hypothetically and in past time. The same is true of D. 29.2.76.1 and D. 39.5.25 (book 6). In D. 45.1.108 (book 10) the facts are given in a positive form and the act took place in the past. Oddly enough, however, the facts are repeated in the answer in a hypothetical way. In D. 46.1.44 (book 11) the facts are given positively and in the past. Thus, of the eight questions in the texts, the fact situations are given positively and in the past in four (including the case where the question is repeated hypothetically in the answer), hypothetically and in the past in three, and hypothetically and in the present in one. Thus, only half of these questions have the particular form which appears in all of those where there is a switch to the third person.

Of the four texts where there is a switch from 'I' to 'you' (which, I repeat, may be a special case) one, D. 41.2.23.2 (book 1) has the facts hypothetical and in the past tense; three, D. 45.1.105 (book 2); D. 18.1.65 (book 11); and D. 19.2.51.1 (book 11) positive and in the past tense.

The regularity of the pattern of the questions in those texts where the answer switches to the third person, when compared with the lack of pattern in those where is no such switch, can hardly be regarded as coincidental. At the same time, the existence of a pattern in the questions which is related to the form of the answers means that we can exclude the idea that the form of the answers is the result of interpolation [4]. The compilers would have had no inducement to alter the form of the answer — since any interpolation would be the result of a desire to shorten a text, clarify it or alter a decision — because of the form of the question. It must be significant,

---

versa). The change is very natural in a question-answer context and may be a form with a different significance. [4] This is not to suggest that in some texts the substance too, that, although in a number of texts the fact situations leading to the question are stated in the third person, the answer never then switches to the first or second person. Yet such a switch would have been just as likely to occur if changes of person were the result of interpolation. But, on the other hand, one cannot say that it is the form of the question which causes the switch to the third person. First, because it is impossible to see why this form, and not another form of question, should induce that particular kind of answer. Secondly, though this is not so strong, because such a question does not always lead to the switch. This means that the form of the question and answer must be attributable to the situation behind the posing of the question. And that this situation is different from that behind the posing of at least some of the questions where the answer does not switch to the third party.

In Javolenus' *libri epistularum* I suggest — though no strict proof is possible — that the form of question with the facts stated positively in the first or second person and answer in the third person occurs when an actual question which has arisen in practice is put to Javolenus, most likely by a client. First, because the positive form suggests an actual case. Secondly, the switch to the third person is peculiarly appropriate and tactful in such circumstances because it is more abstract and also the jurist dissociates himself from the accuracy of the statement of facts. Javolenus is carefully not saying « Your legal position is such and such » since the actual facts may not be as presented to him. At the same time he tactfully avoids « So far as the facts which you have given are concerned, your position is such and such ». Another way of achieving the same object may be, as in D. 45.1.108, to repeat in a hypothetical form the facts which were given positively in the question. Thirdly, Javolenus never expresses any hesitation as to his decision in these texts whereas he does so in some others [5]. This, too, is what we would expect in answers to clients' problems but not necessarily, for instance, in replies to students' question. Fourthly, in none of these texts is there anything which could suggest that they were not practical questions put by clients. D. 8.4.5, for exemple, may show a client asking a question which is of immediate importance to him and at the same time raising a rather different but connected point which he thinks may affect him in the future. D. 41.3.21 may show an actual *bonae fidei possessor* who leased the estate to the true owner asking about his existing legal position and wondering whether he can get out of his difficulties by selling to the owner [6].

may not have been altered. [5] D. 18.1.64; D. 18.1.65; D. 41.2.23.2; D. 45.1.105.

[6] The person of the seller is not mentionend in the reply to the second question.

Index of Texts

I. LEGAL SOURCES

A. PRE-JUSTINIANIAN WRITERS AND COLLECTORS

Digesta (continued)

Digesta (continued)

II. NON-LEGAL SOURCES

GREEK AND ROMAN WRITERS